# American Philanthropy at Home and Abroad

# American Philanthropy at Home and Abroad

*New Directions in the History of Giving*

Edited by
Ben Offiler and Rachel Williams

BLOOMSBURY ACADEMIC
LONDON · NEW YORK · OXFORD · NEW DELHI · SYDNEY

BLOOMSBURY ACADEMIC
Bloomsbury Publishing Plc
50 Bedford Square, London, WC1B 3DP, UK
1385 Broadway, New York, NY 10018, USA
29 Earlsfort Terrace, Dublin 2, Ireland

BLOOMSBURY, BLOOMSBURY ACADEMIC and the Diana logo are trademarks of
Bloomsbury Publishing Plc

First published in Great Britain 2023
This paperback edition published 2024

Cover image: Making friends with the sea. These orphan children at Marathon, Greece,
were brought from the interior of Asia Minor by the Near East Relief and never saw the sea
before, 1915/16. Photograph https://www.loc.gov/item/2002695431.

A catalogue record for this book is available from the British Library.

A catalog record for this book is available from the Library of Congress.

ISBN: HB: 978-1-3501-5195-6
PB: 978-1-3503-2982-9
ePDF: 978-1-3501-5196-3
eBook: 978-1-3501-5197-0

Typeset by Deanta Global Publishing Services, Chennai, India

To find out more about our authors and books visit www.bloomsbury.com and
sign up for our newsletters.

# Contents

**Challenging philanthropy**

# Figures

# Contributors

**Amanda Niedfeldt** is Impact and Partnership Development Officer at the University of Exeter. She received her PhD from the University of Minnesota-Twin Cities in 2021.

**Ben Offiler** is Senior Lecturer in History at Sheffield Hallam University. His research interests include US foreign relations, American and international philanthropy, modernization and development, and US-Iranian relations during the Cold War. He is the author of *US Foreign Policy and the Modernization of Iran: Kennedy, Johnson, Nixon and the Shah* (2015).

**Bridget Bennett** is Professor of American Literature and Culture at the University of Leeds. Her publications include *Ripples of Dissent* (1996); *The Damnation of Harold Frederic* (1997); *Grub Street to the Ivory Tower* (1998); *Special Relationships: Anglo-American Affinities and Antagonisms, 1854–1936* (2002); *Twelve Months in an English Prison* (2003, two volumes); *Transatlantic Spiritualism and Nineteenth-Century American Literature* (2007) and two editions for the Macmillan Press, Walt Whitman, *Leaves of Grass and Selected Poems* (2019), and Willa Cather, *My Ántonia* (2019).

**Emma Long** is Associate Professor of American History and Politics at the University of East Anglia. Her interests include the US Supreme Court, the Constitution and the modern history of American evangelicalism and their engagement with political activism. She is the author of *The Church-State Debate: Religion, Education, and the Establishment Clause in Postwar America* (2012) and *Lobbying for the Lord: The National Association of Evangelicals and the Growth of Post-war Evangelical Political Activism* (forthcoming).

**Karen Patricia Heath** is a stipendiary lecturer in history at Lady Margaret Hall and a senior research fellow at the Rothermere American Institute, University of Oxford. She specializes in twentieth- and twenty-first-century history, and her research interests include the history of institutions, arts policymaking and the politics of outer space.

**Kevin E. Grimm** is Associate Professor of History at Regent University, Virginia Beach. He is the author of *America Enters the Cold War: The Road to Global Commitment, 1945–1950* (2017), and he has published or has forthcoming articles in *Labor History*, the *Journal of Contemporary History* and the *Journal of West African History*. He has written several book chapters, including one on the historiography of US-Third World relations in the Blackwell Companion volume to the Eisenhower presidency. His research considers the various relationships between United States and international labor organizations, development and modernization ideas, and African nations during the 1950s and 1960s.

**Linda L. Johnson** is Professor Emerita, Department of History, Concordia College – Moorhead, Minnesota. She is a historian of modern Japan, currently researching US-Japanese cultural diplomacy.

**Margaret Nettesheim Hoffmann** is Associate Director of Career Diversity for the Humanities Without Walls consortium based at the University of Illinois at Urbana-Champaign and Director of the Career Diversity Initiative at Marquette University. Her research tracks the transformation of philanthropy in the Unites States during the Gilded Age and Progressive Era with a special focus on political discourses critical of private giving to public institutions. She is the co-author of *For the Benefit of All: A Fifty-Year History of the Faye McBeath Foundation* (2016), which tracks the impact of philanthropic foundations in the city of Milwaukee during the late twentieth century.

**Miguel Hernandez** is Lecturer in American History at Aberystwyth University in Wales. His research centres on the history of American race relations and organized white supremacist movements in the twentieth century. He is the author of *The Ku Klux Klan and Freemasonry in 1920s America* (2019).

**Rachel Williams** is Lecturer in American History at the University of Hull. Her research interests include antebellum reform, the Civil War and nineteenth-century evangelicalism.

**Scott P. Libson** is the librarian for history, Jewish studies and religious studies at Indiana University Bloomington. His research and writing focus on the boundaries between religious and secular philanthropy in the United States during the Gilded Age and Progressive Era.

# Acknowledgements

The editors would like to thank the contributors to this collection and everyone who attended or presented at the New Directions in American Philanthropy conference at Sheffield Hallam University in 2017, especially Inderjeet Parmar who has provided encouragement and support throughout the process of editing this book. Special thanks also to Maddie Holder and Abigail Lane at Bloomsbury for their advice, expertise and patience. Finally, the editors are grateful to the Economic History Society and SHU for providing funds to organize the original conference from which this volume has grown.

# Introduction

## Ben Offiler and Rachel Williams

'Who can doubt', Merle Curti wrote in 1957, exhorting fellow historians to subject philanthropy to scholarly scrutiny, 'that the character and dimensions of American civilization may be illuminated by sustained inquiries into American experience in giving?'[1] Scholars responded with gusto to his challenge. Several classic texts defined the field in the 1960s. Robert H. Bremner's *American Philanthropy* (1960) sought to synthesize nearly two centuries of American do-gooding, while in the same year, Charles Foster and Clifford Griffin published competing accounts of religious reform between the revolution and the Civil War that sparked a still-simmering debate about the extent to which reform activity – and by extension, charity and philanthropy – were vehicles for social control and outlets for the status anxiety of philanthropic footsoldiers.[2] Curti himself broadened the geographic scope of inquiry yet further with his *American Philanthropy Abroad,* published later that decade.[3] Six decades on, the question of what philanthropy is, what it does, and to what effects, continues to engross and divide historians of America.[4]

In 2017, we invited an international group of scholars to Sheffield Hallam University, UK, to present research on the many manifestations of American philanthropy in the United States and beyond. The papers presented by these scholars – eleven of which are collected here in expanded form – illustrated both the challenges and the possibilities of philanthropy history. By engaging with examples as far back as the eighteenth century, our presenters revealed both continuities and evolutions in ideas about the definition of philanthropy, the motivations and justifications that drove philanthropic behaviour, and the modes and methods through which philanthropic impulses were expressed over the course of American history. Moreover, by encouraging scholars to think broadly about the spaces in which American philanthropy happened, the conference revealed the rich potential of exploring intellectual, ideological and methodological currents between domestic and international iterations of philanthropy. Before engaging with the perennial issue of how to define philanthropy, we will briefly outline important and emerging themes and questions in the history of philanthropy, demonstrating the vitality and diversity of the field and highlighting the interventions and emphases of the contributors in this volume. As the historiography reveals, scholars and practitioners have engaged with a multitude of ideas about the purpose, principles and definition of philanthropy through a wide variety of activities and projects both within the United States and across the globe.

For many years, numerous historians of philanthropy focused on the prominent individuals and activities associated with the so-called Big 3 Foundations established by wealthy benefactors in the first decades of the twentieth century: the Rockefeller Foundations, Ford Foundation and Carnegie Corporation. Considering the sheer scale of philanthropic endeavours that these organizations engaged in over the years, it is little wonder that they, and the business magnates that ran them, have received considerable attention, positive and negative.[5] Scholars of philanthropic foundations have interrogated their involvement in a number of realms, from education to arts patronage to international development to public health and more besides.[6]

In the early twentieth century a number of foundations, including the Big 3, channelled significant financial support into the realms of public schooling and higher education helping to establish modern science and social science networks. Scholars such as Alice O'Connor and Donald Fisher have highlighted the progressive values that guided these foundations, while acknowledging the deep influence they acquired concerning the structure and direction of research within university social science departments.[7] Others have examined the complex nature of the relationships between foundations and scientists, variously describing these as ones of 'partnership' or 'patronage', noting the opportunities, challenges and criticisms that they cultivated.[8] Nor were the humanities left untouched; Karen Ferguson and Noliwe Rooks have revealed the extent to which the Ford Foundation engaged with and ultimately shaped both African American studies and Black Power within the United States.[9] The continuing reliance of academic research on the support of philanthropic foundations has raised thorny questions about academic freedom and independence, hidden agendas and the replication of cultural assumptions and hegemonies. These questions become yet more potent when applied to the work of foundations overseas. Historians Maribel Morey and Tiffany Willoughby-Herard, for example, have both sought to complicate the narrative of foundation benevolence by exposing the Carnegie Corporation's endorsement of scientific racism and white supremacy at home and abroad.[10]

The chapters in this collection frequently engage with the actions of foundations, and with their attendant critiques; however, Carnegie, Ford and Rockefeller are not the primary focus of this collection. Rather, this book is part of a renewed scholarly trend that seeks to move beyond the Big 3, while at the same time acknowledging their significance and that of foundations more broadly to the story of US philanthropy. In particular, recent scholarship has embraced a more diverse and contingent understanding of what philanthropy is, and who we consider a philanthropist. Increasingly, historians are paying greater attention to how intersections of race, class and gender shaped philanthropic activity and discourse and impacted the (two-way) relationship between the donor and the recipient. For instance, while older, narrower definitions of philanthropy tended to focus on white, middle- and upper-class actors, casting people and communities of colour primarily as passive recipients of aid, new work pays greater attention to the vital contributions of people of colour to charity and reform work, and to debates about the purpose and methods of philanthropy.

Some historians have revealed how African Americans asserted their own agency in response to white northern philanthropic efforts to reform Black education in the South, while others have noted that such projects extended to and intersected with similar scientific surveys and programmes of uplift in Africa.[11] Meanwhile, Julie Reed's *Serving the Nation* (2016) explores Cherokee construction of a system of welfare provisions and protections, while Anelise Hanson Shrout has situated nineteenth-century native philanthropy as a political tool to assert autonomy and express solidarity with other marginalized and oppressed peoples.[12] Black philanthropy has also received increasing attention from scholars such as Evan Faulkenbury who explains how the Voter Education Project contributed to the southern Black freedom movement at the height of the classic Civil Rights movement in the 1960s.[13] Further emphasizing – and celebrating – the agency and philanthropy of Black Americans, Tyrone McKinley Freeman's new biography of Madam C J Walker highlights the close links between her entrepreneurship and her charity work and activism.[14]

Indeed, biography has frequently been a useful method for historians to explore the relationship between class, gender, race and forms of giving.[15] Profiles of prominent women philanthropists have emphasized the importance of women in shaping philanthropic discourse and have demonstrated that public giving, especially before the turn of the twentieth century, represented a rare outlet for women's political expression and organization. For instance, scholars have used the stories of women like Ellen Browning Scripps and Mary Elizabeth Garrett to illustrate the many areas of American life that their philanthropy touched, from abolition to suffrage, from labour and medicine to science, the arts and women's education.[16] Kathleen McCarthy, too, has argued that the flourishing of American arts and culture in the nineteenth century relied in no small part upon philanthropic activity – including the foundation of cultural institutions and the patronage and sponsorship of middle- and upper-class women donors.[17] Yet philanthropy was not the sole preserve of elite women. Historians like Lori Ginzberg, Anne Boylan and most recently Carolyn Lawes have explored how involvement in volunteer reform associations – including the campaigns for temperance and abolitionism – represented a palatable public outlet for the perceived moral superiority of women before the Civil War, and helped lay the groundwork for women's political organization in the latter half of the nineteenth century.[18] During the Civil War, women mobilized in large numbers to relieve the suffering of soldiers, refugees and orphans, framing their labours as expressions of patriotic commitment and staking a claim for benevolence, reform and charity as a field of endeavour best populated by women.[19] Yet, as historians in this collection demonstrate, women's involvement in philanthropy did not fade away with the rise of the foundation and the acquisition of the franchise. Even so, charity has traditionally been coded in gendered terms as sentimental and feminine, often an expression of religious faith, while philanthropy, especially foundation philanthropy, is considered more objective and rational. Recent scholarship has sought to destabilize this association of religion with charity alone as numerous studies highlight the intersection between religion and philanthropy.

The antebellum reform movements that aimed to transform the world, and not merely relieve suffering, before the Civil War relied not only on postmillennial theological pronouncements but also on armies of dedicated volunteers whose donations and organizing efforts sought to create a utopia in America.[20] Many of these individuals were driven by both their faith and a love of humanity. In recent decades, scholars have demonstrated the importance of 'humanitarianism' as a motivating and organizing principle for philanthropic work and thought. Far from being a twentieth-century invention, humanitarianism emerged before the revolution as a moral vocabulary that insisted upon the equality of souls.[21] Nicole Eustace has convincingly demonstrated the potential of emotions history as a framework to understand evolving ideas about humanity, moral and civic duty, and natural rights – all ideas which nourished benevolence in the early Republic.[22] Yet, as Susan Ryan and others have noted, the language of humanitarianism from its inception was loaded with assumptions of cultural superiority and racialized prejudices that were in turn baked into benevolent activity.[23] In the wake of conflict and disaster in the early twentieth century, humanitarianism remained a powerful but contextually contingent justification for philanthropic activity in many forms and places.

The history of both humanitarianism and philanthropy has always had an international dimension; since the creation of the United States, the philanthropic efforts of its citizens – from missionaries and voluntary aid societies to charities and foundations – have looked beyond its own borders. Amanda B. Moniz finds the origins of global American philanthropic endeavours in the reactions to the revolution by situating British and American activists as part of a wider international network of humanitarianism.[24] Other scholars, such as Emily Conroy-Krutz, have recounted how during the early Republic Christian missionaries motivated by religious, philanthropic and imperial impulses negotiated the new country's standing in the world.[25] Similarly, Ian Tyrrell illustrates the centrality of moral reform to the work of missionaries in the late nineteenth and early twentieth centuries, which influenced political and social developments both within and beyond the United States.[26] Missions continued to provide women, who were less likely than men to be involved in formal diplomacy, opportunities to influence and shape US relations with the wider world.[27] David A. Hollinger, David P. King and Heather D. Curtis have also explored the legacy and influence of Protestant and evangelical missions in shaping American liberalism at home and US humanitarianism and aid abroad.[28]

Towards the beginning of the twentieth century, the work of missionaries began to intersect with that of philanthropists and others who sought to provide either relief to disaster-struck areas or development programmes to those in need, especially in the corner of the globe referred to as the Near East.[29] As the United States became increasingly embroiled in global politics in the mid-twentieth century due to its engagement in the Second World War and Cold War, voluntary associations such as the American Red Cross continued to play a pivotal role in shaping US foreign relations, providing emergency relief and influencing international development.[30] Some scholars, such as Stephen R. Porter, have seen in these philanthropic efforts of multiple state and non-state actors the origins of an imperfect and idealized 'benevolent empire'. Sarah B. Snyder has explored the role of non-state actors, including philanthropic NGOs, in advocating human rights in US foreign relations. Others, most notably Edward H. Berman and Inderjeet Parmar, have criticized the Big 3 Foundations in particular for adopting policies that sought to maintain and extend US hegemony in the developing world under the guise of altruistic benevolence.[31]

As the above-mentioned survey suggests, any work purporting to address philanthropy must first grapple with the continuing conundrum of definition. Questions of who does philanthropy, under what aegis, where, towards whom and with what effects (intended or otherwise) are taking historians in increasingly exciting and diverse directions and are destabilizing narrow, traditional definitions which tended to focus on the actions of elite and middle-class white actors, often operating within the parameters of 'the foundation'. Embracing the instability of the *language* of philanthropy further enriches this expanding field of inquiry. While 'philanthropy' in the twenty-first century may conjure up an image of detached managerialism, super-wealthy donors and long-term infrastructural projects, often in the realm of international development, in the most literal translation of the word – an interpretation proudly adopted by self-confessed practitioners in the early Republic – 'philanthropy' encompassed any act which deliberately expressed a love of humanity. Actors and recipients involved in 'giving', broadly defined, used a range of terms interchangeably, and frequently inconsistently, to describe their behaviour. Throughout the eighteenth and nineteenth centuries, 'philanthropy' competed and overlapped with 'charity', 'reform' and 'benevolence' – what Anelise Shrout calls a 'constellation of terms' that broadly described acts of giving or of conscious and public dedication to the improvement of the world.[32] As scholars in our collection demonstrate, we might add to this list words like 'voluntarism', 'humanitarianism', 'aid' and more besides. This terminological fluidity serves to challenge the hard chronological and philosophical line drawn by earlier scholars between 'charity' – with its associations of emotionalism (frequently coded as feminine), an overarching religiosity, and its ultimate aim of urgently and directly alleviating short-term suffering – and 'philanthropy' – a supposed invention of the late nineteenth century driven by bureaucratization, professionalization, secularization and masculinization, and increasingly associated with structural solutions and corporate giving.[33] This collection – in line with the new directions outlined earlier – seeks to question the usefulness and accuracy of this teleology.

As the chapters here illustrate, older ideas about charity and benevolence did not vanish; philanthropy in the twentieth century, for instance, still encompassed acts of voluntarism, drew upon the contributions and directions of women, and still wrestled with the role of religion in defining its remit and parameters. The 'philanthropists' profiled herein do not fit one neat mould but, regardless of the time and spaces in which they operated, are drawn from many walks of life. Nor did they understand and justify their work in identical ways, beyond perhaps a shared underlying conviction (sometimes shaken by experience) of the goodness and necessity of their actions. Moreover, their work – whether engaged in local acts of kindness, the management of international projects, the day-to-day running of benevolent programmes, or the loftier articulation of the meaning and purpose of philanthropy – did not travel along a one-way street, but was frequently bound up in dynamic and transformative encounters with the proposed beneficiaries of this work, in unexpected and sometimes troubling ways. The chapters presented here demonstrate the possibilities of using 'philanthropy' as a framework to understand American ideas about community, civic responsibility, national identity, inequality, friendship and the meaning of humanity – and the ways since the eighteenth century in which these ideas have evolved, intersected and even fragmented at home, abroad and in the spaces between.

The first section considers the interplay between religion – specifically, Protestant Christianity – and philanthropy, a fraught and often controversial relationship. Our authors here grapple with how assumptions of cultural and moral superiority have underpinned much Christian philanthropy; assumptions which were often thrown into sharp relief by encounters with other religions, cultures and political ideologies. Chapter 1 addresses the work of the United States Christian Commission, a civilian relief agency established by northern Protestant evangelicals, during the American Civil War. As Rachel Williams reveals, while the USCC was primarily concerned with ministering to Union troops, it faced challenges to its remit and even accusations of disloyalty when it extended its philanthropy to Confederate troops. In response, USCC workers employed scriptural justifications to cast their work with enemy troops as not only spiritually but also politically necessary for the salvation of the Union. Williams's chapter provides a case study of an organization caught between antebellum models of voluntary 'benevolence' and newly professionalized charity activity and suggests that philanthropy was never politically neutral, even when those engaged in it attempted to frame it as such.

In Chapter 2, Scott Libson considers the work of the American Committee for Armenian and Syrian Relief, later incorporated as Near East Relief, in the wake of the Armenian Genocide. ACASR attempted, in order to avoid sectarian division and appeal to a wide constituency of donors as possible, to frame their work as 'non-religious'. At the same time, they drew on implicitly and explicitly Christian imagery and what Libson calls a 'vague religiosity' to legitimize their work, seeking to harness the sentimental power of religion through fundraising campaigns like 'Golden Rule Sundays'. According to Libson's work, the framing of giving as a universal moral good demonstrates that disaggregating religion and philanthropy altogether was a tall order in the first decades of the twentieth century. In so doing, moreover, Libson challenges a persistent historiographical binary that has defined philanthropic activity as either religious or secular.

Chapter 3, similarly, explores the international dimensions of religious philanthropy. Focusing in particular on Italy and Colombia, Emma Long discusses the efforts of the Evangelical Foreign Missions Association to protect religious liberty for Protestants in Catholic countries in the middle decades of the twentieth century. For these missionaries, protecting religious freedoms – not least the right to worship freely and openly – was an act of philanthropy as profound and necessary as establishing schools and orphanages. Yet, in navigating local laws and customs to assert the religious freedoms of both missionaries and local residents, evangelicals were prompted to reassess the robustness of America's own religious liberty protections. Long reveals that evangelical interactions with the specific legal and judicial contexts of Italy and Colombia fuelled not only a closer relationship with the federal government but also a growing suspicion of Catholic influence in the United States.

The second section considers the establishment of cultural networks and communities as motors and conduits of philanthropy and provides insights into the physical spaces in which philanthropy– not least intellectual and cultural activities funded and influenced by philanthropic individuals and organizations – took place. The three chapters here interrogate the operation of wealth and power in forming and shaping cultural institutions, the role of culture in politics, activism and diplomacy and the frequently ambivalent relationship between public and private funding for arts and culture. In Chapter 4, Bridget Bennett explores the radical potential – and limitations – of libraries as 'unquiet' spaces where dissenting voices can be preserved, amplified and placed in conversation with others. Bennett focuses on the Quaker abolitionist Anthony Benezet and his close association with the Library Company of Philadelphia, and on Wilson Armistead, a Leeds-born merchant and anti-slavery activist who sought to promote Benezet's work and legacy as a philanthropist. Libraries, print culture and literacy played crucial roles in creating transatlantic networks of readers and thinkers in a period in which abolition was what she calls 'the most significant philanthropic concern of the nineteenth century'. Bennett thus reveals the processes by which philanthropic intellectual currents, and international abolitionist communities, were democratized, diversified and expanded in the decades before the Civil War.

By the mid-twentieth century, public discussion about the purpose and position of cultural institutions in American life had intensified considerably. The political implications of the ambivalent relationship between art and philanthropy attracted increasingly intense scrutiny in the Cold War era. Karen Patricia Heath's chapter, the fifth in this volume, reveals how the demise of federally funded New Deal art projects, and a growing atmosphere of anti-communist anxiety, gave rise to new debates about arts patronage and the intersection between the cultural and political spheres in the early Cold War. Heath teases out tensions between public and private funding, and between populism and elitism, through her focus on the conservative arts foundation established by supermarket tycoon George Huntington Hartford II in 1948. As with the libraries of Bennett's chapter, the physical spaces and buildings of the Foundation are a crucial part of the story. Located in the Santa Monica hills, the Foundation espoused an anti-modernist aesthetic vision that chafed against a perceived north-eastern artistic elite, and championed what Hartford believed to be wholesome, intelligible art. Heath not only illustrates that arts patronage represents an important lens through which to understand the heterogeneity of mid-century conservatism but also stresses the necessity of positioning the arts, and the politics of arts funding, more centrally into histories of philanthropy.

The relationship between culture, politics and philanthropy in the Cold War forms the backdrop for the final chapter in this section, too; this time, however, we look abroad to West Berlin where, as Amanda Niedfeldt details, the Ford Foundation expended over $6 million over a quarter century, establishing a raft of cultural centres in the early 1960s, including an Artist-in-Residence Programme and the Berlin Literary Colloquium. The Ford Foundation's presence in West Berlin, Niedfeldt argues, complicates prevailing understandings of Cold War philanthropic foundations as unquestioning conduits for US government money and fronts for CIA agendas. Instead, the Foundation navigated tricky relationships between its own trustees and managers, the US and West German governments, the artists it funded, and the Berlin public, demonstrating not only the complexity of soft diplomacy in these decades but the continuing value of scrutinizing the work and operations of major philanthropic foundations like Ford.

The third section explores how philanthropists, philanthropic organizations and other non-state actors engaging in philanthropic activity have contributed to US cultural diplomacy and international development in the twentieth century. Each chapter highlights how different philanthropic endeavours sought to not only improve the lives of the recipients of support but also responded to and, to varying degrees, sought to shape the political and international context in which they operated. Linda Johnson examines the evolution of fundraising strategies for Tsuda Umeko's Women's English Language Academy (JEJ), a Tokyo women's college, in the early twentieth century to assess its implications for US-Japanese cultural diplomacy. In 1924, led by Japanese-American activist Yonako Abiko, JEJ fundraising became a platform for opposition to Japanese exclusion legislation by capitalizing on Tsuda's prestige and the reputation of her school as a 'Bridge Across the Pacific' that educated a network of pro-American women teachers throughout Japan. Johnson argues that during a period of increasing acrimony between the two nations, educational philanthropy became a gender-specific approach to US-Japanese cultural diplomacy and immigration-policy advocacy. Drawing on US foreign relations history and transnational American studies, Johnson evaluates the contradictions of moral uplift discourse within the American philanthropy tradition.

Ben Offiler examines the origins of the Near East Foundation's rural welfare programme in Iran from the initial invitation by the Iranian government to conduct a survey of rural conditions within the country in 1943 through to the provision of Point Four funds by the Truman administration that allowed for a significant expansion of NEF activities in the early 1950s. During this period, the NEF embarked on a series of education, agricultural and sanitation projects to help improve the living conditions of rural Iranians. The chapter argues that while the NEF's small-scale, incremental approach to development gained widespread acclaim and brought it to the attention of the US Department of State, it also laid the groundwork for future challenges as government funding necessitated a shift towards larger, nationwide programmes. Offiler also suggests that although it focused primarily on the daily experiences of rural Iranians, the NEF implicitly aligned itself with the Truman administration's broader strategy of containing communism, thereby highlighting the intersection between private philanthropy and US foreign policy.

Kevin Grimm addresses the myriad small ways that the AFL-CIO and the International Confederation of Free Trade Unions, an umbrella pro-Western labour group, aided numerous African Union movements during the 1950s and 1960s. In doing so, the chapter provides a material history of the philanthropic efforts of American trade unions, detailing specific examples of activities, including book donations, provision of cars for transportation, and money for legal defence funds or to support striking workers. Grimm demonstrates the level of African engagement and agency in relation to American and Western philanthropy, as well as shedding light on an informal and somewhat haphazard method of philanthropy by Western NGOs in the labour sphere as they sought to coax African unions into the Western fold.

The final section addresses two examples of 'challenging philanthropy'. Margaret Nettesheim Hoffmann explores a case study that challenges the very concept of philanthropy as being a social good. In 1915, the United States Commission on

Industrial Relations produced a report highly critical of the growing influence of philanthropic foundations. The commission chairman, Frank P. Walsh, highlighted the pernicious link between foundation activities and growing industrial unrest, which was a reaction to the perceived exploitation of labourers and the working classes. For the first time in American history, in an extensive and detailed report, a federal task force directly linked the history of labour unrest to the activities of philanthropic foundations. As Nettesheim Hoffmann indicates, Walsh, a committed progressive, rejected the idea that philanthropic foundations were a force for good or aligned with progressive values. Instead, Walsh condemned the growth of capital, income inequality and the concentration of wealth within the hands of a very few powerful individuals. Philanthropic foundations were being used, according to Walsh, to provide capitalists with a mechanism to further consolidate their wealth, avoid government and public oversight, and strengthen their political influence. By shedding light on the complex relationships of the individuals involved in producing the Commission's report, Nettesheim Hoffmann demonstrates how foundations were simultaneously subject to robust critique by progressives like Walsh but also able to deflect scrutiny of links between their philanthropy and the exploitation of workers.

In turn, Miguel Hernandez's chapter presents a challenging case of philanthropy by examining the ways in which the Ku Klux Klan used tactics and discourse associated with charitable giving to cultivate a positive image. During the Progressive Era, as philanthropic foundations increasingly exerted influence over civil society, many Americans continued to engage in voluntarism through their participation in and fundraising for communitarian organizations and fraternities. In an era before social security, fraternities such as the Freemasons or the Odd Fellows provided invaluable relief for their own members through mutual aid insurance and for the wider public by raising funds for charitable projects such as orphanages and hospitals. Although as an organization the Klan of the 1920s is remembered more for its racist ideology and violent vigilantism, the order's founders had also created the movement as a fraternity, emulating other established orders of the period. By definition, fraternities were exclusionary both in terms of their membership and their charitable giving. The Klan's growth into a mass movement in the years after the First World War was predicated on its status as a fraternity and its widely publicized donations to schools or churches. Hernandez argues that the Second Klan, with its nearly four million members, was able to wield considerable influence and raise substantial funds to combat the perceived roots of America's ills in this rapidly changing decade. By detailing how this ethnically exclusive and racist fraternity employed charity and philanthropy to build its membership, fend off public criticism and defend white Protestant American interests, Hernandez further complicates the notion and narrative of philanthropy as an act of altruism or benevolence.

By drawing out common themes and threads within and between these very different case studies, geographic locations and time periods – that is, by eschewing a straightforwardly chronological structure – these four sections demonstrate the variety and richness of American philanthropy and its histories. As the work showcased here demonstrates, questions of what constitutes philanthropy, what social purpose it serves, who engages in it and for what reasons, remain applicable and relevant across time and space, and so by decentering a teleological interpretation of the evolution of philanthropy in America and by Americans we hope not only to demonstrate the benefits of embracing a broad definition of philanthropy but to highlight the ways in which cultural assumptions and biases have often shaped philanthropic impulses, the potency of debates over the relationship of religion and voluntarism to philanthropy, and the enduring importance of the interplay between the domestic and international to understanding how and why philanthropists sought, at the heart of it, to improve their version of the world.

# Notes

1  Merle Curti, 'The Field of American Philanthropy as a Field of Research', *American Historical Review* 62, no. 2 (1957): 352–63, 363.
2  Robert H. Bremner, *American Philanthropy* (Chicago: University of Chicago Press, 1960); Charles I. Foster, *Errand of Mercy: The Evangelical United Front, 1790–1837* (Chapel Hill: University of North Carolina Press, 1960); Clifford S. Griffin, *Their Brothers' Keepers: Moral Stewardship in the United States, 1800–1865* (New Brunswick: Rutgers University Press, 1960). For the critique of the 'social control' thesis, see especially Lois W. Banner, 'Religious Benevolence as Social Control: A Critique of an Interpretation', *Journal of American History*, 60, no. 1 (1973): 23–41.
3  Merle Curti, *American Philanthropy Abroad: A History* (New Brunswick: Rutgers University Press, 1963).
4  See, for instance, *Philanthropic Foundations: New Scholarship, New Possibilities*, edited by Ellen Condliffe Lagemann (Bloomington: Indiana University Press, 1999); *Charity, Philanthropy, and Civility in American History*, edited by Lawrence J. Friedman and Mark D. McGarvie (Cambridge: Cambridge University Press, 2003); Kathleen D. McCarthy, *American Creed: Philanthropy and the Rise of Civil Society, 1700–1865* (Chicago: University of Chicago Press, 2005); Oliver Zunz, *Philanthropy in America: A History* (Princeton: Princeton University Press 2012).
5  A sample of work addressing the history, organization and influence of Rockefeller, Ford and Carnegie, as well as the lives of John D. Rockefeller, Henry Ford, and Andrew Carnegie and their families, includes Frederick P. Keppel, *The Foundation: Its Place in American Life* (New York: MacMillan Company, 1930); John T. Flynn, *God's Gold: The Story of Rockefeller and His Times* (New York: Harcourt, Brace & Co., 1935); Raymond Fosdick, *The Story of the Rockefeller Foundation* (1952); David Lanier Lewis, *The Public Image of Henry Ford: An American Folk Hero and His Company* (Detroit: Wayne State University Press, 1976); John Ensor Harr and Peter J. Johnson, *The Rockefeller Century* (New York: Scribner, 1988); Ellen Condliffe Lagemann, *The Politics of Knowledge: The Carnegie Corporation, Philanthropy, and Public Policy* (Chicago: University of Chicago Press, 1989); Ron Chernow, *Titan: The Life of John D. Rockefeller, Sr.* (New York: Vintage Books, 1998); David Nasaw, *Andrew Carnegie* (New York: Penguin Books, 2006); Eric John Abrahamson, Sam Hurst and Barbara Shubinski, *Democracy and Philanthropy: The Rockefeller Foundation and the American Experiment* (New York: The Rockefeller Foundation, 2013); Patricia L. Rosenfield, *A World of Giving: Carnegie Corporation of New York, A Century of International Philanthropy* (New York: PublicAffairs, 2014).

6 For a sample of work that critiques contemporary philanthropy and foundations, see Sarah Reckow, *Follow the Money: How Foundation Dollars Change Public School Politics* (New York: Oxford University Press, 2013); Erica Kohl-Arenas, *The Self-Help Myth: How Philanthropy Fails to Alleviate Poverty* (Oakland, CA: University of California Press, 2015); Lisa McGoey, *No Such Thing as a Free Gift: The Gates Foundation and the Price of Philanthropy* (New York: Verso, 2015); Rob Reich, Chiara Cordelli and Lucy Bernholz, *Philanthropy in Democratic Societies: History, Institutions, Values* (Chicago: University of Chicago Press, 2016); Megan Tompkins-Stange, *Policy Patrons: Philanthropy, Education Reform, and the Politics of Influence* (Cambridge, MA: Harvard Education Press, 2016); David Callahan, *The Givers: Wealth, Power, and Philanthropy in a New Gilded Age* (New York: Penguin Random House, 2017); Rob Reich, *Just Giving: Why Philanthropy is Failing Democracy and How It Can Do Better* (Princeton: Princeton University Press, 2018); Anand Giridharadas, *Winners Take All: The Elite Charade of Changing the World* (New York: Penguin Random House, 2019).

7 Alice O'Connor, *Social Science for What?: Philanthropy and the Social Question in a World Turned Rightside Up* (New York: Russell Sage Foundation, 2007); Donald Fisher, *Fundamental Development of the Social Sciences: Rockefeller Philanthropy and the United States Social Science Research Council* (Ann Arbor: University of Michigan Press, 1993). More broadly, the embrace of science, data and the social sciences in the Progressive Era changed methodological approaches to the relief of suffering, with profound ramifications for social welfare policy and for the categorization of the 'deserving poor'. See Brent Ruswick, *Almost Worthy: The Poor, Paupers, and the Science of Charity in America, 1877–1917* (Indianapolis: University of Indiana Press, 2013); Elizabeth N. Agnew, *From Charity to Social Work: Mary E. Richmond and the Creation of an American Profession* (Chicago: University of Illinois Press, 2004).

8 Robert E. Kohler, *Partners in Science: Foundations and Natural Scientists, 1900–1945* (Chicago: University of Chicago, 1991); Mark Solovey, *Shaky Foundations: The Politics-Patronage-Social Science Nexus in Cold War America* (New Brunswick: Rutgers University Press, 2013). For further reading on philanthropy and American social sciences see Martin Bulmer, *The Chicago School of Sociology: Institutionalization, Diversity, and the Rise of Sociological Research* (Chicago: University of Chicago Press, 1984); *Pittsburgh Surveyed: Social Science and Social Reform in the Early Twentieth Century*, edited by Maurine W. Greenwald and Margo Anderson (Pittsburgh: University of Pittsburgh Press, 1996); Dorothy Ross, *The Origins of American Social Science* (New York City: Cambridge University Press, 1991); Alice O'Connor, *Poverty Knowledge: Social Science, Social Policy, and the Poor in Twentieth-Century U.S. History* (Princeton: Princeton University Press, 2002).

9 Karen Ferguson, *Top Down: The Ford Foundation, Black Power, and the Reinvention of Racial Liberalism* (Philadelphia: University of Pennsylvania Press, 2013); Noliwe Rooks, *White Money/Black Power* (New York City: Penguin Random House, 2006).

10 Maribel Morey, *White Philanthropy: Carnegie Corporation's An American Dilemma and the Making of a White World Order* (Chapel Hill: University of North Carolina Press, 2021); Tiffany Willoughby-Herard, *Waste of a White Skin: The Carnegie Corporation and the Racial Logic of White Vulnerability* (Berkeley: University of California Press, 2015).

11 Joan Malczewski, *Building a New Educational State: Foundations, Schools, and the American South* (Chicago: University of Chicago Press, 2016); Eric Anderson and Alfred A. Moss, Jr., *Dangerous Donations: Northern Philanthropy and Southern Black Education, 1902–1930* (Columbia, Missouri: University of Missouri Press, 1999);

Kenneth James King, *Pan-Africanism and Education: A Study of Race Philanthropy and Education in the Southern States of America and East Africa* (Oxford: Clarendon Press, 1971); Helen Tilley, *Africa as a Living Laboratory: Empire, Development, and the Problem of Scientific Knowledge, 1870–1950* (Chicago: University of Chicago Press, 2011).

12  Julie L. Reed, *Serving the Nation: Cherokee Sovereignty and Social Welfare, 1800–1907* (Norman: University of Oklahoma Press, 2016); Anelise Hanson Shrout, 'A "Voice of Benevolence From the Western Wilderness": Native Philanthropy and Political Critique in the Trans-Mississippi West', *Journal of the Early Republic* 35, no. 4 (2015): 553–78.

13  Evan Faulkenbury, *Poll Power: The Voter Education Project and the Movement for the Ballot in the American South* (Chapel Hill: University of North Carolina Press, 2019).

14  Tyrone McKinley Freeman, *Madam CJ Walker's Gospel of Giving: Black Women's Philanthropy During Jim Crow* (Chicago: University of Illinois Press, 2020).

15  See for instance, Ruth Crocker, *Mrs Russell Sage: Women's Activism and Philanthropy in Gilded Age and Progressive America* (Indianapolis: University of Indiana Press, 2008).

16  Molly McClain, *Ellen Browning Scripps: New Money and American Philanthropy* (Lincoln: University of Nebraska Press, 2017); Kathleen Waters Sander, *Mary Elizabeth Garrett: Society and Philanthropy in the Gilded Age* (Baltimore: Johns Hopkins University Press, 2020). Indeed, the education of women and girls has been a focal point for numerous women and organizations throughout the nineteenth and twentieth century. *Women and Philanthropy in Education*, edited by Andrea Walton (Bloomington: Indiana University Press, 2005).

17  Kathleen D. McCarthy, *Women's Culture: American Philanthropy and Art, 1830–1930* (Chicago: University of Chicago Press, 1991) and *Noblesse Oblige: Charity and Cultural Patronage in Chicago, 1849–1929* (Chicago: University of Chicago Press, 1982). See also Linda Dowling, *Charles Eliot Norton: The Art of Reform in Nineteenth Century America* (Durham: University of New Hampshire Press, 2007). For another perspective that emphasizes the role of philanthropy and patronage in the realm of literature, see Francesca Sawaya, *The Difficult Art of Giving: Patronage, Philanthropy, and the American Literary Market* (Philadelphia: University of Pennsylvania Press, 2014).

18  Lori Ginzberg, *Women and the Work of Benevolence: Morality, Politics, and Class in the Nineteenth Century United States* (New Haven: Yale University Press, 1990); Anne M. Boylan, *The Origins of Women's Activism: New York and Boston, 1797, 1840* (Chapel Hill: University of North Carolina Press, 2003); Carolyn Lawes, *Women and Reform in a New England Community, 1815–1860* (Lexington: University Press of Kentucky, 2000).

19  Jeanie Attie, *Patriotic Toil: Northern Women and the American Civil War* (Ithaca: Cornell University Press, 1998); Judith Giesberg, *Civil War Sisterhood: The US Sanitary Commission and Women's Politics in Transition* (Boston: Northeastern University Press, 2000).

20  Robert H. Abzug, *Cosmos Crumbling: American Reform and the Religious Imagination* (Oxford: Oxford University Press, 1994); Steven Mintz, *Moralists and Modernizers: America's Pre-Civil War Reformer* (Baltimore: Johns Hopkins University Press, 1995); Philip F. Gura, *Man's Better Angels: Romantic Reformers and the Coming of the Civil War* (Cambridge, MA: Harvard University Press, 2017).

21  See for instance Peter Stamatov, *The Origins of Global Humanitarianism: Religion, Empires, and Advocacy* (Cambridge: Cambridge University Press, 2013); Michael Barnett, *Empire of Humanity: A History of Humanitarianism* (Ithaca: Cornell University Press, 2011).

22  Nicole Eustace, *Passion is the Gale: Emotion, Power, and the Coming of the American Revolution* (Chapel Hill: University of North Carolina Press, 2012). See also Elizabeth B. Clark, "'The Sacred Rights of the Weak': Pain, Sympathy, and the Culture of Individual Rights in Antebellum America', *Journal of American History* 82, no. 2 (1995): 463–93.

23  Susan Ryan, *The Grammar of Good Intentions: Race and the Antebellum Culture of Benevolence* (Ithaca: Cornell University Press, 2003).

24  Amanda B. Moniz, *From Empire to Humanity: The American Revolution and the Origins of Humanitarianism* (Oxford: Oxford University Press, 2016).

25  Emily Conroy-Krutz, *Christian Imperialism: Converting the World in the Early American Republic* (Ithaca: Cornell University Press, 2018). For more on early international philanthropic networks see Mary Kathleen Eyring, *Captains of Charity: The Writing and Wages of Postrevolutionary Atlantic Benevolence* (Durham: University of New Hampshire Press, 2017).

26  Ian Tyrrell, *Reforming the World: The Creation of America's Moral Empire* (Princeton: Princeton University Press, 2010).

27  Laura R. Prieto, 'Introduction: Women and Missionary Encounters with Foreign Nationalism in the 1920s', *Diplomatic History* 43, no. 2 (2019): 237–245; Barbara Reeves-Ellington, 'American Women Missionaries on Trial in Turkey: Religion, Diplomacy, and Public Perceptions in the 1920s', Ibid: 246–64; Connie Shemo, 'Imperialism, Race, and Rescue: Transformations in the Woman's Foreign Mission Movement after World War I', Ibid: 265–81; Rui Kohiyama, 'The 1927 Exchange of Friendship Dolls: U.S.-Japan Cultural Diplomacy in the Inter-War Years', Ibid: 282–304.

28  David A. Hollinger, *Protestants Abroad: How Missionaries Tried to Change the World but Changed America* (Princeton: Princeton University Press, 2018); David P. King, *God's Internationalists: World Vision and the Age of Evangelical Humanitarianism* (Philadelphia: University of Pennsylvania Press, 2019); Heather D. Curtis, *Holy Humanitarians: American Evangelicals and Global Aid* (Cambridge, MA: Harvard University Press, 2018).

29  Michael Limberg, 'Abundant Life: U.S. Aid and Development in the Near East, 1919–1939' (Ph.D. diss., University of Connecticut, 2018); J. Charles Schencking, 'Giving Most and Giving Differently: Humanitarianism as Diplomacy Following Japan's 1923 Earthquake', *Diplomatic History* 43, no. 4 (2019): 729–57; Guy Aiken, 'Feeding Germany: American Quakers in the Weimar Republic', *Diplomatic History* 43, no. 4 (2019): 597–617.

30  Julia F. Irwin, *Making the World Safe: The American Red Cross and a Nation's Humanitarian Awakening* (Oxford: Oxford University Press, 2013); Joshua Hideo Mather, 'Citizens of Compassion: Relief, Development, and State-Private Cooperation in U.S. Foreign Relations, 1939-1973', (Ph.D. diss., St. Louis University, 2015); *Rachel M. McCleary, Global Compassion: Private Voluntary Organizations and U.S. Foreign Policy since 1939* (Oxford University Press, 2009). For more on the domestic role of voluntary associations, see Elisabeth Clemens, *Civic Gifts: Voluntarism and the Making of the American Nation-State* (Chicago: University of Chicago Press, 2020).

31  Stephen R. Porter, *Benevolent Empire: U.S. Power, Humanitarianism, and the World's Dispossessed* (Philadelphia: University of Pennsylvania Press, 2016); Sarah B. Snyder, *From Selma to Moscow: How Human Rights Activists Transformed U. S. Foreign Policy* (New York: Columbia University Press, 2018); Edward H. Berman, *The Influence of the Carnegie, Ford, and Rockefeller Foundations on American Foreign Policy: The Ideology of Philanthropy* (Albany: State University of New York Press, 1983); Inderjeet Parmar, *Foundations of the American Century: The Ford, Carnegie, and Rockefeller Foundations in the Rise of American Power* (New York: Columbia University Press, 2012).

32  Anelise Shrout, 'Time, Talent, and Treasure: Philanthropy in the Early Republic', in *A Companion to US Foreign Relations: Colonial Era to the Present*, vol. 1, ed. Christopher R. W. Dietrich (Hoboken: John Wiley and Sons, 2020): 45–65, 49.

33  As Benjamin Soskis has noted, this binary is not the creation of historians. Self-proclaimed 'philanthropists' then and now have constructed and articulated a rationale for their actions against what they have condemned as 'charity' in order to legitimize their work, while practitioners of 'charity' have conversely sought to issue a corrective to the perceived managerial excesses and institutional coldness of 'philanthropy'. Soskis, 'Both More and No More: The Historical Split between Charity and Philanthropy', *Hudson Institute*, 15 October 2014. Available online: https://www.hudson.org/research/10723-both-more-and-no-more-the-historical-split-between-charity-and-philanthropy (accessed 30 October 2021). On the distinction between charity and philanthropy, see also Jeremy Beer, *The Philanthropic Revolution: An Alternative History of American Charity* (Philadelphia: University of Pennsylvania Press, 2015). An early attempt to complicate the particularly gendered nature of this binary is Elisabeth Israels Perry, 'Men are from the Gilded Age, Women are from the Progressive Era', *Journal of the Gilded Age and Progressive Era* 1, no. 1 (2002): 25–48.

# Religion and philanthropy

# 1

# Heaping coals of fire on the enemy's head

## The political uses of Christian benevolence in the Civil War

Rachel Williams

Shortly after the Battle of Gettysburg, a young Philadelphia minister called John Scott sat with a group of wounded Confederates. He was trying to get them to pray for their immortal souls: they were trying to convince him to get them some tobacco from the hospital stores. Scott struck a bargain. 'Well, if you all read the 14th Chapter of John's Gospel', he told them, 'tomorrow I will bring you the tobacco faithfully.' Both parties kept their side of the bargain, and when Scott next visited the Rebel patients, he was delighted to find 'they had read the New Testament every day and had made up their minds to serve the Lord with all their hearts, the Lord being their helper'. Scott recorded the rest of their conversation in a handwritten report reflecting on his work at Gettysburg. 'I asked them if they was not tired with the service of so unholy a war,' he wrote. 'They all answered in the affirmative. I then asked them if they would not be glad that this unholy war was brought to a close and us all to become one people again, they said yes.'[1]

John Scott was a delegate of the United States Christian Commission, an evangelical relief organization set up by northern clergy and laymen to minister to Union troops during the American Civil War. Over the course of a period of around two weeks in September 1863, Scott worked among the wounded still recuperating in the hastily assembled hospitals outside the Pennsylvania town. In the exit report submitted at the end of his service, he estimated that he had personally spoken with upwards of one hundred men, led several prayer meetings, delivered three sermons and liberally distributed hymn books, Bibles and religious tracts to the men he encountered. His meeting with the wounded Confederates was only one small part of his service, yet he wrote at length and with pride about his successful use of prayer, compassion and mercy to erode his impromptu congregation's dedication to the Confederate cause. He proposed a motion to them: 'that we all come back again and be one people as we was before.' This entreaty, Scott recalled, was met with a chorus of emphatic 'ayes'.

Scott's apparently sincere belief in this mass repentance strikes the modern reader as naïve: he showed no awareness that his (literally captive) audience's acquiescence might have been driven more by their quest for tobacco than by a genuine rejection of the Confederacy. Yet Scott's report offers more than an insight into the author's optimism. It – and the wider work of the Christian Commission – reveals much about the nature of philanthropic activity during the American Civil War, and the ideological tensions and practical challenges faced by philanthropic actors. The Civil War created new and often unanticipated needs, and (especially in the North, where there already existed a robust and well-networked charitable tradition) catalysed what George Frederickson called an 'organised response to suffering'.[2] Philanthropic organizations emerged – or adapted – in an attempt to meet these needs, on both the home and battlefronts.[3] These organizations attempted to harness the conflict to further their own agendas, writing political and – as we will see – religious narratives onto the war and positioning their actions and contributions as central to the successful execution of these visions.

The United States Christian Commission was a case in point. One of several large, non-governmental bodies established by northern civilians during the sectional conflict with the aim of aiding the Union war effort, the Christian Commission (USCC), was established in late 1861 by a group of white evangelical Protestants, most of whom had some ties to the Young Men's Christian Associations. YMCA branches had emerged in major American cities in the decade before the Civil War, their proponents motivated by concern for the moral health of newly arrived urban migrants who, shorn of the guidance of familial networks, were considered susceptible to temptation and vice.[4] The roots of the USCC went back further than the 1850s, however. The organization, in both its personnel and its methods, built on established antebellum patterns of 'philanthropy', a word proponents and critics used interchangeably with 'benevolence' and 'charity' to describe a staggering range of activities aimed at improving and ultimately perfecting the world.[5] Largely undertaken by middle-class volunteers alarmed at how urbanization, immigration and industrialization were apparently creating and compounding poverty and lawlessness, philanthropic work became increasingly organized and bureaucratized in the northern states before the Civil War.[6] Philanthropic activities ran the gamut from conservative, paternalistic attempts at imposing a moral vision based on sobriety, industry and piety, to advocating the radical dismantling and reinvention of existing social structures. Yet whether encouraging a stricter observance of the Sabbath, distributing Bibles, establishing utopian communities or campaigning against prostitution, intemperance or slavery, what united Americans engaged in 'philanthropy' before the Civil War was the ardent belief, as Wendy Gamber puts it, that 'a better world was not only possible but also inevitable'.[7] Much of this philanthropic activity drew upon the religious enthusiasm of the Second Great Awakening, and in particular the urgent millennialism of the flourishing evangelical churches, which posited that human beings must play an active role in preparing the way for Christ's Second Coming.

The Protestant evangelicals associated with the Christian Commission drew on this same 'mixture of anxiety and hope' in their work.[8] They saw the Civil War as an unparalleled opportunity to convert the entire Union army to Christianity, and to begin a snowball effect that would transform and redeem the world, ridding the earth of sin and bringing about the Second Coming of Christ. As the Commission president, dry goods merchant George Hay Stuart – a leading light of the Sunday School movement before the war – claimed: 'the harvest is ripe as well as great, and the sickle should be vigorously thrust in with the least possible delay.'[9] Fuelled by this confidence and energy, the USCC head office in Philadelphia sent a total of approximately 5,000 volunteer workers – known as delegates – to the Union armies for six weeks at a time to minister to the spiritual and bodily needs of Union soldiers and to encourage men in their struggle towards conversion. These delegates (who were, with only a handful of exceptions, men) were primarily evangelical clergymen, theological students and lay preachers associated with northern congregations. Reflecting the roots of the organization in the pre-war YMCAs, most were compelled to volunteer their services by their concerns over the moral health of young men removed from the spiritual guidance of their families and thrust into the unfamiliar environment of the army camp, a place associated not only with physical danger but with sinful temptations such as profanity, gambling and intemperance.

The Christian Commission's work on and near the battlefield included a range of spiritual and bodily ministries designed not only to promote the comfort and well-being of Union soldiers but also to maintain moral standards in the armies, and to urge soldiers to consider the state of their souls, to reject the vicious temptations of the army camp, to repent of their sins, and to turn to Christ. The varied ministries performed by Christian Commission delegates on the battlefront included disseminating Bibles, Testaments, religious tracts, hymn books and religious newspapers, organizing prayer circles and Bible reading groups, holding religious services, praying with the ill, injured, or dying, presiding over funeral services, distributing food, drink and clothing in hospitals, managing portable libraries of appropriate religious and moral literature, and writing letters on behalf of the incapacitated. There was an overtly political motive to this religious philanthropy. The members of the Commission were politically aligned with the Republican Party and the Union cause; few were ardent abolitionists in the Garrisonian mould, but most evinced a robust opposition to slavery, and moreover were firm in their belief that the Union was a political entity ordained by God and crucial to the salvation of the world. They subscribed to the 'redeemer nation' vision of America, which held that the United States and its social and political systems represented the pinnacle of human endeavour, and would eventually, by example and strenuous evangelizing, transform the rest of the world into a utopia ready and worthy to welcome Christ.[10] Therefore, ensuring that the northern armies emerged victorious from the struggle to salvage the American experiment was crucial, and the Commission believed they had an important role to play in bringing that victory about. For USCC delegates, the remaking of Union bodies symbolized and hastened the renewal and reparation of the nation and the Christian values it was assumed to embody. In ministering visibly and relentlessly to northern troops, they cast the Federal soldier as the saviour, not only of the American Union but also of the divine mission bestowed upon the United States by the Almighty: to convert the entire world to evangelical Christianity and catalyse the millennium. The philanthropic remit of the USCC, therefore, hinged upon the conflation of piety and patriotism. One Executive Committee member loftily described the USCC as 'one of the grandest special works ever opened to Christian patriots'.[11]

Casting ministry among Union soldiers as both spiritually and politically righteous was relatively straightforward. However, the chaos of war frequently brought Commission delegates into contact with enemy soldiers. Whether in hospitals, prison stockades, transport depots or on the battlefield in the aftermath of combat, it was near impossible for delegates to avoid Confederate personnel, whom they invariably found in a state of vulnerability and need. These unexpected and unregulated encounters – and the ways in which they strained the fusion of piety and patriotism embedded in the USCC's mission – are the subject of this chapter. When faced with Confederates in need, Commission leaders found that their religious and political agendas did not always neatly align, and they confronted pressing questions from sceptical critics and irate donors about the purpose and worth of their philanthropic endeavours. How much autonomy ought philanthropic organizations be granted in their operations? How was philanthropic labour at the coal face – especially when performed by volunteers – monitored and regulated? Most importantly, who was a worthy recipient of aid? The heightened political polarizatioh of the wartime scenario lent questions surrounding the purpose of organizations like the Christian Commission an added piquancy. This was a time when new philanthropic models – increasingly bureaucratic, professional and secularized – were emerging in competition.[12] Rival organizations, most notably the United States Sanitary Commission, dismissed the USCC's work as sentimental and amateurish. Within this competitive philanthropic landscape, encounters between Christian Commission delegates and Confederate soldiers raised difficult questions for the delegates. On the one hand, making the choice to extend their aid to Rebel troops was consistent with Christian teaching on compassion and mercy. On the other hand, these acts of mercy could just as easily be interpreted as overt betrayals of the Union war effort. This prompted agonizing at all levels of the USCC's operation. Executive Committee members, fighting to demonstrate that the USCC's brand of benevolent voluntarism still had a role to play in improving American society, struggled to neutralize scandalous rumours that called the Commission's loyalty to the Union into question. At the same time, ordinary delegates brought to their work their own interpretations of benevolent duty and devised a scriptural justification that framed their work with Confederates as both pious and patriotic. The work of the Christian Commission – and in particular its contentious work among Confederate soldiers – illustrated that philanthropy, regardless of its intentions, can never be apolitical.

The question of how to treat enemy combatants was not merely one for individual delegates to weigh against their consciences. Rather, this question was part of a larger public debate about the meaning and limits of loyalty in the Civil War. Treason (theoretically a capital offence) became a malleable vocabulary employed inconsistently and zealously by people from all walks of life to condemn and police the supposedly disloyal behaviour – and even thoughts and words – of others.[13] As William Blair explains, what constituted treasonous action was unclear, and 'routine activities considered personal in peacetime became potentially dangerous in a civil war'.[14] Arguably, religious ministers were held to even higher standards than others, given their public status and role as community spokespeople. The behaviour and political sympathies of northern ministers, Sean Scott has recently noted, was closely monitored by their congregations and the wider public, and instances of apparent disloyalty were punished with ostracization, removal from the pulpit, or even arrest.[15] That is to say, Christian Commission delegates had to tread carefully. Within the heightened spiciness of wartime public discourse, the Christian Commission feared that acts of personal ministry to individual Rebel soldiers might be interpreted as expressions of disloyalty. The USCC had been founded to further the military and spiritual victory of the United States and cast the secession of the Confederate states as not only a rebellious act but also an overtly sinful one that rejected God's plan for the nation, and jeopardized the project of perfecting the world. Ministering to the perpetrators of this 'wicked' rebellion could serve to undermine the Union war effort, and cast serious doubt upon the dedication of the Commission and its workers to the Republican project.

And yet delegates were given very little guidance on how they should deal with the enemy. Applicants were asked to provide a letter of reference attesting to their good Christian character, and their membership of an evangelical congregation. They were expected to be fit, healthy men who would obey without question the instructions of Commission superiors. Even more importantly, given the notorious impatience certain generals displayed towards meddling, do-gooding non-combatants on the battlefront, they were expected to respect the army chain of command, and, in the paper commission issued to each delegate upon commencement of their service, 'in general strictly to observe all Army and Navy regulations, and abstain from casting reflections upon the authorities, military, medical, and clerical'.[16] Given the potentially disastrous reputational consequences of offering aid to Confederate troops (not to mention the Executive Committee's fondness for specific and copious instructions), it is surprising that delegates were not issued with clearer guidance regarding their behaviour towards the enemy. Delegates' loyalty to the Union cause was largely taken for granted (in some cases, this faith was misplaced, as we will see later), and at no point were delegates explicitly forbidden from ministering to Confederate troops. Rather, the issue was entrusted to their best personal judgement. Delegates were obliquely charged with doing 'whatever the case might demand, or Christian sympathy might devise'.[17]

These vague directions are all the more surprising considering the Commission's fears that their work might be misconstrued or misappropriated for ungodly ends were not without foundation. On several occasions, as frantic letters between Executive Committee members revealed, delegates were suspected of harbouring Rebel sympathies, and some were accused of applying for a commission as a pretext for espionage. This was a legitimate concern. The respect, and the assumption of righteousness, afforded to men of the cloth, meant that ministerial credentials provided an ideal smokescreen for would-be spies: the Confederate scout and Methodist preacher Thomas Conrad, for instance, notoriously used his position to deflect suspicion.[18] The USCC itself fell foul of southern spies masquerading as delegates and taking advantage of the relative immunity this identity provided. On one occasion, Confederate sympathizers marked their wagon – assumed to be carrying illegal goods or stolen information – with the initials 'USCC' to bamboozle Union forces, and the Commission concluded regretfully that 'the name of the Commission was frequently counterfeited by those who had no sympathy with our Government'.[19] Some delegates actively sought out Confederate troops for ministry and aid at the expense of Union men. William Schaeffer, labouring at a hospital in Frederick, Maryland, reported one of his colleagues to the USCC head office, recommending that the man be dismissed and complaining that the man 'wears the [Christian Commission] Pin and gives *all* his attention to the Rebels . . . our men feel this very tenderly, they are very sensitive on that point'.[20] Summarily dismissing another offender, Commission president George Stuart wrote angrily, 'under no circumstances are ministrations to be at a sacrifice to our own brave Union soldiers. We commission none but loyal delegates'.[21]

In addition to these individual rogue delegates, the Commission found itself embroiled in a string of scandals that demonstrated just how damaging and costly accusations of disloyalty, whether founded or not, could be. The response to these incidents illustrated the potency and bitterness of public discourse surrounding treason; it also proved that philanthropic actors found themselves increasingly held to account, with their methods, aims, and recipients monitored and policed by a public ever more sceptical of the motives of self-appointed administrators of benevolence. Notably, the scandals in question occurred in spring 1865, when Union victory was secure, and the question of suitable recrimination and punishment for the defeated South was taking on a new urgency. As northerners debated the terms of surrender and the proportionality of prosecuting Confederate politicians and military leaders for treason, the interactions of northern aid workers with enemy personnel received greater public scrutiny and were subject to stronger censure when found wanting or suspicious.

Hamstrung by Grant's ten-month siege of Petersburg, Richmond finally fell on 3 April 1865, precipitating a mass military and civilian evacuation from the beleaguered Confederate capital, and leaving those too poor or weak to flee with little recourse to aid. Fires set by the retreating Confederate forces devastated large portions of the city, and crime, food shortages and inflation reached extreme levels among both impoverished whites and newly emancipated African Americans.[22] The Christian Commission immediately sent delegates to Richmond to minister to Grant's armies now billeted in the city, and to the remaining Confederate troops (many of them convalescing in Richmond's huge Chimborazo hospital). Soon, these delegates were engaged in alleviating the civilian crisis and smoothing the transition to peacetime, demonstrating compassion across sectional lines. Initially, delegates in Richmond dealt with individual cases, like Mary Bell, a Confederate widow granted a railroad pass to safety in Memphis by Joseph Albree.[23] However, with the plight of civilians showing little sign of abating, and with destitute citizens flocking to makeshift USCC stations in search of food and clothing for their families, the delegates in Richmond, led by two field agents from Massachusetts, Edward Williams and Samuel Fitz, set about distributing supplies to women and children in a more organized fashion.[24] 'During these eventful days', Williams remembered, 'the Commission was ready with willing hands and abundant stores, to comfort and relieve the suffering'.[25] The USCC set up depots distributing food to stranded and impoverished civilians, and delegates worked closely with local ministers to identify families in dire need, visiting individual houses and devising a ticket system to ensure basic foodstuffs like flour were distributed as fairly as possible.[26] A defunct soup kitchen was taken over and reopened under USCC management.[27] 'It is wonderful how those poor starving women + hungry little children instinctively come to the Christian Commission for help,' Robert Patterson wrote to a colleague a week into the work, reporting that his team had swiftly exhausted the stores on hand.[28]

But while the work in Richmond was well organized and apparently appreciated by recipients – 'there were multitudes who appreciated most thoroughly our entire mission', Samuel Fitz reflected – it was not without its critics.[29] In May 1865, reports in the *Chicago Tribune*, the leading Republican daily in Illinois, accused the USCC of diverting funds intended for Union soldiers to feed Rebels.[30] While it was conceded that women and children in need were indeed entitled to Christian aid, one *Tribune* writer complained that 'no able-bodied Rebel should be supported from any eleemosynary fund'.[31] Certainly, the work at Richmond did not only benefit non-combatants. The collapse of the Confederacy in the spring of 1865 meant that in the weeks following the surrender soldiers were overwhelmingly left to their own devices to cope with the psychological and material burdens of defeat.[32] Faced with thousands of wounded Rebels recuperating in the hospitals around Richmond, or surrendered troops trying to reach home, delegates provided food and clothing, reading and writing material and a place of shelter for Confederate soldiers waiting to travel back to their home states.[33] They also organized regular prayer meetings for all military personnel – federal or Confederate – passing through the city. These activities fed critics' claims that 'influential' or 'unrepentant' Rebels had benefited from funds contributed by loyal northerners. The *Tribune*, incensed by this prospect, condemned the white population of Richmond as 'a haughty, insolent tribe . . . who cannot understand how they are under any obligations to anybody for the food or raiment donated to them'.[34] Not only did the *Tribune* call the Commission's competence into question, ridiculing the USCC's plan to 'buy the allegiance of these Rebels' as 'simple-minded but transparent folly', but the newspaper also called the loyalty and integrity of the workers involved into question.[35]

Attacks on the Commission's actions warned that well-meaning donors would be tarnished by their association with the Commission, and admonished the Commission for abusing their donors' trust by diverting funds and re-allocating resources that had initially been donated by patriotic northerners wanting to support the Union cause. Commission secretary Lemuel Moss, upon hearing of the rumours circulating in the *Tribune*, was anxious to refute these accusations and to clarify the Commission's stance on ministering to Confederates (whether civilians or soldiers). 'What was done by us did not intrench either upon our proper work or upon the funds contributed for it,' he wrote to his colleague Robert Patterson. 'We did not feed influential or unrepentant Rebels, but the starving citizens of a desolate and conquered city'.[36] Patterson himself wrote to the *Tribune* to deny the claims. Stressing that aid had been given only to those in direst need, Patterson tried to reassure readers in Chicago and beyond that the USCC had done 'just what any humane person would have done'.[37] The scandal, and the Commission's attempts to neutralize this negative publicity, demonstrate that northerners disagreed – often vehemently – over what constituted acceptable philanthropic activity, and who was a worthy beneficiary of this philanthropy.

At the same time, another kerfuffle in Richmond hammered home how damaging suspicions of disloyalty could be to an organization's reputation. Barely a fortnight after the Confederate surrender, six delegates who had been working in Richmond paid an impromptu visit to pay their respects to Robert E. Lee, general-in-chief of the defeated Confederate armies, at his home near the fallen Rebel capital. The meeting was apparently short but cordial, with Lee praising the work of charitable organizations such as the Christian Commission. When news of this meeting reached the northern press, the fallout was swift and damaging. While Lee's reputation as the embodiment of Old South chivalry and as a Christian man of honour forced by his conscience to bear arms against his country persisted for many northerners after Appomattox, others were not so forgiving. Republican and abolitionist newspapers gladly condemned Lee as a traitor and a hypocrite and were happy to tar the Christian Commission delegates who visited him with the same brush.[38] One Boston newspaper denounced the incident as 'one of the most shameful pieces of flunkeyism' and asked indignantly, 'didn't these men have a particle of shame in their natures, or are they anxious to once more hear the crack of the slave-holder's whip all over the country, as well as in Congress?'[39] Another scathing editorial read: 'if they truly represent the Christian Commission, then the Christian Commission does *not* truly represent the loyal North, which sent that Commission into the field, and hitherto has supported it by generous contributions.'[40] The *NY Independent* built on this accusation that public trust and funds had been abused: 'Hundreds of thousands of dollars have been poured into its treasury in aid of this work, and now the agents paid from that treasury forsake the hospital, abandon the bedside of the dying Union soldiers in Richmond, to pay a visit of "respect" to Robert E. Lee!'[41]

The Executive Committee was frantic at the wave of criticism directed their way. Lemuel Moss, mortified to hear that one of his own congregation had been among the wayward group, wrote to Edward Williams, the field agent in charge of operations in Richmond, 'it has occasioned the greatest scandal throughout the country + the severest censure. Scarcely a paper, secular or religious, has not noticed + condemned it in unmeasured terms.'[42] Williams, Moss and other high-ranking members of the Commission soon began devising schemes to, as one member said, 'save a miserable scandal from doing us harm'.[43] Much was at stake. Emotions were at a fever pitch as the war ended, and popular perceptions that the terms of surrender had been too lenient, rumours of the suffering endured by Union prisoners of war at Confederate hands and the assassination of Abraham Lincoln, all served to fuel northern anger.[44] In a bid to prevent this anger being funnelled towards the USCC, the guilty delegates were swiftly and publicly dismissed from the Commission's service, and the president of the Commission, George Stuart, hastily sent a strongly worded denunciation of those involved to the influential editor of the *New York Herald*, James Gordon Bennett, distancing the Commission from the delegates' errant actions and accusing them of 'an utter misapprehension of the work for which [they were] sent to the army'.[45] While it was clear the delegates had no ulterior motive in visiting Lee, the fallout of even this isolated and fairly innocuous incident was enough to call the loyalty of the entire Commission into question in the eyes of the northern press.

The controversies surrounding the USCC's presence in Richmond demonstrate that the northern public – and the secular and religious press alike – took a keen interest in the affairs of large charitable endeavours like the Christian Commission. Philanthropic activity undertaken in the name of, and funded by, the Union citizenry was scrutinized, critiqued and – wherever a whiff of treason or disloyalty could be detected – publicly and scathingly held to account. Evidently, displaying compassion towards the enemy was a dangerous game for northern charity workers. But, having been instructed to act according to 'God and their own consciences', Christian Commission delegates did not ignore the Confederate soldiers they encountered. Many of them were simply unable or unwilling to turn away from men in need, regardless of their political and sectional affiliations.[46] Walter Carter, a delegate from Wisconsin, found his heartstrings tugged by the wretched sight of hundreds of wounded men, 'loyal and Rebel, white and black', strewn across the lawn of a formerly grand mansion near Aiken's Landing, Virginia, in September 1864. In Carter's view, what united them was not political or denominational allegiance, but their shared 'moans of agony and cries of help'.[47] Another delegate at Point Lookout, Maryland, similarly stressed the universality of his ministry and his commitment to aiding anyone in need: 'We preached in the chapel, we preached in the hospital, and we preached in the prison. We preached to our own men and we preached to the Rebels, and wherever we went the dullest eyes brightened and welcomed our coming.'[48]

While in the above-mentioned examples delegates flattened their work with Confederates into a narrative of indiscriminate compassion that did not discern between Confederate and Union, some delegates reported going out of their way to minister explicitly to Confederates, and to treat them kindly. While working at Fairfax Courthouse, Edward Williams – who, as we have seen, would learn just how toxic interactions with the enemy could become – took time away from his work among Union wounded to take refreshments to a group of Rebels. When he distributed a cup of coffee to an enemy colonel, the man expressed surprise, saying, 'Well, this beats me. We don't treat our prisoners so.'[49] At Phillipsburg, in a scene of 'singular solemnity', A. M. Palmer baptized a North Carolinian man who was close to death.[50] Another delegate, encountering a South Carolinian prisoner, recalled how he and his co-workers 'gave him refreshing drink, laid him in cool shade, giving him good counsel', making the most of the opportunity to begin a conversation about the state of the man's soul.[51] For some delegates, ministering to enemy soldiers did engender some soul-searching about the right course of action. Working in various aid stations along the Susquehanna River in 1863, E. Clark Cline reflected on his decision to help enemy prisoners of war: 'although we felt they were enemies to us and our beloved country', he ultimately concluded, 'they were our fellow men suffering far from home and friends, and we could do no less.'[52]

In their accounts of working with Confederate troops, delegates frequently reflected on their motivations for ministering to Rebels, advancing justifications for undertaking this work, and spelling out the results they hoped to achieve. Given that a large proportion of the evangelical volunteers who constituted the USCC's workforce were preachers or theological students, it was natural that they repeatedly and consciously turned to Scripture to explain their attitude towards the enemy. In particular, delegates turned to Romans 12, where Paul commands his audience: 'if thine enemy hunger, feed him; if he thirst, give him drink.' This snippet was echoed constantly in the recollections of delegates. At Gettysburg, George Duffield, a Presbyterian minister from Adrian, Michigan, came across a group of wounded Confederates lying on the bare ground in a barn. He took it upon himself to share food and drink with the men, and recalled, 'the distribution of the bread was in solemn silence, reminding me strangely enough of distributing on a communion-day the emblems of Christ's body and blood, as well as of the command, "if thine enemy hunger, feed him; if he thirst, give him drink."'[53] Similarly, another delegate, working at an ambulance depot overseeing hospital transports, related the following conversation with a wagon driver appalled at the suggestion that he offer some comfort to a Southerner:

> 'Have you any wounded in this wagon, driver?' 'Yes, two; one a Reb, and one of ours.' 'Well, give each of them a cup of that punch.' 'What! Give punch to Rebs?' 'Why not? If the man is fainting, it won't hurt him.' 'That is new doctrine,' said an officer, standing by. 'That is the Christian Commission doctrine. If thine enemy hunger, feed him. If he thirst, give him drink.' 'Well,' said he, after a moment's reflection, 'I go in for that Commission.'[54]

The phrase was employed so often in delegate writings that the title of one chapter of a post-war commemorative volume compiled by the Commission was simply: 'Prisoners: If Thine Enemy Hunger, Feed Him.'[55] Paul's advice on philanthropic action – unlike the second commandment, to 'love thy neighbour as thyself' – explicitly set aside the recipient of aid as an enemy, rather than merely a neighbour or a stranger. The frequent invocation of this verse by USCC delegates helped them to rationalize their distribution policy, maintaining their political allegiance and preserving their patriotism intact by condemning Confederate subjects as enemies, even as they ministered to their bodily needs.

For delegates who sought to justify this controversial ministry, the wider context of this verse helps explain how providing aid to the enemy, far from being an act of potential treason, actually constituted both piety and patriotism of the purest order:

> [19] Dearly beloved, avenge not yourselves, but rather give place unto wrath: for it is written, Vengeance is mine; I will repay, saith the Lord. [20] Therefore if thine enemy hunger, feed him; if he thirst, give him drink: for in so doing thou shalt heap coals of fire on his head. [21] Be not overcome of evil, but overcome evil with good.

While the 'if thine enemy hunger, feed him' refrain appeared most commonly, delegates who quoted from the verse in their reports would no doubt have been aware of the long passage and its implications. According to Paul in this passage, aid rendered to an enemy would constitute a purifying fire cleansing the recipient's conscience and eliciting remorse and shame for his crimes. Therefore, for the USCC, what appeared to be selfless acts of kindness and compassion were also calculated to undermine the subject's loyalty to the Confederacy and to encourage repentance for his disobedience. By embodying Christian benevolence, delegates believed that they might dispel southern misconceptions about northern godlessness and cruelty (and, by comparison, cast the South in a poor light), remind Confederates of their shared American heritage and provoke in the recipients of their aid sufficient guilt and remorse that they would ultimately renounce the shameful sin of rebellion.

Several delegates endorsed this patriotic weaponization of benevolence in their recollections. The words of one prisoner from Tennessee emphasized the power of Christian compassion to erode dedication to the cause of secession: 'how kind you Northern people are! [. . .] I used to have a prejudice against you, but since I have been in the army, and have seen what you do for the soldiers, I think you are a wonderful people.'[56] Another delegate, Joshua Cowpland, expressed his belief 'that many of the prisoners will bear away to their homes undying memories of the attentions of Northern Christians'.[57] This interpretation was not confined to the private writings of individual delegates: the Commission leadership wholeheartedly and publicly approved this instrumentalization of its work. An annual report published in 1863 and widely distributed to evangelical congregations across the North concluded, 'in many instances kindness to [Confederates] has opened their hearts, and induced free expression of penitence as well as gratitude'.[58] A year later, the Executive Committee boldly claimed that their organization was 'acting an important part in showing the South the groundlessness of its hatred to the North'.[59] Humanizing the Union by overcoming evil with good – that is, debunking myths that all northerners were cruel, mercenary and godless – was considered vital to diluting Confederate adherence to their cause. In emphasizing their role in bringing about political repentance, Commission workers cast their philanthropy, not as disinterested, apolitical or neutral, but as explicitly and actively political.

In their recollections, delegates frequently framed these moments of political repentance as conversions – crises of conscience in which remorse and shame gave way to eventual relief and ecstasy. What is striking in many of these reports is the visceral and involuntary emotional response of the penitent Rebel. There are clear echoes, in these reports of grown men moved to tears, of the conversion narratives which were a fixture of evangelical revivalism during the Second Great Awakening.[60] As John Corrigan and others have argued, displays of emotion 'announced religious faith and spiritual striving', and were signs that a sinner's struggle to accept the grace of the Holy Spirit had reached its climax.[61] Christian Commission delegates employed the structure and language of antebellum conversion narratives to remark not only upon the tearful anguish of *spiritual* conversions to which they bore witness during the Civil War, but also of the *political* conversion of repentant Confederates. For instance, P. B. Thayer, working with the wounded at Martinsburg, recalled a rough, violent Confederate moved to tears by the kindness of the Commission. 'I am no coward,' the man said; 'I can face the enemy and not wink; but this kindness kills me, it breaks me all to pieces.'[62] Like other delegates, Thayer implied that the resolve and loyalty of Confederate soldiers could be undermined and fatally compromised, not by increasing their suffering, but rather by alleviating it, and by demonstrating the compassion and Christianity of the North. In several accounts, the powerful and transformative impact of Christian compassion on the enemy soldiers exposed to it was manifested in their visibly emotional responses. Men broke down and sobbed as they gratefully and incredulously received kindness and aid from their supposed enemy. 'When we're wounded, you come to us here not like angels, but like the

Lord Jesus Christ himself, washing our feet', one weeping Confederate, wounded at Antietam, told Reverend D. Merrill, 'and I can't stand it – I can't stand it'.[63] Another, a South Carolinian taken prisoner at Gettysburg, was overcome by the kindness of a delegate who offered him a handkerchief steeped in cologne, saying, 'I can't understand you Yankees; you fight us like devils, and then you treat us like angels. I am sorry I entered this war'.[64]

When their subjects did not express their repentance verbally or through tears, delegates looked for other signs that their commitment to the Confederate cause was waning. Observing Union and Confederate patients converse cordially together gave delegates hope that 'henceforth all would be Union men, true to the starry banner of Freedom'.[65] Even more encouraging was the receptivity of Rebel soldiers to the printed material handed out by Christian Commission delegates. Distributing religious literature – in the form of denominational newspapers, tracts, Bibles, prayer books and hymn books – was a huge part of the delegate's daily routine, with delegates asked to record carefully the numbers of texts disseminated. The emphasis placed upon colportage by the Christian Commission reflected their belief that reading, and reflecting upon that reading, could serve to hasten spiritual awakening and eventual conversion.[66] However, the texts distributed by delegates also served patriotic ends; hymn books were frequently organized around political themes such as 'battle', 'patriotism' and 'victory', and prayer books and Bibles printed for the Commission were embossed on the cover with the American flag.[67] While committed Rebels refused to accept these books, wishing to avoid any association with the United States, one delegate reported that, at Camp Douglas, 'few now remain who have not become possessors of the books and flag'.[68] As with Scott's tobacco deal which opens this chapter, the delegates here chose to interpret small gestures such as these, not as pragmatic and cynical attempts by prisoners to find any means of alleviating boredom, but as meaningful signs that men were embracing both Christianity and the United States. 'It was truly pleasant', one delegate reported, 'to see the "Christian Banner" with its stars and stripes lying upon the face of one who had so recently been fighting against it'.[69]

The delegates who performed this work were frequently convinced that they were actively contributing to Union victory. This may appear at first glance hopelessly naïve. The Confederates to whom Commission workers ministered were vulnerable and isolated; convincing a handful of prisoners or wounded men to renounce secession could hardly have a tangible impact on the overall strength or lethality of the southern armies. Yet delegates displayed remarkable patience in suggesting that the spiritual warfare they performed against Confederate souls acted as a vital and potent counterpoint to the physical warfare being waged by the Union army against their bodies. 'The Day of Judgement alone will reveal the worth of the great missionary work of the Christian Commission here,' William Paddock wrote while stationed at the prisoner of war camp at Fort Delaware. Using the verb 'disarm' in both a military and an emotional sense, he continued, 'That it disarms our enemies more than the weapons of our national warfare we daily hear'.[70] Thomas Rogers, a delegate from Hoosick, New York, was even more convinced that his work with wounded Confederates in hospitals in City Point, Virginia, was helping to win the war and to win it righteously. 'I am firm in my conviction that the US Christian Commission is doing much to bring this rebellion to a close,' he wrote in his exit report. Like Paddock, he considered the moral work of the Commission a necessary complement to armed combat. He continued:

> It enlightens the prisoners, it lays before them facts and dispels the dark clouds of prejudice and error that obscure their vision.... While the army wages war against the enemy and slowly but steadily presses on to victory, the Christian Commission, with quiet but powerful advance, pours the healing oil of Christian sympathy into the wounds of the soldiers, strengthening our men in their cause, but disarming by their kindness the most bitter enemies of our Union.[71]

The volunteers of the Christian Commission, as they encountered enemy soldiers, began to improvise a 'weaponised' benevolence which aimed through overbearing kindness to convert Confederates away from rebellion and towards evangelical Christianity. Through these efforts, the solitary kindness of individual delegates towards the enemy became subsumed into a wider political narrative. Piety once again became patriotic and was framed as contributing directly to the defeat of the South and the restoration of the Union. Christian philanthropists like the workers of the Christian Commission used religious benevolence as a political tool to demonstrate the piety and righteousness of the North, to convince Rebels of the errors of their ways, and to smooth the path from war to reconciliation. Needless to say, this agenda largely failed in the years following Appomattox. However, the Commission's concerns over their public reputation and attempts to justify their loyalty and their relevance demonstrate that Civil War philanthropy was never neutral, and was always concerned with imposing a specific political, social and religious vision onto the broken nation.

# Notes

1  John Scott, report, September 1863, Delegates' Statistical Reports; United States Christian Commission Records, 1861–1866; Records of the Adjutant General's Office; Record Group 94; National Archives Building, Washington, DC. Hereafter USCC.

2  George M. Frederickson, *The Inner Civil War: Northern Intellectuals and the Crisis of the Union* (Chicago: University of Illinois Press, 1965), 98.

3  See, for instance, Jeanie Attie, *Patriotic Toil: Northern Women and the American Civil War* (Ithaca: Cornell University Press, 1998); Robert H. Bremner, *The Public Good: Philanthropy and Welfare in the Civil War Era* (New York: Alfred A. Knopf, 1980); Judith Ann Giesberg, *Civil War Sisterhood: The U.S. Sanitary Commission and Women's Politics in Transition* (Boston: Northeastern University Press, 2000).

4  Paul Boyer, *Urban Masses and Moral Order in America, 1820–1920* (Cambridge. MA: Harvard University Press, 1978), 108–20; Allan Stanley Horlick, *Country Boys and Merchant Princes: The Social Control of Young Men in New York* (Lewisburg: Bucknell University Press, 1975), 227–45.

5  Susan M. Ryan, *The Grammar of Good Intentions: Race and the Antebellum Culture of Benevolence* (Ithaca: Cornell University Press, 2003), 10.

6  See, for instance, Robert H. Abzug, *Cosmos Crumbling: American Reform and the Religious Imagination* (Oxford: Oxford University Press, 1994), 77–124; Phillip F. Gura, *Man's Better Angels: Romantic Reformers and the Coming of the Civil War*

(Cambridge, MA: Belknap Press of Harvard University Press, 2017), 14–18; Ronald G. Walters, *American Reformers, 1815–1860* (New York: Hill and Wang, 1978).

7   Wendy Gamber, 'Antebellum Reform: Salvation, Self-Control, and Social Transformation', in *Charity, Philanthropy, and Civility in American History*, ed. Lawrence J. Friedman and Mark D. McGarvie (Cambridge: Cambridge University Press, 2003), 131.

8   Stephen Mintz, *Moralists and Modernizers: America's Pre-Civil War Reformers* (Baltimore: Johns Hopkins University Press, 1995), xiii.

9   George Stuart, circular, 7 January 1865, Scrapbooks; USCC.

10  Sacvan Bercovitch, *The American Jeremiad* (Madison: University of Wisconsin Press, 1978), 174; James H. Moorhead, *American Apocalypse: Yankee Protestants and the Civil War, 1860–1869* (New Haven: Yale University Press, 1978), 42–66; Harry S. Stout, *Upon the Altar of the Nation: A Moral History of the Civil War* (London: Penguin, 2006), 72, 188–9.

11  'Instructions to Delegates', pamphlet, n.d.; Reports; USCC.

12  On the rivalry between the USCC and the Sanitary Commission, see Attie, *Patriotic Toil*, 157–64; Frederickson, *Inner Civil War*, 108–11.

13  Robert M. Sandow, 'Introduction', in *Contested Loyalty: Debates over Patriotism in the Civil War North*, ed. Sandow (New York: Fordham University Press, 2018), 1.

14  William A. Blair, *With Malice Toward Some: Treason and Loyalty in the Civil War Era* (Chapel Hill: University of North Carolina Press, 2014), 37.

15  Sean A. Scott, '"Patriotism Will Save Neither You Nor Me": William S. Plumer's Defense of an Apolitical Pulpit', in *Contested Loyalty*, ed. Sandow, 172–3.

16  'Commission no. 66', n.d.; Scrapbooks; USCC.

17  'Instructions to Delegates', pamphlet, n.d.; Reports; USCC.

18  Michael J. Sulick, *Spying in America: Espionage from the Revolutionary War to the Dawn of the Cold War* (Washington: Georgetown University Press, 2012), 63–71, 93–9.

19  *United States Christian Commission Second Annual Report* (Philadelphia: The Commission, 1864), 78.

20  William S. Schaeffer, report, 13 August 1864; Delegates' Statistical Reports; USCC.

21  George Stuart to Reverend Dillon, 8 August 1864, Letters Sent; USCC.

22  Stephen V. Ash, *Rebel Richmond: Life and Death in the Confederate Capital* (Chapel Hill: University of North Carolina Press, 2019), 225–30; Mary A. DeCredico, *Confederate Citadel: Richmond and its People at War* (Lexington: University of Kentucky Press, 2020), 124–48; Ernest B. Ferguson, *Ashes of Glory: Richmond at War* (New York: A. A. Knopf, 1996), 341–58.

23  Lemuel Moss to Joseph Albree, 8 April 1865, Letters Sent; USCC.

24  Robert Patterson to 'Jacob', 13 April 1865, Letters Sent; USCC. See also E. F. Williams, 'US Christian Commission', *Richmond Whig*, 29 April 1865, 3.

25  Williams, quoted in *United States Christian Commission Fourth Annual Report* (Philadelphia: The Commission, 1866), 107.

26  George Stuart to C. R. Robert, 24 April 1865; Letters Sent; USCC.

27  'Local and Other Items', *Bangor Daily Whig and Courier*, 13 May 1865, 2; 'News from Richmond', *Baltimore Sun*, 6 May 1865, 4.

28  Robert Patterson to 'Jacob', 13 April 1865, Letters Sent; USCC.

29  *Fourth Annual Report*, 134.

30  Gordon Mayer, 'Party Rags? Politics and the New Business in Chicago's Party Press, 1831–1871', *Journalism History* 32, no. 3 (2006): 141–4.

31   'Feeding Influential Rebels', *Chicago Tribune*, 20 May 1865, 2.
32   Kevin Levin, '"When Johnny Comes Marching Home": The Demobilization of Lee's Army', in *Virginia at War: 1865*, ed. William C. Davis and James I. Robertson, Jr. (Lexington: University Press of Kentucky, 2012), 85–102; Yael Sternhell, *Routes of War: The World of Movement in the Confederate South* (Cambridge, MA: Harvard University Press, 2012), 165.
33   *Fourth Annual Report*, 101–9, 134–7.
34   'Feeding Influential Rebels', 2.
35   'Northern Flunkyism', *Chicago Tribune*, 2 May 1865, 2.
36   Lemuel Moss to Robert Patterson, 29 May 1865, Letters Sent, USCC.
37   'Feeding Influential Rebels', 2.
38   Cayce Myers, 'Southern Traitor or American Hero? The Representation of Robert E. Lee in the Northern Press from 1865 to 1870', *Journalism History* 41, no. 4 (2016): 215–16.
39   'Review of the Work', *Flag of our Union (1854–1870)*; 20 May 1865, 20.
40   'General Lee and the Christian Commission', in *The Independent . . . Devoted to the Consideration of Politics, Social and Economic Tendencies, History, Literature, and the Arts*, 4 May 1865, 17, 857.
41   'Gen Lee – The Christian Commission', from the *NY Independent*, reprinted in *The Liberator*, 19 May 1865, 1.
42   Lemuel Moss to E. F. Williams, 6 May 1865, Letters Sent; USCC.
43   Edward Smith to William Ballantyne, 3 May 1865, Letters Sent, USCC.
44   Caroline E. Janney, *Remembering the Civil War: Reunion and the Limits of Reconciliation* (Chapel Hill: University of North Carolina Press, 2013), 46–55; Thomas Reed Turner, *Beware the People Weeping: Public Opinion and the Assassination of Abraham Lincoln* (Baton Rouge: Louisiana State University Press, 1982), 25–52.
45   George Stuart to James Gordon Bennett, 3 May 1865, letters sent; USCC. George Stuart, undated circular, letters sent, USCC.
46   'Instructions to Delegates', pamphlet, n.d.; Reports; USCC.
47   Walter Carter, quoted in *Christ in the Army: A Selection of Sketches of the Work of the US Christian Commission* (Philadelphia: JB Rodgers, 1865), 94.
48   *Second Annual Report*, 180.
49   Edward Parmelee Smith, *Incidents among Shot and Shell* (Philadelphia: J B Lippincott, 1869), 157–8.
50   A. M. Palmer, report, 20 July 1853, Delegates' Statistical Reports, USCC.
51   W. W. Condit, report, 20 May 1864, Delegates' Statistical Reports; USCC.
52   E. Clark Cline, report, 7 September 1863, Delegates' Statistical Reports; USCC.
53   Smith, *Incidents among Shot and Shell*, 80.
54   Robert Patterson, 'At the Front', in *Christ in the Army*, 91.
55   Ibid., 113.
56   Smith, *Incidents among Shot and Shell*, 283.
57   Joshua P. Cowpland, report, 6 August 1863, Delegates' Statistical Reports; USCC.
58   *United States Christian Commission First Annual Report* (Philadelphia: The Commission, 1863), 13.
59   *Second Annual Report*, 78.
60   Elizabeth B. Clark, '"The Sacred Rights of the Weak": Pain, Sympathy, and the Culture of Individual Rights in Antebellum America', *Journal of American History* 82, no. 2 (1995): 476–7; Nathan O. Hatch, *The Democratization of American Christianity* (New Haven: Yale University Press, 1989), 105.

61 John Corrigan, *Business of the Heart: Religion and Emotion in Nineteenth Century America* (Berkeley: University of California Press, 2002), 221–2.

62 Smith, *Incidents among Shot and Shell*, 384.

63 *Christ in the Army*, 114–15.

64 Smith, *Incidents among Shot and Shell*, 177.

65 *Fourth Annual Report*, 161.

66 Isabelle Lehuu, *Carnival on the Page: Popular Print Media in Antebellum America* (Chapel Hill: University of North Carolina Press 2000), 22–4; David Paul Nord, 'Religious Reading and Readers in Antebellum America', *Journal of the Early Republic* 15, no. 2 (1995): 241–72. As Sonia Hazard has recently noted, not only were the texts themselves important to processes of conversion but so too were the interactions between the distributor and the recipient of religious reading matter (in this case, between the delegate and the soldier). Hazard, 'Evangelical Encounters: The American Tract Society and the Rituals of Print Distribution in Antebellum America', *Journal of the American Academy of Religion* 88, no. 1 (2020): 200–34.

67 *Hymnbook for the Army and Navy* (New York: American Tract Society, 1863), 2. Many of the songs in this collection blurred the line between hymn and anthem, for instance 'My Country, Tis of Thee' and 'God Save the State.'

68 *Second Annual Report*, 220.

69 *Fourth Annual Report*, 183.

70 William Paddock, quoted in *Second Annual Report*, 143–4.

71 Thomas Rogers, report, 23 August 1864; Delegates' Statistical Report; USCC.

# 2

# 'Ministry of helpfulness'

## Near East Relief and Protestant philanthropic secularism, 1915–30

### Scott P. Libson

'A very disturbing man.' That was William Millar's assessment of James Barton in 1916. Barton had apparently gotten into Millar's head with stories of the Armenian Genocide. 'Even after I did [fall asleep] in the wee small hours', Millar continued, 'I still heard the sobs and groans of women and children.'[1] The conversation was tactical. Millar was an expert fundraiser, general secretary of the interdenominational Laymen's Missionary Movement, which had been founded a decade earlier to encourage businessmen to give more money to foreign missions. Barton wanted to exploit those skills for his own organization, the American Committee for Armenian and Syrian Relief (ACASR, later and better known as Near East Relief or NER).[2] The non-profit was providing emergency relief and would become one of the largest international non-governmental organizations before the Second World War. The organization described itself as 'non-religious' and preferred to identify as simply 'American'. The talk apparently worked. Months later, Millar was helping the committee raise $30 million.

Barton's disturbance of Millar's sleep recalls the sentimentalist appeals that already had a long history by 1916. Scholars rightly point out that such sentimentalism has often justified colonialism; instilled a sense of noblesse oblige; or distracted the wealthy from nearby needs that might attract less attention.[3] Even then it was controversial, 'under constant fire by foundation administrators', according to NER associate general secretary Barclay Acheson. But, he asserted, 'the public was cold unless their emotions, sympathies or religious convictions were touched'.[4] NER appealed to all those convictions. That may explain why scholars have called it both a 'Protestant missionary philanthropic organization'[5] and the critical organization that ushered in the professionalized, bureaucratic and secular philanthropies of the twentieth century.[6] Barton called it 'positively Christian without a taint of sectarianism or propaganda' and a 'ministry of helpfulness'.[7] It would claim a role as a spiritual leader, but of no particular sect, and work towards well-being in general.

As indicated by the various ways that historians have characterized NER, whether or not it is defined as a religious organization matters, and it also mattered a century ago. When the Commonwealth Fund asked for advice about whether to fund NER, a consultant demurred. The 'Protestant missionary interests' that controlled NER 'have forfeited the confidence of impartial observers by . . . a markedly sentimental approach'. Religious philanthropy continues to spark periodic controversies, whether the Bush-era 'faith-based initiative' programme or Samaritan's Purse, an evangelical philanthropy, offering medical assistance during the COVID-19 pandemic.

One ought not to ignore either the religiosity or the non-religiosity of NER. It is within that perceived division, which I call Protestant philanthropic secularism, that we can better understand interwar American philanthropy. Protestant secularism, an analytical lens in religious studies that understands secularism within the individualistic and private religious practices associated with Protestantism, has helped to explain the underlying religiosity or reliance on religion in some parts of society identified as secular or non-religious. Charles McCrary and Jeffrey Wheatley, however, have argued convincingly that scholars should focus on what Protestant secularism does as opposed to what it is.[8] I employ Protestant philanthropic secularism to describe NER's attempt to remain self-consciously above religious sectarianism and yet entirely dependent upon it. Religion was often omnipresent and yet consciously minimized for NER, both essential and a barrier to growth. After years of working with or within religious institutions, NER leaders realized the economic and political power that came with secularism and they harnessed it for their philanthropic purposes, but they also depended on religion as a motivating factor in philanthropic activity.[9]

The religious landscape of American philanthropy has attracted renewed attention in recent years.[10] Like this recent work, I challenge the binaries that other scholars have drawn to distinguish religious and secular philanthropy.[11] One history of NER, for instance, makes a strong argument for the centrality of the post-First World War Eastern Mediterranean (especially local people there) in the history of humanitarianism, but juxtaposes the religious figures who ran the organization and the 'modern' relief workers.[12] As illustrated later in the chapter, that distinction merits more nuance. NER might fit better within Rachel McCleary's category of 'faith-founded' organizations, but it preceded her period of study and, significantly, the organizers would not have recognized NER within any of her categories.[13]

Several factors prompted NER's Protestant philanthropic secularism. First, NER could not have existed without American Protestant foreign missions. The organization sought a rapid response in a region that had been of interest primarily to missionaries and their supporters. Missionaries had experience responding to atrocities and did not see NER as an aberration from missions work. Second, NER officials could easily employ generic Christian imagery and terminology, because they did not substantially distinguish 'non-religious' from ecumenical Christian. The organization used both 'non-religious' and 'non-sectarian' to describe itself and often expressed what it identified as universal moral codes in explicitly Christian terms. Third, NER tapped into long-standing American prejudices against Muslims, particularly the 'terrible Turk', in order to raise additional funds. It frequently referenced its aid to Jews and Muslims as well as Christians, in keeping with its self-identity as 'non-religious', but it devoted far more attention to the latter. Through its fundraising appeals, NER attempted to persuade Americans (presumed to be Christian) of their responsibility to Armenian Christians. Protestant philanthropic secularism served that goal.

## Foundational beliefs

Chairman James Levi Barton (1855–1936) exemplified the religious leadership of the 'non-religious' NER. A Vermont-born Quaker who became a Congregationalist minister and missionary, Barton had spent seven years in the Ottoman Empire before becoming a foreign secretary for the American Board of Commissioners for Foreign Missions in 1892. Like most mission board officers, he faced continual frustrations at financial shortfalls. Throughout the first decade of the twentieth century, Barton and many of his NER colleagues assisted with numerous endeavours to promote interdenominational cooperation and build greater giving for missions. The genocide of Armenians that began in 1915, though, sparked more decisive and permanent action. During the last two decades of Barton's life, NER dominated his attention and his obituaries typically began with those accomplishments.

Numerous historians have told the story of the Armenian Genocide, the horror that prompted the ACASR to form.[14] The ACASR's origins stem from a cable Ambassador Henry Morgenthau sent to Woodrow Wilson's old friend Cleveland H. Dodge pleading for help. Dodge quickly turned to James Barton.[15] Barton and several others met in Dodge's offices in New York on 16 September 1915. By the end of the day, they had formed the Armenian Relief Committee, which became the ACASR later that year, NER in 1919 and finally the Near East Foundation in 1930.[16] As it formed to respond to Morgenthau's plea, it intended to do little more than raise funds and share information. Initially relying on large donors, particularly the Dodge family and the Rockefeller Foundation, the ACASR raised nearly $1 million within ten months.[17] As the depths of the crisis became clearer, the scope of relief work expanded and the organization set up relief centres in the region to provide food, clothing, shelter and basic medical care to displaced persons. By the end of the First World War, the work was increasingly focused on orphans, with a goal of providing industrial education to encourage 'self-support' and eventually, paternalistically, to train a new generation of leaders. When Congress incorporated the organization in August 1919, NER was employing over 500 relief workers.[18]

Nearly all of the founding ACASR members had some association with missions and most came from mainline Protestant denominations. As noted earlier, James Barton became the chairman of the new organization. The wealthy Dodge family, several of whom joined the committee, co-owned the Phelps Dodge mining company and had long supported American foreign missions. Other participants included four mission board officials, four men actively involved in the American College for Girls (an offshoot of the Woman's Board of Missions); and John Mott, a YMCA and Student Volunteer Movement leader. Charles Vickrey, of the Missionary Education Movement, would become the organization's general secretary in May 1916. All had supported greater interdenominational cooperation, Mott most prominently. Except for Vickrey, none of the mission movement officials quit his day job to work for the ACASR.[19]

Barton's identification of NER as a 'ministry of helpfulness' pointed to two essential qualities of the organization: its vague religiosity ('ministry') and its emphasis on outsider aid ('helpfulness'). Distribution teams in Turkey, Syria, and Persia (work later expanded into Greece and Palestine) consisted exclusively of Americans, almost entirely missionaries or individuals with ties to missions. In part, necessity dictated this scenario since Constantinople, preoccupied with war, refused to admit new relief workers. Even after 1918, though, when NER began sending hundreds of new workers, a large number had ties to missions. The organization rarely highlighted those ties, preferring to focus on missionaries' language and vocational knowledge, which allowed NER to describe them as 'technically trained'. James P. McNaughton, for instance, had taught in Western Anatolia for decades until the start of the war. He went back to Turkey in 1919 as one of 'five technically trained relief workers' with 'many years experience as a relief worker in the Orient'.[20]

Part of the argument for a purely secular NER rests on the claim that some relief workers, like Dr Mabel Elliott, in contrast to administrators in New York, were 'not amateur idealists or zealous missionaries, but rather pragmatic and results-oriented professionals'.[21] This is a false dichotomy. Although Elliott was not herself a missionary, both she and the NER administrators embraced secularism that idealized American society and its perceived Protestantism in the interests of their philanthropic goals.

Elliott memorialized her experiences with NER in *Beginning Again at Ararat* (1924), published by Fleming Revell. Missionaries had long favoured this premier American evangelical publishing house and the book opens with an appreciation by Grace Kimball, a famed American Board medical missionary during the massacres of Armenians in the 1890s. Kimball had set up 'industrial bureaus' that provided income and training in a variety of technical fields, a practice favoured by NER for many years.[22] Not surprisingly for a Revell memoir, Elliott's own words seem most at odds with any attempt to bifurcate religion and secularism. Like the NER administrators, Elliott asserted an 'American humanitarian exceptionalism', which she linked with Christianity.[23] 'The real meaning of the American work in Armenia [was] not the multitudes that were saved from starvation, nor the tens of thousands of little children bathed and clothed and fed . . . but the great fact of Christ's spirit working through the machinery of the modern world.' That machinery included modelling a 'Christian home', a traditional role for missionary women. Janet MacKaye, Elliott asserted, created a particularly wholesome environment, 'dress[ing] [the children] as cunningly as any American mother' and granting them 'interest and affection'.[24]

These parallels between Elliott and missionaries do not indicate that Elliott was a 'zealous missionary'. She was not, but nor did she embrace pure bureaucratic secularism. Elliott, like many NER administrators and relief workers, was neither a sanctimonious missionary nor a militant secularist and would not have recognized a spectrum between those two. Instead, they thought in terms of 'progress', which they paternalistically believed would make the Near East look increasingly like Western Protestant societies.

## All American Armenian-Syrian Relief Days

NER administrators and relief workers thoroughly believed in 'Americanism', a word that reached the apex of its popularity in the years during and after the First World War. While some of their contemporaries defined Americanism precisely (if not uniformly), NER offered no such precision, preferring to let their supporters choose a definition.[25] To achieve its goals, NER sought the support of political leaders from local mayors to presidents who helped legitimize that American identity. It built a fundraising network across the country and tried to make Americans feel obliged to donate. Many of these tactics mimicked those of the American Red Cross (ARC) and the comparison was one that NER actively encouraged.

Armenian supporters successfully lobbied Congress to raise money for the ACASR in 1916, leading President Wilson to announce Armenian-Syrian Relief Days on 21 and 22 October. It was not a very tough sell; all sides accepted the merits of the appeal, though some quibbled about the precedent and process. The weekend dates consciously connected the fundraiser with religion. 'These funds will be mostly collected in churches,' Miran Sevasly told the House Committee on Foreign Affairs, and the resolution would 'have a great moral effect on the people'.[26] Many Red Cross chapters, Boy Scout troops and public schools helped raise money. Nearly every piece of publicity mentioned politicians' endorsements and the ACASR advised speakers to reference the Wilson proclamation and the support of local officials. Trolleys in Brooklyn, Toledo and other cities provided free advertising for the day. The ACASR published notices in both religious and secular presses, underlining the attempt to operate both within and beyond religious establishments.[27]

At the urging of Henry Morgenthau, the ACASR set an ambitious goal of raising $5 million. It established local auxiliaries to help reach the goal and make the campaign a national endeavour, suggesting that public officials run the auxiliaries and schedule meetings in a city hall or statehouse. Like earlier fundraising efforts (including those of *The Christian Herald*, the tuberculosis Christmas seals or the Every Member Canvass), the ACASR hoped local efforts on the Armenian-Syrian Relief Days would create a national, social obligation to give, akin to the 'culture of giving' that Olivier Zunz has associated with this time period. In later years, the ACASR would encourage communities to compete with each other by placing advertisements that read, 'other cities and states have met their full quota with a substantial overage' in contrast with $x$ city, which 'lacks $ . . . of reaching the quota'.[28]

The Armenian-Syrian Relief Days were not enough to raise $5 million, partly because of ACASR's poor planning and partly Wilson's mixed motives in picking a date two weeks prior to the 1916 election. Only $500,000 had arrived by early November, so the ACASR decided to continue the campaign through Thanksgiving. The food-based holiday allowed the ACASR to appeal to Americans' sense of guilt, using images of gluttony to contrast with starving Armenians.[29] More directly relevant, the ACASR was cooperating with the ARC and the US government to fill a navy ship with foodstuffs, oil and clothing to send to Beirut. Extending the fundraising efforts helped the ACASR continue to advertise the relief ship.[30] In the future, Thanksgiving would become an annual period of fundraising for the ACASR.

After further delays, the Thanksgiving ship became a Christmas ship, which presented new opportunities to integrate generic Christian rhetoric into fundraising. The ACASR advertised this portion of the fund drive as 'a Christian ministry' and circulated 'Christmas checks' to support the ship. Though the 'checks' contained clearly recognizable Christian imagery, the 'non-religious' ACASR encouraged supporters to distribute them in both religious and secular contexts, including church pews, Sunday Schools, theatre programmes, banks, hotels, labour organizations and department stores. One side of the check depicted a large red Greek cross with equidistant arms, remarkably similar to the symbol of the ARC. The overlap was unlikely to have been happenstance. In addition to the widespread recognition of the Red Cross symbol, the ACASR was soon mimicking the Red Cross uniform. Although the two organizations were cooperating on the relief ship operation, they remained entirely separate organizations and the pledge was to go exclusively to the ACASR.[31]

The Armenian-Syrian Relief Days were a mixed blessing for the ACASR. The organization failed to reach its monetary goal and the Christmas ship was a major disappointment. The *Caesar* set sail with $250,000 in supplies and politicians' messages of support, but the German policy of unrestricted submarine warfare began before the ship reached Beirut. After months of waiting in Alexandria, the ACASR sold the *Caesar*'s cargo to the ARC for $127,200.[32] On the other hand, the fundraiser brought national attention and governmental support to an organization that had just marked its one-year anniversary. Collaboration with Washington would continue, including a 1917 edition of the Armenian-Syrian Relief Days. When the ACASR first sought congressional incorporation in 1918, it noted the relief days to demonstrate long-standing federal approval of the work. Despite the failure to raise $5 million during a months-long campaign, ACASR officials soon decided to aim far higher.[33]

## The $30 million campaign and the visual culture of NER

It took two years for the ACASR to raise $5 million, including the first Armenian-Syrian Relief Days when they tried to raise the amount in two days. Nevertheless, the organization set a wildly optimistic goal of raising $30 million. They clearly needed help and turned to William Millar to manage the campaign. Millar's oversight led to a professional, national drive that aligned itself with common conceptions of American patriotism. Building on the Armenian-Syrian Relief Days, the organizational apparatus reached across the country and asked everyone to give. All three living presidents (Wilson, Taft and Roosevelt) endorsed the effort and the ACASR never missed an opportunity to publicize that support. By May 1919, $22 million had already been subscribed.[34]

As part of the fundraiser, the organization prepared a national visual campaign that borrowed from wartime propaganda posters. Prominent artists like Ethel Betts, W. T. Benda and Douglas Volk combined folk art with modern advertising techniques and used an established medium (posters) and modern reprography to reach a national audience. The posters followed a developing field of humanitarian imagery that addressed viewers with simple, direct images of individuals to spur actions to prevent further suffering. The posters' pathos, repeatedly using the word 'perish' (e.g. 'Lest We Perish' and 'They Shall Not Perish') followed patterns of using images to articulate 'pain's inexpressibility', in Elaine Scarry's words.[35] The subtle linguistic differences between 'they' and 'we' played with a Euro-American perception of Armenians as both 'western' and 'oriental'.[36] The ACASR remained a private philanthropy, but it depended heavily on the perception of a patriotic, moral and fraternal obligation to donate.[37]

Benda's 'Give or We Perish' (Figure 2.1) literally illustrated the perceived contradictions apparent in the Western gaze on Armenians. On the one hand, the woman in his sketch paid close attention to her appearance. With a bracelet on her left wrist and possibly a bob haircut, the woman epitomized what historian Peter Balakian has described as 'pop culture figures who appear more as damsels in distress from pulp fiction or silent film'.[38] On the other hand, she has clutched her outerwear (which may be a shawl or a blanket) as one would when faced with a desperate cold and the text underscored that desperation. Benda illustrated the woman to be both highly personal and yet nondescript, a detailed study of a white, average Jane. Whether viewers considered the details of Benda's sketch misses the point. It clearly expressed the deplorability of suffering, solved by giving.

Though created for the same fundraising campaign, William Gunning King's 'Lest They Perish' (Figure 2.2) could not have differed more from the Benda poster. Benda's

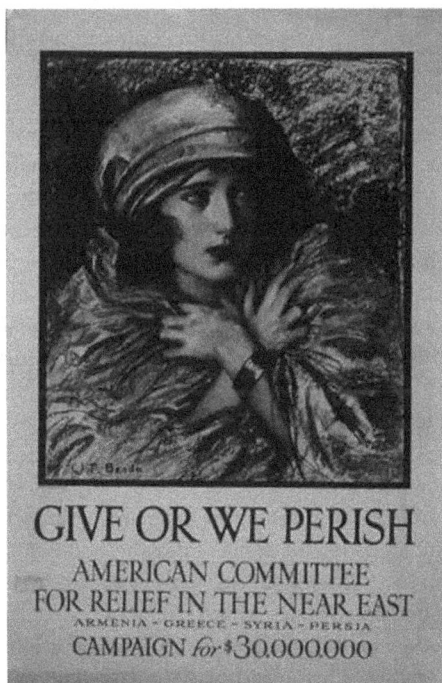

**Figure 2.1** Wladyslaw T. Benda, 'Give or We Perish', American Committee for Relief in the Near East, 1917. Library of Congress Prints and Photographs Division.

**Figure 2.2** W. B. King, 'Lest They Perish', American Committee for Relief in the Near East, 1917–19. Library of Congress Prints and Photographs Division.

black and white portrait with no visible background contrasted with King's clear, beautifully coloured scene of a woman carrying a child. Though both texts included the word 'perish', the verb's subject notably changed between the two advertisements. The visual differences between the images point to a more profound distinction. Benda's average Jane became a defined 'other' in King's painting. King drew her with a traditional yellow and white scarf tightly covering her head and a baby on her back. Middle-class Americans, for whom these posters were made, greatly preferred bassinets and perambulators by the end of the nineteenth century.[39] The background desolation (unlike the abstraction of Benda's background) connoted a war zone, far from the tranquil United States that most wealthy American donors experienced. The text in King's painting, unlike that in Benda's drawing, underlined the otherness of the woman and child. They were a 'they'.

The $30 million campaign also prompted a cinematic project: *Ravished Armenia*. Premiering on 15 January 1919, the movie (and the book of the same name) told the story of a sixteen-year-old girl named Aurora Mardiganian, who survived the genocide and fled to the United States with the help of the ACASR. Rather than hire professional actors, producer William Selig (who gave a portion of the profits to the ACASR, but did not otherwise involve it) cast Mardiganian to portray herself in this traumatic story. He then took her around the country to appear in person (and relive the trauma) as the film debuted in various cities. She later claimed that she had not understood the contract she was signing. The film title, promotional posters and film itself all identified Turks as sexual predators. All tacitly or explicitly also emphasized the victims as Christians. The movie's opening scene, Easter Sunday, 1915, depicted a row of naked, crucified women. In fact, Selig had planned for additional scenes of sexual violence, more fitting with Mardiganian's memory of actual events, but the film's screenwriter balked.[40]

Though *Ravished Armenia* and the various posters differed greatly from each other, they collectively made a visual case for American Christians to support the Armenian Christian victims of Muslim oppression. Depicting Armenians as both 'western' and 'foreign', the visual imagery claimed both religious and cultural similarities with Americans, but also underlined the different circumstances that Armenians faced. Other posters, like Herman Pfeifer's 'The Child at Your Door', reinforced both the proximity and distance of those in need. The production of the movie points to this interplay, with an Armenian actress who came to the United States and became something of a film star, albeit unintentionally. All of the images depicted women and children as victims. The motif of the defenceless female victim long preceded the genocide and was associated with Western portrayals of Turks as both lustful and heartless.[41] Both of these elements, the victims' religious identity and their presumed dependency as women and children, became critical components in the congressional action that converted the ACASR into NER.

## 'We cannot be Christians alone': Incorporating the Golden Rule

On 6 August 1919, following the $30 million campaign, Congress incorporated the ACASR under the name Near East Relief. Since the ACASR had always said it represented the nation as a whole, the incorporation affirmed its long-standing identity. Indeed, 'recognizing this committee as the representatives of the people of the United States' (and the accompanying 'prestige') was the major, if not the sole, purpose. The act did not 'involve one penny from the Treasury of the United States', Sen. Albert Cummins confidently asserted.[42] Cummins was technically right, but the federal government did provide numerous financial benefits. Between 1919 and 1920, the government gave NER $12.8 million worth of foodstuffs and more food, medicine and other gifts-in-kind would follow.[43]

Neither the act of incorporation nor the first NER charter referenced religion at all and though the named trustees included a large number of mission movement men (Anna Pennybacker, Eva Perry Moore, and Mary Woolley were the first women to be elected trustees in 1924), they also included political leaders of various faiths, as well as Cardinal James Gibbons and Rabbi Stephen Wise.[44] Support for Armenians, at least in the abstract, bridged many divides (fundamentalist/modernist, Republican/ Democrat). As Charlie Laderman has argued, though, divisions over the form of that support informed opposing US foreign policies during the critical interwar period.[45] This would have been an ideal moment to move away from religion entirely, but, in fact, that path was not within the realm of possibility. Religion was too essential to the concept of philanthropy for it to be ignored.

The congressional incorporation debates, which occurred during and after the First World War, exemplify why NER could not so easily move away from its religious ties. Wartime Americanism and patriotism, for NER, were entangled in religion, particularly generic Christianity. The United States had decided not to declare war on the Ottoman Empire, partly because of pressure from American missionary and philanthropic societies, including the ACASR.[46] Such a declaration nevertheless remained possible in mid-1918, making the transmission of money to the Ottoman Empire a potentially counterproductive endeavour.[47] Charles Vickrey assured Congress that the ACASR work was 'pro-ally, in capital letters', because all funding went through the War Trade Board for the benefit of 'pro-ally races'. William Peet quickly clarified, 'the recipients of our benevolent work in the Ottoman Empire are from the Christian races and that means they are strongly pro-ally'.[48]

After incorporation, NER fundraising continued to blend moralism and generic Christian rhetoric. The largest annual fundraising drive in the mid-1920s was Golden Rule Sunday. The event, like the Armenian-Syrian Relief Days, occurred between Thanksgiving and Christmas, which allowed publications to contrast American 'material prosperity' with the 'moral obligations' to 'those less fortunately placed'.[49] Participants served meals akin to what the children in NER orphanages were eating. In some cities, local committees arranged for donations of food and facilities and then sold dinner tickets. Other participants, including the Rockefellers, ate meagre meals at home and donated their savings.[50] Though the practicalities of the fundraiser had little to do with religion, its name pointed to a broader significance. 'It is hoped that many will use it as a day for reviewing the year's receipts and expenditures, measuring each item of the year's budget by the Golden Rule to ascertain whether we are practising the Golden Rule in our stewardship of funds.'[51] Elsewhere, NER claimed it valued the 'spiritual and educational values' that Golden Rule Sunday would instil even more than the 'financial returns'.[52]

NER identified Golden Rule Sunday as a financial lifeline. Prior to the first International Golden Rule Sunday on December 2, 1923, the organization faced a deficit of $1.5 million and 'a marked downward trend throughout the preceding three years' following the windfall that all philanthropic organizations received during the Great War.[53] By early 1927, NER held a surplus of around $300,000. The organization attributed about one-third of its total receipts of $11 million during that period directly to Golden Rule Sunday. Even the Rockefeller philanthropies, which generally refused to donate to NER due to disagreements with the organization's leadership, viewed the annual fundraiser as 'a highly successful money raising scheme', indeed 'the most successful method employed by the Near East Relief in the raising of its funds'.[54]

Media coverage of Golden Rule Sunday, which NER cultivated with care, helped corroborate the claim that the organization represented all Americans in its work. The *New York Times* claimed the first event in 1923 was being 'observed all over America', with over a million participants, including President Calvin Coolidge and members of his cabinet.[55] *Good Housekeeping*, *The Literary Digest* and other popular periodicals, as well as radio programmes, also covered Golden Rule Sunday. The participation of

Jackie Coogan, the 'best-loved boy in America', attracted particular notice. Known today for his portrayal of Uncle Fester in *The Addams Family* (1964–6), the child-star Coogan travelled around the country on a 'Children's Crusade of Mercy'. He had recently co-starred with Charlie Chaplin in *The Kid* (1921), playing an abandoned boy saved by Chaplin's Tramp character. Other celebrities, including baseball slugger Ty Cobb, appeared on Coogan's tour. In the lead-up to Golden Rule Sunday, Coogan boarded a ship to bring donations of clothes and money to the Eastern Mediterranean himself.[56]

One of the more common Golden Rule Sunday advertisements was an illustration depicting children climbing a steep slope with the words, 'Don't Let Go! LIFT' in the upper left.[57] All of the children are light-skinned. The central figure is a male dressed in shorts, a long-sleeved shirt, with a neckerchief, reminiscent of a Boy Scout uniform. Below him are numerous children, mostly girls. Above him, the hand of Uncle Sam reaches down to help him up. The Boy Scout uniform affirmed the acceptability of the aid recipients. In fact, the Boy Scouts of America actively participated in the planning and promotion of Golden Rule Sunday, further establishing NER in middle-class society. In addition, the Boy Scouts operated in the Near East and urged American boys to donate their uniforms to Armenians.[58]

The symbolism went further, though, with allusions to the Bible. The mountain recalled the most famous of Armenian mountains, Ararat, the supposed final resting place of Noah's ark. On Ararat, God presented Noah with the possibility of rebuilding after the devastating flood that nearly obliterated humanity. Americans would have understood the reference. According to Herbert Hoover,

> Probably Armenia was known to the American school child in 1919 only a little less than England. The association of Mount Ararat and Noah, the staunch Christians who were massacred periodically by the Mohammedan Turks, and the Sunday School collections over fifty years for alleviating their miseries – all cumulate to impress the name Armenia on the front of the American mind.[59]

Only Uncle Sam's arm extends into the frame of the NER publication. Like the Christian God, he is a faceless being on high, offering salvation.[60]

Unlike in the Christian story, though, the road to salvation was through wealth. The message of the image matched other publications. For example, a poem entitled 'Keep Their Star of Hope Shining' (referring to the star worn by NER relief workers), described 'tortured Armenia, pillaged, war-worn' encouraged by the 'Star of Hope . . . put in the sky by America's pity. . . . Give, oh America, give of your riches, that Armenia's Star of Hope fade not from her heaven forever!' Without American gifts, Armenian children 'will struggle and grope in the blackness of night, homeless, despairing of life'.[61] 'Don't Let Go! LIFT' inflated the value of American givers even further. At the end of a brochure, just before an ersatz check that donors were to use as a symbol of their pledge, the association with God turned explicit. 'If YOU could be God', the brochure asked the reader to contemplate, what would be done to help the orphans? 'No – you can never be God, but made in His image you may be like Him.' Lifting or giving, in other words, sanctified the giver.[62]

Golden Rule Sunday played on the contradictions of a 'non-religious' organization deeply tied to Protestant Christianity. In responding to the question 'what is International Golden Rule Sunday', General Secretary Charles Vickrey wrote, 'It is a test of our religion. Whatsoever else may be included in or omitted from our creeds, we all believe in the Golden Rule.'[63] Elsewhere, NER claimed the Golden Rule was 'a common denominator of all religions' and a 'universally accepted standard of conduct for all people.'[64] That universality supposedly demanded social engagement. Future Nobel Laureate John Mott (who had been with NER from the start, but was not deeply involved) called on supporters of NER to get out into the world. 'We cannot be Christians alone. We have got to have the Golden Rule.'[65] Whether or not the Golden Rule was 'a common denominator of all religions', locating a shared basis for giving was fundamental to the organization. Mott's statement points to the philanthropic secularism of Golden Rule Sunday. It assumed a vague religiosity, one that accommodated a variety of belief systems, and combined it with a recognition of the common humanity of all peoples.

## Conclusion: Secularizing philanthropy and nurturing religion

As James Barton entered retirement in the late 1920s, he looked back on his years with the American Board and NER. He saw a transformation in philanthropy, but not a radical shift. Indeed, looking back on the formation of the ACASR with two decades of hindsight, Barton became only more enthusiastic about the mutually beneficial value of religious and secular philanthropy. The founders of the American Board had selected its name in 1810 with the hope it would serve as a philanthropy of all Americans. A century later, Barton instilled that hope in NER. After a trip to the Near East in 1919, Barton wrote, 'I have come back with the conviction that unless America, great benevolent America, is ready to respond to the cry of Armenia . . . there will be no other relief for them.'[66] Five years later, he seemed satisfied with the results. The orphans in the care of NER had become 'living, breathing, trusting children of American philanthropy. . . . The Near East Relief received its commission from the generous heart of America to save these children for themselves and for the land of their sorrow.'[67]

In 1924, the same year Barton expressed this optimistic message, NER commissioned a report on early childhood education, child welfare, and 'religious nurture'. The orphanages would eventually close, so NER was considering its future role in the region. For years, it had endeavoured to raise a generation of 'modern' leaders, a 'quasi-colonial' idea reflected in the title of NER's publication, *The New Near East*.[68] James I. Vance, a Southern Presbyterian pastor, authored the report on religious nurture. He concluded that NER had entered 'a great missionary opportunity, for only religion can give the training and grow the character that is needed'. Missions would produce leaders to bring about positive change in the region, Vance claimed.[69] A subsequent report called the children 'the spiritual seed corn of the Near East'.[70]

Neither the project nor the methods differed substantially from the contemporary mainline foreign mission movement, which had been in a period of profound transformation since at least 1910. Missionaries very much wanted to be 'modern' themselves and to spread that modernity. James Barton wrote an essay on the subject less than a year before the formation of the ACASR. He disparaged 'fanatical, . . . irresponsible missionaries', favouring 'more sympathetic relations with the non-Christian world' that promoted social change over direct personal conversion. 'Salvation for the life that is now', he wrote, not for 'the world to come'.[71] As Ussama Makdisi has argued, this turn away from proselytization would eventually convert missionary institutions from their imperialist origins into sites of anti-colonial activism in the Islamic world, mostly due to the local people who lived and learned there.[72]

Categorizing philanthropies as religious or secular rarely offers much insight, particularly in the first decades of the twentieth century. Even mainline missionaries were trying to find some middle ground. James Barton believed he had found that middle, what I call Protestant philanthropic secularism, with NER. Given Barton's background and given that of his colleagues, it should come as no surprise that the 'non-religious' NER was anything but divorced from religion. At the same time, claiming to be 'non-religious' opened the door to a more inclusive future, one more fully adopted when the Near East Foundation took over for NER in 1930.

# Notes

1 William Millar to James Barton, 14 April 1916, American Board of Commissioners for Foreign Missions Archives, 1810–1961, ABC 11.4, box 5, folder 7, Houghton Library, Harvard University (hereafter ABCFM Archives).

2 I use the name NER throughout this chapter, except when writing specifically about the pre-1919 organization.

3 Samuel Moyn, 'Spectacular Wrongs', review of *Freedom's Battle: The Origins of Humanitarian Intervention*, edited by Gary J. Bass, *The Nation* 287, no. 11 (13 October 2008): 32–5.

4 Barclay Acheson diary, 1 June 1926, Near East Foundation records, Accession 2009:104, RG 1, series 12, box 3, folder 25, Rockefeller Archive Center.

5 Peter Balakian, 'Photography, Visual Culture, and the Armenian Genocide', in *Humanitarian Photography: A History*, ed. Heide Fehrenbach and Davide Rodogno (New York: Cambridge University Press, 2015), 110.

6 Keith David Watenpaugh, *Bread from Stones: The Middle East and the Making of Modern Humanitarianism* (Oakland: University of California Press, 2015), esp. 2. For Watenpaugh, Acheson was one of the few administrators who advanced that modernization project. Ibid., 186–7.

7 'Expressions of Conviction', [1930], ABC 11.4, box 2, folder 13, ABCFM Archives; James L. Barton, *Story of Near East Relief* (New York: Macmillan, 1930), 14.

8 Charles McCrary and Jeffrey Wheatley, 'The Protestant Secular in the Study of American Religion: Reappraisal and Suggestions', *Religion* 47, no. 2 (April 2017): 256–76.

9 David P. King, 'Religion, Charity, and Philanthropy in America', in *The Oxford Encyclopedia of Religion in America*, ed. John Corrigan (New York: Oxford University Press, 2018), 511–36.

10  Heather D. Curtis, *Holy Humanitarians: American Evangelicals and Global Aid* (Cambridge, MA: Harvard University Press, 2018); Shai M. Dromi, *Above the Fray: The Red Cross and the Making of the Humanitarian NGO Sector* (Chicago: University of Chicago Press, 2020); David P. King, *God's Internationalists: World Vision and the Age of Evangelical Humanitarianism* (Philadelphia: University of Pennsylvania Press, 2019).

11  See, for example, Jonathan Levy, 'Altruism and the Origins of Nonprofit Philanthropy', in *Philanthropy in Democratic Societies: History, Institutions, Values*, ed. Rob Reich, Lucy Bernholz, and Chiara Cordelli (Chicago: University of Chicago Press, 2016), 19–43; Robert Payton, 'Philanthropic Values', in *Philanthropic Giving: Studies in Varieties and Goals*, ed. Richard Magat (New York: Oxford University Press, 1989), 29–45.

12  Watenpaugh, *Bread from Stones*. Even though there were inevitable differences between NER workers and their administrators, both perspectives matter, and the administrators played particularly significant roles in shaping American perspectives of humanitarianism.

13  Rachel M. McCleary, *Global Compassion: Private Voluntary Organizations and U.S. Foreign Policy since 1939* (Oxford: Oxford University Press, 2009), 11–15.

14  Among the best is Ronald Grigor Suny, *'They Can Live in the Desert but Nowhere Else': A History of the Armenian Genocide* (Princeton: Princeton University Press, 2015), esp. ch. 5–7.

15  Barton had already tried, unsuccessfully, to form a committee when Morgenthau's cable arrived. In his memory, he was the one who provided the main impetus for forming the ACASR despite not being included or mentioned in Morgenthau's cable. James Barton, 'Autobiographical Notes', [1934?], 250, ABC 11.4, box 12, folder 2, ABCFM Archives.

16  The organization also used the name American Committee for Relief in the Near East during a major fundraising campaign in 1919, discussed at length later.

17  While Dodge contributed heavily to the organization until he died in 1926, the Rockefellers greatly slowed their giving after 1917.

18  Near East Relief, *Hand Book*, 1920, MRL 2: Near East Relief Committee Records, series 2, box 8, folder 4, The Burke Library Archives at Union Theological Seminary (hereafter NER Records).

19  Several scholars incorrectly assume that Barton had quit the American Board. Peter Balakian, for example, identifies Barton as the 'former secretary of the American Board'. In fact, he travelled from Boston to New York almost every month to attend ACASR/NER meetings. Balakian, 'Photography, Visual Culture, and the Armenian Genocide', 101.

20  'Another Life Boat', ACASR *News Bulletin* 24 (May 1919): 1–2.

21  Watenpaugh, *Bread from Stones*, 94.

22  See, for example, 'Relief Work at Van, Eastern Turkey', *Missionary Herald* 92, no. 6 (June 1896): 234.

23  Watenpaugh, *Bread from Stones*, 109.

24  Mabel Evelyn Elliott, *Beginning Again at Ararat* (New York: Fleming H. Revell Company, 1924), 184–5, 308.
       The scholarship connecting missions, 'civilization' and domesticity is extensive. See, for example, Barbara Reeves-Ellington, Kathryn Kish Sklar and Connie Anne Shemo, eds, *Competing Kingdoms: Women, Mission, Nation, and the American Protestant Empire, 1812–1960* (Durham: Duke University Press, 2010).

25  Jonathan Hansen, 'True Americanism: Progressive Era Intellectuals and the Problem of Liberal Nationalism', in *Americanism: New Perspectives on the History of an Ideal*, ed. Michael Kazin and Joseph Anthony McCartin (Chapel Hill: University of North Carolina Press, 2006), 73–89.

26  *Relief of Armenians: Hearings Before the Comm. on Foreign Affairs*, 64th Cong. 5 (1916) (statement of Miran Sevasly, chairman of the Armenian National Union).

27  Frederick Lynch, circular, 20 November 1916, series 1, box 4, folder 6, NER Records; Memoranda, September-October 1916, series 1, box 2, folder 1, NER Records; Charles Vickrey to W. W. Rockwell, 23 October 1916, series 1, box 2, folder 1, NER Records.

28  'Suggestions to Guide in the Organization of an Auxiliary Committee for Armenian and Syrian Relief', n.d., series 1, box 3, folder 4, NER Records; 'Memoranda Concerning Follow-Up Campaign', 28 March 1919, Near East Foundation records, Accession 2010:002, RG 2, box 1, Rockefeller Archive Center (hereafter NEF Records, Acc 2010). Although *The Christian Herald* did not organize local committees, the publication circulated nationally and it printed long lists of donors along with their home cities. Curtis, *Holy Humanitarians*, 30, 47–53; Scott M. Cutlip, *Fund Raising in the United States: Its Role in America's Philanthropy* (New Brunswick: Rutgers University Press, 1965), 53–8; Olivier Zunz, *Philanthropy in America: A History* (Princeton: Princeton University Press, 2012), ch. 2.

29  For example, War Relief Committee of Milwaukee, circular, [1916?], series 1, box 4, folder 14, NER Records. See also 'Workers Bulletin No. 2', 2 November 1916, series 1, box 2, folder 1, NER Records.

30  'Workers Bulletin No. 2'; ACASR Minutes, 11 October 1916, box 1, NEF Records, Acc 2010; 'Memoranda for Appropriation Committee Meeting', 27 October 1916, box 1, NEF Records, Acc 2010.

31  'The Star of Hope in the East', ACASR *News Bulletin* 3, no. 9 (February 1919): 1–2; 'Peace and Good Will to the Land of the Christ Child', ca. December 1916, series 1, box 4, folder 6, NER Records.

32  'Christmas Ship Off for Beirut Today', *New York Times*, December 17, 1916; 'Teutons Refuse to Pass U.S. Warships', *Washington Post*, 22 March 1917; ACASR minutes, 13 September 1917, box 1, NEF Records, Acc 2010.

33  *Hearings on S. 4785 Before the Senate Comm. on the Judiciary*, 65th Cong. 6h (1918) (statement of Charles McFarland); ACASR Executive Committee minutes, 25 February 1917, box 1, NEF Records, Acc 2010.

34  See October 1918 through May 1919 issues of the ACASR *New Bulletin*.

35  Heather D. Curtis, 'Depicting Distant Suffering: Evangelicals and the Politics of Pictorial Humanitarianism in the Age of American Empire', Article, *Material Religion* 8, no. 2 (July 2012): 154–83, Scarry quoted on 63, https://doi.org/10.2752/1751834 12X13346797481032.

36  'We' (as in 'lest we perish') refers to Armenians, but, as noted later, that ambiguity is precisely the point. Jo Laycock, *Imagining Armenia: Orientalism, Ambiguity and Intervention* (Manchester: Manchester University Press, 2009), esp. ch. 1.

37  Pearl James, 'Introduction: Reading World War I Posters', in *Picture This: World War I Posters and Visual Culture*, ed. Pearl James (Lincoln: University of Nebraska Press, 2009), 1–3, 6; Christopher Capozzola, *Uncle Sam Wants You: World War I and the Making of the Modern American Citizen* (Oxford: Oxford University Press, 2008), 6–8; Curtis, *Holy Humanitarians*, 22–4, 30, 283–4.

38  Balakian, 'Photography, Visual Culture, and the Armenian Genocide', 105.

39 Susan J. Pearson, "Infantile Specimens': Showing Babies in Nineteenth-Century America', *Journal of Social History* 42, no. 2 (Winter 2008): 345.

40 Anthony Slide, 'Introduction: A History Lesson', in *'Ravished Armenia' and the Story of Aurora Mardiganian*, ed. Anthony Slide (Jackson: University Press of Mississippi, 2014), 10–17; Benedetta Guerzoni, 'A Christian Harem: *Ravished Armenia* and the Representation of the Armenian Woman in the International Press', in *Mass Media and the Genocide of the Armenians: One Hundred Years of Uncertain Representation*, ed. Joceline Chabot et al. (Houndmills, Basingstoke, Hampshire: Palgrave Macmillan, 2016), 59–66.

41 Guerzoni, 'A Christian Harem', 55–6; James, 'Images of Femininity in American World War I Posters', 283–8; Keith David Watenpaugh, 'The League of Nations' Rescue of Armenian Genocide Survivors and the Making of Modern Humanitarianism, 1920–1927', *The American Historical Review* 115, no. 5 (December 2010): 1337.

42 *Hearings on S. 4785 Before the Senate Comm. on the Judiciary*, 65th Cong. 6h (1918) (statement of Sen. Hoke Smith); 58 Cong. Rec. 2545 (1919) (statement of Sen. Albert Cummins).

43 James Barton, 'Near East Relief—Looking Backward and Forward', NER Board of Trustees minutes, 6 February 1930, box 1, NEF Records, Acc 2010.

44 'The religious diversity of the NER leadership, 'of every religious denomination and almost every creed in America', was noted as a point in favour of incorporation in Congress. 57 Cong. Rec. 838 (1918) (statement of Rep. Andrew Jackson Montague).

45 Charlie Laderman, *Sharing the Burden: The Armenian Question, Humanitarian Intervention, and Anglo-American Visions of Global Order* (Oxford: Oxford University Press, 2019), esp. 198–9.

46 Lloyd E. Ambrosius, 'Wilsonian Diplomacy and Armenia: The Limits of Power and Ideology', in *America and the Armenian Genocide of 1915*, ed. Jay Winter (New York: Cambridge University Press, 2003), 115–16; Laderman, *Sharing the Burden*, 115–16 convincingly argues the missionary lobby was only one factor in Wilson's decision making.

47 Laderman, *Sharing the Burden*, 120–30.

48 *Hearings on S. 4785 Before the Senate Comm. on the Judiciary*, 65th Cong. 6h (1918) (statements of Charles Vickrey and William Peet).

49 'Propose New Plan for Raising Fund', *Boston Globe*, 24 September 1923; 'Sincere Thanksgiving', *The New Near East* 10, no. 6 (December 1925): 3–4.

50 John D. Rockefeller, Jr. to Charles Vickrey, 4 December 1923, series 2, box 7, folder 6, NER Records; 'First American Golden Rule Dinner', *The New Near East* 9, no. 8 (October 1924): 17–18; Charles Vickrey, 'The Golden Rule, A.D. 1925', *The New Near East* 10, no. 5 (September 1925): 3–4.

51 'Suggestions and Meditations for Golden Rule Sunday', Golden Rule Docket, May 1924, 10, series 2, box 7, folder 7, NER Records.

52 *Report of International Golden Rule Sunday Observance, 1926* (New York: Near East Relief, [1927]), 2.

53 Ibid., 5. Rapid expenditures following the Great Fire of Smyrna, which began in September 1922, caused much of the deficit, and prompted a donation from the Laura Spelman Rockefeller Memorial, but those facts do not negate the importance of Golden Rule Sunday for NER fundraising.

54 Report Assessing Donation Request from the Golden Rule Foundation, 29 May 1929, Office of Messrs. Rockefeller records, series Q, box 41, folder 359, Rockefeller Archive Center.

55  Note that the population was around 100 million, so if the *Times*'s numbers were accurate, it represented about a 1 per cent participation rate. 'Golden Rule Sunday', *New York Times*, 30 November 1923; 'America Observes 'Golden Rule' Day', *New York Times*, 2 December 1923; 'Million Americans and Near East Poor', *New York Times*, 3 December 1923.

56  Bulletin to Advisory Committees of the Religious Bodies and Other Cooperating Religious Leaders, 21 June 1924, series 2, box 7, folder 9, NER Records; 'The Golden Rule Crusade', *The New Near East* 9, no. 7 (September 1924): 12, 18; 'The Golden Rule Campaign', *The New Near East* 11, no. 2 (December 1927): 4.

57  'Don't Let Go! LIFT!' *The New Near East* 10, no. 10 (December 1926): cover.

58  'Boy Scouts, Here and There', *The New Near East* 9, no. 2 (February 1924): 12–13; Barton, *Story of Near East Relief*, 390.

59  Quoted in Karine V. Walther, *Sacred Interests: The United States and the Islamic World, 1821-1921* (Chapel Hill: University of North Carolina Press, 2015), 292.

60  'Suggestions and Meditations for Golden Rule Sunday', Golden Rule Docket, May 1924, 30, series 2, box 7, folder 7, NER Records.

61  'Keep their Star of Hope Shining', [1922?], series 2, box 8, folder 4, NER Records.

62  'Suggestions and Meditations', 30.

63  Charles Vickrey, 'International Golden Rule Sunday', Golden Rule Docket, 8, series 2, box 7, folder 7, NER Records.

64  'Cooperation of Organizations in Near East Relief', n.d., 46, series 2, box 7, folder 14, NER Records; 'A World Observance', *The New Near East* 10, no. 5 (September 1925): [2]. See also 'Golden Rule Living', *The New Near East* 9, no. 1 (January 1924): 3; 'The Universal Creed', *The New Near East* 10, no. 6 (December 1925): [2]; 'Divided in Creeds, United in Deeds', *The New Near East* 11, no. 2 (December 1927): 17.

65  'Extracts from Address by John R. Mott at National Golden Rule Committee Luncheon', 20 May 1924, series 2, box 7, folder 7, NER Records.

66  'East and West—At Last the Twain Have Met', ACASR *News Bulletin* 29 (September 1919): 5.

67  James Barton, 'Living, Breathing, Trusting Children', *The New Near East* 9, no. 4 (April 1924): 2.

68  Watenpaugh, *Bread from Stones*, 123.

69  Paul Monroe, R. R. Reeder, and James I. Vance, *Reconstruction in the Near East* (New York: [Near East Relief], 1924), 22.

70  George Stewart, 'Section II of Report to Survey Committee of the Near East Relief', 1925, series 2, box 7, folder 11, NER Records.

71  James Barton, 'The Modern Missionary', *Harvard Theological Review* 8, no. 1 (January 1915): 1–17, quotes on 2, 4, 15. The more famous articulation of this point was Howard Bliss, 'The Modern Missionary', *Atlantic Monthly* (May 1920): 664–75.

72  Ussama Samir Makdisi, *Faith Misplaced: The Broken Promise of U.S.-Arab Relations: 1820-2003* (New York: PublicAffairs, 2010), 3.

# 3

# Philanthropy as exchange

## American missionaries and the international religious liberty debate

Emma Long

Is missionary work philanthropy? It hasn't traditionally been seen that way, especially by those outside of the missionary enterprise. And missionaries themselves might well object to the secular implications of the term to describe what is, at its core, a deeply religious enterprise. But if taking the broadest definition of philanthropy, an act or gift done or made for humanitarian purposes, then some missionary work is and has been undoubtedly philanthropic. The extent of non-evangelizing activity by missionaries has waxed and waned over time, subject to distinct criticism at times and actively encouraged at others, but throughout history missionaries brought more than just their faith.[1] As Robert Speer, secretary of the Presbyterian Board of Foreign Missions, one of the largest denominational missions boards of the early twentieth century, noted, missions 'successes' included not only souls won to Christ but also colleges, universities, schools, hospitals, dispensaries and publishing houses.[2] Mainline Protestant missions influenced by the Social Gospel movement in the so-called 'heyday' of missionary activity, roughly from 1880 to 1930, focused with particular intensity on social reform and 'good works', but missions of all faiths and denominations have, to some extent, combined elements of social service and evangelism. As Bob Pierce, founder of World Vision International, today the largest Christian humanitarian organization in the world, argued: 'You can't preach to people whose stomachs are empty. First, you have to give them food.'[3] As a result, while not all missionary work is philanthropic in nature, much of it does incorporate philanthropic elements, whether from necessity or intent.

But missionaries brought more than hospitals, schools and orphanages; they also brought ideas, beliefs and values. In some circumstances this influence was positive, empowering socially marginalized and disfavoured individuals and communities, laying foundations for mass movements, encouraging critiques of Western imperialism, developing radical thinking and encouraging national self-determination for developing nations.[4] But more often the influence was parochial and culturally specific, to the detriment of indigenous populations. With good reason has missionary history, as Lamin

Sanneh noted, traditionally been linked to colonial history.[5] Anthropologists in the final quarter of the twentieth century explored and exposed the variety of ways in which missionaries abroad imposed their own cultures on those with whom they worked, while scholars spurred on by the Civil Rights Movement and American Indian Movement noted the many ways in which missionaries at home decimated Native American and African American cultures, all adding to the image of missionaries as narrow-minded purveyors of cultural destruction.[6] Portrayals of missionaries in popular culture embedded such views in public consciousness while scholars, as William Hutchison observed, tended to overlook missionary history because, unable to cast missionaries entirely as villains as a result of their undeniable hard work and self-sacrifice, they were nevertheless embarrassed by missionary attitudes towards other faiths and cultures.[7] Missionaries and cultural imperialism, it appeared, went hand-in-hand.

While some of this might be evidence of the secular academy's historical unwillingness to take religion seriously as a motive for action, missionaries themselves provided ample support for viewing themselves as cultural imperialists. Although missions workers had been raising the occasional searching question about their methods and activities since the mid-nineteenth century, doubts about the missionary enterprise were exemplified by the 1932 publication of *Re-Thinking Missions*, subsequently known as the Hocking Report, after the chair of the committee which produced it, Harvard University philosopher, William Ernest Hocking.[8] Funded by John D. Rockefeller, the laymen's committee was intended to analyse the condition of Protestant missions and outline an approach for the future. Although the report did not question the fundamental legitimacy of missions, it did raise questions about some of the traditional assumptions made by missionaries, including a parochial tendency to look down on other faiths and a failure to understand that others held to their faiths with equal sincerity as Christians to theirs. It also challenged the traditional view that Christianity was intended or entitled to displace the other developed religions of the world. Although it outraged many, especially fundamentalists who saw in it a call for relativism in questions of faith, the Hocking Report said little that had not been asked by missionaries for decades and it raised questions about the role and purpose of missions that saw mainline Protestant denominations slowly reduce their missions activity in the second half of the twentieth century. It also contributed to the sense that missionaries tended to be conveyors of a faith deeply shaped by their cultural background.

For American missionaries, the connection between faith and culture has been particularly close, driven in part by an understanding of the United States as a covenantal nation endowed with God's favour which emerged with particular force during the Second Great Awakening of the early nineteenth century. The emergence of scientific racism in the late nineteenth and early twentieth centuries which held white Westerners superior in almost all respects and then the development of American international power as a result of the Second World War and the Cold War further connected faith and national identity. American missionaries were shaped by the nation's power and implicated by it, and, as 'American power and responsibility became the new normal' after 1945, the connections between Christianity and Americanism that had been an inherent part of missionary activity from the beginning became more obvious.[9] Evangelical missionaries were particularly susceptible to what

Richard Pierard called 'a syncretic confusion of Christianity and America'.[10] Largely untroubled by the consequences of the Hocking Report, arguing that their focus on saving souls rather than on social welfare activities left them untainted by the risk of cultural imperialism, missionaries' conviction that evangelical Protestantism held the answer to salvation nevertheless combined with a growing sense of American global dominance in an increasingly bipolar world. Not until the Lausanne Congress of 1974 would evangelicals acknowledge, 'Missions have all too frequently exported with the gospel an alien culture, and churches have sometimes been in bondage to culture rather than Scripture.'[11]

The middle decades of the twentieth century then, the period between the emergence in the early 1940s of a self-conscious evangelical movement, which dismissed claims of missionaries' cultural interference, and the Lausanne Covenant of 1974, offer a useful period in which to consider the question of evangelical missionaries, American identity and philanthropy. This chapter challenges an implicit assumption in the broad definition of philanthropy, and in the associated understanding of missionary activity, that the relationship only went one way, from provider to recipient. While acknowledging American evangelical missionaries' implicit cultural biases, it draws on Daniel Bays and Grant Wacker's understanding of missions as sites of cultural exchange to argue that the relationship between the missionaries and the people they served was more complex and more interactive, what I've termed philanthropy as exchange.[12]

The chapter uses a case study, the Evangelical Foreign Missions Association (EFMA), which by the 1970s was one of the largest missions organizations in the United States, its parent organization, the National Association of Evangelicals (NAE), and the missions they served in the mid-twentieth century. As the group that experienced the most growth in missionary numbers after 1945, evangelicals offer a dynamic case study for this period. At the same time, their focus on soul-winning, and denial of participation in culturally influencing activity, helps to show both the intertwining of Christianity and Americanism and the way in which experiences shaped missionaries abroad separate from a self-conscious understanding of their cultural impact. To trace and explore the nature of this exchange, the chapter uses evangelical campaigns for religious liberty for Protestant minorities abroad, especially those in Catholic countries. Religious liberty was important to Americans in the 1940s and 1950s. It was one of the four freedoms used by President Franklin Roosevelt to define American aims during the Second World War and yet reports from around the world in the years following the war's conclusion suggested it was under threat from both communism and government action.[13] As such, it was very much in the public consciousness, even as debates about the proper relationship between church and state emerged in the United States. EFMA and the NAE came to see it as one of the benefits missionaries could bring, alongside more traditional philanthropic activities such as schools and orphanages. Using these examples we can see that while the missionaries brought their own cultural assumptions to the missions fields, once there, they were required to engage with the political, legal and social cultures of the nations in which they served, and this engagement fundamentally shaped the missions, organizations and thinking about religious liberty, with consequences for missionaries, missions and the United States more generally.

# American missionaries as cultural imperialists?

'There is', the NAE and EFMA's Clyde Taylor observed in 1959, 'the basic resentment on the part of our European leaders of evangelists and pastors coming over to these countries from either England or the United States. They feel that they are old historic churches and countries and do not need folks to come over and help them do their job.'[14] Taylor's comment came in response to complaints from a Salvation Army colleague in Italy that certain American missionaries were alienating their Italian colleagues with their attitudes and behaviour.[15] Nor was the difficulty limited to Italy. As Allen Koop observed, evangelical missionaries in post-war France found little traction for their work, seen as no different from the American technicians, economic advisers, businessmen and military personnel who were already intervening in French economic and political life.[16] And it was not only in Europe that missionaries found such a response. In Colombia, the government lost no opportunity to accuse Protestant, especially American evangelical, missionaries of cultural invasion and damage. '[I]t is unfortunate that at a time when the country is making such remarkable progress and advance, there should still be planned the sending of missions to us as if it concerned a savage nation,' President Gustavo Rojas Pinilla lamented in November 1953.[17] The following year, Minister of Foreign Affairs Evaristo Sourdis asserted, 'it is injurious to the dignity of Colombia as a sovereign nation . . . to be considered as a country to be conquered in respect to religion'.[18] In the view of those on the outside, therefore, post-war American evangelical missionaries were little different from their predecessors in their sense of cultural superiority.

American values and assumptions clearly underlay much of the work done by missionaries. Notable for the rarity of its self-reflection was a 1954 comment by Stanley Rycroft of the mainline Board of Missions of the Presbyterian Church in the United States: 'We shall have to think through quite carefully this whole problem. We may be a little unfair sometimes when we apply to some other country the standards of our own.'[19] Despite the fact that many NAE and EFMA officials and their in-country counterparts had significant experience of the life and culture of other nations, they showed little apparent willingness to acknowledge the complexities of being a religious minority in nations where religion and national culture, as well as religion and politics, were so intertwined. Claims by government officials and religious leaders that missionary activity risked damage to the national culture were too often dismissed by evangelicals as poor cover for the influence of the Catholic Church. At the same time, they drew on explicitly American-centric definitions of religious liberty. Protestants were, they asserted, being consistently denied, 'liberty of press, liberty of public assembly, and liberty of education'.[20] Much of the evangelical missionary campaign for religious liberty abroad was conducted in terms that reflected another Rycroft comment: 'Would it be too much to ask that Protestants should enjoy the same freedom to proselytise in Colombia that the Roman Catholics do in Protestant USA?'[21] As Americans, brought up with such rights and assumptions, it is perhaps not surprising that evangelicals turned first to definitions with which they were most familiar but it provided further evidence for those who saw in the activity of American missionaries an attempt to shape the world in the image of the United States.

A closer look, however, suggests that the story is rather more nuanced. American values were part of evangelicals' earliest interventions abroad because missionaries called on the American government to defend their rights as *American citizens* living in other countries. Calls on the State Department to protect missions' property, release individuals who had been imprisoned, and protest cases of physical harm were made on the understanding that people and property were protected by American laws.[22] But American treaty provisions were of no use in protecting non-American Protestants and evangelicals' language was beginning to expand beyond protests about American citizens. 'It is one thing to ask missionaries to leave', a colleague wrote to Taylor in 1953, 'but it is an entirely different thing to interfere with the freedom of worship of a local Protestant church which is a self-governing body made up of local Colombian believers.'[23] '[T]his case does not only involve us, but by implication it involves religious freedom for every other non-Catholic group in Italy', argued Earl Smith for the Church of Christ in Italy, a sentiment reinforced by Frank Gigliotti who indicated that the aim of the NAE was not only liberty for EFMA-affiliated missionaries but also 'religious liberty . . . for Italy'.[24] These broader aims were reflected in responses from the State Department to requests for action and support. 'While the Embassy will always be ready to extend the fullest protection to American interests, it must avoid exposing itself to the grave and politically damaging charge of interference in internal Italian affairs. . . . It is, therefore, difficult to intervene on behalf of Protestant missionaries who are Italian citizens', US ambassador to Italy, Claire Boothe Luce, reminded one correspondent.[25] 'The problem', a State Department official responded to an enquiry about why the government was not doing more to help Protestants in Spain, 'is difficult to solve in view of the fact that it involves Spanish nationals, and, therefore, is an internal matter within the jurisdiction of the Spanish Government.'[26] Such comments suggest that evangelicals, who had perhaps once regarded the problems in these countries as difficulties preventing their missionaries from carrying out their roles, were increasingly regarding the restrictions on Protestants in a broader sense of restrictions on groups of national believers. This in turn forced them to understand the limits to American influence: they, as Americans, might be able to help facilitate resolutions but they could not solve the problems by outside influence: they had to engage with the laws and governments of the countries in which they served.

Perhaps the best example is the actions of evangelicals in Italy who turned to the nation's courts to fight their cause. Because the problems facing some Protestant denominations were rooted in the law, it would take the courts to gain what they required: 'clarification and rewriting of the Penal Code and the education of the Civil authorities to obey the law in conformity of the new Constitution.'[27] This was not the imposition of an American understanding of religious liberty but a campaign to encourage the Italian courts to interpret existing laws in ways that allowed greater freedom to national Protestants. Although largely funded by US-based denominations, the legal office set up in 1953 by the Italian equivalent of the NAE, the Federal Council of Evangelical Churches in Italy, was primarily intended, as W. Dewey Moore of the Italian Baptist Mission explained, to 'enable our Italian brethren to carry on more effective work through a full-time legal service' and to 'speak with one intelligently-informed voice . . . in all matters that have to do in any way with religious liberty'.[28] The aim was to give Italian Protestants a voice to speak on their own behalf, not to have missionaries speak for them. Leading figures in US-based missionary organizations, including EFMA, were certainly in regular correspondence with one another but this was in addition to, not in place of, work by Italian Protestants in their own defence.

Writing about the first decade of NAE activity, James DeForest Murch observed the work of evangelical missions: 'They have been depending too much on the work of *foreign* missionaries.'[29] The above-mentioned examples indicate that missionaries were increasingly looking beyond those national borders and coming to see their fights abroad as a crucial battle for the right to religious liberty on behalf of *all* evangelical Protestants. Further evidence comes from evangelical willingness to evoke the Universal Declaration of Human Rights (UDHR) and call on the UN to intervene to defend the rights of religious minorities. Given evangelicals' general suspicion of the UN and the fact they had forcefully objected to the adoption of the UDHR, their willingness to call upon both was surprising but also indicated a pragmatic understanding that this might help them achieve their goals of protecting national Protestants.[30] This is important in challenging the perception of missionaries as little more than carriers of their own cultural assumptions. Without denying the clear influence of American ideals of religious liberty on evangelical missionary thinking, their actions were also increasingly shaped by an understanding of both the *national* context in which they were working and the *limits* of American power and authority. In drawing on the legal frameworks in each country, and in calling on the UDHR, evangelical missionaries were actively engaging with non-American sources of authority for their defence.

## Missions as exchange

As can clearly be seen, American missionaries certainly took their cultural assumptions with them into the field. But, perhaps inevitably, those assumptions ran up against the cultural, legal and political behaviours and traditions in the countries in which they served. The interaction between the two perspectives led to what this chapter refers to as philanthropy as exchange: that is, as missionaries increasingly engaged with the issue of religious liberty for Protestants and used the tools available to them within each country, the lessons they learned had a crucial impact on missionaries and those back home who supported them. American missionaries never entirely abandoned their Americanism, nor perhaps would it be realistic to expect that they would, but a closer look at their work indicates that the relationship was more complex than a simple attempt to impose American concepts of religious liberty. The influence went both ways, and missionaries were shaped by their experiences abroad as much as they shaped their communities. Three examples, drawn primarily from the NAE's work in and on behalf of Italy and Colombia, illustrate this exchange: defining the boundaries of religious liberty, deepening their anti-Catholicism and increasing their perceptions of the government as an ally in their fight.[31]

Evangelicals' battles for religious liberty abroad forced them to think carefully about the meaning of religious freedom and how it was protected. They were not questions that needed asking in the United States where evangelicals were protected by the First Amendment and by their position as part of the dominant religion. But as a minority faith in countries where the majority religion and national culture were intimately intertwined, evangelicals faced challenges. When political leaders claimed repeatedly that their nation's laws protected religious liberty, the burden was on the missionaries to show why the restrictions imposed on them went beyond the protection of 'public order' or safety and pushed into the realm of what they termed 'persecution'. At the heart of evangelical objections was an American opposition to an established church, but it was based less on American constitutional theory and more on very specific experiences of missionaries abroad.

NAE correspondence with colleagues abroad was full of claims that local and national government officials were unfairly wielding their power of approval to restrict the activities of evangelical missionaries and delegitimize their efforts. The problems began early, they claimed, with the government using visas and residence permits as a way to discriminate against Protestants. 'The Colombian government is refusing visas to every ordained clergyman who applies,' Taylor complained to a colleague in May 1955.[32] W. Dewey Moore wrote to Taylor in April 1953 that the Italian government's reasons for denying residence visas to five of their missionaries were 'a bit "fishy"' since all but one of the individuals facing difficulties were 'Protestant religious workers'.[33] Once missionaries were able to enter the country, however, their concerns expanded to other areas of government control over the religious life of their citizens. Restrictions on where Protestants could meet and worship, the enforced closing of churches with no clear reason provided, the imprisonment of ministers and the closing or forbidding of Protestant schools, hospitals and orphanages were among the most common complaints expressed to the NAE. In each case the problem was government action that restricted the ability of individuals to follow their faith. From the denial of access to water for a Protestant building, to the taxing at crippling levels of non-recognized denominational buildings, from government foot-dragging in regards to requests for authorization to build or operate churches, schools, and hospitals to low-level harassment by local officials in areas where evangelical churches operated, including warnings not to hold religious services and the occasional arrest of individuals for preaching, speaking or handing out religious literature in public spaces, evangelicals saw myriad examples of what could happen when the secular authority was given too much power over the living out of individual faith.[34] Only harm could come from giving the government too much authority to regulate the practices of individual and communal faith. 'We are convinced', Taylor protested to the State Department, 'that a determined effort is being made, first in Colombia and later perhaps to be carried out through the rest of the Latin American countries, of a definite attack on the Protestant minorities.'[35]

'The situation in Colombia has gone from one of violent persecution to legalized restriction and curbing of the religious freedom of non-Catholics,' noted Stanley Rycroft, while the UK-based Evangelical Alliance asserted, 'There is a new effort to clothe the persecution with an air of legality . . . the government is attempting to strangle Protestantism by "legal" means.'[36] Their experiences made evangelicals acutely sensitive to issues of religious liberty. It was not only a reminder that the rights taken for granted by American citizens within the United States were not available to all around the world or reinforcement of the importance of the American principle of separation of church and state, but that these experiences illustrated how seemingly neutral laws, such as operating permits, could be used in practice to limit religious freedom. This was especially important in the United States given the enormous growth of government since the New Deal of the 1930s. As the government expanded into new areas of American life, evangelicals feared that religious liberty might be at risk. '[T]his basic American heritage of freedom is imperilled by subtle [*sic*], insidious trends and influences that dangerously tend toward the state restricting and controlling . . . religion,' the NAE stated in 1959, noting 'growing concern' about government actions.[37] Minimum wage and overtime laws threatened the right to voluntary religious service, anti-discrimination legislation in relation to the mails risked the freedom to 'expose the heresies' of other faiths,[38] and social security reform raised the spectre of government redefining church roles according to the NAE throughout the 1950s. Rather than simply seeing such reactions as conservative opposition to government growth, evangelical sensitivity can be seen as a concern that without close attention, laws might be used, deliberately or inadvertently, to limit religious freedom at home, just as their missionaries experienced abroad.

Underpinning these actions was a long-standing evangelical concern about the influence of the Catholic Church in US politics and government, a concern exacerbated by missionary experiences of religious liberty in Catholic countries. The situation was seen by American Protestants to be so severe that in 1947 a small group, including Taylor and other NAE leaders, came together to form Protestants and Other Americans United for the Separation of Church and State (POAU), an interest group dedicated to maintaining the separation of church and state and religious liberty by primarily opposing Catholic involvement with government.[39] 'Catholicism everywhere in the world', POAU's executive director Glenn Archer warned, 'is seeking to dominate national capitals through the techniques of politics, labor, publicity, and censorship.' 'Will Roman clericalism', he asked, 'someday dominate our own beloved country?'[40] If such a reality were to be avoided, Archer argued, Americans of all faiths would need to be vigilant and to resist even the smallest attempts to challenge the separation of church and state at home. Of particular concern in the late 1940s were proposals to provide federal funding for education, sparked in part by concern that the nation's education system needed reinforcing if the country was to win the Cold War. Such proposals were largely supported by the Catholic Church, which pushed for the inclusion of its own extensive school network, and was opposed by Protestants who interpreted them as the entering wedge in the collapse of church-state separation. Protestants were particularly alarmed when, in 1947, the US Supreme Court permitted New Jersey to reimburse parents from tax funds for the costs of sending their children to religious schools via public transport, seeing the first gap in the wall of separation between church and state.[41] The mainline *Christian Century* called *Everson* 'the thin edge of the wedge which would ultimately crack open the Constitution', while the NAE's Clyde Taylor grimly concluded it was simply 'the first battle' in the war. But evangelicals and some mainline Protestants were under no illusions about the significance of *Everson*. As Archer told the NAE: '[T]he Catholic demand for bus funds is part of a world pattern.'[42]

Evangelicals were already convinced as a result of the experiences of their missionaries in Catholic countries, which had deepened their suspicion to almost conspiratorial levels. Early complaints about individual priests riling up mobs of locals to attack Protestant churches or encouraging violence against missionaries and their congregations slowly turned by the 1950s into claims of a more pernicious and dangerous influence of the Catholic Church over government policymaking. In Italy, Taylor expressed concern about 'the very serious problem of clerical infiltration and control in government'.[43] When schools, hospitals and orphanages were closed, denied licences to operate or prevented from being created at all, evangelicals complained that local officials were paying too much attention to the local clergy. When the national government closed churches belonging to the Churches of Christ and the Assemblies of God, evangelicals saw the influence of the Catholic Church behind the action. 'The hand of the Minister of the Interior is becoming more and more heavy with all the weight of the Vatican back of it', the Foreign Missions Board of the Southern Baptist Convention reported to Taylor.[44] In Colombia, Taylor observed that President Pinilla 'feels that he must have the support of the Roman Catholic Church to stay in power'.[45] When the government in 1953 closed large sections of the country to anyone other than Catholic clergy following agreements with the Vatican, evangelicals were quick to argue that this was further evidence of the tactics employed by the church when it had power and influence.

The scope and tone of their discussions suggested evangelicals saw some kind of religious Domino Theory at play in their battles over religious liberty. In a confidential report to evangelical missions in October 1953, the NAE wrote: 'from official sources we have been informed that they are convinced that Colombia is but the exper[i]mental ground where the "Catholic Action" of the Roman Catholic Church is working out its future strategy for all of Latin America'.[46] '. . . [A]s the battle goes in Rome, so it will go on in South and Central America, and in Spain, Portugal and other Catholic-dominated regions', warned Gigliotti.[47] This was much more than just a fight for Colombia or Italy; it had consequences for the rest of the world including, possibly, the United States. Missionary experiences abroad were lessons to be learned, evangelicals argued, to ensure that the United States did not go the same way. Although evangelical hostility towards Catholicism pre-dated these post-war debates, the battles for religious liberty that evangelicals perceived as fights against the hierarchy of the Catholic Church fundamentally expanded and deepened their anti-Catholicism at home. It thus provides another example of how missionary activity abroad shaped those who remained at home.

Coming to see the involvement of the US government as a benefit to their aims was a third and final element that evangelicals learned as a result of their engagement with Protestants abroad. This engagement is important in the context of evangelical history. Scholarship largely holds that evangelical engagement with national-level politics did not begin in earnest until at least the late 1960s.[48] Although free from the party politics that would characterize the New Christian Right from the 1970s onwards, the NAE's extensive engagement with the federal government, especially the State Department, from the late 1940s in regards to religious liberty issues tied to missionary activity suggests, in fact, that evangelicals were quite deeply engaged with politics at least a decade earlier and that missionary engagement abroad was a significant part of what prompted that engagement in the first place. As evangelicals lobbied against US government policies that appeared to violate their concept of the separation of church and state, such as federal funding for education or the appointment of an envoy to the Vatican, that connection with government became increasingly important on the domestic front too.

The NAE's first approach to the State Department came in 1946 over the denial of visas to missionaries to enter Colombia.[49] The successful resolution of that difficulty, and those that followed, played a major role in convincing evangelicals that the government was worth working with. As Taylor wrote to a colleague in July 1954: 'I believe in helping the Government whenever we can, because we certainly expect them to help us.'[50] It was visa issues that prompted evangelicals to reach out to the US government that was crucial. Visas and re-entry permits fell under the heading of consular and diplomatic activity, issues that required government involvement but which did not reflect requests for special treatment. Visa issues were also among the least complicated for the State Department to address, requiring relatively limited action for a significant success rate.[51] This success worked to convince evangelicals who were new to this direct contact that working with and through the government could bring tangible benefits. '[T]he State Department', Taylor informed evangelicals in 1949, 'is willing at every level to go to the defense of American citizens who may be missionaries, and American organizations who may be Mission Societies, where they may legally and diplomatically intervene on our behalf.'[52]

Evangelical calls on the US government expanded rapidly from the late 1940s onwards as first violence and then legal restrictions impacted missionary work. Over time, Taylor and others at the NAE built strong relationships with key figures in the State Department and American embassies and action by the government in response to requests, such as demanding an investigation into the vicious beating of Rev. Julius Allen DeGruyter of the World Wide Evangelization Crusade in Colombia in 1955, formal and informal requests to reopen churches and schools, or quiet requests for protection for people and property, helped to reinforce evangelicals' belief that the government was a valuable ally. The new American ambassador, Taylor confided to a colleague in Colombia, 'certainly is on our side of the fence. . . . I am sure he will do everything he can to advance our cause.'[53] In Italy too, the NAE noted the 'the fine cooperation . . . received from Ambassador James Dunn in Rome and other members of the U.S. Embassy' regarding the ongoing difficulties for evangelicals and praised the 'sincerity and genuineness of our friends in the State Department'.[54] Even in Spain, where the NAE acknowledged that the United States had little influence, Taylor noted that the embassy staff were 'all very much on our side of the fence'.[55] 'We have some very wonderful friends there,' Gigliotti informed NAE president Thomas Zimmerman about the State Department, 'Clyde Taylor and the Washington office are in touch with all of them'.[56]

As Axel Schäfer has noted, NAE successes 'generated an awareness of the opportunities provided by working with government agencies'.[57] As evangelicals expanded their engagement with the government at home through participation in social service funding programmes, informal networks such as International Christian Leadership and the prayer breakfast movement, or via publicity, protest, and calls for evangelical letter-writing campaigns on issues such as federal aid to education, President Truman's firing of General Douglas MacArthur, or the existence of an American envoy to the Vatican, the opportunities for success increased and they moved further and further into political activity. Their engagement with the State Department was only part of this process but, as one of the earliest formal connections made by the newly formed NAE, it played a significant role. And as evangelicals became increasingly politically active, their engagement became more and more influential and so the lessons learned over visa issues and calls for protection for missions became more valuable.

# Conclusion

There is no doubt that American evangelical missionaries serving abroad in the decades after the Second World War brought with them their cultural background and assumptions, whether that was about the possibilities of American power and influence around the world, or in thinking about religious liberty in terms defined by the American experience under the First Amendment. But many, as Hutchison argued, also brought a 'sensitivity' to the dilemmas of cultural interaction that should not be overlooked.[58] Missionary pressure played an important role in pushing countries like Colombia, Italy and Spain to become more protective of minority religious rights in the mid-twentieth century. Meanwhile, missionary experiences shaped both the missionaries and those at home who supported them. The example of religious liberty battles for minority Protestant groups abroad is only one small example of a range of ways in which missionaries were shaped by their experiences, but it helps to show clearly how philanthropic missionary work abroad could have an impact back home in the United States and indicates that missionaries could and did learn from the people and cultures around them.

Those influences, like the impact of the missionaries themselves, could be both positive and negative. Long inclined to reach across national borders to see transnational communities of faith, religious liberty debates encouraged evangelicals to look outwards and build more extensive connections to people who shared their faith. It also encouraged evangelicals to understand that events around the world had significance for the United States too, but in terms that were not limited to Cold War rhetoric in which the United States was in the leadership role. Their campaigns also forced them to think carefully about what religious liberty actually meant, especially when those debates became more prominent in American society as a result of *Everson* and the battles over federal funding for education. As a result, when evangelicals protested such programmes, they did so not as a knee-jerk reaction to policies to which they objected, but with positions that had been shaped and informed by the missionary experience abroad and a determination that they should not be repeated at home. Significantly, the defence of missionaries brought evangelicals, the NAE included, into contact with the federal government. As the number of successful interventions increased, so too did evangelical confidence in the government as a reliable ally. This would have major consequences for the political activism of evangelicals on domestic issues from the 1950s onwards, encouraging them to turn to the government as a way to achieve their aims. While they were not always, even often, successful, the confidence they built and the connections they developed would be the foundations on which the New Christian Right would build in the last quarter of the twentieth century. Finally, illustrating that exchange was not always positive, missionary experiences abroad deepened evangelical distrust of the Catholic Church to almost conspiratorial levels. This anti-Catholicism had a profound effect on American law and politics in the middle of the twentieth century, from Supreme Court cases in which Protestant-Catholic antipathy formed the context, to outright battles over federal funding for education or the ability of a Catholic to become president. Seen solely in domestic terms, evangelical anti-Catholicism appears hysterical and overblown; placed in its international context their position becomes more understandable, if no more defensible.

That American evangelical missionaries acted as agents of US cultural power and influence in the world in the period after the Second World War is well documented and not in doubt. But in focusing on what missionaries brought with them, alongside their faith and philanthropic actions, we should not lose sight of the fact that missions were also sites of exchange in which missionaries learned, and the knowledge and understanding gained they took home with them with important consequences for the United States.

# Notes

1 For a good survey of changing attitudes towards social engagement by missions see William Hutchison, *Errand to the World: American Protestant Thought and Foreign Missions* (Chicago: University of Chicago Press, 1987).

2 Robert E. Speer, *Missionary Principles and Practice* (New York: Fleming H. Revell, 1910), 501–2, quoted in Hutchinson, 100.

3 Pierce quoted in David King, *God's Internationalists: World Vision and the Age of Evangelical Humanitarianism* (Philadelphia: University of Pennsylvania Press, 2019), 110.

4 See, for example, chapters by Everett Wilson and Lamin Sanneh in Joel Carpenter and Wilbert Shenk eds, *Earthen Vessels: American Evangelicals and Foreign Missions, 1880–1980* (Grand Rapids: William B. Eerdmans Publishing Co., 1990), and those by Mark Hanley, William Svelmoe and Scott Flipse in Daniel Bays and Grant Wacker, eds, *The Foreign Missionary Enterprise at Home: Explorations in North American Cultural History* (Tuscaloosa: University of Alabama Press, 2003).

5 Lamin Sanneh, 'Mission and the Modern Imperative – Retrospect and Prospect: Charting a Course', in Carpenter and Shenk, 301–3. Some have argued that philanthropy itself includes elements of imperialism. See, for example, Peter Buffett's description of 'Philanthropic Colonialism' or Ashley Smith on 'humanitarian imperialism'. Peter Buffett, 'The Charitable-Industrial Complex', *New York Times*, 26 July 2013; Ashley Smith, 'Humanitarian Imperialism and its Apologists', *International Socialist Review*, Vol. 67 (September 2009).

6 For a good overview of anthropological criticisms of missionary work see Sarah Ruble, *The Gospel of Freedom and Power: Protestant Missionaries in American Culture*

*After World War Two* (Chapel Hill: University of North Carolina Press, 2012), 91–120. On nineteenth century missionary impact on minority groups at home see Heather Curtis, *Holy Humanitarians: American Evangelicals and Global Aid* (Cambridge, MA: Harvard University Press, 2018), 191–8, 330–1 (for an introduction to relevant scholarship).

7  Hutchison, *Errand to the World*, 1–2. Examples of missionaries in recent popular culture include novels such as Barbara Kingsolver, *The Poisonwood Bible* (London: Faber & Faber, 1999), and films including *The Mosquito Coast* (1986) and *At Play in the Fields of the Lord* (1991).

8  William Ernest Hocking, *Re-Thinking Missions: A Laymen's Inquiry after One Hundred Years* (New York: Harper and Brothers, 1932). On the Hocking Report and its impact, see Hutchison, *Errand to the World*, 158–75; Grant Wacker, 'Second Thoughts on the Great Commission: Liberal Protestants and Foreign Missions, 1890–1940', in Carpenter and Shenk, 293–5. See also the life and writings of Pearl Buck, a Pulitzer and Nobel Prize-winning writer and child of missionaries to China who, in later life, became increasingly critical of the missionary enterprise. Grant Wacker, 'The Waning of the Missionary Impulse: The Case of Pearl S. Buck', in Bays and Wacker, 191–205.

9  Ruble, *The Gospel of Freedom and Power*, 2, 22. For studies of the complex interplay of faith, philanthropy and Americanism in missions work at either end of the long twentieth century, see Curtis, *Holy Humanitarians* and King, *God's Internationalists*.

10  Richard Pierard, 'Pax Americana and the Evangelical Missionary Advance', in Carpenter and Shenk, 164–5.

11  'The Lausanne Covenant' (1974) available online at https://www.lausanne.org/content /covenant/lausanne-covenant#cov (accessed 15 April 2020).

12  Bays and Wacker, eds, 8.

13  See, for example, Robert Root, 'Twilight of Religious Liberty', *Christian Century*, 16 April 1947, 491–3; 'Terror Sweeps Colombia', *Christian Life*, October 1950, 27; 'Red China's Captive Americans', *Life*, 19 May 1952, 51–5; 'Burial Above Ground', *Life*, 8 September 1952, 126–46.

14  Clyde Taylor to Norman Marshall, 12 May 1959, Papers of the Evangelical Fellowship of Missions Agencies, Billy Graham Center Archives, Wheaton College (hereafter EFMA Papers) Box 104, File 6.

15  International Secretary to Norman Marshall, 2 April 1959, EFMA Papers, Box 106, File 6.

16  Allen Koop, 'American Evangelical Missionaries in France, 1945–1975', in Carpenter and Shenk, 180–202. Of course, the predominance of Catholicism in France might also account for some of the French disinterest in Protestant missionary activity.

17  Quoted in NAE press release, 6 November 1953, EFMA Papers, Box 3, File 26.

18  Frank Hall, 'Colombian Hits Persecution Cry', *The Tablet* (Brooklyn, NY), 5 February 1955, EFMA Papers, Box 85, File 4.

19  Stanley Rycroft to Claud Nelson, 17 November 1954, EFMA Papers, Box 85, File 1.

20  CEDEC Statement on Colombia, 7 April 1954; NAE press release, 28 April 1954. Both EFMA Papers, Box 85, File 2.

21  Stanley Rycroft to Claud Nelson, 17 November 1954, EFMA Papers, Box 85, File 1.

22  These included Treaties of Friendship, Navigation and Commerce with both Colombia and Italy, as well as the peace treaty the United States signed with Italy at the end of the Second World War.

23  Harold Commons to Clyde Taylor, 20 October 1953, EFMA Papers, Box 84, File 23.

24  Earl Smith quoted in Church of Christ News Release, 25 September 1952 and Frank Gigliotti to Charles Fama, 13 May 1953. Both EFMA Papers, Box 104, File 5.

25  Clare Boothe Luce to Brooks Hays, [u.d., April 1953?], Americans United for the Separation of Church and State Papers, Mudd Manuscript Library, Princeton University (hereafter Americans United Papers), Box 23, File 17.

26  William B. Macomber, Jr to Catherine May, 25 February 1959, EFMA Papers, Box 88, File 12. See also Howard Cook to Rev. Gardener Winn, 2 January 1953, General Records of the Department of State, Record Group 59, National Archives at College Park, College Park, MD (hereafter State Department Records), Central Decimal Files 1950–1954, Box 5030 (Declassification No.: NND842913).

27  Special Meeting of the NAE Commission on Evangelical Action, 6 November 1951, EFMA Papers, Box 2, File 50.

28  W. Dewey Moore to Clyde Taylor, 17 April 1953, EFMA Papers, Box 104, File 5. For a brief survey of success before the courts prior to 1953 see Federal Council of Evangelical Churches in Italy, "Religious Intolerance in Italy 1947–1952", Papers of the National Association of Evangelicals (hereafter NAE Papers), Buswell Library, Wheaton College Special Collections, Box 104, File 6.

29  James DeForest Murch, *Cooperation Without Compromise: A History of the National Association of Evangelicals* (Grand Rapids: William B. Eerdmans Publishing Co., 1956), 107 (emphasis in original).

30  Evangelicals argued the UDHR failed to properly recognize the source of rights by asserting that rights inhered in man and not that they were granted by God. Sue Nichols, 'Evangelical View of Human Rights Expressed by NAE', *United Evangelical Action*, 15 December 1949, 3–4.

31  Italy and Colombia were, of course, not the only countries in which evangelical missionaries served, nor were they the only countries in which religious liberty was an issue. But the work on behalf of Protestants in these two nations in particular account for a large proportion of the material in the NAE and EFMA archives which indicates that they took up a large proportion of the organizations' time and resources.

32  Clyde Taylor to W. Stanley Rycroft, 31 May 1955, EFMA Papers, Box 85, File 3.

33  W. Dewey Moore to Clyde Taylor, 17 April 1953, EFMA Papers, Box 104, File 5.

34  See, for example, Sidney Correll, 'Protestant Purge is on in Spain', *United Evangelical Action*, 1 August 1952, 3–4; Herman Parli, 'Why Italy Persecutes the Protestants', *United Evangelical Action*, 15 October 1952, 3–4; 'How Rome is Strangling Protestantism in Spain', *United Evangelical Action*, 1 October 1953, 7–8; Clyde Taylor, 'Roman Catholic Persecution in Colombia', *United Evangelical Action*, 15 November 1957, 3–4; 'Are Colombian Protestants Being Persecuted?', *United Evangelical Action*, 1 July 1958, 4–5, 15.

35  Clyde Taylor to Albert Gerberich, 7 October 1953, EFMA Papers, Box 84, File 23.

36  Stanley Rycroft, 'Is Religious Freedom a God-Given Right', *National Council Outlook*, April 1954, 22; John Savage, Evangelical Alliance press release, 24 March 1954. EFMA Files, Box 85, File 2.

37  General Convention Business Minutes, 9 April 1959, 4, NAE Papers, Box 34, File 6.

38  Report of the Board of Administration to the 1949 annual conference, conference booklet, April 1949, 17, NAE Papers, Box 40, File 1.

39  The organization still exists, although it has dropped the opening words, and its early anti-Catholicism, and is now Americans United for the Separation of Church and State, or simply Americans United. See the organization's home page at https://www.au.org/. International developments played a role in the organization's

discussions: at its first, informal, meeting one of the agenda items was 'The Italian Constitution', presented by Gigliotti. See 'Informal Conference on Church and State', Agenda, and POAU Manifesto, Americans United Papers, Box 16, File 10. For a good introduction to POAU's anti-Catholicism, see Steven Green, *The Third Disestablishment: Church, State, and American Culture, 1940–1975* (New York: Oxford University Press, 2019).

40  Glenn Archer, '"The Cure for Clericalism"', speech to the 1961 NAE Conference, 13 April 1961, EFMA Papers, Box 17, File 4.

41  *Everson v. Board of Education* 330 US 1 (1947).

42  Charles Clayton Morrison, 'Supreme Court Widens Breach in the Law', *Christian Century*, 19 February 1947, 227; EFMA Report to the Executive Committee of the NAE, March 1947, NAE Papers, Box 60, File 16; Glenn Archer, 'The Cure for Clericalism'.

43  Clyde Taylor to Luther Smith, 19 February 1960, EFMA Files, Box 104, File 7.

44  George Sadler to Clyde Taylor, 20 November 1951, quoting Dewey Moore, EFMA Files, Box 2, File 49.

45  Clyde Taylor to Rev. J. Hubert Cook, 30 September 1953, EFMA Files, Box 84, File 23.

46  Anon, 'Confidential News Report', 30 October 1953, EFMA Files, Box 3, File 26.

47  Frank Gigliotti to Clyde Taylor, 24 May 1951, EFMA Files, Box 2, File 49.

48  Some studies which have begun to challenge this include: Kevin Kruse, *One Nation Under God: How Corporate America Invented Christian America* (New York: Basic Books, 2015); Axel Schäfer, *Piety and Public Funding: Evangelicals and the State in Modern America* (Philadelphia: University of Pennsylvania Press, 2012); Matthew Avery Sutton, *American Apocalypse: A History of Modern Evangelicalism* (Cambridge, MA: Belknap Press, 2014); Daniel K. Williams, *God's Own Party: The Making of the Christian Right* (New York: Oxford University Press, 2010).

49  Clyde Taylor to EFMA Missions members, 1 August 1946, EFMA Papers, Box 1, File 4. See also Memorandum of Conversation, 9 May 1946, State Department Records, Central Decimal Files 1940–1949, Box 1667 (Declassification No.: NND812044).

50  Clyde Taylor to Robert Lazear, Jr., 14 July 1954, EFMA Papers, Box 84, File 24.

51  'Such intervention was always informal, and invariably successful', reported the Charge d'Affaires in Colombia, Thomas Maleady, in June 1954: 'My intervention in each instance was confined simply to requesting action on applications already filed, and at no time did any foreign official evidence any feeling that my action was unwelcome.' Foreign Service Despatch, 2 June 1954, State Department Records, Central Decimal Files 1950–1954, Box 930 (Declassification No.: NND969002).

52  EFMA Report to the NAE Board of Administration, April 1949, Papers of Herbert J. Taylor, Billy Graham Center Archives Wheaton College, Box 66, File 22; Report of the Executive Secretary to the 1950 EFMA Convention, EFMA Papers, Box 210, File 1.

53  Clyde Taylor to Robert Lazear, 16 November 1951, EFMA Papers, Box 84, File 21.

54  Special Meeting of the NAE Commission on Evangelical Action, 6 November 1951, NAE Papers, Box 2, File 50; Frank Gigliotti to Clyde Taylor, 2 May 1951, EFMA Papers, Box 2, File 49.

55  Clyde Taylor, Confidential Report on Spain, 17 August 1953, EFMA Papers, Box 88, File 6.

56  Frank Gigliotti to Thomas Zimmerman, 14 August 1961, EFMA Papers, Box 4, File 21.

57  Schäfer, *Piety and Public Funding*, 99.

58  Hutchison, *Errand to the World*, 205.

# Cultural networks

# 4

# Transatlantic abolition and the unquiet library

## Print culture and the making of a 'celebrated philanthropist'

Bridget Bennett

Libraries have long been viewed as locations of peaceful – even silent – work, as well as critically important sites of sociability. While the physical site of the library is frequently a place of sanctuary and quiet repose, a repository for archives and books, it simultaneously nurtures radical exchanges and loud dissent. Productive noise can emerge in meetings, reading groups and especially in the written texts that are produced as a consequence of immersion in libraries and then are studied in, or borrowed from, them. Libraries are places for undertaking the kind of work which can lead to disturbance, restlessness, activity and noise outside of their bounded spaces. The library is, in other words, fundamentally *unquiet*, though library users can also choose to experience it as a restful retreat. Indeed, the British Library's current podcast series 'Anything but Silent' acknowledges this, demonstrating the multiple ways in which libraries empower their users. Libraries have often provided crucial resources for individuals involved in social justice, inspiring them and bringing them together in person or through print. Likewise, public libraries in particular have had a long and well-established relationship with philanthropy via donations and fundraising activities.[1] Philanthropy, broadly defined as the love of mankind, was chiefly understood in the nineteenth century as having a relationship to charities and to agents and agencies of reform.[2] It is not a term we might immediately associate with the abolition of slavery. Instead, we might think of its connections to corporate and individual giving. However, the word 'philanthropy' was used in the nineteenth century to suggest an interest in the well-being of others, specifically those who were held in enslavement. Without a doubt, abolition was the most significant philanthropic concern of the nineteenth century. Philanthropy, therefore, connects libraries to abolition and anti-slavery in important ways. Here I focus especially on the role of libraries and the impact of print culture in the transatlantic abolitionist campaigns of the eighteen and nineteenth centuries. While print culture made a major contribution to the abolition of slavery in the United States, it is what I call the *unquiet library* which played a key role in making that possible.[3]

In what follows I consider the contributions made by two Quaker men to transatlantic abolition via their connections to print culture and libraries. One was Anthony Benezet the French-born Philadelphian educationalist. The other was a Leeds-born merchant named Wilson Armistead who so admired Benezet's example that he produced a mid-century edition of his memoirs to keep his memory alive. They were both committed library users who valued their library memberships. Benezet was both a member (and the first librarian) of the Library Company of Philadelphia (founded in 1731) one of the earliest and most important subscription libraries in the colonies. Evidently, Wilson Armistead understood the relationship of empowerment until the end of his life, publishing a pamphlet titled 'Public Libraries for Liberia and Sierra Leone' (1865) three years before his death. He was a member of the Leeds Library (founded in 1768) the oldest surviving proprietary subscription library in Britain. Both the Library Company and Leeds Library were vitally important to the social and intellectual networks of the cities in which they were located.[4] They were key sources of information and printed matter for both men, and also gave them access to like-minded people. Though Armistead and Benezet had quiet demeanours, they were fearless and noisy in their contributions to the print public sphere, intervening when they saw injustice at work. The libraries and their resources accelerated their very unquiet forms of activism, which were largely focused on anti-racist and abolitionist writing. Benezet framed his interventions on slavery and injustice in relation to sound; in a letter on the slave trade to the Quaker abolitionist Richard Shackleton dated 6 June 1772, he asked rhetorically, 'Can we be both *silent* and *innocent* spectators?'[5] They both used networks of printers, booksellers, libraries, purchasers and readers to disseminate their writings. They also relied upon friends and acquaintances to carry letters and printed texts across the Atlantic to petition for change; Benezet's assiduity in this regard was particularly well known. Benjamin Rush, his friend and fellow member of the Library Company of Philadelphia, wrote:

> If a person called upon him who was going [on] a journey, his first thoughts usually were, how would he make him an instrument in its favour; and he either gave him tracts to distribute, or sent him letters by him, or he gave him some commission on the subject, so that he was the means of employing several persons at the same time, in various parts of America, in advancing the work he had undertaken.[6]

Clearly, Benezet understood the possibilities offered by mobile individuals in an era before the establishment of a reliable postal system. This enabled him to build his activism very widely. David Crosby writes that

> He was not content with speaking or publishing; he conducted a powerful lobbying campaign, creating networks of Quakers and other like-minded reformers to approach opinion makers, legislators, officials, churchmen, and any others in the colonies and in Europe who were in a position to influence policy.[7]

In all these respects then, it is appropriate to think of Anthony Benezet (as Wilson Armistead and others certainly did) as a philanthropist. Armistead was probably familiar with Benezet's reputation for piety and activism from an early age, through his membership of the Society of Friends. It is possible, though probably unverifiable, that Armistead accessed the English edition of Roberts Vaux's *Memoirs of Anthony Benezet* (1817) from the Leeds Library. Vaux was a well-known philanthropist himself, actively involved in penal reform, education and abolition, and his book was the most significant source of information on Benezet. The Leeds Library possessed a copy of an English edition, published in 1817 by W. Alexander, a York-based Quaker publisher. This extended the American edition in ways set out in an anonymous preface:

> In reprinting these interesting Memoirs, the Editor has incorporated with the text some very long notes, which he found in the original; and has also made many small corrections; but the general arrangement remains unaltered. The Editor has also added some extracts from a letter written by Anthony Benezet to John Pemberton, of which he possessed a manuscript copy.[8]

The library cannot trace any definite date of receipt; the catalogue's first mention of the book is 1836. Since Armistead became a member of the library in 1844, it would certainly have been possible for him to access it there. However, given its Quaker subject matter, it might also have been part of his personal library, which contained other books about Friends. He donated at least two foundational Quaker works from his own collection to the Leeds Library; the journal of George Fox (1694) and Robert Barclay's *An Apology for the True Christian Divinity* (1678). This is part of a long-standing pattern of Quaker ownership (or authorship) of works on notable members of the Society of Friends. For instance, the Philadelphian-based Vaux published *Memoirs of the Lives of Benjamin Lay and Ralph Sandiford* (1815) two years before his book on Benezet. Both Sandiford and Lay were uncompromising British-born Quakers who moved to Philadelphia and agitated for abolition, often to the fury of slaveholding Quakers. Inspired by Vaux's work, Armistead would go on to produce an updated and revised edition of his own, *Memoirs of Anthony Benezet* (1859). He further developed the expanded English edition of 1817 writing,

> The scarcity of the original memoir of this good man, long out of print, has induced the compiler to issue the present volume, which is considerably enlarged, and somewhat improved in form, believing that the example of so humble, active, and practical a Christian, is more worthy of being known and imitated at the present day, when such labours as he was engaged in are as much needed as at any former period.[9]

The particular qualities he notes here – 'humble, active and practical a Christian' – were all ones he especially valued and indeed shared. They all have a powerful relation to the way philanthropy was understood. A key definition of philanthropy links it to *practical benevolence*, something Armistead also acknowledges in relation to the 'practical . . . Christian' Benezet. When he draws special attention to the idea of emulation he might easily be talking about how he personally responded to the other man's example. In addition, he explicitly draws attention to what he calls Benezet's 'enlightened and unbounded philanthropy' and to his personal benevolence, which he argues is 'usually combined in the characters of the most noted philanthropists'.[10] The British Quaker was inspired by the example of Benezet's contribution to the earlier phase of the campaign for the abolition of slavery and wanted to revive his memory and work for a new generation of abolitionist activists.

## Anthony Benezet's funeral and the unquiet library

However Armistead first encountered Vaux's work, it is clear from the two prefaces quoted earlier that Vaux's original text was adapted after it crossed the Atlantic. This process of adaptation can be further traced in an abiding anecdote about Benezet's funeral, an event that became famous for its simplicity and size. The anecdote was repeated, with slight variations, in multiple texts over the next few years, in this manner making its way to England. Eventually, as I will shortly outline, it made a textual return to Philadelphia and then travelled South, after abolition, into the Freedmen's schools being set up in the post Emancipation South. Benezet's biography was used to suggest what the contours of an exemplary life might be; he did not strive after wealth or self-aggrandizement but instead pursued disinterested duty, underpinned by his deep ethical convictions. His history offers a counter to the capitalist ethos which was increasingly determining how character was judged on both sides of the Atlantic. What starts as an anecdote with specific personal details was adapted over time as local references lost their specific and recognizable meaning. Eventually what remains is a vital message about Benezet's chosen role as abolitionist, educator and philanthropist. The subtle textual changes in multiple descriptions of the same event reveal about the way editors altered texts to suit their particular audiences. They also provide a good example of the way that Benezet's posthumous reputation for philanthropy was sustained within the medium of print, including via libraries, as abolition moved even more substantially into its transatlantic phase after his death in 1784.

The description of his funeral first appeared at the end of a short piece published by Benjamin Rush who became an active abolitionist after the dead Benezet appeared to him in a dream. Rush later described this in a strange story titled 'The Paradise of Negro Slaves – A Dream' (1787), published in the *Columbian Magazine*. A few years later, in a description of Benezet's funeral, he noted:

> Colonel J__n, who had served in the American army, during the late war, in returning from the funeral, pronounced an eulogium upon him. It consisted only of the following words: 'I would rather,' said he, 'be Anthony Benezet, in that coffin, than George Washington with all his fame.'[11]

As one of the signers of the Declaration of Independence, Rush was well-placed to reflect upon the disjunction between Washington's 'fame' and magnificent funeral and Benezet's very different send-off. While about 4,000 people attended Washington's funeral, which went ahead with considerable pomp and formality, Benezet's was attended by about 400 Blacks and a smaller number of whites, showing the mutual respect and understanding between Benezet and the community whose rights he upheld and sought to foster. The anecdote subsequently appeared in Lindley Murray's *The Power of Religion on the Mind* (1787). Murray a fellow Quaker, had been born in Pennsylvania in 1745 and pursued a successful career as a lawyer before retiring to York in 1794. The following year he published his hugely influential *Grammar of the English Language*, using the significant earnings it brought him to fund philanthropic projects, including abolition work, penal reform and the care of those with mental illnesses. He would undoubtedly have consulted Benezet's own works (perhaps in a library) – *An Essay on Grammar* (1778) and *The Pennsylvania Spelling Book* (1778).

Meanwhile, the anecdote about Benezet made its way into Vaux's 1817 *Memoir*, then languishing for a few years before reappearing in the work of the American engraver and historian John Barber. He first used it in his *An Account of the Most Important and Interesting Religious Events* (1834) before reusing it in a book he edited with Elizabeth Barber, *Historical, Poetical and Pictorial American Scenes* (1851). This illustrated book was comprised of accessible short pieces, aimed at a Christian audience. Barber and Barber write:

> An American officer of the Revolutionary army, in returning from the funeral, pronounced a striking eulogium upon him. 'I would rather,' said he, 'be Anthony Benezet, in that coffin, than the great Washington with all his honours.'[12]

The words are largely the same as they were in Rush's original. However, the officer is now anonymized and the army has been revised from 'the American army, during the late war', to an 'American officer of the Revolutionary army'. Armistead's later version of the anecdote is very similar, suggesting that as well as knowing Vaux's work he may have been familiar with the Barbers' book. He writes:

> An officer, who had served in the American army during the revolutionary war, in returning from the funeral, pronounced a striking eulogium upon him. It contained but a few words: 'I would rather,' said he, 'be Anthony Benezet, in that coffin, than the great Washington with all his fame!'[13]

Here the 'Revolutionary army' becomes 'the American army during the revolutionary war', giving the anecdote additional context, and implying its connection to an earlier point in history. He changes 'honours' to 'fame', perhaps imagining that this would be more recognizable to a British audience with less immediate knowledge of, or personal relationship to, George Washington. Perhaps he was also being sensitive to an audience that was on the losing side of the war! He retains the addition of the adjective 'striking' to emphasize the significance of the unnamed officer's comments.

A key reason these writers could access the works through which the anecdote travelled, and from which they made their revisions, was that they all had access to a range of different libraries, of various types and scales. The word 'library' can refer to a personal library as it does in Walter Benjamin's essay 'Unpacking my Library', which describes the process of organizing his books after a period of storage. As he unpacks, his interest in the contents of his collection is reignited. He sees his books as containers of ideas but also as material objects with rich individual histories and characteristics. But he is particularly interested in an intimate and highly personal relation to the materiality of books, their haptic and tactile qualities. He depicts the passion of the collector for her or his books – their covers, pages, markings as well as contents.[14] Private collections can indicate social class and education or can be ostentatious symbols of wealth – of conspicuous display. One of the best fictional examples of this is Jay Gatsby's showy library in *The Great Gatsby* (1925). Described as 'a high Gothic library, panelled with carved English oak, and probably transported complete from some ruin overseas', it is full of books with uncut pages.[15] This signifies their purely decorative use – the books have never been read. Though Benjamin argues that personal libraries do not have to be made exclusively of works the collector has read (indeed he argues that this is emphatically not the case) Gatsby's uncut pages reveal that he has never intended to read them. James Gatz reinvents himself as Jay Gatsby through his shows of wealth, yet his carefully curated life is always on the cusp of falling apart. The owl-eyed man who the narrator encounters in the library during one of Gatsby's parties intimates this while returning a volume to the shelves, noting that 'if one brick was removed the whole library was liable to collapse'.[16] Gatsby's library emphasizes the way he uses his possessions to hide his previous identity for the sake of social cachet, and his love for Daisy Buchanan. It is part of his elaborate theatrical performance, with books as props, rather like the vast collection of shirts he displays when he eventually invites her into his house.

Libraries are (and have always been) locations of sociability and activity in which relationships with real and virtual others are cultivated and sustained. They can be physical locations of sociability providing sanctuary for those who may face persecution elsewhere. These may include the melancholy and introverted, as Herman Melville playfully suggested in the opening pages of *Moby Dick* (1850) in which the (now deceased) fictional Sub-Sub Librarian is credited as being the source of the list of extracts about whales that opens the novel. Yet though the Sub-Sub has searched through multiple volumes, he has not produced the last word, or what Melville calls 'veritable gospel cetology'. There is always more to be found, as *Moby Dick* reveals in its digressive pages, and some (though certainly not all) of this is to be found in libraries. David Reynold writes that Melville celebrated the value of serendipity in collecting sources,

> Melville himself was a lynx-eyed reader, quick to discover literary possibilities in randomly acquired minor literature. Many of his works are heavily indebted to his variegated reading which seems to have been done in the spirit of a character in *White-Jacket* who says that 'public libraries have an imposing air, and doubtless contain invaluable volumes, yet, somehow, the books that prove most agreeable, grateful, and companionable, are those we pick up by chance here and there; . . . those which pretend to little, but abound in much'.[17]

More commonly than the idea of a personal collection, the word 'library' refers to something more widely accessible – a communal or public collection of printed matter. In this meaning, scale is less important than function and impact. Recently the bestselling novel *The Librarian of Auschwitz* recounts the story of Dita Kraus's role in caring for a tiny and precious collection of eight books hidden in Block 31 of the camp at Auschwitz-Birkenau. These are used as educational tools for the young Jewish children of the camp and remind the prisoners who encounter them of a world beyond its fences and gates. The library's limited contents were supplemented by the knowledge and memories of prisoners whom Kraus called living libraries.[18] The combination of the tiny collection of printed texts and embodied knowledge forms a singularly unquiet library that must be protected at all costs. At the same time, since it is clandestine, it is also quiet, and knowledge of its existence is dangerous to its users.

It is the idea of the size that the novelist Hilary Mantel recollects when she describes her small (and disappointingly dull) school library as a 'suitcase library'.[19] While it was particularly limited, no library (except perhaps Jorge Luis Borges's imaginary library in his 1941 story 'The Library of Babel') can contain all that has been written, for as Alberto Manguel writes, libraries are not 'exclusionary'. He notes:

we know that every orderly choice, every catalogues realm of the imagination, sets up a tyrannical hierarchy of exclusion. Every library is exclusionary, since its selection, however vast, leaves outside its walls endless shelves of writing that, for reasons of taste, knowledge, space and time, have not been included. Every library conjures up its own dark ghost; every ordering sets up, in its wake, a shadow library of absences.[20]

It is possible that Mantel's early experience of the limitations of the library allowed her to identify with Toni Morrison's famous provocation that we must write the books we want to read if they haven't yet been written. Walter Benjamin made a similar point when he argued that 'Of all the ways of acquiring books, writing them oneself is regarded as the most praiseworthy method'.[21] Celebrated library users who decided to write the books they wanted to read (in this sense) include the exiled Karl Marx, whose quiet hours working in the reading room of the British Library produced *Das Kapital* (1867).

Libraries are invaluable resources, especially for those not wealthy enough to buy books. Active and engaged citizenship is frequently produced and nourished by libraries and their holdings. Publicly funded libraries are a testament to the recognition that this is a public good. Ali Smith's recent collection *Public Library and Other Stories* (2015) champions public libraries by presenting a collage of reflections on public libraries by other people, especially writers and short stories about books. In her book *Why Women Read Fiction*, Helen Taylor draws attention to the comments of Borges (who was also the Librarian of the National Library of Argentina from 1955 to 1973) who argued, she writes, 'that he always imagined Paradise as a kind of library' adding,

he is not alone. Described by the Library Campaign as 'the bedrock of a nation's entire culture strategy', my correspondents dubbed it 'a magical community space' and 'sacred pleasure palaces' which 'opened a world beyond where I was and allowed me to wonder about lives different from mine'.[22]

Access to the books in libraries and to the buildings in which they are housed allows readers to imagine the possibility of other kinds of geographies, systems and worlds to those within which they themselves live out their daily lives. Repressive regimes often regard this as profoundly dangerous and try to exert discipline and control. To this end, there is a long tradition of banning, censoring or burning books, while the libraries and the buildings that contain them have frequently been destroyed by invading armies or repressive regimes. This reminds us of the ways that libraries are symbols of intellectual liberty and good community, which often makes them threatening to those in power. Attacks on libraries remind us that history often repeats itself. Indeed, libraries are often key sites of contestation within culture wars and actual wars. Wai Chee Dimock opens her influential book *Through Other Continents* with a description of the destruction of the Iraqi National Library and the Islamic library of the Religious Ministry on 14 April 2003. She uses this to reflect on the 'ontology of time', showing how the Iraqi population and US forces differently interpreted this event.[23] While the US forces understood their task through the present, she argues that Iraqis were reminded of the moment in 1258 when the Mongol army had destroyed the same library. For them, the attack had its roots deep in a historical past whose records were held within the library itself, as well as within public memory.

The subversive possibilities of libraries come from a combination of their holdings with the opportunities they give (as physical locations) for the like-minded to unite, to think, to plan and to remember. In the acknowledgements to her classic work *The Feminine Mystique* (1963), Betty Friedan made a point of stating the importance of the New York Public Library:

> Without that superb institution, the Frederick Lewis Allen Room of the New York Public Library and its provision to a writer of a quiet work space and continuous access to research sources, this particular mother of three might never have started a book, much less finished it.[24]

Years earlier, the novelist and activist Lydia Maria Child relied on the holdings of libraries to research and write her work, recognizing that her gender significantly restricted her access to print culture. As a child, she had encountered the books in her brother's personal library – in the absence of a library of her own – and later in her life, she was able to avail herself of his growing personal library (numbered somewhere between seven and eight thousand works at his death in 1863). George Ticknor, who was closely involved with the Boston Athenaeum, was a key figure behind the foundation of the Boston Public Library leaving it a collection of his Spanish and Portuguese books in his will, extended Child free library privileges at the Boston Athenaeum. This was something only ever offered to one other woman. But when she published *An Appeal in Favor of that Class of Americans called Africans* (1833), which advocated for the immediate emancipation of the enslaved without compensation to slaveholders, he was outraged. Her uncompromising writing discomforted and disturbed some, while delighting others. Her work was, without doubt, unquiet, and the Athenaeum withdrew her access to its resources, presumably to silence her. Maria Weston Chapman rapidly led a campaign among her abolitionist supporters to purchase her a membership. But the Athenaeum once more refused to allow her access. Though deeply frustrated, she thanked her supporters for their backing, exclaiming, 'I have never in my whole life, met with anything that gratifies me more, or affected me so deeply'.[25] A woman who had grown up with access to books always at one remove, appreciated their subversive power.

Even when they are excluded from libraries or from normal life, readers have historically tried to find ways to access the books that give them hope in times of anguish, understanding that reading and the knowledge it brings can provide solace as well as suggest possibilities of resistance and revolution. Manguel argues that,

> every library, including those under strictest surveillance, contains secretly rebellious texts that escape the librarian's eye. As a prisoner in a Russian camp . . . Joseph Brodsky read W.H. Auden's poems, and they strengthened his resolve to defy his jailers and survive for the sake of a glimpsed-at freedom. Haroldo Conti, tortured in the cells of the Argentinian military of the 1970s, found solace in the novels of Dickens, which his jailer had allowed him to keep. For the writer Varlam Chamalov, sent by Stalin to work in the gold mines of Kolyma because of his 'counter-revolutionary activities,' the prison library was itself a gold mine that 'for incomprehensible reasons had escaped the innumerable inspections and "purges" systematically inflicted on all of Russia's libraries.'[26]

Yet even when no library can be accessed, the contents of books can be recollected and reconstituted for new purposes as they were by the living libraries Kraus discusses. The writer Hisham Matar describes the way his father Jaballa, whose 'literary memory was like a floating library', recited aloud 'the elegiac Bedouin poetry of the alam' in his solitary prison cell in the notorious Abu Salim jail in Libya rather than the modern and modernist poems he also knew by heart.[27] Remembering this older tradition of poetry that 'privileges the past over the present' enabled him to reflect upon a history that went back to a period well before the birth of the Gadaffi regime which imprisoned him. The longevity of that tradition, and the contents of the works themselves, gave the prisoners hope. Jaballa Matar's recitations, listened to in silence by other prisoners in their own cells, spoke of other times, as well as better places than the cells in which they were imprisoned. This provided solace and countered authoritarian violence, suggesting the possibility that times could change and improve.

Of course, there are also libraries that are more obviously and overtly unquiet, too. A prime example is the People's Library of Occupy Wall Street, founded in September 2011 and physically removed by the New York Department of Sanitation when they cleared Zuccotti Park. The volunteer librarian William Scott noted, in a manner recalling both Walter Benjamin and Abraham Lincoln:

> I love books – reading them, writing in them, arranging them, holding them, even smelling them. I also love having access to books for free. I love libraries and everything they represent. To see an entire collection of donated books, including many titles I would have liked to read, thoughtlessly ransacked and destroyed by the forces of law and order was one of the most disturbing experiences of my life.

. . . With public libraries around the country fighting to survive in the face of budget cuts, layoffs and closings, the People's Library has served as a model of what a public library can be: operated for the people and by the people.[28]

While the police dismantled the library, the poet and fellow librarian Stephen Boyer recited poetry at the top of his voice. Scott writes that some of the police listened to (and were moved by) the words and the performance of resistance they witnessed. This reminds us that if poets are, as Shelley argues in 'The Defence of Poetry' (1821) – the 'unacknowledged legislators of the world', their words have the capacity to make lasting meanings and to disrupt the acts of the otherwise powerful. The recitations of Boyer and Jaballa Matar both disturbed the quiet, but also created moments of quiet and reflective listening. In short, libraries are both places of certain kinds of quiet but more importantly they are unquiet locations that foster noisy activity and challenge well beyond themselves. As Bella Bathurst has written, 'The libraries' most powerful asset is the conversation they provide – between books and readers, between children and parents, between individuals and the collective world. Take them away and those voices turn inwards or vanish. Turns out that libraries have nothing at all to do with silence.'[29]

## Anthony Benezet: 'Celebrated philanthropist'

So far this essay has shown the significance of libraries throughout history; how they are perceived by users and by those who feel threatened by them; and how they provide tools for radical personal transformation. All of these understandings of how the library is *unquiet* relate to the way that the contents of a library can produce radical and positive change. However, there are more uncomfortable elements of libraries that also need to be acknowledged. Libraries have often been exclusionary both in terms of who can become a member, such as Lydia Maria Child. In addition, since curatorial practices are never neutral, this impacts upon whose voices are contained and preserved within their collections as Borges suggests in his resonant term 'a shadow library of absences'. In a period in which scholars and activists are increasingly probing the histories of public and private institutions such as universities, libraries are not, and should not be, exempt from scrutiny. The histories of libraries often reveal their connections to unethical practices and individuals. By examining the historical conditions within which libraries were founded and financed, we can find many examples of libraries being used for purposes of self-aggrandizement. The case of the steel magnate and library philanthropist Andrew Carnegie is instructive here. He is probably the single most significant library philanthropist in history, though the Bill and Melinda Gates Foundation's Global Libraries initiative is another vast philanthropic project, which has supported public libraries for about two decades. Having made his fortune, Carnegie resolved to give away his money, believing firmly that philanthropy should help those who help themselves. This doctrine corresponded with a belief in the importance of self-education and self-reliance and he believed that free library provision could be at the heart of this kind of personal transformation. He donated more than $41 million dollars for the erection of 1,679 libraries in 1,412 US towns between 1886 and 1917. In addition, he funded libraries in Belgium, France, Ireland, Serbia and the UK. Yet, his devotion to libraries was second to his commitment to making money, and his transition from extreme poverty to colossal wealth was in part a result of his notoriously poor treatment of those who worked for him.[30] While many welcomed his philanthropic largesse, others refused to participate in such a system of giving and receiving, feeling disquieted by the disjunction between the public good libraries purport to perform, and their often disavowed or unacknowledged origins in exploitative workplace practices and the pockets of unethical tycoons.

Despite these necessary caveats, it is important to note that the two libraries especially used by Armistead and Benezet helped to create a critically understudied transatlantic connectedness that continued despite a dominant wider political culture which sometimes encouraged national separation and hostility. As we have seen, they were key to underwriting the philanthropic activities of abolitionists. Exploring the histories and legacies of sites such as libraries reminds us of their valuable and unquiet contribution to freedom of thought and expression. However, we should remember that subscription libraries were not open to all and that it was not until the development of a public library system that fuller possibilities of freely accessible libraries emerged. Though libraries have been important throughout history for dissidents and for radical and reforming movements, they have also been implicated in white supremacy and murky and exploitative business practices. More particularly for what is being discussed here, scholars have been exploring the foundational relationship between slavery and early American libraries for some time with disturbing consequences. Recently, Sean Moore has provocatively claimed that libraries 'stood at the nexus of two major branches of transatlantic commerce: the book trade and the slave trade'.[31] This was certainly true of the Library Company of Philadelphia. Located in a key centre of book production and circulation, it was a vital and progressive intellectual and social resource for many. Yet it was founded by a group of individuals who included both abolitionists and slaveholders. This means that the library's history, like those of many august institutions was indebted to the system of slavery. Benjamin Franklin himself, its key founder, was a slaveholder and dealer until the late 1750s, though Benezet was instrumental in turning him into an abolitionist.

Benezet's work and personal example underpinned the abolitionist activity of the eighteenth century and helped pave the way for nineteenth-century abolition. Yet despite his importance, his reputation faded in the early nineteenth century before a series of closely related publications revived it once more. The circulation of a number of texts that were accessible in the holdings of libraries amplified his connection to philanthropic projects. One of them included the only known image of him and named him explicitly as a 'celebrated philanthropist'. He was extremely resistant to sitting for his portrait, arguing that he was too ugly for any visual representation to be preserved.[32] In consequence, since no illustrations, drawings or paintings were produced within his lifetime the only image (Figure 4.1) is an imaginative fantasy produced decades after his death. It provides insight into how he was perceived. Though its accuracy should not be relied upon, its iconography and symbolic message are instructive. It first appeared in *Historical, Poetical and Pictorial American Scenes*. It depicts a pedagogical

**Figure 4.1** Unknown artist, 'Anthony Benezet Instructing Coloured Children', in John W. Barber and Elizabeth G. Barber, *Historical, Poetical and Pictorial American Scenes* (New Haven: J. W. Barber, 1850).

moment. Benezet sits on a stiff-looking wooden chair at the very centre of the portrait. On his left is a table on which a closed volume, an inkwell and two quill pens are either ready to be used – or perhaps have just been put down. In his lap there is an open book, its words visible though not actually legible. Two young Black children, a girl and a boy, stand by his knees. The writing implements may be theirs – one is slightly smaller than the other, as if reflecting the respective sizes of the children. Equally, they might have been used by Benezet to pen one of his abolitionist or educational works. While the boy points at the book, presumably parsing it for himself after an earlier lesson, the girl looks directly and intently at the adult man who returns her gaze thoughtfully, as if fully engaged. Benezet's right hand is elevated, the index finger pointing upwards. Quite possibly he is engaging in religious instruction and has moved from the words on the page to some kind of exegesis. Certainly, the image represents figures in harmony not only with each other but also with the reading and writing objects around them. The link between each element of the scene is made visible by the physical connectedness of the three bodies and their relationship to the written work. The shoulder of the girl touches that of the boy, while his finger points at both the page and simultaneously to Benezet's left hand which is holding a book that might be part of his personal library. This connects the boy with the man, refusing the divides of race and age, while it also provides a conduit between the man and girl.

The books, pens and implied discussion are central to the image's message of cross-racial and intergenerational sociability and to the process and importance of acquiring and disseminating knowledge. The two children are becoming literate; in consequence of this newly acquired skill, their lives will be transformed. Alongside a personal change, literacy will produce a far broader political revolution, allowing them to advocate for themselves in the print public sphere. The pens and books provide the physical tools the children will be able to use to undertake imaginative journeys of self-representation, leading to self-reliance. The particular link between the three is their access to print culture: the books bring them together. Overall, the iconography recalls the fact that Benezet was highly regarded as a teacher, especially by the African American community. His reputation as an educator lived on and was revived in the work of Armistead and others.

His teaching career had commenced in 1739 when he started to work in the Germantown Academy, in Pennsylvania. Following a period working at the Friends' English Public School in Philadelphia, he founded a school for girls in 1755. By this time, he had also been teaching African Americans for five years, in evening classes he led when his routine work was over. Increasingly, he recognized that he had found his vocation. He went on to establish the first day school for African Americans in Philadelphia in 1770. His success in this area is evident; many of his students would go on to becoming notable abolitionists, including Absalom Jones, Richard Allen and James Forten. The image celebrates his role as a teacher and also highlights a broader idea. His personal desire to teach came from a more deeply rooted appreciation of the way in which literacy and accessible books would be central to eventually overturning slavery and building a more equal civil society. Therefore, it is unsurprising that the image is accompanied by a caption explicitly naming Benezet as a 'celebrated philanthropist'.[33] This undoubtedly alludes in part to his personal virtue and reputation for benevolence. His long-standing work with African Americans, as well as with Acadian refugees to Philadelphia from Canada in 1756, was well-known. His many written anti-slavery works included his treatise 'An Epistle of Caution and Advice Concerning the Buying and Keeping of Slaves' (1754). His influential essay 'A Caution and Warning to Great Britain and Her Colonies of the Calamitous State of the Enslaved Negroes' (1766–7) marshalled considerable evidence to make a strong argument for abolition, while his *Some Historical Account of Guinea* (1771) would be profoundly important to Olaudah Equiano.[34] He founded the Society for the Relief of Free Negroes Unlawfully Held in Bondage which would become, after his death, the Pennsylvania Society for Promoting the Abolition of Slavery. The image of Benezet as a 'celebrated philanthropist' thus brings together the key elements with which this essay is particularly engaged: transatlantic abolition understood as a form of philanthropy, and its relation to the creation and circulation of transatlantic print culture, underpinned by libraries and the connectedness they enable.

The publication of the *Historical, Poetical and Pictorial American Scenes* took place during a critical juncture in transatlantic abolitionist labour. In September of that year, the Fugitive Slave Law was passed, enabling fugitives to be returned to enslavement even if they were in free states. Clearly, at a moment in which abolitionists were especially addressing the treatment of fugitives as well as the educational opportunities for free Blacks, the model of Benezet was powerfully enabling. He believed that equal access to education would challenge white supremacy and lead to a demonstration of the equality of Blacks and whites. Such evidence would in turn be one element of an incontestable argument against slavery and discrimination on the grounds of race. Thus, teaching was the first part of a process leading to ethical, political and social transformation. The image is probably intended to suggest his idiosyncratic pedagogic methodology, one which relied on a model of kindness and personal humility rather than authoritarianism. This is not something usually associated with the unquietness I have been focusing on, though through its profound connection with the power of literacy as an individual and political tool, it does have the idea of production of disturbing the status quo at its heart. Despite the progressive message about racial equality, he personally espoused, the image itself hints at a hierarchical depiction of White Christian patriarchal benevolence, centred on access to books. The paternalistic top-down message of the illustration is at odds with the model of self-help premised on education, literacy and equal access to power that Benezet's educational efforts promoted.

Armistead's book would be the basis for another work on Benezet, published by a Germantown-based philanthropic organization, the Benezet Auxiliary Freedmen's Relief Association. Germantown (where Benezet had first started his work as an educator) is well-known for its contribution to anti-slavery and abolition. The Germantown Quaker Petition Against Slavery (1688) was the first organized protest against slavery in the colonies. The association intended the example of Benezet's life and teaching to be made available to the next generation through the medium of a new memoir. The anonymous preface notes that the book is intended as an inspiring gift to teachers in the South, working in Freedmen's schools:

> The following narrative, chiefly drawn from a small volume, entitled, 'Anthony Benezet, from the Original Memoir, Revised, with Additions, by Wilson Armistead,' was read at a late meeting of the Benezet Auxiliary Freedmen's Relief Association, and is printed by the Association, in the hope that a short sketch of one of the pioneers in the anti-slavery cause might be acceptable to the teachers engaged in the Freedmen's schools in the South, as a token of sympathy for them, in their labour of love, from some of their friends in the North.[35]

So, while Armistead had hoped that Benezet's life and work would be an example to inspire abolitionists, the association, in turn, wanted teachers and the newly emancipated to be similarly inspired. It is tantalizing to think this 'token of sympathy . . . in their labour of love' being carried into the Freedmen's schools in the South to disseminate Benezet's message of equality, and activism. This language suggests connections to definitions of philanthropy which ally it to the love of mankind, while intimating a more radical agenda of self-help that moves it away from White paternalism into Black activism. W. E. B. Du Bois, a great admirer of Benezet's work with Black children, praised the contribution made by school teachers in the South in the period of reconstruction. He noted that 'Behind the mists of ruin and rapine waved the calico dresses of the women who dared, and after the hoarse mouthings of the field guns rang the rhythm of the alphabet'.[36] Acquiring literacy and having access to books and education gave the possibility of personal and national transformation. He argues:

> The greatest success of the Freedmen's Bureau lay in the planting of the free school among Negroes, and the idea of a free elementary education among all the

classes in the South. . . . The opposition to Negro education in the South was at first bitter, and showed itself in ashes, insult, and blood; for the South believed an educated Negro to be a dangerous Negro. And the South was not wholly wrong; for education among all kinds of men always has had, and always will have, an element of danger and revolution, of dissatisfaction and discontent. Nevertheless, men strive to know.[37]

Du Bois's sense of the relationship between knowledge and 'danger . . . dissatisfaction and discontent' – a condition of righteous unquiet political unrest – is at the heart of the exhilarating possibilities offered by literacy and by books and libraries. Indeed, the verb form of the word 'unquiet' is defined as meaning 'to disturb the quiet of; to disquiet'. It is this very condition of powerful self-awareness and intellectual desire which literacy, books and libraries foster.

Learning to read was a powerful form of resistance for formerly enslaved individuals and the wider Black community.[38] The relationship between literacy, agency and the desire for citizenship was well-recognized by activists. Harriet Jacobs and her brother John S. Jacobs together ran the Anti-Slavery Reading Rooms above the offices of Frederick Douglass's *North Star* newspaper in Rochester, from 1849 to 1850. Jacobs' own first person account of her enslavement repeatedly showed just how powerful a tool her literacy had been to produce her own emancipation and subsequently represent her experience. Yet in texts authored by White writers, White characters were often depicted as teaching Blacks in a manner that elevated the teacher and demeaned the taught. Take this well-known example from Harriet Beecher Stowe, whose family was well-known as social reformers and educators. Early in *Uncle Tom's Cabin* (1851–2) the thirteen-year-old Master George is depicted in the eponymous cabin, teaching the adult Tom to read. Tom and his wife Chloe regard George's skill with a kind of respect that reinforces hierarchical racial positioning. Tom looks at George 'with a respectful, admiring air' while Chloe says 'How easy white folks al'us does things!'[39] This representation implies that it is a lack of skill rather than opportunity and systemic racism which excludes the enslaved from literacy. Tom eventually learns to read, but it is a slow process. The process of acquiring literacy is a key trope in many of the slave narratives and abolitionist texts that proliferated in the 1840s and 1850s. Refusing the enslaved access to literacy was a way of maintaining white supremacy. While Stowe depicts Tom's literacy as a route towards teaching the enslaved to embrace Christian lives in which earthly sacrifice leads to eternal salvation, more radically, Frederick Douglass made his own acquisition of literacy central to a radical understanding of self-emancipation and uplift. In chapter seven of the *Narrative of the Life of Frederick Douglass, an American Slave* (1845) he describes the way he developed stratagems in order to learn to read and write once he realized that his enslaver was fearful of what an educated enslaved person might become. He shows the way his understanding of the empowering possibilities of reading and writing grew throughout his childhood, in the process making a wider argument for other African Americans. In particular, he depicts literacy as a tool allowing the enslaved access to forms of self-representation. His well-known encounter with Caleb Bingham's educational volume *The Columbian Orator* gave him access to arguments for emancipation made by an enslaved individual himself, enabling him to marshal arguments against enslavement in a fuller way than he has previously done, but also filling him with disquiet and despair at his own position.

Wilson Armistead evidently believed that reviving attention to Anthony Benezet's activism, beliefs and personal example was timely and important. His memoir helped to revive the American's posthumous reputation for a mid-century audience in a period of intensive abolitionist activity. He reminded his readers of Benezet's critical contribution to the earlier phase of abolition, which led to the 1807 Slave Trade Act. This renewed focus on Benezet in the mid-century period was part of a wider strategy to stimulate interest in the multiple ways in which abolitionists could be activists. His personal activism was a testament to the continuing importance of Benezet's example. He founded the Leeds Anti-Slavery Society in 1853, and his wife Mary Armistead was its librarian. He also produced a series of books that reminded readers of key figures from the past including James Logan the celebrated Quaker bibliophile. Logan chose the first forty-three volumes for the Library Company of Philadelphia and on his death bequeathed his own extensive personal library (now the Loganian Library) to the Library Company. Armistead also wrote about the achievements of people of African heritage such as Paul Cuffee, a devout Quaker, abolitionist and a merchant. It seems extremely probable that Armistead's influential work *A Tribute for the Negro* (1848) took inspiration in part from Benezet's earlier writing. Because he understood the importance of libraries, Armistead passed his library membership to his sons when he died. In this way, the Leeds Library served as a means through which his memory (as an activist and father) survived. He gave his sons access to the physical site of the library while it, in turn, provided them with the possibility of accessing the voices and history it held, if they should so choose. This is an example of the kind of practical teaching Benezet would have appreciated for he had earlier stipulated in his own will that his estate should go to his wife, and then (after her death) be directed towards the education of African Americans. He left his personal library to the Society of Friends Library in Philadelphia.[40] It is highly fitting that using the resources of the many different kinds of unquiet libraries in which we continue to conduct our work enables us to keep the memories of Armistead and Benezet alive and preserve the records of their philanthropic labours.

Action and benevolent giving underwrote the philanthropic work of abolition. The strategies of abolitionists were varied including the use of print culture to create a transformed political and social climate. Many abolitionists used their relationships with faith communities to build opposition to slavery beyond their immediate circles. Their membership in such groups gave them religious and moral authority. Yet it also provided access to transnational networks of like-minded people. Religious nonconformists, especially in Pennsylvania and Yorkshire (both places with significant Quaker populations) created alliances based both on progressive religious and political commitments to dissent and commercial connections. Much of this is well documented, however, there is still a good deal to be discovered about both the way that engaged citizenship and habits of independent thought were fostered and neglected figures who are starting to have new attention paid to them. In this context, a growing number of works are bringing new attention to Benezet's life and work.[41]

The extent to which discussions about anti-slavery and abolition shaped the eighteenth and nineteenth centuries cannot be understated. Abolition brought together campaigners on both sides of the Atlantic, sometimes using existing networks established via trade and by religious affiliations, especially to the Society of Friends. Benezet was one of the most important figures to first recognize how such transatlantic connectedness could be mobilized politically, to further the cause of abolition. His intellectual labour made him a highly effective and influential abolitionist. The impact of his writing created a climate of intense activism, mobilizing others to work for the cause, noisily and actively. His writing was vitally connected both to his long-standing interactions with the Black community and his immersion in the holdings of the Library Company of Philadelphia. Library collections make it possible to trace the textual history of his abolitionist beliefs. Yet it is important to imagine the ways in which his face-to-face conversations with this community profoundly shaped his intellectual and ethical landscape. This is harder to trace because of gaps in the archive. A combination of conviction and personal regular engagement with African Americans, not just solitary immersion in print cultural productions, reinforced Benezet's abolitionism. Print culture was an important source for him, but his arguments were fortified and given life by these vital personal interactions. His Black interlocutors were living libraries with invaluable experiences. Their knowledge and their acts of resistance were as foundational to him as the books he read. He drew direct attention to this in one of the last pieces he published, the 1783 'Short Observations on Slavery'.[42] Benezet understood that the kinds of works he was able to undertake had a crucial connection to the experiences and knowledge of non-Whites. As Manisha Sinha has recently argued, the 'actions of slave rebels and runaways, Black writers and community leaders, did not lie outside of but shaped abolition and its goals'.[43] While many stories of human interaction and movement can be traced through the holdings of the unquiet libraries in which scholars undertake research, other stories still remain outside of their boundaries. In order to remedy and correct our understandings of the past, we must continue to acknowledge and address this. Furthermore, libraries themselves also need further investigation if we are better to understand their role in redressing the democratic deficit experienced by nonconformists and dissenters such as Armistead and Benezet and, even more particularly, by the enslaved individuals whose rights were abrogated by the system of slavery.

# Notes

I would like to acknowledge the support of the Leverhulme Trust for a Major Research Fellowship which made this work possible. I thank Iona Bennett for her careful and generous reading of an earlier draft of this essay, and Ben Offiler and Rachel Williams for all their work and encouragement.

1  Kathryn Dilworth, 'Philanthropy in Public Libraries: its Impact on Community Well-Being Missions', *International Journal of Community Well-Being* (2021): 1–19. https://doi.org/10.1007/S42413-021-00140-8.

2  Robert H. Bremner, *American Philanthropy* (Chicago and London: University of Chicago Press, 1960); *Giving: Charity and Philanthropy in History* (New Brunswick and London: Transaction Publishers, 1996).

3  The idea of the unquiet library is one I initially started to develop in 'Guerrilla Inscription: Transatlantic Abolition and the 1851 Census', *Atlantic Studies: Global Currents* 17, no. 3 (2020): 375–98.

4  Sean Moore writes that 'almost all Philadelphia reading eventually led back to the Company, establishing it not only as the central space of reading in the city, but also as a powerful social network of the literate and, usually, wealthy population'. Sean D. Moore, *Slavery and the Making of Early American Libraries: British Literature, Political Thought, and the Transatlantic Book Trade, 1731–1814* (Oxford: Oxford University Press, 2019), 174.

5  Wilson Armistead, *Anthony Benezet: from the Original Memoir: Revised, with Additions* (London: A. W. Bennett and Philadelphia: Lippincott and Co., 1859), 26.

6  Quoted in Maurice Jackson, *Let This Voice be Heard: Anthony Benezet, Father of Atlantic Abolitionism* (Philadelphia: University of Pennsylvania Press, 2009), xiii.

7  David L. Crosby, *The Complete Antislavery Writings of Anthony Benezet, 1754–1783* (Baton Rouge: Louisiana State University Press, 2013), 2.

8  Roberts Vaux, *Memoirs of the Life of Anthony Benezet* (York: W. Alexander, 1817), 1.

9  Armistead, *Anthony Benezet*, vi.

10 Ibid., 16, 76.

11 Benjamin Rush, 'Biographical Anecdotes of Anthony Benezet' [15 July 1788] in *Essays, Literary Moral and Philosophical* (Philadelphia: Thomas and William Bradford, 1806): 302–4, 304.

12 John W. Barber and Elizabeth G. Barber, *Historical, Poetical and Pictorial American Scenes; Principally Moral and Religious; Being a Selection of Interesting Incidents in American History: to which is added a Historical Sketch, of each of the United States* (New Haven: J.H. Bradley and Cincinnati: Johnson and Brother, 1851), 56.

13 Armistead, *Anthony Benezet*, 138.

14 Walter Benjamin, 'Unpacking my Library', in Hannah Arendt, ed., *Illuminations* trans. H. Zohn (New York: Shocken Books, 1969): 59–67.

15 F. Scott Fitzgerald, *The Great Gatsby* (London: Vintage Books, 2010), 38.

16 Ibid. The owl-eyed man says, 'This fella's a regular Belasco. It's a triumph. What thoroughness! What realism! Knew when to stop, too – didn't cut the pages. But what do you want? What do you expect?'

17 David S. Reynolds, *Beneath the American Renaissance: The Subversive Imagination in the Age of Emerson and Melville* (Oxford and New York: Oxford University Press, 2011), 4.

18 Antonio Iturbe, *The Librarian of Auschwitz*, trans. L Zekulin Thwaites (London: Ebury Press, 2019), 25.

19 Helen Taylor, *Why Women Read Fiction: The Stories of Our Lives* (Oxford: Oxford University Press, 2019), 66.

20 Alberto Manguel, *The Library at Night* (New Haven and London: Yale University Press, 2006), 107.

21 Benjamin, 'Unpacking my Library'.

22 Taylor, *Why Women Read Fiction*, 63.

23 Wai Chee Dimock, *Through Other Continents: American Literature Across Deep Time* (Princeton and Oxford: Princeton University Press, 2006), 2.

24 Betty Friedan, *The Feminine Mystique* with an introduction by Lionel Shriver (London, New York, Toronto, Dublin, Camberwell, New Delhi, Rosedale and Johannesburg: Penguin Classics, 2010), 3.

25 Carolyn L. Karcher, *The First Woman of the Republic: A Cultural Biography of Lydia Maria Child* (Durham and London: Duke University Press, 1994), 221.

26  Manguel, *Library at Night,* 114–15.

27  Hisham Matar, *The Return: Fathers, Sons and the Land in Between* (London: Penguin Books, 2016), 58–9.

28  Karen Mc Veigh, 'Destruction of Occupy Wall Street 'People's Library' Draws ire', *The Guardian*, 23 November 2011. Available online: https://www.theguardian.com/world/blog/2011/nov/23/occupy-wall-street-peoples-library (accessed 30 October 2021).

29  Bella Bathurst, 'Secret Life of Libraries', *The Guardian*, 30 April 2011. Available online: https://www.theguardian.com/books/2011/may/01/the-secret-life-of-libraries/ (accessed 30 October 2021).

30  Manguel, *Library at Night,* 96–104; Abigail Ayres Van Slyck, *Free to All: Carnegie Libraries and American Culture, 1890*–1920 (Chicago and London: University of Chicago Press, 1995).

31  Moore, *Slavery and the Making of Early American Libraries,* 1.

32  Jackson, *Let This Voice be Heard,* 20.

33  Barber and Barber, *Historical, Poetical and Pictorial American Scenes,* 56. The Barbers were father and daughter.

34  Crosby, *Antislavery Writings of Anthony Benezet;* Moore, *Slavery and the making of Early American Libraries,* 166–200.

35  Anonymous, *Life of Anthony Benezet* (Philadelphia: Sherman and Co., 1867), 3.

36  W. E. B. Du Bois, *The Souls of Black Folk*, edited by B. Hayes Edwards (Oxford: Oxford University Press, 2007), 23. See also *The Philadelphia Negro: A Social Study* (1899).

37  Du Bois, *Souls of Black Folk*, 27.

38  Elizabeth McHenry, *Forgotten Readers: Recovering he Lost History of African American Literary Societies* (Durham and London: Duke University Press, 2002).

39  Harriet Beecher Stowe, *Uncle Tom's Cabin*, edited by. E. Ammons (New York and London: W.W. Norton and Company, 1994), 18.

40  Henry J. Cadbury, 'Anthony Benezet's Library', *Bulletin of Friends Historical Association* 23, no. 2 (Autumn 1934), 63–75.

41  Irv A. Brendlinger, *To be Silent Would be Criminal: The Antislavery Influence and Writings of Anthony Benezet* (Lanham: Scarecrow Press. 2006); Jackson, *Let This Voice Be Heard;* Crosby, *Antislavery Writings of Anthony Benezet;* Marie-Jeanne Rossignol and Bertrand Van Ruymbeke, eds, *The Atlantic World of Anthony Benezet (1713–1784): From French Reformation to North American Quaker Antislavery Activism* (Leiden: Brill, 2016).

42  Crosby, *Antislavery Writings of Anthony Benezet,* 233, 243.

43  Manisha Sinha, *The Slave's Cause: A History of Abolition* (New Haven and London: Yale University Press, 2016), 2.

# 5

# Towards a cultural counter-establishment

## Huntington Hartford and his eponymous foundation, 1948–65

### Karen Patricia Heath

Looking back on his art patronage, heir to the Atlantic & Pacific Tea Company (A&P) supermarket fortune, George Huntington Hartford II (b.1911–d.2008), commonly known as Huntington or 'Hunt' Hartford, explained how he sought to create a cultural counter-establishment in the United States in the years after the Second World War:

> I think that my interest in the arts really started with my concern about what I felt was happening in the society . . . a lot of the things I saw in the 20th century . . . the emphasis seemed to be sometimes on ugliness. . . . I've always felt that artists can be and should be the leaders of society . . . that there is some kind of tie-in between morality and the arts.[1]

Hartford's dream was to aid the American cultural folk that he admired, to encourage their creation of what he considered traditional, beautiful, 'moral', and intelligible art forms, and hence to shape American public taste in accordance with his own philosophy.[2] In Hartford's mind, he would stand as a bulwark against what he viewed as north-eastern elitism, particularly the activities of those New York artists, critics, dealers and curators, who advocated what he deemed obscurantist abstraction or modernism, with potentially dangerous communist leanings.[3] To do just that, he wrote a pamphlet entitled *Has God Been Insulted Here?* (1951), a tract called 'The Public Be Damned' (1955), and eventually a book, *Art or Anarchy? How the Extremists and Exploiters Have Reduced the Fine Arts to Chaos and Commercialism* (1964).[4] He also established a range of new arts institutions to try to spark a conservative arts renaissance across the country, most notably the Huntington Hartford Foundation (1948–65) based in Rustic Canyon near Los Angeles, California, that provided fellowships to American artists, writers and musicians.[5]

Huntington Hartford's life and times have been the subject of considerable press coverage, but his philanthropic activities in aid of the arts have yet to be subjected to serious historical consideration.[6] Scholars of arts patronage have, in the main, focused on federal initiatives during the New Deal years, or on the government's Cold War cultural-diplomatic efforts abroad, rather than the anti-communist art affairs of private patrons at home.[7] Meanwhile, the history of the modern American right has frequently emphasized conservative success in electoral politics to the detriment of analysing failure in the cultural arena.[8] Although a smaller body of work examines the growth of conservative philanthropic foundations and think tanks in the post-war years, the arts receive short shrift in this literature.[9]

This chapter accordingly examines Hartford's artistic endeavours and the activities of his foundation to illuminate an alternative trajectory for a nascent cultural counter-establishment that was distinct from the rise of the modern American political right. It starts by setting the scene with an analysis of the nature, trajectory and status of the politics of arts funding in post-war America. It then moves on to assess Hartford's conservative vision for the arts and to explain how, and to what ends, the Huntington Hartford Foundation situated itself within the broader political, artistic, social, cultural and economic milieu. Next, it analyses the impact of anti-communism at the Foundation through the lens of the institution's application system and overarching advisory structure. Finally, the chapter considers the populist tenor of Hartford's efforts via an analysis of his popular image and arts wars over fellowships.

## The politics of arts patronage in post-war America

In the late 1940s and into the 1950s, the cultural status and political meaning of modernism in general, and abstraction in particular, was far from settled. In the visual arts, the abstract expressionism of Jackson Pollock – that is, the spontaneous application of swathes of paint on massive canvases – garnered considerable acclaim from the cultural establishment in the nation's art capital of New York City.[10] It was also a highly popular art form with those federal bureaucracies that sent exhibitions abroad in order to contrast American freedom of expression with Soviet totalitarianism.[11] But modernism did not play so well in Peoria: certainly, there was a sense that it was a difficult kind of art, one that was somewhat unintelligible and inaccessible – an art for the highbrow who favoured Pablo Picasso, rather than the lowbrow who enjoyed commercial art akin to that of Norman Rockwell, while the middlebrow kept to such Grant Wood classics as his famous *American Gothic* (1930).[12] Modernism, whether in the visual arts, literature, music or elsewhere, was somewhat of a confusing topic for the layman and hence something of a mystery to those who were not trained or otherwise educated in this specialized field.

Still, what the public wanted to view or experience in terms of the arts is a much harder question to answer. It would be more accurate to ask, 'Who even cared?', for few ordinary Americans gave much thought to how the creative artist might survive, or what a specific art form should look like. Gallup polling data from 1949 suggests that the arts were a minority activity, and when asked if they would like to try writing a novel, painting a picture, acting in a theatre, or playing the piano, only the musical option encouraged half of the respondents to reply in the affirmative.[13] A myriad of art magazines existed during this period, such as *Art News*, *Music Journal* and *Theatre Arts*, but these were specialist periodicals, produced principally for the professional or the highly interested amateur. The public mostly gained their views from such mainstream sources as Henry Luce's popular *Life*, a magazine that emphasized biographical details, monetary value and insider knowledge, rather than the formal qualities of art.[14] In the national press, *The New York Times* offered the standard for cultural criticism (and listings of events), but even within such illustrious pages, the arts rarely made it to the front of the newspaper. Instead, educative articles were relegated to the Sunday magazine, such as one penned by New York City's controversial Parks Commissioner, Robert Moses, who as late as 1959, was still writing in truth that the 'little men and women have still to be sold on culture'.[15]

Meanwhile, the *American Artist* faced persistent problems, specifically the four key practical elements that all creative types consistently need to produce their best work: sufficient money, the right space, enough time and suitable interactions. These were not new issues, but they were magnified given that in the 1930s, President Franklin D. Roosevelt had created jobs for artists, writers, musicians and theatre folk and in so doing, birthed a new cultural generation (for without access to the New Deal projects, many would have been forced to either suffer in penury or turn their hand to alternative work, such as teaching).[16] But the president's federal arts projects were highly unpopular with conservative critics, who long complained about waste and supposed Roosevelt propaganda. It was therefore no surprise when in 1939, Congress finally cut appropriations for the Federal Theatre Project on the basis of suspected communist subversion: the remaining projects limped on into the Second World War, but their operating principles shifted from relief to patriotic support, and when the war ended, their doors closed too.[17] The New Deal federal arts projects raised expectations for enhanced public subsidy, higher income levels and additional employment opportunities in the arts, but in the post-war period, the recipients of federal arts beneficence were cut adrift as government funding evaporated.

Congressional debate, however, did not dry up. On the right, conservatives such as Representative George Dondero, a Republican from Royal Oak, Michigan, complained regularly on the House floor that abstract art was 'shackled' to Soviet communism, and hence highly suspect.[18] However, on the opposite end of the ideological spectrum, domestic liberals such as Senator Jacob Javits, a Republican from New York, Senator Claiborne Pell, a Democrat from Rhode Island, and Representative Frank Thompson Jr., a Democrat from New Jersey, frequently introduced government arts bills into their respective houses in the 1950s.[19] At the presidential level, views on modern art were similarly mixed. Democratic president Harry S. Truman played the piano, appreciated the 'wonderful' music of classical composers such as Mendelssohn, Beethoven, Mozart, Bach and Chopin, and disdained what he termed 'ham and egg' art (i.e. 'so-called pictures that look as if they had stood off and thrown an egg at them').[20] But Truman was also a Cold Warrior who well understood that the Soviet system dictated what art ought to be produced, and he publicly contrasted communism to the American form of democracy that protected the rights of the individual artist and freedom of expression.[21] Republican president Dwight D. Eisenhower subsequently took a similar line: he was an amateur artist who excelled in traditional, representational art such as landscapes and portraiture, considered certain modern forms to be more of a 'lampoon' than the kind of art that 'America likes', but he, too, went on record as stating that he would never wish to act as a 'censor'.[22] Politically then, a Cold War consensus dominated the politics of art, for most politicians, of whatever stripe, focused on the use of art as a weapon abroad in the battle against totalitarianism. The *domestic* politics of art was thus something of a tangential issue in the 1950s, despite a few Dondero-esque complaints about supposedly Red art, and the efforts of those big-government types who fondly looked back to the New Deal federal arts projects of the 1930s and sought to resurrect them.

Meanwhile, arts patrons in the private sector, and those who worked for them, had long sought to ameliorate fiscal problems for artists, particularly through arts residencies of varying duration, such as those offered by the MacDowell Colony in Peterborough, New Hampshire (founded by philanthropist Marian MacDowell in 1907) and Yaddo in Saratoga Springs, New York (founded by financier Spencer Trask and his wife, the writer Katrina Trask, in 1926).[23] Two of the 'Big Three' major general-purpose philanthropies, the Rockefeller Foundation (created in 1913), and the Ford Foundation (created in 1936), were also active in the arts, and provided matching funds to act as seed funding or pump primers, particularly in the case of the performing arts.[24] Most philanthropies tended to focus on public health, welfare and education though, rather than the arts. Those that did, were rarely willing to take creative risks, and instead supported safe and established institutions such as art museums, ballet companies and symphony orchestras, rather than new experiments undertaken by untried and untested individual artists.[25]

Concurrently, arts controversies sprung up in communities across the country from New York City, to San Francisco, to Dallas, as grassroots anti-communists sought to root out supposedly subversive cultural types and their content in the early Cold War years.[26] Southern California was a particularly heated battlefield, as the Red maelstrom and subsequent blacklisting that embraced the Hollywood Ten was equally alive and well in the broader Los Angeles art world. Throughout the later 1940s and into the 1950s and 1960s, members of the area's dominant, representational landscape school, plus academicians, and groups such as the Society of Western Artists, frequently picketed exhibitions of supposedly subversive or un-American art, while the city council, the Los Angeles Police Department, and the county board of supervisors, clamped down on freedom of artistic expression, most notably in the coffeehouses, such as around Venice, where the countercultural Beat authors were known to frequent.[27]

The post-war years were thus exciting, albeit quite complicated years to be an arts patron. The winds of art politics and funding blew in predominantly anti-communist swirls and eddies at both the national and the local level. The federal government took the arts seriously as a propaganda tool abroad, but this did not mean that most ordinary Americans wanted to practice, appreciate or, most importantly, publicly fund the arts themselves. Modernism was not yet in the mainstream, and for many, the intricacies of art world debates were somewhat obscure and uninteresting. In a domestic sense, there was an obvious federal financial vacuum after the last New Deal projects that persisted throughout the war years finally ended, although this was not the case on the international stage, as various government agencies, both covertly and overtly, utilized the arts as a Cold War weapon. Artists sought support and assistance, while philanthropists, patrons and other funders were unable to provide sufficient support. The political right champed at the bit about modernism as Communistic, while those on the other end of the ideological spectrum sought permanent governmental arts funding structures. It was into this morass that Huntington Hartford stepped in 1948 when, as founder and trustee, he officially opened the Huntington Hartford Foundation for artists, writers and musicians.

## Huntington Hartford's vision for the arts

Foundations are bodies that do not easily fit into definitional categories, and from the outset, the Huntington Hartford Foundation was no exception. It was set up initially as a trust with Hartford as founder and trustee. Hartford sought seclusion, beauty, a tolerant climate and accessibility for his foundation.[28] The estate he found in Rustic Canyon in the Santa Monica mountains near Pacific Palisades was all this and more.[29] It was just a couple of miles from Sunset Boulevard, but so secluded. It had once been a religious colony and was therefore quite autarchic. There was a water supply, electrics, some lodgings and appropriate fencing. A second estate was duly purchased, which included an early American style ranch house plus guest houses, and behind the houses, servants' quarters and other buildings. The landscaping was beautiful and well-suited to artistic reflection and production.[30]

In terms of the aesthetics of the actual buildings, Hartford engaged Lloyd Wright, son of famed architect Frank Lloyd Wright, to redesign the cottages for fellows and to re-envision the road layouts. At first glance, this might seem an unusual aesthetic choice for Hartford to make, given that Wright's work looks to the untrained eye to be purely ultra-modernist, but the result of the project was no accident. As architectural historian Thomas S. Hines has noted, Wright showed a 'concern for the problem of the good and beautiful surviving and triumphing over the hostile and violent' and he creatively explored the intricate relationships between modernism and regionalism.[31] Such sentiments fitted well with Hartford's own philosophy to preserve the best of the past while encouraging experimentation, and Wright's use of oblique angles echoed the surrounding landscape, enhanced the view of the Santa Monica hills, and fit well into the contemporaneous Los Angeles architectural scene.

Hartford needed to attract artists, writers and musicians to attend his new foundation, but the problem was that in the early Cold War years, there were very few conservative magazines of the arts to advertise these fellowships. William F. Buckley Jr. did not found that popular bastion of conservative commentary *National Review* until 1955, and besides, the focus for that magazine was *politics* – defined as foreign policy, key domestic issues and partisan politics – rather than cultural, social or artistic affairs.[32] Few conservative intellectuals gave much thought to the arts in this period, and those that did, such as the conservative moralist and critic Russell Kirk, were busy lamenting a discernible lack of suitable arts patrons in America, not advertising the few artistic residencies that were available.[33] A few specialist magazines *did* offer positive coverage of the Huntington Hartford Foundation (and hence served as a prompt to applications), but magazines such as *American Artist*, which emphasized representational art, were an exception to the general rule of a vacuum on the publishing right when it came to matters aesthetic.[34]

That left Hartford with the mainstream glossies, such as *Life*, that served upwardly mobile middle-class Americans, or non-ideologically aligned, professional art journals, for example *Opera News*. Given the bent and target audiences for these magazines, most coverage of the new foundation emphasized the patron's endeavour on behalf of American artists, rather than his conservative desires. Instead of undertaking investigative reportage, as a later generation of journalists might have done, writers highlighted the idyllic lifestyle on offer at the Foundation, or what was variously termed 'Parnassus, USA', 'Paradise' or the 'Artists' Shangri-La'.[35] The mainstream media and the arts press thus covered the Huntington Hartford Foundation in the context of long-running institutions such as MacDowell and Yaddo: few looked in detail at who chose the Hartford fellows, the kind of cultural folk who attended, or the type of art that they produced. Fast-forward to the 1960s, and Hartford's efforts might have appealed to editors as a vision of intelligible art, accessible literature and tonal music, among a sea of Bohemian confusion and artistic communes. But in the 1950s, Hartford's desire for 'wholesome' art as opposed to the 'vulgar' was considered an amusing and light-hearted affair, and his resultant foundation to be the interesting foible of a slightly eccentric millionaire, not part of a broader Culture War.[36]

From a fiscal perspective, Hartford was an old-school paternalist, a philanthropist who had inherited his millions and was intent on spending it for what he deemed the greater cultural good of the nation. The Huntington Hartford Foundation accordingly included a swimming pool, a library, and other leisure facilities for the resident fellows to use, provided full funding to ensure that an individual might survive completely on that stipend, *and* included certain expenses for art supplies. Unfortunately, Hartford gave little thought to practical financial matters and was notoriously bad with money: his foundation had no endowment, investments or other securities and was instead wholly reliant upon Hartford's personal gifts for its continued existence. It is worth noting too, that on the subject of government aid to the arts, Hartford was equally sanguine: he did not stand against President Lyndon B. Johnson's new federal bureaucracy for the arts, the National Endowment for the Arts that was created in 1965, and indeed, was eventually appointed by President Richard M. Nixon to serve on that agency's National Advisory Council. Hartford's philosophy might therefore best be described as a big-patron one that believed in both private philanthropy and public support, that is, a mixed arts economy.

Like other major arts patrons of the era, Hartford also eschewed partisan politics. Indeed, an analysis of the Huntington Hartford Foundation Records, 1948–65, held at the University of California, Los Angeles (UCLA) Library Special Collections in Los Angeles, indicates that the Foundation enjoyed art world networks and entanglements, rather than right-wing political ones.[37] Certainly, there is little evidence of deep engagement with Red hunters in the arts, and none with any right-wing groups or individuals such as the John Birch Society (founded in 1958) – a grassroots organization that might have been expected to take an interest in the activities of what was *de facto* an artistic commune.[38] Hartford's aim was to create a counter-establishment in a cultural sense, not to secure the election of right-wing politicians at the national, state or local levels, hence there was little reason for the Foundation to engage with the broader political right, or *vice versa*.

Philosophically and practically then, Huntington Hartford and his foundation operated within the boundaries of the established arts world, but this does not make him any less important for scholars of conservatism to study. Hartford was a well-known public figure who was frequently covered by the press, an heir who was able to fund his own projects and sought to make a difference to American society and cultural life. Although his aims were not political in a partisan sense, he was committed to a cause, and that was the promulgation of an anti-modernist aesthetic vision, for his foundation to support traditional, beautiful and intelligible art *and* to grow what he considered a potentially welcoming audience for these art forms among ordinary Americans. And yet, to reach the public, he needed to engage with those individuals, magazines and venues he saw as representative of a New York cultural elitism that he detested. Just as conservative political think tanks struggled to remain relevant during a period when public policymaking skewed in a liberal and technocratic orientation, the Huntington Hartford Foundation also had to work hard to make an impact at a time when the arts world tended towards modernist abstraction.[39]

## Of applicants, advisory councils and anti-communism

Huntington Hartford did not initially think hard or strategically about institutional structures or policy precedents as he set out to create his foundation: he was in a hurry, and keen to get started as quickly as possible. Hartford duly appointed Polish émigré, cheesecake *impresario*, Hollywood socialite, and latterly artist Michael Gaszynski as the Foundation's first director (1948–53).[40] In the first year of operation, Hartford decided to award scholarships to graduate students in the fine arts at leading universities and colleges, or as the *Los Angeles Times* put it, 'to establish a school of geniuses'.[41] That this was Hartford's decision is important to note, as it indicates how intricately he was involved in the minutiae of decision making – Hartford wanted to know precisely where his funds were going. But very quickly, it became clear that the patron had other demands on his time and that Gaszynski would need to begin to draw up formal guidelines and invent processes for choosing suitable fellows. The Foundation's first application form was a short one, and it noted that fellowships were open to US citizens and foreign-born artists who were permanent residents and had applied for citizenship.[42] To qualify, an artist needed to have a definite work project that was beyond the research stage, and also to answer in the negative the question, 'Are you a member of any organization which advocates the overthrow of the United States government by force or violence?'[43] The application form also asked potential fellows to provide several professional referees who would comment on the applicant's talent, ability and achievement, alongside their disposition, temperament and moral character, that is, whether the individual would work well in a group setting and not bring opprobrium down on the Foundation through unsuitable behaviour and a lack of self-discipline.[44]

Upon Gaszynski's resignation to pursue other business interests, Hartford chose classical composer and academic John Vincent, Professor of Composition at UCLA, as the Foundation's second and last director (1953–65).[45] Gaszynski managed the day-to-day operations of the estate and formulated initial foundation policies, procedures and priorities in tandem with Hartford, but it was Vincent who shared and sought to implement Hartford's conservative vision for the arts. Unlike Gaszynski who was an entrepreneurial businessman, Vincent was a cultural conservative who believed in preserving the best of the past, of tradition, and America's heritage, while also supporting new, experimental works that would stand the test of time.[46] In his own field, Vincent was best known for his book, *The Diatonic Modes in Modern Music* (1951), and for his melodious, romantic and old-fashioned diatonic-modal music compositions.[47] But he was also a populist who sought to educate the public in the wonders of classical music, to find a balance between low culture and high culture, or as he put it, the 'too trite, too obvious, too commonplace' and the 'too abstruse, too abstract, too obscure'.[48] In this respect, Vincent's world view sat well with Hartford's own and boded well for the two men working creatively together.

One of the most important problems that Vincent needed to solve concerned Hartford's insistence that applicants send in a handwritten letter because he was deeply interested in the controversial field of graphology, that is, the pseudo-scientific analysis of handwriting patterns and characteristics to discern personality, and in this case, fitness to obtain a foundation fellowship.[49] Although the writing sample was never the sole criterion for an acceptance or rejection, the request caused major headaches because certain applicants either objected on principle or failed to send along a letter that Hartford deemed long enough to be subjected to graphological analysis. Vincent, therefore, found it necessary to walk a tightrope between keeping Hartford happy on the one hand, and avoiding a veritable cursive controversy on the other. If Vincent did not formulate his request pointedly enough he often received another typed letter, but if he were too specific, the Foundation might end up as a laughing stock.[50] Fortunately, and no doubt due to Vincent's tact in dealing with both Hartford and potential fellows, no major controversy erupted over the handwriting question. Surprisingly, Hartford's personal involvement in the running of the Foundation did not receive much opprobrium either. Not until the 1960s did Representative Wright Patman, a populist Democrat from Texas, undertake a concerted effort to analyse the activities of the nation's philanthropies, and when he did, the major headlines concerned the revelation that the J. M. Kaplan Fund was a conduit for Central Intelligence Agency monies.[51] Considering these revelations, possible arguments about graphological decision making and the intricacies of patron involvement undoubtedly paled into insignificance.

Vincent did, however, take steps to ensure that the Foundation operated in a manner akin to other arts residencies and foundations. When he took over as director, he set about establishing a National Advisory Council composed of distinguished representatives of the arts.[52] These positions were largely honorary, rather than substantive though: the council served as an esteemed group of arts boosters, not as a decision-making body. Over the years, members included philanthropist Marian MacDowell, artists Thomas Hart Benton, Edward Hopper and Norman Rockwell, composers Leonard Bernstein, Richard Rodgers and William Schuman, and architect Edward Durrell Stone, among several other notables in the serious world of the arts. Such individuals were pleased to offer their names in support of the Foundation's work but were hardly likely to find the time to wade through applications or involve themselves in discussions over what did or did not qualify as an acceptable standard of work for receipt of a fellowship. The National Advisory Council was rarely asked for or offered guidance, instead, the glittering names served to enhance the reputation of the Foundation.[53] That said, there were exceptions to this hands-off behaviour, particularly when it came to the subject of potential Red subversion in the arts.

The noted sculptor and anti-communist Wheeler Williams was one of the more active members of the National Advisory Committee.[54] In the fall of 1956, he wrote to Vincent, and not for the first time, with a helpful offer: he would be *delighted* to vet foundation applicants for potential communist leanings:

> [I would] . . . greatly appreciate knowing names of at least the sculptors and painters who apply for fellowships before decision is made so that I could have their names screened for confidential reports as to possible front or subversive connections which might lead to subsequent reflection. . . . The Foundation is too wonderful in concept and in reality to risk any such possibility which might impair its fine potential.[55]

In the face of Williams's anti-communist sentiment, Vincent obligingly wrote back:

> We share with you the desire to keep out of the Foundation all Communists and subversives. We are constantly vigilant and do everything we can to protect the Foundation. Your kind offer of help is much appreciated, and I shall refer to you any case that seems suspicious. My assistant and I keep our ears to the ground and would be aware if someone got by our screening process and began spreading dangerous propaganda at the Foundation.[56]

This exchange demonstrates the vitality of the communist issue within the Foundation and without, but also Vincent's administrative competence and arms-length relationship with grassroots anti-communist arts activists. The director was as good as his word, in that he wrote to the Internal Security Division at the Department of Justice in Washington, DC, to obtain an up-to-date list of subversive organizations, but he did not take up Williams' offer to vet potential applicants.[57] When it came to the question of choosing fellows, Vincent created a National Advisory Council to enhance the status of the organization, but he did not wish to encourage individuals such as Williams to start major arts wars over potentially subversive forms or supposedly Red artists, musicians or writers. Instead, he chose a middling anti-communism that only nominally toed the line of those further to the right.

We are accustomed to thinking of anti-communism as the glue that held the modern American right together, yet when it came to the internal functioning of this cultural foundation, anti-communism was sometimes resisted by conservatives.[58] Like other arts organizations, such as museums, libraries and charities, the Foundation was subjected to external anti-communist influence, but although Vincent felt the need to respond politely to Williams, he did not take him up on his Red-driven offer of assistance, even though he, and the organization's patron, were both cultural conservatives. We must therefore be careful to appreciate the heterogeneity of conservatism in the Cold War era, including its multifaceted cultural varieties, and to evaluate anti-communist activities that do not fit comfortably into existing narratives.[59] As Lizabeth Cohen, among others, has argued, the Cold War does not tell the full story, the 1950s were not always conformist or stifling, and, in this case, a conservative in a position of power practised a form of collaborative resistance against anti-communism that defies easy labelling.[60]

## He who plays the populist piper

Although Hartford wished to retain the final ability to make decisions on fellowship applications, even he did not have the time to study each one thoroughly. The Foundation needed admissions committees for each discipline represented, namely art, literature and music, and like the National Advisory Council, these bodies enhanced the reputation and status of the institution. The admissions committees ultimately comprised several notable individuals who served terms of indiscriminate length, *de facto*, at Hartford's pleasure. Committee members were supposed to confidentially evaluate materials and reach a consensus, then to offer Hartford recommendations, but instead, the director often acted as a moderating force between Hartford and the committees. Of the three, it was the Art Advisory Committee that was the most tempestuous due to Hartford's strong belief that abstract art was communist-inspired, morally reprehensible and a form of domestic subversion that ought not to be supported by his foundation.

The first Art Advisory Committee consisted of Lloyd Goodrich, associate director of the Whitney Museum in New York City, plus Californians Arthur Millier, art critic for the *Los Angeles Times*, Donald Bear, director of the Santa Barbara Museum of Art, Kenneth Ross, general manager of the publicly funded Los Angeles Department of Municipal Arts, and Millard Sheets, chairman of the Art Department of Scripps College, Claremont.[61] West-Coast locals, therefore, outnumbered New York art establishment types on the committee, as was the case with the first fellowships. Los Angeles painter Jacob Richard, Santa Barbara wood engraver Victor Podoski, and painter and student from the University of Arizona, Stanley Fabe, were the initial recipients of Hartford's *largesse*, and the Foundation proudly presented the work of the last two at an exhibition in Esther's Gallery in Los Angeles from 17 to 30 November 1950.[62] In making his appointments and initial choices, Hartford showed his determination to build up a viable West-Coast alternative to the dominance of New York art critics and what he perceived as the north-eastern establishment.

Problems began, however, in November 1951, when Hartford penned a tract concerned with what he saw as a decline in literary standards and corresponding levels of morality in American society.[63] The piece was entitled *Has God Been Insulted Here?*, and Hartford mailed out around 4,000 copies to newspaper and magazine editors across the country.[64] In it, he decried the vulgar in modern art, argued that the abstract artist sought to undermine the established order, and attacked the work of notable modern adherents such as Cubist Pablo Picasso.[65] The pamphlet was accompanied by a letter that declaimed 'corruption' and 'decadence' in the arts.[66] Up until this point, Hartford had taken little personal interest in the choices of his Art Advisory Committee, but now he looked at their decisions anew and decided to refuse awards to two applicants whose abstract work he disliked for all of the usual reasons.[67] As a result, all of the artist board members resigned.

From a practical perspective, the Foundation now needed to appoint a new Art Advisory Committee. To avoid further problems, subsequent boards were carefully stacked with members who were screened for their aesthetic and political leanings, as Vincent poured over exhibition catalogues, published writings and even collected sensibilities to determine an individual's true sentiments. In the case of gallerist and curator Ala Story, for example, Vincent's recommendation to Hartford noted that her art collection leaned 'heavily toward the traditional . . . and representational' and that her 'central tendency' was towards 'the accomplishments of the past'; two sentiments that were close to Hartford's own personal beliefs.[68] Hartford was still prone to gripe though when the voting on fellowships did not go his own way: on one occasion he apparently wrote to Vincent, 'Perhaps I should do away with the Art Committee entirely and make all the decisions?' Vincent responded that Hartford might count on him 'one hundred percent' and that the two of them ought to meet to have a 'good talk' and 'map out a plan which would obtain the results you wish'.[69] Vincent took Hartford's complaints seriously as epistolary outbreaks that threatened to undo the Foundation's policymaking structures and he carefully managed and mollified the patron whenever possible. Thus, although such comments would seemingly indicate the veracity of long-standing populist critiques of foundation activity, namely that the patron threatened to subvert the democratic process, it is likely that Hartford was merely letting off steam, rather than making a serious suggestion. Certainly, boards persisted, as did Hartford's public populist pronouncements.

Next, Hartford continued with his attack against 'these contemporary abstractions . . . you can't make head or tail of' in the pages of the conservative magazine *American Mercury*, with the March 1955 article, 'The Public Be Damned'.[70] Two months later, Hartford reportedly paid $25,000 for this piece to be published for a wider audience by way of advertisements in the major New York newspapers.[71] In this essay, Hartford cemented his role as an arbiter of taste who was determined to maintain the public good. Despite his millions and ability to place expensive adverts in the mainstream press, Hartford considered himself a man of the people, and he felt that it was his duty to warn the 'intelligent reader' about the 'fiasco' of modern art and the art critics who 'are quite free to make their own standards and establish their own little dictatorship'.[72]

The critic and former art board member Arthur Millier responded in the *Los Angeles Times* that Hartford's views were 'nonsense!', while *Time* took a populist view that Hartford's aesthetics were problematic, but that encouraging greater public participation was good, noting slyly that his arguments contained enough grains of truth to 'rattle those ivory towers from which weird obscurities are foisted on the public'.[73] Letter writers to *The New York Times* were similarly divided, but in a paradoxical manner: one reader considered Hartford's views 'a transgression of our traditional heritage of freedom of expression' and suggested that the author 'damns himself by his own intolerance and demand for conformity' while another considered his attack on the establishment 'long overdue'.[74] Such comments illuminate a classic problem in the elitist and populist debate: on the one hand, Hartford's comments were potential evidence of the takeover of a suspect, monied elite, yet on the other hand, he was standing up to existing elites and making a principled attack on behalf of the common man.

Matters were not improved for Hartford's critics with the publication of his magnum opus, *Art or Anarchy?: How the Extremists and Exploiters Have Reduced the Fine Arts to Chaos and Commercialism* (1964).[75] This work saw Hartford utilize as yet unmade critical disdain as a selling point, for even the adverts for the book proclaimed that it would attract bad reviews and be 'assailed by the "establishment"', as indeed it was.[76] The grounds for these critical commentaries on Hartford's work ranged the gamut though, from the serious-minded to ridicule. Some scholars did take Hartford seriously, such as art historian and chairman of the art department at Williams College in Massachusetts, S. Lane Faison Jr., who complained about the book's lack of substance and noted grudgingly that the 'germs of truth' within it might have been 'better expressed'.[77] Others were sharper in their disapproval, with art critic Brian O'Doherty complaining that

> Hartford making like a thinker is first-class entertainment, a disarming parable of incompetent goodwill. His heart is always in the right place. It's his head that's in trouble.[78]

When it came to public criticism then, critiquing Hartford was something of a challenge, to say the least. The final two pieces are particularly notable for their coverage of Hartford's views and yet the multitude of diverging interpretations that might be drawn from them. The first was a *Life* article from February 1952 that saw an unsmiling Hartford standing in front of 'vulgar' abstract *versus* 'wholesome' representational pieces, juxtaposed between another image of an artist sketching a nude at the Foundation, plus an image of the cover of *Has God Been Insulted Here?*[79] For some, Hartford's posturing with works that he termed good and bad art might have been reminiscent of the Nazi Degenerate Art Exhibition of 1937, but suffice to say that the jumble of imagery left much to the *Life* reader to discern for themselves.[80] The second was satirical journalist Tom Wolfe's coverage of Hartford as the 'Luther of Columbus Circle' in the *New York Herald Tribune* in late February 1964.[81] Although the lead quotation read, 'I thought a museum ought to have organ music', Huntington Hartford said, 'it's really like a church' – such subtle sarcasm was no doubt missed by some readers (including Hartford himself, who later offered the piece as recommended reading for those who wished to know 'what makes me tick').[82] That said, what is most interesting is that the commentary on Hartford did not attack his mere existence as a rich donor. Such coverage was not indicative of a robber baron attack that begrudged Hartford his money, complained about tax avoidance or argued that Hartford was seeking to improve his public image through arts support.

To a degree, Hartford's writings were useful to the Foundation, in that he acted as a lightning rod for critiques, meaning that the Foundation itself was able to operate with little public scrutiny or controversy, to in effect, continue with its business under the radar. Although the full foundation records for fellowship decisions will not be available until 2050, it is likely that fellows hailed from a variety of different backgrounds and ran the gamut across the arts. Most importantly, they were able to pursue their arts without being told what to do or how to produce. If the Foundation had been a federal grant-making body that chose specific projects and organizations to fund, rather than a foundation that offered residencies, the critical coverage of the output would no doubt have been far more pointed, potentially in terms of waste and boondoggling, or pork and patronage. Discussions about taxpayers' expenses and the activities of government employees would have likely made the Foundation more newsworthy. With just a few exceptions, press coverage tended to focus on Hartford himself, as journalists preferred to engage with the individual patron's taste and desires rather than to look behind the scenes at the actual fellows themselves.

Although investment in individuals who were known for their potential or *de facto* communist sympathies were no doubt avoided, the resulting art was far from middle-of-the-road, and a wide variety of different art forms were produced at the Foundation. C. Wright Mills wrote *The Power Elite* (1956) on a fellowship, while Ernst Toch composed his Pulitzer Prize-winning Third Symphony, and Edward Hopper painted a watercolour that earned him a $2,000 Hallmark Award.[83] Since the recipients included writers, it is little wonder that publicity for the Foundation was good: it was mainly left to individual artists who had attended to sing the praises of the Foundation.[84] Again, what is most noticeable here is the absence of critiques. There was little discussion concerning debates over favouritism in the selection process, instead, those newspaper reports and magazine articles that did cover the Foundation emphasized long-standing Old West tropes such as the tension between individual and community, that is, the isolation of the location *versus* aspects of communal living.[85] One of the last fellows to attend the Foundation serves to sum up the diversity of residents: a Catholic Sister named Glady Ann who was avant garde in her lifestyle and abstract in her works.[86]

In addition to the fellowships, from 1953 onwards, the Huntington Hartford Foundation also made awards for proven accomplishment and distinguished contributions to the arts by notable individuals, who were then encouraged, but not necessarily required, to reside at the estate for a short period of time. Initially, separate prizes were awarded in the fields of art, literature and music but subsequently, only one award was made annually. Of the awards to artists, the first one was made in 1954 and given to painter George Biddle, who worked for six months at the Foundation on a series of paintings of life in Haiti.[87] The second art award winner in 1955 was artist Andrew Wyeth, who did not visit the Foundation because his detailed art was 'so closely associated' with his own region of New England.[88] The third art recipient in 1956 was Edward Hopper, who enjoyed a period on the estate where he painted works such as *California Hills* (1957), a watercolour of the landscape behind the Foundation. The last of the art recipients in 1957 was Salvador Dali.[89] Subsequent awards were made in the fields of either literature or music, with the last such being made in 1964. Such awards indicated the flexibility of Hartford's conceptions of beauty, tradition and moralism, ranging from Biddle's social realism to Wyeth's hyperrealism, and Dali's surrealism.

By the mid-1960s, however, it was clear that the Foundation was in financial trouble, and Hartford told Vincent that he needed to sell the estate. The operating costs were around $100,000 per annum, but the real problem was that Hartford's proclivity for cultural institution building had placed him in an over-extended financial position with his other projects.[90] Vincent tried to persuade his other employer, the UCLA, to buy, but the Regents only wished to accept the Foundation as a donation, and Hartford needed the funds. At one point, there was a suggestion that a solution might be worked out with the cooperation of the State Park Commission and the State Arts Commission, but these musings ultimately came to naught, as did the initial interest of actor Cary Grant.[91] The Foundation was eventually sold for a loss of over $1 million when it was bought for a reported $700,000 cash by John M. Morehart, a local real estate developer, to be used as a residency by his family.[92] The doors finally closed in July 1965. Looking back on his activities in *Esquire* in the later 1960s, Hartford referred to himself as 'Horatio Alger in reverse' and noted with pique that at least in making his errors, they were usually 'big enough to make news!'[93]

As Steve Fraser and Gary Gerstle have noted, the study of ruling elites has been overshadowed in recent history by a movement towards identity history, while those who do take up the subject usually argue 'against its salience for grasping the essentials' of American history.[94] The case of Hartford indicates the persistence of conflicts between populism and elitism and the complications of that narrative when members of the elite undertake populist attacks against other elites. In this respect, Hartford's activities fit well in this long-standing pattern of American life.

In describing his own beliefs, Huntington Hartford once noted that, 'I'm a little bit somewhat to the right of . . . Atilla the Hun; but not quite as bad as his friend H. L. Hunt'.[95] This comment was followed by a list of problems that Hartford discerned in American society and culture, ranging from 'the trouble with the kids' of the 1960s, down to what he described as 'destructive forces' such as Supreme Court Chief Justice Earl Warren and *The New York Times* magazine section, alongside the Woodstock music festival, the Black Panthers and tenured professors.[96] Without a doubt, Hartford was a conservative, but he was a cultural conservative, not the feared ruler of a tribal empire or a financier of the far-right, and these comments on the general cultural milieu were unusual, for he usually focused solely on aesthetic concerns. Hartford's millions meant that he was the early Cold War era's most notable advocate for the traditional, the beautiful and the easily intelligible populist art forms. But although he used his funds to attract publicity, his foundation was never able to make quite the splash that he sought, nor to marshal a substantial following of advocates who supported his views. Hartford aspired to spread the achievements of his own preferred artists and art forms for the benefit of ordinary Americans, but his foundation was far from in charge of an American public taste. In his attempt to create a cultural counter-establishment, Hartford was ultimately unsuccessful.

When we think of conservative institutions in this period we tend to think of philanthropic foundations or think tanks with expressly political concerns, such as formulating and pushing political conservatism and public policy, and also of those that were successful, that, as Jason Stahl has put it, 'forever alter American political culture in a more conservative direction'.[97] We do not think of conservative art patrons or philanthropists with cultural, rather than discretely political goals, because the emphasis is so often on political organizing and American political culture, rather than culture per se. Although the Huntington Hartford Foundation lasted only fifteen years, it made a difference in the lives of many artists and contributed to the broader fabric of American culture and society. It might not have been central to the activities of the political right, but it did make a difference.

The case of the Huntington Hartford Foundation suggests the existence of modern American conservatism in forms that are detached from party politics, and indeed, eschew the political sphere altogether. From Hartford's point of view, he was up against an incarnation of what later conservatives would term the liberal media elite, and he sought to build a counter-establishment of artists, musicians and literary folk, who would engage with a broader public that, he hoped, would awaken and grow increasingly sceptical of leading art critics, museum professionals and their choices. Such a finding indicates that Hartford's sustained art critical efforts in the post-war era were not merely eccentric mutterings, but rather a moment in a critical tradition of attacks that are now beginning to be documented by scholars.[98] They were neither unlikely to ever evolve into a political movement nor was the Foundation ever able to move away from being a vehicle mainly for Hartford's own personal beliefs.

Throughout his life, Hartford aimed to challenge what he perceived as north-eastern elitism, specifically the ability of the New York art establishment to define what was good in American art. Hartford wanted to raise the level of the arts in his own image, towards the traditional, and to shift the country culturally in a right-wards direction and away towards the West-Coast. His efforts to educate the public received mixed reports, but he certainly gained considerable press coverage for his efforts. Despite the tinkerings of a far from hands-off patron, the Foundation sailed an erstwhile conservative course that, in the main, avoided the shoals of both anti-communist attacks and potential communist controversies. Bar one mass resignation, subsequent choices for advisory councils and boards, alongside fellowships and awards, rarely caused much controversy, and in general, the coverage of foundation awards was positive.

The Foundation provided spaces and places for artists to experiment, to engage in creative work, to grow and then to engage and enter the public sphere. While Hartford wrote and made public comments that provided intellectual underpinnings for a nascent form of cultural conservatism, the Foundation equipped and helped train pools of artists and served as a suitable environment for minds to meet. Those who attended enjoyed opportunities to network, collaborate, meet like-minded individuals and feel like a part of a supportive community. The quality of the art produced no doubt varied, and Hartford sometimes meddled in decisions made by bodies that were instituted to avoid patron dominance, but artists had the opportunity to try, and that is what really matters. Producing art requires great risk, for to create, artists must have the ability to fail, and Hartford understood this. After all, to create, artists all need money, the right space, enough time and suitable interactions, and for a short while, Hartford provided. Although what precisely happened next to those who won fellowships is yet to be documented by scholars due to the inaccessibility of archival material, the Foundation clearly helped tide some artists over during a crucial period. When the fellowship files are unlocked it will be easier for historians to discern what happened next to those artists who benefited from Hartford's funds. As it stands, it is likely that the contribution that an heir such as Hartford made to artists' lives ultimately provided the basis for some to develop and take their place within the separate ranks of the political right, and that for others their primary allegiance was to their art.

Creativity is central to human life, but too often the arts are relegated to a non-essential in the history of philanthropy, while in studies of arts patronage, smaller foundations who operated domestically have been overlooked in works that focus on the role of the federal government, such as the activities of the National Endowment for the Arts.[99] So too, scholars of conservatism have frequently treated the right as predominantly political in conception, one that grew up from the grassroots, but in such analyses (as in the contrasting literature that emphasizes elites), the history of the arts is usually absent.[100] We need to be open to seeing arts battles as an important part of American history, no matter the subfield. The Huntington Hartford Foundation was an effort to respond to a problem that was national in origin – that of support for the *American Artist*. In its years of operation, from 1948 to 1965, the Foundation was not competing with a publicly funded federal system of arts patronage. Instead, it operated in lieu of a governmental system and assisted artists in a barren period after the New Deal federal arts projects of the 1930s, and prior to the creation of the National Endowment for the Arts in 1965. In this respect, it helped to prepare the way for the modern state to play a substantive role in the arts.

Art permits us to communicate, to live, to experience the full range of human emotions, and Hartford provided artists with opportunities, and art was made. Whether the resulting works were good or bad, or popular or unpopular, is not the right question to ask. No matter the source of funding, be it public support or private philanthropy, or a combination of the two, no exercise is without problems, and Hartford tried on behalf of artists, art and the American public, and the choices the Foundation made were ultimately far from one-dimensional in terms of the arts produced. And that is as it should be: a mixed funding model for artmaking with a diversity of sources encourages artists to create different art forms within a democratic society.

# Notes

1 Huntington Hartford, interview by Paul Cummings, 19 May 1970, transcript, 1, Reference Department, Archives of American Art, Smithsonian Institution, Washington, DC.

2 Huntington Hartford, interview by Paul Cummings, 19 May 1970, transcript, 2, Reference Department, Archives of American Art, Smithsonian Institution, Washington, DC.

3 Huntington Hartford, interview by Paul Cummings, 19 May 1970, transcript, 2, Reference Department, Archives of American Art, Smithsonian Institution, Washington, DC.

4　Huntington Hartford, *Has God Been Insulted Here?* (New York: Private Printing, 1951), Huntington Hartford, 'The Public Be Damned', *American Mercury*, March 1955: 36, and Huntington Hartford, *Art or Anarchy? How the Extremists and Exploiters Have Reduced the Fine Arts to Chaos and Commercialism* (Garden City: Doubleday & Company, Inc., 1964).

5　On Hartford's other projects see Jack Long, 'How to Be Happy Though Rich', *Playbill*, 16 November 1959, 5, 7–11, 13, 43, 45–7.

6　For a journalistic overview see Lisa Rebecca Gubernick, *Squandered Fortune: The Life and Times of Huntington Hartford* (New York: G. P. Putnam's Sons, 1991). For an art historical approach see Sandra Zalman, 'Modern Art, Inc.: The Museum of Modern Art v. Huntington Hartford', *Grey Room* 53, no. 1 (Fall 2013): 33–59.

7　On the New Deal arts projects see Nick Taylor, *American-Made: The Enduring Legacy of the WPA: When FDR Put the Nation to Work* (New York: Bantam Books, 2008). On the Central Intelligence Agency see the now classic Frances Stonor Saunders, *Who Paid the Piper?: The CIA and the Cultural Cold War* (London: Granta Books, 1999). On the United States Information Agency see Michael L. Krenn, *Fall-Out Shelters for the Human Spirit: American Art and the Cold War* (Chapel Hill: University of North Carolina Press, 2005). And on the State Department see Penny M. Von Eschen, *Satchmo Blows up the World: Jazz Ambassadors Play the Cold War* (Cambridge, MA: Harvard University Press, 2004).

8　See for example Donald Critchlow, *The Conservative Ascendancy: How the Republican Right Rose to Power in Modern America* (Lawrence: University Press of Kansas, 2011). There are a few exceptions. On conservative cultural criticism see Robert M. Crunden, *The Superfluous Men: Conservative Critics of American Culture, 1900–1945* (Austin: University of Texas Press, 1977). And for an analysis of a conservative foundation with interests in the arts see John J. Miller, *A Gift of Freedom: How the John M. Olin Foundation Changed America* (San Francisco: Encounter Books, 2006).

9　See for example Jason Stahl, *Right Moves: The Conservative Think Tank in American Political Culture Since 1945* (Chapel Hill: The University of North Carolina Press, 2016), Steven M. Teles, *The Rise of the Conservative Legal Movement: The Battle for Control of the Law* (Princeton: Princeton University Press, 2012), and Jean Stefanic and Richard Delgado, *No Mercy: How Conservative Think Tanks and Foundations Changed America's Social Agenda* (Philadelphia: Temple University Press, 1996).

10　See for example 'Jackson Pollock: Is he the Greatest Living Painter in the United States?', *Life*, 8 August 1949, 42–3, 45. On the growing cultural dominance of New York in this period see Serge Guilbaut with Arthur Goldhammer, *How New York Stole the Idea of Modern Art: Abstract Expressionism, Freedom, and the Cold War* (Chicago: University of Chicago Press, 1983).

11　See Eva Cockroft, 'Abstract Expressionism, Weapon of the Cold War', *Artforum* xii, no. 10 (June 1974): 39–41.

12　Russell Lynes, 'Highbrow, Lowbrow, Middlebrow', *Harper's Magazine*, February 1949, 19–28. Russell Lynes, 'High-Brow, Low-Brow, Middle-Brow', *Life*, 11 April 1949, 99–102.

13　George Gallup, ed., *The Gallup Poll: Public Opinion 1949* (Wilmington: Scholarly Resources Inc., 1980), 2: 866.

14　Sheila Webb, 'Art Commentary for the Middlebrow: Promoting Modernism & Modern Art through Popular Culture – How Life Magazine Brought "The New" into Middle-Class Homes', *American Journalism* 27, no. 3 (Summer 2010): 121.

15  Robert Moses, 'Needed: New Medicis for Art Centers', *The New York Times*, 10 May 1959, SM24.

16  On the most well-known of the New Deal arts projects, namely the Federal Art Project (FAP), the Federal Theatre Project (FTP), the Federal Writers' Project (FWP), and the Federal Music Project (FMP) of the Works Progress Administration (WPA) see, respectively, Jonathan Harris, *Federal Art and National Culture: The Politics of Identity in New Deal America* (Cambridge: Cambridge University Press, 1995), Barry Witham, *The Federal Theatre Project: A Case Study* (Cambridge: Cambridge University Press, 2003), David A. Taylor, *Soul of a People: The WPA Writers' Project Uncovers Depression America* (Hoboken: John Wiley & Sons, Inc., 2009), and Kenneth J. Bindas, *All of This Music Belongs to the Nation: The WPA's Federal Music Project and American Society* (Knoxville: The University of Tennessee Press, 1995).

17  Richard D. McKinzie, *The New Deal for Artists* (Princeton: Princeton University Press, 1973): 149–71.

18  See for example George Dondero, 'Modern Art Shackled to Communism', *Congressional Record*, House of Representatives, 81st Congress, 1st Session, 16 August 1949, 95: 11584–7.

19  On their respective arts activities see Jacob K. Javits with Rafael Steinberg, *Javits: The Autobiography of a Public Man* (Boston: Houghton Mifflin Company, 1981): 305–19, G. Wayne Miller, *An Uncommon Man: The Life and Times of Senator Claiborne Pell* (Hanover: University Press of New England, 2011): 115–23, and Augusta E. Wilson, *Liberal Leader in the House: Frank Thompson Jr.* (Washington, DC: Acropolis Books, 1968): 92–8.

20  Harry S. Truman, 'The President's News Conference' Conference', *The American Presidency Project*, 21 February 1946, https://www.presidency.ucsb.edu/documents /the-presidents-news-conference-422. And Harry S. Truman, 'Remarks at a Ceremony in Observance of National Music Week' Week', *The American Presidency Project*, 9 May 1951, https://www.presidency.ucsb.edu/documents/remarks-ceremony -observance-national-music-week.

21  Harry S. Truman, 'Inaugural Address', *The American Presidency Project*, 20 January 1949, https://www.presidency.ucsb.edu/documents/inaugural-address-4.

22  Dwight D. Eisenhower, 'The President's News Conference' Conference', *The American Presidency Project*, 1 July 1959, https://www.presidency.ucsb.edu/documents/the -presidents-news-conference-252.

23  On MacDowell see Carter Wiseman, ed., *Place for the Arts: The MacDowell Colony, 1907–2007* (Peterborough: MacDowell Colony, 2006). On Yaddo see Micki McGee, *Yaddo: Making American Culture* (New York: The New York Public Library, 2008). Note that in 2020, the MacDowell Colony dropped the second part of its name to avoid any associations with long-standing histories of racism, imperialism, hierarchy and exclusion in the arts. See Julia Jacobs, 'MacDowell Colony Drops the Word "Colony", Citing "Oppressive Overtones"', *The New York Times*, 7 July 2020, https:// www.nytimes.com/2020/07/07/arts/design/macdowell-arts-colony-name-change .html.

24  On Ford and Rockefeller see Richard Schechner, 'Ford, Rockefeller, and Theatre', *The Tulane Drama Review* 10, no. 1 (Autumn 1965): 23–49.

25  Julia L. Foulkes, '"The Weakest Point in Our Record": Philanthropic Support of Dance and the Arts', in *Patronizing the Public: American Philanthropy's Transformation of Culture, Communication, and the Humanities,* ed. William J. Buxton (Lanham: Rowman & Littlefield Publishers Inc., 2009): 300–24.

26  See Jane de Hart Mathews, 'Art and Politics in Cold War America', *The American Historical Review* 81, no. 4 (October 1976): 762–87.

27  Sarah Schrank, 'The Art of the City: Modernism, Censorship, and the Emergence of Los Angeles's Postwar Art Scene', *American Quarterly* 56, no. 3 (September 2004): 673.

28  John Vincent, 'History of the Huntington Hartford Foundation', Fall 1953, 1, Folder 7 John Vincent's 'History of the Huntington Hartford Foundation', (1954), 1187 General Files, Box 1, Huntington Hartford Foundation Records, 1948–1965, UCLA Library, Department of Special Collections, Manuscripts Division, Charles E. Young Research Library, Los Angeles, California.

29  On the history of the local area see Betty Lou Young with Thomas R. Young, *Rustic Canyon and the Story of the Uplifters* (Santa Monica: Casa Vieja Press, 1975).

30  John Vincent, 'History of the Huntington Hartford Foundation', Fall 1953, 1, Folder 7 John Vincent's 'History of the Huntington Hartford Foundation', (1954), 1187 General Files, Box 1, Huntington Hartford Foundation Records, 1948–1965, UCLA Library, Department of Special Collections, Manuscripts Division, Charles E. Young Research Library, Los Angeles, California.

31  Thomas S. Hines, 'The Blessing and the Curse', in *Lloyd Wright: The Architecture of Frank Lloyd Wright Jr.*, ed. Thomas S. Hines and Eric Lloyd Wright with Alan Weintraub (London: Thames & Hudson, 1998): 12, 13.

32  William F. Buckley Jr., 'Publisher's Statement', *National Review*, 19 November 1955, 6.

33  Russell Kirk, 'The Passing of the Patron', *America*, 21 September 1957, 641–3.

34  Val Telberg, 'Creative Paradise in California', *American Artist*, October 1954, 41–3, 71.

35  Bradford Smith, 'Parnassus, USA', *The Saturday Review*, 2 August 1958, 7–9, 40–41, Peter Jona Korn, 'Artists' Shangri-La: A Paradise Almost Lost', *Musical Courier*, 6 February 1949, 6–9, and Helena Frost, 'Artists in Paradise', *Opera News*, 27 February 1965, 6–11.

36  'Art Trouble in Paradise: Modernism Upsets Grocery Heir's Eden', *Life*, 4 February 1952, 76–9.

37  Huntington Hartford Foundation Records, 1948–1965, UCLA Library, Department of Special Collections, Manuscripts Division, Charles E. Young Research Library, Los Angeles, California.

38  On Robert Welch and the John Birch Society see D. J. Mulloy, *The World of the John Birch Society: Conspiracy, Conservatism and the Cold War* (Nashville: Vanderbilt University Press, 2014).

39  Stahl, *Right Moves*, 3, 7–46.

40  'People Are Talking About: In Hollywood', *Vogue*, 1 April 1948, 194.

41  'Genius School Gets Preliminary Nod', *Los Angeles Times*, 9 March 1949, 2. '"School for Genius Aim of Heir to A. & P. Fortune"', *The New York Times*, 6 February 1949, 29.

42  First Application Form, undated, 1, Folder 1 Printed Matter Samples, 1187 General Files, Box 21, Huntington Hartford Foundation Records, 1948–1965, UCLA Library, Department of Special Collections, Manuscripts Division, Charles E. Young Research Library, Los Angeles, California.

43  First Application Form, undated, 2, Folder 1 Printed Matter Samples, 1187 General Files, Box 21, Huntington Hartford Foundation Records, 1948–1965, UCLA Library, Department of Special Collections, Manuscripts Division, Charles E. Young Research Library, Los Angeles, California.

44 Referee Request, 'Confidential Report on Candidate for Fellowship', undated, Folder 1 Printed Matter Samples, 1187 General Files, Box 21, Huntington Hartford Foundation Records, 1948–1965, UCLA Library, Department of Special Collections, Manuscripts Division, Charles E. Young Research Library, Los Angeles, California.

45 'John Vincent, Composer, Headed Music Department at U.C.L.A.', *The New York Times*, 25 January 1977, 36.

46 John Vincent, 'The Composer: Artist or Scientist?', *Newsletter of American Symphony Orchestra League*, July-August 1963, 27.

47 John Vincent, *The Diatonic Modes in Modern Music* (Berkeley: University of California Press, 1951).

48 John Vincent, 'How an Audience Influences the Composer', *Hollywood Bowl Magazine*, 12, 14, 16 July 1949, 35.

49 First Application Form, undated, 2, Folder 1 Printed Matter Samples, 1187 General Files, Box 21, Huntington Hartford Foundation Records, 1948–1965, UCLA Library, Department of Special Collections, Manuscripts Division, Charles E. Young Research Library, Los Angeles, California. He eventually wrote a book on the subject: Huntington Hartford, *You Are What You Write* (New York: Macmillan, 1973).

50 Letter, John Vincent to Huntington Hartford, 23 October 1964, 1, Folder 3 Hartford, Huntington Corresp. With Vincent (1964–1965), 1187 General Files, Box 17, Huntington Hartford Foundation Records, 1948–1965, UCLA Library, Department of Special Collections, Manuscripts Division, Charles E. Young Research Library, Los Angeles, California.

51 Nancy Beck Young, *Wright Patman: Populism, Liberalism, and the American Dream* (Dallas: Southern Methodist University Press, 2000): 207, 212. For lengthy letters, questionnaires, and financial reporting between John Vincent and Wright Patman see Folder 9 Congressional Correspondence, 1187 General Files, Box 14, Huntington Hartford Foundation Records, 1948–1965, UCLA Library, Department of Special Collections, Manuscripts Division, Charles E. Young Research Library, Los Angeles, California.

52 Memorandum, most likely John Vincent to Huntington Hartford, undated, Folder 9 National Advisory Council 1, 1187 General Files, Box 19, Huntington Hartford Foundation Records, 1948–1965, UCLA Library, Department of Special Collections, Manuscripts Division, Charles E. Young Research Library, Los Angeles, California.

53 On the economics of cultural prestige see James F. English, *The Economy of Prestige: Prizes, Awards, and the Circulation of Cultural Value* (Cambridge, MA: Harvard University Press, 2009).

54 On Williams's activities in the service of conservative, anti-communist art forms and artists see Karen Patricia Heath, 'Conservative Artists in the 1950s: The Limits to Success', in *Rethinking American Conservatism*, ed. Tom Packer and Philip Davies (London: Institute for the Study of the Americas, 2020), 1, 2, 14, 16, 18.

55 Letter, Wheeler Williams to John Vincent, 13 September 1956, 1, Folder 10 National Advisory Council 2, 1187 General Files, Box 19, Huntington Hartford Foundation Records, 1948–1965, UCLA Library, Department of Special Collections, Manuscripts Division, Charles E. Young Research Library, Los Angeles, California.

56 Letter, John Vincent to Wheeler Williams, 28 September 1956, Folder 10 National Advisory Council 2, 1187 General Files, Box 19, Huntington Hartford Foundation Records, 1948–1965, UCLA Library, Department of Special Collections, Manuscripts Division, Charles E. Young Research Library, Los Angeles, California.

57 Letter, John Vincent to Internal Security Division, United States Department of Justice, 20 April 1960, Folder 4 General Correspondence, 1187 General Files, Box 19, Huntington Hartford Foundation Records, 1948–1965, UCLA Library, Department of Special Collections, Manuscripts Division, Charles E. Young Research Library, Los Angeles, California.

58 See most notably Lisa McGirr, *Suburban Warriors: The Origins of the New American Right* (Princeton: Princeton University Press, 2001).

59 For instance, Lary May, ed., *Recasting America: Culture and Politics in the Age of Cold War* (Chicago: University of Chicago Press, 1989), Elaine Tyler May, *Homeward Bound: American Families in the Cold War Era* (New York: BasicBooks, 1988), and Stephen J. Whitfield, *The Culture of the Cold War* (Baltimore: Johns Hopkins University Press, 1991).

60 See Lizabeth Cohen, *A Consumers' Republic: The Politics of Mass Consumption in Postwar America* (New York: Knopf, 2003). Also Peter Filene, "'Cold War Culture" Doesn't Say It All', in *Rethinking Cold War Culture*, ed. Peter Kuznick and James Gilbert (Washington, DC: Smithsonian Institution Press, 2001).

61 'Board Named to Select Artists for Fellowships', *Los Angeles Times,* 5 November 1950, 39.

62 'Four Winners of Hartford Award Named', *Los Angeles Times,* 13 July 1950, A1. Press Release, November 1950, 2, Folder 2 Publicity, 1187 General Files, Box 21, Huntington Hartford Foundation Records, 1948–1965, UCLA Library, Department of Special Collections, Manuscripts Division, Charles E. Young Research Library, Los Angeles, California.

63 Huntington Hartford, interview by Paul Cummings, 19 May 1970, transcript 2, 3, Reference Department, Archives of American Art, Smithsonian Institution, Washington, DC.

64 Huntington Hartford, interview by Paul Cummings, 19 May 1970, transcript 2, 3, Reference Department, Archives of American Art, Smithsonian Institution, Washington, DC.

65 Hartford, *Has God Been Insulted Here?*.

66 Covering Letter, Huntington Hartford, undated but 1951, Folder 1 Printed Matter Samples, 1187 General Files, Box 21, Huntington Hartford Foundation Records, 1948–1965, UCLA Library, Department of Special Collections, Manuscripts Division, Charles E. Young Research Library, Los Angeles, California.

67 'Art Trouble in Paradise: Modernism Upsets Grocery Heir's Eden', *Life,* 4 February 1952, 76.

68 Letter, John Vincent to Huntington Hartford, 6 September 1963, Folder 2 Hartford, Huntington Corresp. with Vincent (1962–1963), 1187 General Files, Box 17, Huntington Hartford Foundation Records, 1948–1965, UCLA Library, Department of Special Collections, Manuscripts Division, Charles E. Young Research Library, Los Angeles, California.

69 Letter, John Vincent to Huntington Hartford, 23 March 1962, Folder 2 Hartford, Huntington Corresp. with Vincent (1962--1963), 1187 General Files, Box 17, Huntington Hartford Foundation Records, 1948--1965, UCLA Library, Department of Special Collections, Manuscripts Division, Charles E. Young Research Library, Los Angeles, California.

70 Huntington Hartford, 'The Public Be Damned', *American Mercury,* March 1955, 36.

71  Val Duncan, 'Art World Warrior', *Newsday*, 3 May 1960, 48. See for example, Huntington Hartford, 'The Public Be Damned', [advertisement], *The New York Times*, 16 May 1955, 48.

72  Huntington Hartford, 'The Public Be Damned', *American Mercury*, March 1955, 35, 37.

73  'Battlefronts', *Time*, 20 June 1955, 71.

74  James M. Fennelly, 'To the Editor of *The New York Times* [letter]', *The New York Times*, 24 May 1955, 30. Margaret E. Arnold, 'To the Editor of *The New York Times* [letter]', *The New York Times*, 24 May 1955, 30.

75  Hartford, *Art or Anarchy?*

76  'ART OR ANARCHY? Huntington Hartford Speaks Out Against the Extremists of Modern Art – From Picasso on Down', [advertisement], *The New York Times*, 22 November 1964, BR34. See also 'ART OR ANARCHY? Huntington Hartford Asks the Big Question That is Starting an All-Out War!', [advertisement], *The New York Times*, 20 December 1964, BR9.

77  S. Lane Faison, 'Art Things That Bad?', *The New York Times*, 29 November 1964, 22.

78  Brian O'Doherty, 'A Millionaire Art Buff Takes on the Bad Guys', *Life*, 27 November 1964, 12.

79  'Art Trouble in Paradise: Modernism Upsets Grocery Heir's Eden', *Life*, 4 February 1952, 78.

80  On this subject see Olaf Peters, ed., *Degenerate Art: The Attack on Modern Art in Nazi Germany, 1937* (Munich: Prestel, 2014).

81  Tom Wolfe, 'The Luther of Columbus Circle', *New York Herald Tribune Magazine*, 23 February 1964, 13–15, 18.

82  Huntington Hartford, interview by Paul Cummings, 19 May 1970, transcript, 3, Reference Department, Archives of American Art, Smithsonian Institution, Washington, DC.

83  Peter Bart, 'Coast Art Colony Enters 16th Year', *The New York Times*, 19 December 1964, 27.

84  See for example Jona Korn, 'Artists' Shangri-La', 6–9, and Frost, 'Artists in Paradise', 6–11.

85  For an indicative example see Peter Gray, 'A Canyonful of Creativity', *Los Angeles*, June 1962, 62, 64.

86  Dorothy Townsend, 'Nun Finds Right Direction in Artists' Colony', *Los Angeles Times*, 8 August 1965, A1.

87  '3 Get Awards in Arts', *The New York Times*, 10 July 1954, 6. 'George Biddle's Haitian Art to Go on Display', *Los Angeles Times*, 8 May 1955, 32.

88  'Hartford Group Awards Prizes to Arts Figures', *Los Angeles Times*, 6 September 1955, A1. 'Get Hartford Awards', *The New York Times*, 6 September 1955, 29. Letter, Andrew Wyeth to John Vincent, 4 July 1955, Folder 3 Awards (Non-Resident), 1187 Admissions Committees Art, Box 14, Huntington Hartford Foundation Records, 1948–1965, UCLA Library, Department of Special Collections, Manuscripts Division, Charles E. Young Research Library, Los Angeles, California.

89  'Dali Given $5000 Award by Hartford', *Los Angeles Times*, 27 October 1957, E8. 'Dali Gets $5,000 Award of Hartford Foundation', *The New York Times*, 21 October 1957, 16.

90  'Hartford on the Rocks?', *Newsweek*, 7 June 1965, 73–4. 'Harassed Hartford', *Newsweek*, 20 June 1966, 95–6.

91  Charles E. Davis Jr., 'Huntington Hartford Plans to Close Canyon Artists' Retreat', *Los Angeles Times*, 2 May 1965, B5.

92  Charles E. Davis Jr., 'Huntington Hartford's Artists' Retreat Sold', *Los Angeles Times*, 1 July 1965, A3.

93  'Three Misspent Lives: Huntington Hartford', *Esquire*, October 1968, 133.

94  Steve Fraser and Gary Gerstle, 'Introduction', in *Ruling America: A History of Wealth and Power in a Democracy* (Cambridge, MA: Harvard University Press, 2005), 1–2.

95  Huntington Hartford, interview by Paul Cummings, 19 May 1970, transcript, 9, Reference Department, Archives of American Art, Smithsonian Institution, Washington, DC.

96  Huntington Hartford, interview by Paul Cummings, 19 May 1970, transcript, 9, Reference Department, Archives of American Art, Smithsonian Institution, Washington, DC.

97  Jason Stahl, *Right Moves*: The Conservative Think Tank in American Political Culture Since 1945 (The University of North Carolina Press: Chapel Hill, 2016), 3.

98  See for example Kathleen Hall Jamieson and Joseph N. Cappella, *Rush Limbaugh and the Conservative Media Establishment* (New York: Oxford University Press, 2008), Nicole Hemmer, *Messengers of the Right: Conservative Media and the Transformation of American Politics* (Philadelphia: University of Pennsylvania Press, 2016), and Anthony M. Nadler and A. J. Bauer, eds, *News on the Right: Studying Conservative News Cultures* (New York: Oxford University Press, 2020).

99  See for instance David A. Smith, *Money for Art: The Tangled Web of Art and Politics in American Democracy* (Chicago: Ivan R. Dee, 2008).

100  For the two respective approaches see for example Dan T. Carter, *The Politics of Rage: George Wallace, the Origins of the New Conservatism, and the Transformation of American Politics* (New York: Simon & Schuster, 1995) and Kim Phillips-Fein, *Invisible Hands: The Businessmen's Crusade Against the New Deal* (New York: W. W. Norton, 2010).

# 6

# The Ford Foundation's cultural Cold War in Berlin

Amanda Niedfeldt

Suspended between east and west, Berlin repeatedly became the focal point of the Cold War. The Berlin Airlift in 1948–9, the building of the Wall in 1961, and its collapse in 1989, all marked important flashpoints of the conflict. The military manoeuvres were each quickly followed by soft power interventions and investments as the United States and the Soviet Union jostled for influence in the island city. The most discussed cultural intervention on the Western side of the conflict has been the birth of the Congress for Cultural Freedom (CCF) in Berlin in 1950. While the CCF had far-reaching implications for the course of the cultural Cold War, the struggle between the Soviet Union and the United States to win hearts and minds to their causes was but one of several soft power mediations into Berlin's cultural landscape during the 44-year conflict. The CCF's formation had a circuitous influence on the city, but it was the cultural development after the erection of the Wall that had a transformative and lasting impression on Berlin's cultural life. In 1962, in coordination with the US and German governments, the Ford Foundation supported Berlin in establishing three cultural centres, two of which—the DAAD Berlin Artists-in-Residence Programme and the Literary Colloquium Berlin—continue to thrive today.

Research on the Ford Foundation's Cold War activities has shown that while the Foundation worked in tangent with the US government and often pursued the same aims, it kept its distance from open coordination. As scholars such as Kathleen D. McCarthy and Anne Zetsche have shown, Ford worked closely with government agencies from the 1950s through the 1970s, in particular, to coordinate cultural activities and build the soft side of strategic alliances.[1] This working relationship has been best conceptualized as the state-private network, in which staff, primarily people in leadership positions, move between government agencies and foundation boardrooms with ease. Sharing similar backgrounds and values, they inherently work towards similar aims whether direct coordination occurs or not.[2] Yet, despite this, Ford's leadership understood their influence and success was only possible as long as it remained an independent body in the public eye. The Berlin programmes are one of the few times the Ford Foundation collaborated openly with the US government throughout the cultural Cold War. They are, therefore, a useful case study in examining how the state-private network functioned in action. The origin of the Berlin programmes evidences how internal competing priorities within the Foundation influenced outcomes and offers a concrete example of how ideas flowed seamlessly from private to public and back again. Ford's management of the grants' development and its active role in shaping publicity in the city shows how it navigated a strategic and careful public partnership with government entities intended to foster constructive relationships with the US and German governments while maintaining a public presence of independent goodwill.

Ford's cultural investments in Berlin also suggest a more complex reading of the Western cultural Cold War than currently exists. Scholars have clearly established how US government funding subsidized cultural activities in support of their cause. Up to this point, the literature has indicated that philanthropic foundations functioned as fronts or conduits for government expenditure or executors of government initiatives.[3] The Ford Foundation's cultural grants in Berlin challenge this notion. Ford did not act as a conduit of payments or purely accept government direction; rather, the Foundation, including its staff, principles and functions, shaped the investment in its own image, providing guidance to both US and German government officials towards amenable ends. In this way, the Ford Foundation was able to have a more lasting influence than the famed Central Intelligence Agency (CIA) interventions.

## Networked origins

In response to the clandestine Soviet assertion of the Berlin Wall on 13 August 1961, US president John F. Kennedy dispatched Vice President Lyndon B. Johnson and General Lucius D. Clay along with military reinforcements to show American support. Johnson soon returned to Washington, but Clay, a favourite of Berliners for his role in the 1948 Berlin Airlift, stayed on as a special adviser to the president, an emblem of American commitment to the city. The military reinforcements were to remain largely symbolic and governments on both sides of the Cold War were relieved that, despite the tank standoff in October 1961, an armed conflict was avoided. From this point on the division of Berlin was entrenched. The American response to the Wall was measured to boost Berlin's morale and establish that the United States was going to stay in the city, while also clearly demonstrating that they did not want military escalation.[4] With the status of the divided city clarified, its potential as a hot point of the Cold War waned, but the danger that West Berlin would slowly be engulfed by the German Democratic Republic increased. The West quickly got to work promoting investment and cultural activity to create a showcase of all that capitalist society had to offer.

General Clay became a leading advocate for the cultural and financial reinforcement of the city. On 28 May 1962, *The Wall Street Journal* reported that

the U.S. is taking a major hand in a broad campaign, just now developing, to build up West Berlin's resistance against slow erosion in coming years. The campaign begins with the efforts of West Berliners: it rests heavily on massive West

German aid. But it reaches increasingly into the upper echelons of the Kennedy Administration and into U.S. corporate board rooms as well.[5]

As part of the effort, Clay sent a number of letters to influential investors reaching beyond boardrooms and appealing directly to deep philanthropic pockets, particularly for cultural and academic funding. One of these letters went to John J. McCloy at the Ford Foundation. McCloy had served as the United States High Commissioner to Germany from 1949 to 1952 and became a Ford Foundation trustee in the late 1950s. He was supported at the Foundation by Shepard Stone, the director of the International Division with a focus on Europe. Stone had an extensive history with Germany and a hand in shaping its post-war future. He had completed his PhD in Weimar Germany, married a German, and, during the war, worked on intelligence while his wife worked in the Office of Strategic Services, the precursor to the CIA. After the war, he became the 'Chief of Intelligence' for American forces in Germany and was in charge of establishing a free German press, including radio stations and publishing houses. He later served under McCloy as the public affairs director in the High Commission of Germany before following him to Ford.[6] Clay, McCloy and Stone shared the same values and priorities regarding Germany's future and the United States' potential role. As Volker Berghahn and Zetsche have argued, it is clear to see how these men's government work in occupied Germany easily carried over to their efforts and shaping of Ford's funds as they transitioned to civilian life.[7]

Contrary to *The Wall Street Journal* article's claim, however, the cultural wing of the effort had not originated with Clay and was not directed by the US government. In this area of development, Clay served more as a conduit than a driver. In late 1961, Berlin mayor Willy Brandt had met with Stone, the secretary-general of the CCF Nicolas Nabokov, and the congress' CIA liaison Michael Josselson in the CCF's Paris headquarters where it was agreed, as Nabokov summarized, that 'West Berlin should now play an important cultural game to regain some of its lost cosmopolitan glamour'.[8] Nabokov envisioned West Berlin building on its strengths to offer cultural programmes that would attract people from across the world and particularly engage young people. His suggestions became the core principles upon which the programmes were built.

The proposal of cultural investments in West Berlin solved several people's problems. On a personal level, the programmes allowed Nabokov to gain distance from the CCF, of which he was tiring.[9] Politically, the initiatives promised concrete support for West Berlin, quelling both US and German concerns about flight from the city. A Berlin investment also helped assuage internal conflicts at the Ford Foundation. Stone was a committed advocate of the transatlantic cause and worked persistently to gain funding for the CCF and several other cultural projects focused on building transatlantic relations. When in 1958 Stone's International Affairs Division ran into a conflict with the Humanities and Arts Division regarding what types of cultural funding each should pursue, Stone vigorously emphasized that his division should allocate grants in the cultural realm when they are 'directed toward international relations objectives rather than towards the support of the arts for their own sake'.[10] In practice, this meant primarily supporting the exchange of people and the circulation of publications. Stone included an appendix to his letter specifically outlining the US government's activities in the international cultural field to argue that its role was limited and in need of supplementation. He believed that Ford had a powerful role to play by filling the government vacuum in international relations and foreign policy efforts. In his estimation, culture was simply the most pliable tool for the mission.

In the name of US interests, Stone worked closely with Josselson and had been lobbying within the Foundation to secure significant funding for the CCF for a number of years, including a full takeover of the CCF's funding so that the organization did not need to rely on CIA support. He encountered several roadblocks but ultimately made some headway. The main issue was the known fact within the Ford Foundation that the CIA subsidized the CCF. Ford drew a line in 1951 that it would not be a conduit for CIA money. As rumours circulated more fervently in the late 1950s that the CIA funded the CCF, Ford, under the leadership of Henry T. Heald, was increasingly reluctant to fund it, wishing to protect the organization from questionable collaboration with government agencies.[11] Yet, as scholarship on the Foundation's cultural Cold War activities has aptly shown, Ford's international cultural funding aligned closely with US foreign policy aims. McCarthy demonstrates that Ford worked in line with government agencies from the 1950s to the 1970s. Zetsche has specifically illustrated how the Ford Foundation and Stone in particular worked with the German and American governments to build a leadership network and reinforce transatlantic ties. The Ford Foundation may not have served as a conduit for the CIA, but it directed its own resources to support the same causes. Despite concerns Heald may have put forward to deter Stone, Ford granted over $6 million to the CCF during the 1950s and early 1960s, including a grant of $1 million in 1963, which was publicly announced along with part of the Berlin allocation in *The New York Times*.[12]

When the opportunity to pursue the West Berlin programmes arose, it therefore provided a solution for Heald and Stone by serving as a suitable direction for transatlantic investment from both of their perspectives. Stone sought support from several directions to strengthen his argument. Nabokov quickly became a key champion for the programmes and made his case separately to Ford. After the autumn 1961 meeting in Paris, he met with Ford administrator Joseph Slater in January 1962 to advocate for further investment in transatlantic efforts. Clay's letter to McCloy on 5 April 1962 was aptly timed to put more weight into Stone's and Nabokov's argument and urge the project along. Clay wrote to McCloy that his Viability Committee at the US Mission in West Berlin had filtered through the many suggestions for cultural projects that they had received and determined two projects he thought could be well supported by American foundations: a centre for advanced study in the arts and sciences and a centre for urban development.[13] Clay assured McCloy that the Berlin Senate was supportive of the proposals and he expected the exchange could begin for the academic year of 1962-3. These two suggestions were not taken on directly, but their essence was worked into the final programme formation. Clay's letter also underlined the strong political support on the German and US sides for the investment. The project was set in motion.

Over the course of 1962, the International Affairs Division, under Stone's guidance and at the direction of the Board of Trustees, worked to develop a major project proposal for direct investment in West Berlin. The division advised that after several discussions with Brandt and the US and German leadership in Bonn 'a public announcement shortly after the December Trustees meeting would be timely and helpful in the over-all context of the Berlin situation'.[14] The advice was to invest in three areas: American studies at the Free University, artistic exchange and residencies, and an urban studies centre. As a result of these investments, the proposal concluded, 'Berlin, though it may remain an island geographically, would become otherwise a more vigorous part of the mainland of Europe and the world.'[15] Ford appointed approximately $2,000,000 in 1963 to 'help strengthen educational, scientific and cultural institutions in Berlin' focused primarily on three cultural projects: the International Institute for Comparative Music Studies and Documentation, the Literary Colloquium Berlin and the Artists-in-Residence Programme with additional appropriations provided to the Free University, a pedagogical centre and a centre focused on development.[16]

The final grant allocation held the kernels of both Nabokov's and Clay's suggestions with foci on cultural and developmental projects but had strategic adjustments from the Ford Foundation's point of view. Through the consultation process the project had been localized in important ways. The Literary Colloquium was proposed and run by Walter Höllerer, an impresario of German literature with widespread connections both within Europe and the United States. The Artists-in-Residence programme was coordinated with the DAAD. The DAAD provided the administrative support on the ground and then took over the programme after two years. Importantly, the German government and Berlin Senate supported all of the efforts by supplying housing for guests and facilities for the institutes themselves.[17] With a high level of local commitment, the Ford Foundation could be assuaged that they would not get bogged down in years of funding, but act more as seed investors for the new initiatives. In addition, by 1962 the Foundation had already invested $5 million in Germany with about half of this spent in Berlin. The majority of this funding had gone to educational and cultural projects. For example, the Ford Foundation played a key role in the founding of the Free University of Berlin in 1948 when the University of Berlin, now known as Humboldt University of Berlin, was taken over by Soviet forces. The new cultural projects therefore could be seen as shoring up previous investments. Within the next decade, Ford would grant about $5 million more to Germany, most of which was spent in West Berlin. In the final recorded figures of Ford grants in Germany from 1951 to 1978, the Foundation had given $10,446,586 to projects within Germany, $6,166,248 of which was spent in Berlin.[18]

## Strategic distance

Clay had confidently assured McCloy that the Germans were supportive of a large cultural investment, which was true in principle, but there were concerns about who should lead the effort. On 22 September 1961, Brandt led a discussion in the Berlin Senate on the city's cultural future sharing his vision to re-establish West Berlin as a world-class cultural city. All political factions were behind the plans, but both Brandt's party, the Social Democratic Party (SPD), and the Christian Democratic Union

(CDU) emphasized that cultural institutions should inherently be independent and not influenced by the state, raising flags about national interference. In a targeted response, the CDU stated that institutions outside of Berlin should not have more influence over cultural developments in the city than Berliners have themselves, a concern that proved to be well founded. During the meeting, a number of cultural developments were proposed including an educational institute, increased professor and student exchanges, further buildings for the Technical University and a range of other institutions already in existence, including a radio studio for *Sender Freies Berlin*. The Senate eventually funded new construction projects and a version of the educational institute came to fruition via the Ford Foundation grant.[19] While the Senate was behind Brandt's plans, they were wary of who would make decisions about what should be funded and who should take part.

Even though the post-Wall cultural projects had been primarily Nabokov's idea, he proved to be a problematic leader. In late 1962, he stepped back from the CCF and began serving as Brandt's cultural adviser, where he hoped to play a leading role in the cultural initiatives.[20] The Ford Foundation's final allocation effectually cut him off from their funding. All of the key projects had local leaders or hired specialists to handle specific portions of the grant, none of whom was Nabokov. Instead, he took on a more political role acting as a liaison between Brandt, the Senate and the burgeoning cultural institutions. In charge of Berlin's festival weeks, Nabokov coordinated activities and events with the new centres and provided advice and connections to artists and intellectuals who might be suitable for the programmes, but he had no direct monetary or discretionary authority over the new centres' developments. That is not to say his advice and support, drawing on his wide cultural ties, particularly to the CCF, were not helpful or appreciated, but it was also wise of the Ford Foundation to keep him at a plausibly deniable arm's length.

Nabokov was in trusted communication with the Ford Foundation, but there were concerns about his involvement and its impact on Ford's reputation in Berlin more generally.[21] On 12 August 1963, as the programmes got off the ground, Frederick Burkhardt of the American Council of Learned Societies wrote to Shepard Stone to inform him of some conversations he had in Berlin about the progress of the cultural programmes. He reported that one key German official, Hans Wallenberg, was ready to leave the project because of his frustration in working with Nabokov. Burkhardt summarized: '[Wallenberg] is not interested in relations with people who think they know everything and want only admiration (obviously Nicholas).'[22] He further expressed concern that Wallenberg's feelings were shared more widely, reporting, 'Berliners want to know who does the selecting. They think Nicholas Nabokov does it. Brown mentioned, as especially critical, the Reidemeisters of the Dahlem Museum.'[23] Karl Haas, the Ford Foundation's representative in West Berlin, also wrote to Stone and Slater to complain that Nabokov overstepped his bounds and acted damagingly as a representative of the Ford Foundation. He warned:

> it is only natural that in the minds of many Berliners Nicolas is closely associated with the Ford Foundation. It has come to my attention only this weekend that he still speaks out in many circles for the Ford Foundation. I must tell you also

that Nicolas has made innumerable enemies in connection with his plans for the Festspiel-Wochen. Indeed, I believe firmly that, if he goes through with his plans, he will be made impossible in Berlin. This is no longer an undercurrent that I feel but there is open resentment. I mention all this in order to prepare you that somehow any resentment of Nicolas' with or without the Festwochen will reflect upon the Ford Foundation. It is, therefore, without any malice that I warn you that, unless Nicolas is told in clear terms that he is not to identify himself or speak or write to anyone for the Ford Foundation and that the Ford Foundation has only one official representative in Berlin, the seeds that we have sown here will reap ugly fruits. . . . I say, Nicolas is a genius but he is also the embodiment of what is called in the vernacular a big time operator. I know that he has been very helpful to you but we can no longer afford to let him throw his weight around in our name.[24]

While it is tempting to read Haas' warning as one of only personal concern with his own role as the Foundation's representative, he had a clear reason to be worried about Nabokov's involvement and the potential taint he could bring to the project. Nabokov was indeed, as Haas puts it, 'a big time operator', both in the fact that he loved the limelight and used the free-flowing cash of the time to plan elaborate events and also that he was deeply involved with the CCF, had connections to the CIA, and was now cultivating a relationship with the Soviets as he worked for the mayor of Berlin.

Members of the Berlin Senate also questioned his purpose and position in the city raising concerns about his control of the *Festwochen* and influence generally on cultural activities in Berlin. On 3 December 1964, representatives of both the Free Democratic Party (FDP) and the CDU were critical of Nabokov's role. The FDP senator Lischewski thought that Nabokov's influence was too great and that he isolated and ignored the relevant committees, creating suspicion. He further questioned Nabokov's role in the city generally and requested answers about exactly what Nabokov was charged with doing. Either Nabokov should run the festival, Lischewski argued, or he should carry out his official title of International Cultural Relations Advisor, not both and not more than this. The CDU senator Lorenz reminded the Senate that while Berlin is a city open to the world, it also had much to share with the world and Berliners should be more involved and further featured in the festivals than they so far had been under Nabokov. Senator Werner Stein from the SPD defended Nabokov replying that

Without [Nabokov's] wide-reaching international connections, which reach to the best human relationships and the most famous artists of our time, critical parts of the last festival and future festivals would not be realized. . . . Professor Nabokov was and remains the cultural adviser to the Senate. In this role – and about this it must be remembered – after the building of the Wall he, as we ourselves intensively contemplated what we must, should and can do in Berlin, created the famous Ford Foundation program, which was indeed crucial.[25]

There was clear concern about Nabokov's dominant role and uncompromising stances both within the Senate and within the Ford Foundation.

The lack of German involvement in Nabokov's plans was part of the worry, but more concerning were his efforts to build ties with the Soviets, purportedly to arrange for Soviet participation in future festivals. Josselson, the CIA agent imbedded in the CCF, concurred. He was not happy about Nabokov's involvement in Berlin. Nabokov seemed to spend CCF money there, but was becoming more distant in his work with the congress and simultaneously openly courting the Soviet ambassador Pyotr Andreyetvitch Abrassimov. Josselson wrote to warn Nabokov on 29 June 1964 to deter him from travelling to Moscow with Abrassimov:

> Also, please bear in mind that you have many enemies in Berlin who are only waiting for an opportunity to knife you, and in your own interest, you would do well to cut the ground from under these people and their malicious gossip. . . . You could become an unwitting instrument of Soviet policy in Germany. . . . You [have] already made a first step on that direction.[26]

Josselson's warning echoes Haas's statement and the Senate's concern. While Nabokov had Brandt's backing to try to expand cultural relations and he did have some success, having the Leningrad Philharmonic participate in the 1964 festival, the Ford Foundation, the Berlin Senate, and the CIA were on the same page in their condemnation of his behaviour and the potential damage he was causing to the programme and the American presence in Berlin.

## Winning over Berlin

While political battles played out in the background, the Ford Foundation knew it needed to win over the West Berlin and German public in order to ensure their investments would succeed. The main concerns were the selection of the participants and their integration and benefit to West Berlin institutions and the general public. On a trip to assess the progress and needs of the developing project in April 1963, J. E. Slater reported back to Ford headquarters that the project is going well and the aims are correct but cautioned that several delicate balances must be found in order for the project to be a lasting success. He advised that they need to get the support of existing institutions and make sure the participants are well-integrated into Berlin 'to ensure that Ford program will have long-term results by being picked up and supported by permanent institutions.'[27] This was no short order, but is usual of Ford's international projects, particularly in this period. The Foundation did not want to take part in efforts that would require long-term funding but rather desired to provide seed money and hand the institutions off to local officials. The Berlin project succeeded in this by working hand-in-hand with officials in Berlin and coordinating the programmes with the DAAD. Slater was simultaneously aware that the city and larger German cultural community needed to accept the new initiatives as well. He said the programmes should strive to create a balance of participants to include prominent Berliners and international guests along with a mix of traditional and new artists. Importantly they also needed to strive to 'make the results of Ford programs abailable [*sic*] to more than the "elite", "the social set", and "those who can pay". Important to get students and others from entire city involved wherever possible'.[28] While the Foundation was aiming to create renowned institutions that would attract distinguished artists, they also needed to have variety and make the programmes accessible and attractive to the wider public of Berlin.

Since the programme was prepared in just a matter of months, the initial selections were haphazard and impromptu. The first Ford liaison, Moritz von Bomhard, took suggestions from Berliners and then consulted widely to make sure a suggested person was broadly agreeable before sending an invitation.[29] In 1963, the Ford Foundation sent Haas as an official representative to Berlin to assist with the project. Under Haas, the selection process continued to be a consultative process, but was formalized. Ford administrator F. F. Hill wrote specifically in the initial grant request from the appropriated funding on 17 May 1963 that 'A distinguished group of cultural leaders, the heads of the major Berlin educational and scientific institutions, and the DAAD working closely with the [International Affairs] staff would make the selections'.[30] There was some effort at cooperation between the various interested parties with the creation of the Berlin Advisory Council. The council included the Senator for Science and Art, the Senator for Education, the rectors of the Free University and the Technical University, the president of the art academy, the directors of the *Hochschulen*, the director of the Dahlem Museum, the German Opera, the Berlin Symphony and the Schiller Theatre, along with Nabokov.[31] Haas maintained a relationship with Nabokov, people from the Senate and also key Berlin figures on the council.[32]

Despite the Berlin Advisory Council, after a few months in West Berlin, Haas drew a similar conclusion to Slater and emphasized that the artists chosen had to grasp the imagination and support of wider Berlin. He made it clear that in the future Ford should have the ultimate say over the artists chosen with advice from the Berlin Committee and through a clear process to avoid willy-nilly invitations from Berlin senator Adolf Arndt and Nabokov.[33] In a letter dated 29 October 1963, as the programme prepared to hosts its second round of artists, Haas lamented the quality of the initial participants and stated,

It is my conviction . . . that famous leaders in the various disciplines are needed for the program to make a lasting impression. . . . The composition of the program as it stands now has given rise to criticism that it is too esoteric for the Berlin population to fathom; and hence, to make an impression desirable and commensurate with the intention of the grant.[34]

Stone agreed with Haas. Nabokov had a rather different opinion:

*Of course*, we would all have loved to have Braque, Picasso, Chagall, Stravinsky (and perhaps even J.S. Bach and Beethoven and Shakespeare) come to Berlin. But famous old artists do not *move* easily and readily . . . was not one of the main ideas to bring to Berlin not necessarily 'famous' old men, but fresh blood, fresh talent, young people and ideas.[35]

Among the artists first hosted in 1963 were Ingeborg Bachmann, Witold Gombrowicz, Piers Paul Read, Iannis Xenakis and Frederic Benrath. Looking at the artists for 1964–5 it appears Haas and Ford found the following artists more suitable for the Berlin public: W.H. Auden, Igor Stravinsky, Alberto Ginastera, Eric Bentley, Elazar Koppel Benyoetz, Michel Butor, Ruth Francken, Hans Werner Henze and Isang Yun.

In addition to desiring a shift in the choice of artists, in the autumn of 1963, Haas expressed a need to Stone to generate more publicity and interaction between the artists and the Berlin public, a request with which Stone could assist. Stone had ties to the German press, including a close relationship with Countess Marion Dönhoff, the influential editor of *Die Zeit*, and other press contacts from his time serving in the occupation forces in charge of building up Germany's democratic press.[36] When the programmes were in need of positive reports, as Haas suggested, Stone came to the city for a visit. Haas and Höllerer arranged key events for him to attend in order to facilitate a few useful conversations.[37] After a press club dinner, held in early November 1963, Haas reported several requests for interviews to inform the public about the programmes.[38] On 21 November 1963, he wrote again to Slater and Stone, 'My efforts with the press right now I believe are bearing fruits too. I am enclosing the article of "der Tagesspiegel", first of a series of articles in various Berlin papers to show what is really being done.'[39] Haas was also keen to have Stone involved in the Press Ball in January 1964.[40] By February 1964, there was so much press, or as Haas wrote, the press was 'now cooperating fully', producing several articles, that he had to employ a clipping service to keep on top of it. Even U.S magazines such as *Time* and *Life* were sending reporters over to cover it.[41] Peter Nestler, the German administrator put in charge of the program for the DAAD, later commented that this sudden press attention was actually a mistake by Ford. It was, he said,

> a regrettable and fatal error on the part of the Ford administration in Berlin to attack the press for its supposed deficient reporting of until then nonexistent activities, and this at a specially convened press conference. Thereupon the daily press sought out most of the artists who had arrived but were not yet 'at home'. The problems the artists, still struggling with their environment, revealed in these interviews received distorted publicity.[42]

Where Haas and Stone might have seen their influence with the press as a way to raise the profile of Ford's work, Nestler viewed it as an invitation for aggressive scolding, which created more harm than good by shining light prematurely on the developing projects, disproportionately, in his view, focusing on the negative aspects of the programmes.

The Ford Foundation was able to oil the wheels of the press, but the integration of the artists into Berlin's cultural life proved trickier. In a letter from November 1963, Haas reported he had dinner with Berlin senator Blacher and Nabokov. He felt Blacher was 'depressing and devestating [*sic*] in his negative attitude toward anything we do', but nevertheless the talk pointed up certain doubts. Perhaps [Blacher] is not alone in thinking that we are too generous in Berlin and therefore subject to ridicule. Were certainly out to re-appraise our stand here and I believe that the firm guidance of the Artists in Residence program upon which we agreed when you were here, Shep, will do a lot toward giving us proper perspective in the eyes of Berliners.[43]

He further said that getting the Berliners to get involved and befriend the incoming artists 'is harder to move than molasses in January'.[44] An article from *Die Zeit* also reported that it was difficult to integrate the artists and Berliners because of several factors, but primarily the haste with which the programme was planned and the failure to manage expectations: the visiting artists expected a warm welcome and the Berliners were disgruntled because they themselves were not supported by the funding.[45]

Haas's efforts to better manage the expectations of the artists did see, in his estimation, an improvement in the impact of the residencies for 1964 and 1965. Yet the underlying factor remained that during Ford's years of oversight money was given to artists with no guidelines or expectations, bringing artists to Berlin, but for no other purpose than to be present. Integration relied on the goodwill of actors on both sides, which did not always align with the funders' aims. As Haas wrote to the Foundation in February 1964,

I find that it is a mistake to invite artists under conditions unequal anywhere without asking of them the slightest obligation. While it is true that they should be free to create and function anyway they see fit, the resulting tendency in many instances has been to accept the money, live free of any cares for a year, add the invitation by the Ford Foundation as an attractive item of their curriculum vitae and get out.[46]

Haas also found that the stipends were too high, leading to wasted money and further bad stereotypes of Americans just throwing cash around. Some of the artists, he claimed, had never seen so much money and would go on living off their funding for years.

## Conclusion

On 2 October 1964, as the Ford Foundation prepared to hand the cultural programmes officially over to their German counterparts, *Die Zeit* published an article giving the Foundation's grants a positive recount:

It started with General Clay, the personal representative of President Kennedy for problems on Berlin, who described in a private conversation to some gentlemen of the Ford Foundation the situation of Berlin after the erection of the Wall. It was the situation of a divided city which was being deserted by many like a sinking ship. . . . The mighty Ford Foundation, the largest philanthropical organization of the world, picked up this idea and decided to help stop the city from going provincial . . . institutes were founded, a travel program started, scholarships given to promising foreign students and the spectacular artists-in-residence program planned.[47]

Even as Ford was preparing to depart from Berlin, and despite interventions by Nabokov's strong presence, the public narrative centred on the fact that the US government invited the Ford Foundation to support Berlin, implying that the Foundation benignly and good-heartedly obliged, swooping in to quickly solve the city's problems with their expertise. In *Die Zeit*'s version, Ford appears as a gallant hero serving the greater good. This was surely a picture Ford was happy to propagate in the popular imagination. Yet, the evidence is clear that the idea for the programmes actually originated with Ford officials and their covert associates. On the ground, the Foundation carefully managed their official associations, limiting their public relationship with Nabokov while courting German officials and institutions. They were sure to garner positive publicity and remain perceived as passive helpers of a righteous cause, which was possible as a result of their many governmental and institutional connections.

The Ford Foundation's funding of Berlin's cultural programmes in the face of the Wall was not a new direction of investment, but merely a logical extension of efforts already ongoing. In West Berlin, all sides shared the same immediate aims: anchor West Berlin into West Germany and strengthen transatlantic ties. The programmes undoubtedly grew organically from shared interests, but the government-led initiative presented to the public was actually a reversal of the events that had unravelled. Ford coordinated with the governments on their joint aims and public relations needs, blurring their agency in the process. Appearing as an organization of expert assistance, they also played the role on the ground taking control of the programmes. Following their preferred funding model, they appointed their own personnel and identified appropriate local partners for their goals, sidestepping government and compromised figures. The balance of these relationships shows a careful calculation on Ford's part in how they publicly engaged with different entities, strategically cooperating to reach their aims. Finally, Ford's Berlin programmes also suggest it is pertinent to probe the role of Foundations in the cultural Cold War further. The Western side of the cultural Cold War has often been talked about as a government-led initiative with foundations playing the middleman. Ford's agency in Berlin suggests that a rethinking of the role foundations played in the cultural Cold War is needed. The American Foundations and US government certainly held mutual views on the direction of American foreign policy, ideas and personnel moved between them fluidly, but how they functioned differed, resulting in diverse outcomes.

# Notes

1   All uses of Ford in this chapter refer to the Ford Foundation and not the Ford Motor Company.
2   Dwight MacDonald identified early the Ford Foundation's interest in particular to build relationships between the United States and other countries in *The Ford*

*Foundation: The Men and the Millions* (New York: Reynal and Company, 1956). For more information on Ford's cultural work during the Cold War see Anne Zetsche, 'The Ford Foundation's Role in Promoting German-American Elite Networking During the Cold War', *Journal of Transatlantic Studies* 13, no. 1 (2015): 76–95; Kathleen D. McCarthy, 'From Cold War to Cultural Development: The International Cultural Activities of the Ford Foundation, 1950–1980' *Daedalus* 116, no. 1. Philanthropy, Patronage, Politics (Winter, 1987): 93–117. For more on Ford's relationship to the US government see Edward H. Berman, *The Influence of the Carnegie, Ford, and Rockefeller Foundations on American Foreign Policy: The Ideology of Philanthropy* (Albany: State University of New York Press, 1983) and Inderjeet Parmar, *Foundations of the American Century: The Ford, Carnegie, & Rockefeller Foundations in the Rise of American Power* (New York: Columbia University Press, 2014). Berman and Parmar establish the close working relationship of the major American philanthropic foundations with the US government within foreign policy and the United States' relations with the world. Robert F. Arnove et al., *Philanthropy and Cultural Imperialism: The Foundations at Home and Abroad* (Bloomington: Indiana University Press, 1982) richly establish the foundations' wide reach in shaping not just foreign policy, but also educational and social policy within the United States and beyond its borders. For more on the state-private network see Scott Lucas, *Freedom's War: The American Crusade Against the Soviet Union* (New York: New York University Press, 1999) and Helen Laville and Hugh Wilford, eds, *The US Government, Citizen Groups and the Cold War: The State-Private Network* (New York: Routledge, 2006) especially Inderjeet Parmar's chapter, 'Conceptualising the State-Private Network in American Foreign Policy', 13–27.

3  There are several excellent studies on the US-led cultural Cold War including Pierre Grémion, *Intelligence de L'Anticommunisme: Le Congrès pour la liberté de la culture à Paris, 1950–1975* (Paris: Fayard, 1995); Michael Hochgeschwender, *Freiheit in der Offensive? Der Kongreß für kulturelle Freiheit und die Deutschen* (Munich: De Gruyter Oldenbourg, 1998); Frances Stonor Saunders, *Who Paid the Piper? The CIA and the Cultural Cold War* (London: Granta Books, 1999); Lucas, *Freedom's War*; Volker R. Berghahn, *America and the Intellectual Cold Wars in Europe* (Princeton: Princeton University Press, 2001); Giles Scott-Smith, *The Politics of Apolitical Culture: The Congress for Cultural Freedom, the CIA and Post-War American Hegemony* (New York: Routledge, 2002); Laville and Wilford, *The US Government, Citizen Groups and the Cold War*; Hugh Wilford, *The Mighty Wurlitzer: How the CIA Played America* (Cambridge, MA: Harvard University Press, 2008); Greg Barnhisel, *Cold War Modernists: Art, Literature, and American Cultural Diplomacy* (New York: Columbia University Press, 2015). All of these studies acknowledge the presence and even essential role of American philanthropy in pursuing the cultural Cold War, but no one has yet addressed the agency and influential role philanthropic organizations played in the United States' pursuit of artistic and cultural supremacy over the Soviet Union.

4  Frederick Kempe, *Berlin 1961: Kennedy, Khrushchev, and the Most Dangerous Place on Earth* (London: Penguin, 2011), particularly chapters ten and eleven, and David and Deane Heller, *The Berlin Wall* (New York: Walker, 1962).

5  Philip Geyelin, 'Bolstering Berlin: U.S. Big Firms Aid Efforts to Resist Long Period of Red Pressure', *The Wall Street Journal*, 8 May 1962, 1.

6  For more on Stone's experience and ties to Germany see Berghahn, *America and the Intellectual Cold Wars in Europe*.

7   See Berman, *The Influence of the Carnegie, Ford, and Rockefeller Foundations on American Foreign Policy* and Parmar, *Foundations of the American Century* for further analysis.

8   Quoted in Vincent Giroud, *Nicolas Nabokov: A Life in Freedom and Music* (Oxford: Oxford University Press, 2015), 341.

9   Ibid.

10  'International Cultural Activities'. Shepard Stone to D. K. Price. 24 January 1958. Ford Foundation Int. Affairs. FA748. Series I: Admin Papers. Box 3. Folder Programs Cultural Affairs 1957–1962 (2 of 2). Ford Foundation, Rockefeller Archive Center, Sleepy Hollow, NY. Further abbreviated as FF-RAC.

11  Berghahn (1983), especially 220–33. This policy changed when McGeorge Bundy took over as president of the Foundation in 1966. Ford fully funded the CCF as it became the International Association for Cultural Freedom in 1967 under the leadership of Shepard Stone. For more on this transition and the demise of the CCF see Saunders, *Who Paid the Piper?*, Berghahn, *America and the Intellectual Cold Wars in Europe*, and Scott-Smith, *The Politics of Apolitical Culture*.

12  *The New York Times* reported on 10 January 1963 that along with the Berlin allocation, the Ford Foundation gave $1,000,000 to the CCF for activities in Paris. Fred M. Hechinger, 'Ford Foundation Aids West Berlin' *The New York Times*, 10 January 1963, 5. For more on Ford's funding of the CCF, see McCarthy, 'From Cold War to Cultural Development'; Saunders, *Who Paid the Piper?*; Scott-Smith, *The Politics of Apolitical Culture*; Berghahn, *America and the Intellectual Cold Wars in Europe*; Zetsche, 'The Ford Foundation's Role in Promoting German-American Elite Networking During the Cold War'.

13  Clay, Lucius D. Letter to John J. McCloy. 5 April 1962. Ford Foundation History Project Files – Regional. Europe-Correspondence, Board of Trustees Mtg Program Docket (1958), Article Re: Artists-In-Residence & Free University of Berlin Foundation Programs. Box 61. Folder 10, 1. FF-RAC.

14  'Strengthening of Institutions in Berlin'. Ford Foundation Int. Affairs. FA748. Series V: Exchanges. Box 7. Folder: Exchanges 1963–1965 Berlin Artists in Residence – General. FF-RAC.

15  'Strengthening of Institutions in Berlin'. Ford Foundation Int. Affairs. FA748. Series V: Exchanges. Box 7. Folder: Exchanges 1963–1965 Berlin Artists in Residence – General. FF-RAC.

16  Stone, Shepard to Dr J. A. Stratton. 8 December 1965. RE: IA Programs in Berlin. International Affairs – Grants 1951–1978. Grants Involving France and Germany. Ford Foundation Int. Affairs, FA 748, Series III:Grants, Box 4. FF-RAC.

17  First Meeting of the Advisory Group for the Ford Foundation's Program in Berlin. 7 June 1963. Ford Foundation Int. Affairs. FA748. Series V: Exchanges. Box 7. Folder: Exchanges 1963–1965 Berlin Artists in Residence – General. FF-RAC.

18  All investment figures are taken from Summary of FF Grants and DAPs re Germany 1951-March 1978. Folder International Affairs – Grants – 1951–1978 – Grants Involving France and Germany, Box 4, Series III: Grants, FA748, International Affairs, FF-RAC.

19  See *Stenographischer Bericht* Issue 1961, III, *Wahlperiode*, Band III, 52.-80. Sitzung Nr. 19 (70), 22 September 1961. https://digital.zlb.de/viewer/toc/15975510/1/

20  Berghahn, *America and the Intellectual Cold Wars in Europe*, 234; Giroud, *Nicolas Nabokov*, 341–3.

21  Slater, J. E. to Shepard Stone Berlin Program – Additional projects and FF Berlin Appropriation. 25 April 1963. Ford Foundation International Affairs. FA748. Series V:

Exchanges. Box 7. Folder Exchanges 1963–1965 Berlin Artists in Residence – General. FF-RAC.

22 Burkhardt, Frederick to Shepard Stone. 12 August 1963. Ford Foundation Unpublished Records. FA739. Box 75. Folder 001945. FF-RAC.

23 Burkhardt, Frederick to Shepard Stone. 12 August 1963. Ford Foundation Unpublished Records. FA739. Box 75. Folder 001945. FF-RAC.

24 Haas, Karl to Shepard Stone and Joseph Slater. 18 November 1963. Ford Foundation International Affairs. FA748. Series V: Exchanges. Box 7. Folder Exchanges 1963–1965 Berlin Artists in Residence – Karl Haas. FF-RAC.

25 Translation my own. See *Stenographischer Bericht* Issue 1964, IV, *Wahlperiode*, Band II, 24.-44. Sitzung Nr. 19 (42), 3 December 1964. https://digital.zlb.de/viewer/toc /15975510/1/

26 Saunders, *Who Paid the Piper?*.

27 Slater J. E. to Shepard Stone. Berlin Program-General Observations. 25 April 1963. Ford Foundation Int. Affairs. FA748. Series V: Exchanges. Box 7. Folder: Exchanges 1963–1965 Berlin Artists in Residence – General. FF-RAC.

28 Slater J. E. to Shepard Stone. Berlin Program-General Observations. 25 April 1963. Ford Foundation Int. Affairs. FA748. Series V: Exchanges. Box 7. Folder: Exchanges 1963–1965 Berlin Artists in Residence – General. FF-RAC.

29 Von Bomhard, Moritz to Joseph Slater. 1 August 1963. Ford Foundation International Affairs, Program Action No. 63 -351. Berlin Artists-in-Residence Program. FF-RAC.

30 Hill, F. F. to Henry T. Heald. Grant Request – International Affairs, 17 May 1963, 3. Ford Foundation International Affairs, Program Action No. 63 -351A. Berlin Artists-in-Residence Program, FF-RAC.

31 Unsigned report, 1963, 6. Ford Foundation International Affairs, Program Action No. 63 -351. Berlin Artists-in-Residence Program, FF-RAC.

32 Haas, Karl to Shepard Stone. 21 November 1963, 2. Ford Foundation International Affairs, Program Action No. 63 -351. Berlin Artists-in-Residence Program, FF-RAC.

33 Haas, Karl to Joseph Slater. 7 November 1963. Ford Foundation International Affairs, Program Action No. 63 -351. Berlin Artists-in-Residence Program, FF. And Haas, Karl to Hubertus Scheibe. 21 November 1963. Ford Foundation International Affairs, Program Action No. 63 -351. Berlin Artists-in-Residence Program, FF-RAC.

34 Haas, Karl to Shepard Stone and Joseph Slater. 29 October 1963. Ford Foundation International Affairs. FA748. Series V: Exchanges. Box 7. Folder Exchanges 1963–1965 Berlin Artists in Residence – Karl Haas. FF-RAC.

35 Quoted in Giroud, *Nicolas Nabokov*, 344, italics in the original.

36 Berghahn, *America and the Intellectual Cold Wars in Europe*; Zetsche, 'The Ford Foundation's Role in Promoting German-American Elite Networking During the Cold War'.

37 Höllerer, Walter to Shepard Stone. 3 November 1963. 03WH/BM/4, 35, Literary Archive Sulzbach Rosenberg, Germany (LASR).

38 Haas, Karl to Shepard Stone. 18 November 1963. Ford Foundation International Affairs, Program Action No. 63 -351. Berlin Artists-in-Residence Program, FF-RAC.

39 Haas, Karl to Shepard Stone and Joseph Slater. 21 November 1963. Ford Foundation International Affairs. FA748. Series V: Exchanges. Box 7. Folder Exchanges 1963–1965 Berlin Artists in Residence – Karl Haas. FF-RAC.

40 Haas, Karl to Walter Höllerer. 7 January 1964. H521.2186, LASR.

41 Haas, Karl Shepard Stone and Joseph Slater. 3 February 1964, 2. Ford Foundation International Affairs, Program Action No. 63 -351. Berlin Artists-in-Residence Program, FF-RAC.

42 Nestler, Peter. The Berlin Cultural Program 'Artists in Residence' 1963–1966, 8. 1970. Ford Foundation International Affairs, Program Action No. 63 -351. Berlin Artists-in-Residence Program, FF-RAC.

43 Haas, Karl to Shepard Stone and Joseph Slater. 21 November 1963. Ford Foundation International Affairs. FA748. Series V: Exchanges. Box 7. Folder Exchanges 1963–1965 Berlin Artists in Residence – Karl Haas. FF-RAC.

44 Haas, Karl to Shepard Stone and Joseph Slater. 18 November 1963. Ford Foundation International Affairs. FA748. Series V: Exchanges. Box 7. Folder Exchanges 1963–1965 Berlin Artists in Residence – Karl Haas. FF-RAC.

45 'Half-Time at the Ford Foundation: Why Many of the Invited Artists are not Content in Berlin' by Cornelia Jacobsen. *Die Zeit*. 2 October 1964. Ford Foundation: Francis X. Sutton International Division. FA 568. VI-History Project Regional Files. Box 61. Folder 10. FF-RAC.

46 Haas, Karl. General Report. 3 February 1964, 5. Ford Foundation International Affairs, Program Action No. 63 -351. Berlin Artists-in-Residence Program, FF-RAC.

47 'Half-Time at the Ford Foundation: Why Many of the Invited Artists are not Content in Berlin' by Cornelia Jacobsen. *Die Zeit*. 2 October 1964. Ford Foundation: Francis X. Sutton International Division. FA 568. VI-History Project Regional Files. Box 61. Folder 10. FF-RAC.

# Diplomacy and international development

# 7

# Women's educational philanthropy and civil-society diplomacy

## Opposing US legislation prohibiting Japanese immigration while fundraising for a Tokyo women's college, 1900–29

Linda L. Johnson

The 7.9 magnitude Great Kantō Earthquake of 1923 and ensuing fires, which damaged or destroyed three-quarters of the buildings in Tokyo and killed more than 100,000 people, demolished the campus of Joshi Eigaku Juku (JEJ, Women's Institute of English Studies), the Tokyo academy founded by Tsuda Umeko (1864–1929) and supported by US philanthropy for the preceding twenty-three years. American fundraisers then waged a successful six-year campaign to rebuild JEJ, raising the question: during the interwar years, while US-Japanese relations became increasingly acrimonious, particularly over immigration, why did Americans contribute to the rebuilding of a Tokyo women's school, and what were the implications for US-Japanese relations? Historian J. Charles Schencking characterizes the US disaster-relief effort in Japan as a 'unique humanitarian engagement', arguing that the government viewed the unprecedented outpouring of supplies and cash to Japan as a 'panacea to resolve political tensions that had developed between the two countries'.[1] While Schencking focuses on government-mediated aid to Japan, this study analyses US women's educational philanthropy as a gender-specific, civil-society (non-governmental) diplomacy strategy, analysing the backstory of a successful non-governmental, disaster-relief programme. The first three decades of JEJ fundraising illustrate the trajectory identified by educational philanthropy scholar Andrea Walton, from the voluntary giving of time and money because of religious, benevolent and humanitarian ideals, to the organizational innovation brought about by professional fundraising and foundations.[2] Drawing financial support from women's transpacific higher-education associations, progressive political groups, Protestant reform organizations and Japanese-American groups, this study contextualizes historian Ian Tyrrell's analysis of networks of benevolent associations and moral reform organizations, which he describes as having overlapping strategies, tactics and ideologies.[3] Fundraising to establish JEJ, Tsuda mobilized turn-of-the-twentieth-century philanthropists' assumptions that it was their duty to 'uplift' 'darker races' to 'civilization', demonstrating historian Gail Bederman's observation that 'civilization' ideology was protean and contradictory, making it possible to legitimate different claims for power.[4] Contextualizing historian Rotem Kowner's observation that 'Japanese called into question some of the most fundamental racial conventions of the time', Tsuda and her students confounded racial hierarchies, contesting the justification for 1924 legislation prohibiting immigration from Japan.[5] A new era in JEJ fundraising began, when, capitalizing on JEJ's reputation to appeal to Christian donors and represent moderation, fundraisers used the campus rebuilding campaign as a pretext to oppose Japanese exclusion. This study shows that women's international philanthropic fundraising merits consideration as a 'new profession', an 'alternative setting', in which women engaged in international thought and activism in the early twentieth century.[6]

## Tsuda Umeko and the establishment of Joshi Eigaku Juku

In 1871, the Japanese government, promoting *bunmei kaika* (civilization and enlightenment) with an aggressive modernization programme, commissioned Tsuda Umeko to live for ten years with an American family and attend US girls' schools. The arrival of 'the oriental waif' was reported in US newspapers, creating a heroic narrative portraying Tsuda as an 'uplift' luminary.[7] Upon her return to Japan, Foreign Minister Inoue Kaoru recruited Tsuda as a translator and cultural interpreter for his initiative to safeguard Japan's sovereignty by demonstrating that Japan was rapidly becoming 'civilized', meriting parity with Western nations. Because women's status was viewed as a 'civilization' marker, Tsuda taught Japanese dignitaries' wives conversational English and Western social practices.[8] At Western-style receptions hosting foreign dignitaries, Tsuda engaged in the 'affective labor', (essential to both diplomacy and philanthropic fundraising), which required 'emotional resources and communication skills' to promote 'a feeling of ease, well-being, satisfaction'.[9] Appointed head of the English Department at Kazoku Jogakko (Peeresses' School), for which the Empress served as patron, Tsuda became Japan's leading woman, English-language educator.

By 1888, needing an American, post-secondary credential to retain her professional preeminence, Tsuda sought assistance from philanthropist Mary Harris Morris. Morris worked with Philadelphia Quaker 'uplift' charities including Orphans' Asylum, Women's Christian Temperance Union, Howard Home (for women discharged from prison) and Carlisle Indian School. In 1882, Morris established the Women's Foreign Missionary Association, whose 1884 statement, 'Why Should Friends Engage in Foreign Mission Work?' employed the 'rescue' rhetoric of Women's Work for Women (WWfW), with which missionaries spoke of 'uplifting' Asian women by liberating them from male oppression and educating them in Christian colleges.[10]

> The condition of oriental women is degraded. They are denied all education and personal liberty and are literally groaning under the iron heel of man's despotism. For the amelioration of this bondage, every intelligent woman must ardently long

[and realizing] the elevation of woman to be the result of Christian teaching, cannot resist making some effort for the benefit of downtrodden sisters.[11]

Morris arranged for Tsuda to attend Bryn Mawr College on scholarship and in 1889, Tsuda joined the Japanese students whom Morris invited home for dinner and Bible studies, including women who became Japan's first professionals in medicine, social welfare and higher education.

While in the United States, Tsuda began fundraising for Japanese women's education, developing themes that characterized her discourse for the following three decades. She drew on multiple rhetorical strategies from the overlapping, but at times, contradictory, discourses of WWfW and US racial 'uplift'. In 1891, Tsuda and Morris established the American Women's Scholarship for Japanese Women (AWSJW) to educate Japanese women in US colleges. With the goal of an $8,000-endowment, Morris arranged for Tsuda to give 'parlor talks' in the homes of affluent Philadelphians. Appealing to audiences accustomed to missionaries' rhetoric, Tsuda expressed admiration for women's social position in the US, affirmed the growth of Christianity in Japan and asserted that women must achieve parity with men's progress in Japan. The need was 'to educate the Japanese girls according to American methods, to teach them by example and precept the benefit of a Christian civilization'.[12] Tsuda also collaborated with an accomplished US racial 'uplift' rhetorician, Alice Mabel Bacon, with whom she had taught at Kazoku Jogakko in 1882. Bacon, a white woman, taught political economy at the fountainhead of racial 'uplift' schools, Virginia's Hampton Institute and edited their outreach publication, the *Southern Workman*.[13] Teaching the daughters of Japanese nobility had challenged Bacon's assumptions, '"civilization" is so difficult to define and understand that I do not know what it means now as well as I did when I left home'.[14] A native informant for Bacon's book, *Japanese Girls and Women* (*JGW*), Tsuda repeated similar themes in her fundraising speech, 'The Education of Japanese Women'.[15] Tsuda advocated Christian education to develop Japanese women's character, while teaching skills necessary for their financial independence.[16] In contrast to WWfW rhetoric that characterized 'oriental' women as downtrodden victims of male oppression, Tsuda and Bacon highlighted Japanese women's recent social progress, Bacon declaring that while women were becoming educated and undertaking new responsibilities, 'the old politeness and sweetness of manner must not be given up or made little of'.[17] Maintaining traditional standards of upper-class femininity enabled educated women to 'resource respectable subjectivity', appearing less threatening to both race and gender hierarchies.[18] Analogous to racial 'uplift' ideology that identified African American, middle-class professionals as paragons of achievement for their race, Bacon identified samurai women, like Tsuda, as the agents of progress in modernizing Japan.[19] Representing educated, middle-class women as the vanguard of social progress also appealed to Tsuda's Bryn Mawr colleagues, some of whom, served on the AWSJW committee.[20] Tsuda published articles about Japanese women in Christian-mission publications, where the ASWJW was publicized and it was claimed, the recipients would return to Japan to 'form a center for the diffusion of liberal American thought and Christian influence' – the sine qua non of an 'uplift' education.[21]

AWSJW fundraising easily dovetailed with Tsuda's diplomatic initiatives to promote a positive view of Japan. Tsuda was adept at interpreting Japanese militarism in ways

American women might respect, attributing Japan's victories, for example, not to strategy or weaponry, rather, to the wives and mothers who demonstrated 'uplift' virtues of 'self-control and fortitude'.[22] In 1898, Prime Minister Ōkuma Shigenobu invited Tsuda to offer greetings from Japan at the international convention of the General Federation of Women's Clubs in Denver, Colorado, in which 2,700 women's clubs, with 160,000 members were represented. As diplomatic courtesy required, Tsuda expressed Japanese women's gratitude to American women, whose work, she said, had made Japanese women's rapid progress possible. Japanese women were now prepared, Tsuda declared, to 'lend a helping hand and set a bright example to the women of the other lands in the Orient'.[23] The *Denver Republican* reported that Tsuda 'delivered one of the best five-minute speeches, best in composition, delivery, grace, and voice'.[24] Receiving invitations from contacts made in Denver, Tsuda toured British women's colleges, obtaining practical information about the establishment of women's higher-education institutions.

Tsuda began planning for her own school, recognizing her dependence on American financial support because of government-set ten-yen ($5.00) per-term maximums for tuition and a backlash following her resignation from Kazoku Jogakko. Consistent with ideals she expressed in AWSJW fundraising, Tsuda assured supporters that her school would be Christian, focus on teacher preparation and offer English-language instruction at the highest level available in Japan. Illustrating post-colonial theorist Leela Gandhi's observation that 'the 'English text' effectively replaced the Bible – to become the most influential medium for the civilizing mission, Tsuda claimed, 'the teacher even of elementary English in Japan finds that thought which Americans deem almost innate are new, and of deepest interest, to Japanese students'.[25] In 1899, members of the AWSJW committee established the Philadelphia Committee for Miss Tsuda's School; Morris, contributing $1,000 and named chairperson, was unwilling to guarantee ongoing funding, but agreed to assist in raising an initial $4,000.[26] Tsuda looked to her Bryn Mawr classmates to lead JEJ-fundraising campaigns; historian Febe Pamonag notes that appeals were made, not on the basis of Christian evangelism, but the sisterhood of educated women, illustrated by Tsuda's claim that 'schools and students and a true teacher's work are about the same everywhere in the world'.[27]

Tsuda opened JEJ in 1900 – an American school, with an American curriculum and pedagogy – announced in newspapers throughout the United States. Ten students met with Tsuda and Bacon in a rented, dilapidated residence. While Tsuda and Morris's AWSJW committee had, at times, disagreed over the administration of the scholarship, the establishment of JEJ, with its escalating financial needs, further strained their relationship. Tsuda sought to re-direct the AWSJW endowment to support JEJ, while Morris insisted that the scholarship programme continue as advertised. Morris sought to establish JEJ as a Christian-mission school, administered by an American governing board, while Tsuda sought to maintain administrative autonomy. Government regulations prohibited teaching religion and Tsuda recognized that loss of government recognition would jeopardize enrolments and prevent graduates from securing teaching positions.[28] A compromise made Alice Bacon the sole American trustee and Tsuda agreed to return dissatisfied donors' contributions. In 1903, the Philadelphia Committee guaranteed Tsuda 'absolute freedom to implement her plans for JEJ'.[29] While Tsuda freely administered JEJ to maintain government approval, Morris and the

Philadelphia Committee continued to publicize JEJ as a robustly Christian institution. A US publication described Tsuda, a 'true and noble new woman, having experienced the higher and better life, is striving to assist in the uplift of her sisters'.[30]

Government recognition of JEJ as a 'professional training college', in 1904, resulted in larger enrolments and expanded facilities. Tsuda wrote hundreds of letters each month, resulting in a steady stream of campus visitors. Seizing an opportunity to educate students in the 'uplift' imperative of service, Tsuda made JEJ a training ground for charitable fundraising and civil-society diplomacy. Periodically, students planned and performed English-language entertainments to which foreign visitors were invited and tickets sold to pay the JEJ mortgage or benefit Japanese charities. Tsuda boasted to the Philadelphia Committee that 'the girls take great interest in planning and working on [fundraisers,] the committees arrange all the details, programmes, invitations, and staging. It is quite new for Japanese women to work on committees and our girls gain much experience in executive matters'.[31] JEJ achieved greater visibility among educational philanthropists when, in 1905, the YWCA established a Tokyo branch, with Tsuda its president, and in 1907, Tsuda served as an organizer of the World Student Christian Federation conference held in Tokyo, which brought 600 delegates from twenty-five countries. Affiliation with these organizations attracted the attention of philanthropists for whom higher education was their chief Christian evangelization strategy. Japanese, too, began supporting JEJ; the Gaiyukai, thirty women who had lived abroad, donated one-sixth of the total gifts received by JEJ in 1902. An organization of alumnae, patrons, students and faculty, the Dōsōkai, was established in 1905 when there were 180 alumnae, 80 of whom were teachers. Alumnae were urged, not only to make financial gifts but also to volunteer their teaching. Tsuda's dream of a $50,000 endowment, from which she could annually draw $2,000–$3,000, however, eluded her.

The need to appeal to donors, maintain government recognition, enrol the most promising students and place graduates in teaching positions, caused Tsuda to be circumspect about her reputation, as well as those of JEJ students and alumnae. Articulating the 'politics of respectability', Tsuda admonished students on the school's opening day, and regularly thereafter, 'be always gentle, submissive, and courteous as have always been our women in the past'.[32] Fearing bad publicity and government condemnation, Tsuda agonized about alumnae leading the Seitōsha (Bluestockings), who gained notoriety for their critique of the patriarchal family system. In full damage limitation, Tsuda denounced them, 'their doctrines are lawless, and their teachings immoral. They advocate free love'.[33] Tsuda was quick to reassure donors that Western radical thought had no influence on 'our mild, reserved, conservative little ladies'.[34] Consistent with 'uplift' ideology, Tsuda spurned direct, political action, in favour of gradual, social change, declining to participate in the International Woman Suffrage Alliance and the International Peace Committee of Women for Permanent Peace. Her circumspection distorted her representation of JEJ students and marginalized her contribution to gender discourse in modernizing Japan.

A greater threat to JEJ fundraising in the United States was xenophobic opposition to Japanese immigration. Following the 1907 Gentlemen's Agreement, by which Japan prohibited workers emigrating to the United States, the Philadelphia Committee urged Tsuda to undertake an ambitious, US fundraising tour. Embracing 'uplift' perspectives,

Tsuda chronicled her travels for the *Alumnae Report*, reprinted in the United States for fundraising. In Hawaii, she wrote, 'we see the difference between the activity, intelligence, and character of the civilized man, and the indolence, ignorance and the feeble mind of the barbarian.' Travelling in California with her sister, immigration-activist Yonako Abiko, Tsuda expressed awe of what 'cultivators [presumably Japanese immigrants] had accomplished with intelligence, perseverance, and industry. Thus, we Japanese, too, not resting content with the easy work of developing the fertile spots of our own islands, should make the most of the opportunity which we best have to develop Formosa, Korea, and Manchuria.'[35] Tsuda was chagrined when denied service at a San Francisco hotel dining room, but relieved after a Bryn Mawr friend's intervention. On the East Coast, the Philadelphia Committee distributed 'Miss Tsuda's School for Girls', stressing familiar JEJ strengths, Tsuda's American education and strong character, the proven success of JEJ measured in its enrolment growth, and the support of both Japanese and American donors who contributed money and volunteered teaching. For JEJ students, it was claimed, 'the true object of study is not their own personal pleasure or advancement, but the power to help others'. Their fundraising appeal concluded with a plea for a second American intervention in Japan, with women as its beneficiaries. 'Fifty years ago, America forced Japan to open her doors to the world and Japan today is very grateful. May we not hope that Americans will help to open what is best in the Western world to the women of New Japan?'[36] In contrast, Tsuda, speaking to her fellow Bryn Mawr alumnae, declared JEJ students as 'ambitious, fond of study, and eager for any knowledge they can get. I think they must be like the students who were in the first women's colleges here.' Their mastering of English, she claimed, 'helps vastly to bring our nations closer together'.[37] A newly established New York Committee included wealthy, educational philanthropists and YWCA leaders; Grace Dodge and Helen Gould contributed $6,000 to the capital campaign and endowment fund. Culminating their East-Coast tour, Tsuda and Yonako met President Theodore Roosevelt at the White House.

At the invitation of evangelist John R. Mott, Tsuda returned to the United States in 1913 as Japan's representative to the World Christian Students Federation in New York, where 300 delegates from 40 countries met. Coinciding with her fundraising, an adulatory article in *Outlook* (the weekly with the third largest circulation in the United States), 'The New Woman of Japan', captured contradictions that characterized Tsuda's fundraising. JEJ provided a 'thorough training in Western literature and Christian thought' and Tsuda 'opens to her girls the best of Western culture, shows them the ideals of Western womanhood, makes them at the same time hold fast to the old standard of their own country, to the old ideals of politeness and service and self-forgetfulness, and sends them out at once advanced and conservative'.[38] Reflecting changing JEJ-fundraising trends, the New York Committee raised $420, the Philadelphia Committee raised $210, and both were dwarfed by a single gift of $6,000 for the endowment, given by the banker Willard Dickerman Straight and his wife, Dorothy Whitney Straight, a supporter of women's educational and charitable organizations. Other large gifts were given by Anne Wroe Scollay Low, whose husband, Seth Low, was the president of Columbia University and New York City mayor, and Emma R. Kaufman, associate general secretary of the Tokyo YWCA. Writing for the Alumnae Report in 1913, Tsuda expressed gratitude for the $3,000 alumnae had contributed and in a rare statement of equanimity wrote, 'I am very thankful for the prosperity of our school.'[39] This was Tsuda's final, US fundraising tour.

Increasingly incapacitated by illness, Tsuda resigned from the JEJ-presidency in 1919, although she wasn't replaced. The emperor bestowed on Tsuda the Sixth Class, Order of the Precious Crown (awarded exclusively to women). Anna C. Hartshorne, Tsuda's closest collaborator since 1902, substituted for her as a teacher, administrator and host for campus guests. In spite of her absence from the United States, news articles, frequently syndicated, continued to praise Tsuda and JEJ. Reports of Tsuda's Tokyo address, 'The Woman's Movement in Japan', praised her moderate tone, describing her 'manner justly reassuring', reflecting 'the Japanese characteristic of patience'. Approvingly, it was noted that Miss Tsuda insisted, 'there was no woman's movement in Japan in the Western and modern sense'.[40] Apparently referring to an earlier, 1905, fundraising publication, syndicated articles stated, 'today Miss Tsuda is the principal of the most famous girls' school in Japan. Graduates who have been educated according to American methods by Miss Tsuda are now teachers in the higher schools and colleges of the empire.'[41] In an article reprinted from *Outlook,* which reads like a JEJ-fundraising brochure, Anne Swineford observed that 'everyone in Japan knows Miss Ume Tsuda'. Following a brief biographical sketch of Tsuda, emphasizing her American education, Swineford claimed, 'by sheer dint of character she wrought almost unaided a scheme of education'. Neither Tsuda nor JEJ had grown wealthy, 'now and then American friends have sent funds', but the buildings were 'not pretentious'. JEJ was unrivalled, 'her school is now to be regarded as the most advanced in all Japan, her girls the most interesting', and 'the girls come largely from middle-class homes, a Christian school, with daily chapel exercises and regular Bible classes. The list of Miss Tsuda's graduates number hundreds of girls who have become not only advanced women of Japan, but also Christians, and who are the hope of the new Japan.'[42] At the end of JEJ's second decade, 'uplift' philanthropy had brought it financial stability and, in an era of increasing US-Japanese acrimony, a calming reputation for moderation.

## Rebuilding JEJ: The Emergency Committee for Miss Tsuda's School and the Tsuda College Association

With the JEJ campus laid waste by fires that followed the 1923 earthquake, the need for US fundraising had never been greater, but circumstances for fundraising – some unique to JEJ and others representative of national, charitable fundraising trends – had changed. The First World War had undermined the credibility of 'civilization' claims and the Philadelphia Committee, its structure and the donor pool it developed, were too limited to raise the needed $500,000. Moreover, many relief organizations were competing for American dollars. The Japan Relief fund of the ARC collected $11.8 million in six weeks.[43] James H. Collins, surveying post-First World War charitable fundraising in *The Saturday Evening Post,* observed, 'The whole world seems to have turned beggar, and upon the assumption that America alone has a paying job, endeavors to dip into the American pocketbook.'[44] Opposition to Japanese immigration growing, an anonymous author in *Outlook,* cogently summarized 'the Japanese question'. 'Japanese laborers have entered California in such numbers that, with their steady and well-defined policy of becoming landowners, they constitute a danger economically, socially, and politically. The problem is this: Can we Americanize the Japanese now here and those to be born here?'[45] A reassuring answer to that question might both benefit JEJ fundraising and moderate Japanese exclusion discourse.

A month after the earthquake, JEJ faculty member, Anna C. Hartshorne, sailed for the United States to solicit contributions. Joined by Yonako Abiko, they replaced the Philadelphia Committee with the Emergency Committee for Miss Tsuda's School, chaired by industrialist Alba B. Johnson (his wife was Tsuda's Bryn Mawr classmate), Vice Chairman Roland S. Morris (US ambassador to Japan, 1917 to 1920), Treasurer Jerome D. Greene (Rockefeller Foundation trustee) and Secretary Imogene Oakley (Pennsylvania civic leader). Like Tsuda before them, Abiko envisioned the Emergency Committee combining fundraising with diplomacy by educating audiences about Japanese history, culture and modern society.[46] JEJ fundraising was no longer conducted by a local, ladies' missionary society; the Emergency Committee was organized as a non-sectarian, national network, led by prominent men, as well as women, only Hartshorne having personal experience with JEJ operations.

Continuing the Philadelphia Committee's fundraising strategies, however, Hartshorne appealed to its donor base, writing letters and hosting teas. Her pamphlet, 'A Great Thing You Can Help Us to Do: Save Our Souls!' retold Tsuda's heroic life story, narrated challenges establishing JEJ and credited Japanese and US friends for their financial support. She described JEJ as an 'independent Christian philanthropic enterprise', and with wording reminiscent of WWfW, plaintively asked 'will the people of America put out their hands to help, that Tsuda College may be rescued?'[47] Re-creating entertainments staged on campus, Hartshorne recruited alumnae studying on the East Coast to perform at East-Coast women's colleges. While previously successful, however, these activities were time-intensive, yielded relatively small sums and minimally expanded the donor pool. After three years, having collected only half its goal, Hartshorne disbanded the Emergency Committee and returned to Japan, where her arrival was celebrated with an announcement of the Tsuda-Hartshorne Commemorative Fund, its publicity stating, 'Tsuda College is recognized as an international asset, a link between Japan and the English-speaking peoples. The college shall continue to be, as it has been, an interpreter and an agency of genuine friendship between East and West.'[48] In the midst of US-Japanese acrimony, JEJ evoked a nostalgic spirit of cooperation.

After the initial six months organizing the Emergency Committee and speaking at fundraisers in Philadelphia, Boston, New York and Chicago, Yonako Abiko had returned to San Francisco to organize a California branch of the Emergency Committee. Yonako was married to Kyūtarō Abiko, publisher of the *Nichibei Shinbun,* the leading West-Coast Japanese-language newspaper. Their 'uplift' organizations, supporting immigrants' permanent settlement and assimilation, were financed by philanthropist, Shibusawa Eiichi, called 'America's best friend in Japan', who, for the previous eighteen years, had led cultural-diplomatic missions, meeting with American business leaders, to diminish conflicts resulting from Japanese immigration. Recognizing the potential of disaster-relief humanitarianism to serve diplomatic goals, in 1906, Shibusawa had collected relief funds from Japanese business leaders for San Francisco earthquake victims and Kyūtarō, president of the Fukuinkai (Gospel Society) and founding member of the San Francisco Christian Federation, had distributed them. With Shibusawa's financial support, Yonako: established the Joshi Seinen Kai (Young Women's Society), a boarding house for the Japanese picture brides, offering classes in conversational English and American housekeeping; led Nisei Kengakudan, cultural-diplomacy delegations of second-generation Japanese visiting Japan to promote mutual understanding and improve the reputation of Japanese Americans among the Japanese public; and promoted the Tai-Beijin Keihatsu Undō (Campaign to Educate White America) in print media, a useful platform for publicizing JEJ fundraising.[49]

Tsuda having rejected political affiliation and activism, Yonako Abiko embraced them and appropriated the respected Tsuda and JEJ 'brand' to oppose Japanese exclusion. She appointed university officials, who were prominent exclusion opponents, to lead the California branch of the Emergency Committee: Rev. James A. B. Scherer, a missionary in Japan before becoming CalTech president, and David Starr Jordan, Stanford University president, who contributed $15,000 to rebuild the JEJ library. Exclusion legislation threatened the Japanese whom they had recruited to their faculties and student bodies, as well as curtailing the free travel of Japanese nationals conducting cultural diplomacy. Their fundraising pamphlet, 'The Japanese Earthquake – And After', characterized JEJ as 'an international school' and noted that the national committee requested Californians contribute $50,000. The vice president of the San Francisco Chamber of Commerce Robert N. Lynch wrote a letter of support in the Chamber's newsletter, advocating donations as a means of cooperating with the Japanese.[50] When the Emergency Committee disbanded in 1926, the California branch had collected only $18,000.[51] In the centre of anti-immigration agitation and with weak organization, the California branch was unable to significantly expand JEJ fundraising.

Likely on Shibusawa Eiichi's recommendation, Yonako Abiko was, however, instrumental in naming Narcissa Cox Vanderlip the chair of the Emergency Committee's New York branch. Vanderlip (1879–1966) led a new era in JEJ fundraising, having staggering personal wealth, social connections with leaders in international finance as well as political leaders of both parties, and successful experience in organizational development and fundraising. Vanderlip was college-educated, majoring in sociology in one of the early classes of the University of Chicago, leading its YWCA chapter and volunteering in a local settlement house. In 1903, she married Frank A. Vanderlip, assistant treasury secretary in the Republican, McKinley administration and the protégé of James Stillman, whom he succeeded as president of National City Bank. With personal wealth valued at $100 million at the beginning of the twentieth century, Stillman introduced the Vanderlips to his circle of financiers and industrialists, including the Rockefellers, National City Bank's largest customers. At Stillman's urging, the Vanderlips purchased Beechwood, a 100-room, 125-acre, Hudson River estate, which they developed into a perfect venue for business and charitable entertaining. Hosting large numbers of Frank's bank employees' families, Narcissa coordinated transport, booked entertainers, supervised the domestic staff with caterers, and maintained accounts for their galas, which included concerts, vaudeville performances, athletic contests and films. Active in the social ministry of her Swedenborgian church, Narcissa established the Kennedy Street Settlement House in New York City and served as its financial administrator. To educate their six children, as well as those of their affluent Westchester-County neighbours, the Vanderlips established Scarborough Day School in 1913, the first Montessori school in the United States.

Vanderlip's social status and personal wealth facilitated her entry into organizing and fundraising, beginning, in 1915, with the New York campaign for woman's suffrage. Recruited by Vera Whitehouse, chairperson (1916) of the New York State Woman Suffrage Party (NYSWSP), Vanderlip became one of her four 'lieutenants', described by social reformer, Frances Perkins, as 'well-married, rich, and stylish, people who were well-placed and could batter their way into anybody's office or anybody's living room'.[52] Whitehouse declared that the NYSWSP would 'lay aside the tactics of amateurs and work like professionals', her lieutenants conducted door-to-door, as well as telephone canvassing, and raised $682,500 for the 1917 referendum by depending on a small number of women writing large checks.[53] Chair of the Ninth campaign district, which included her affluent, Westchester neighbours, Vanderlip described the canvassing as 'grueling', and appealed to donors, 'let's get through with this now!'[54] Frank Vanderlip contributed $10,000 and Narcissa contributed $7,000, together equalling the gift of the NYSWSP's single largest contributor.[55] Each of the three counties in the Ninth district led by Vanderlip voted for the successful 1917 referendum; Carrie Chapman Catt called the New York state campaign 'the decisive battle of the American woman suffrage movement'.[56]

Following Catt's lead, Vanderlip used the organizing and fundraising knowledge she developed in the suffrage campaign to publicize civilian mobilization programmes and sell war bonds during the First World War. She was appointed by Treasury Secretary William Gibbs McAdoo, Jr, to lead the National Woman's Liberty Loan Committee, for which she worked nationally to organize mass meetings, establish war bond sales centres, and distribute publicity to thousands of women's organization members. Secretary McAdoo praised the committee for having 'paved a new fundraising path'.[57] Thus, Vanderlip became one of the fundraisers whom journalist James H. Collins identified as having transformed fundraising, using mass organization strategies they developed during the war.[58] Having worked with Vanderlip in New York civilian mobilization and war relief projects, Eleanor Roosevelt had been impressed by Vanderlip's profound love for learning, her pragmatic political style, her executive skills, efficiency – and dash.[59] After the war, Vanderlip, became the first chairperson of the New York State League of Women Voters, which she viewed as a model organization, providing women around the world with a vision of democracy and justice that she claimed was 'essential to civilization'.[60] Vanderlip invited Roosevelt to join the League's board, supervising its legislative programme addressing women's working conditions, children's welfare and political reform. Vanderlip credited their League work with having shaped Roosevelt's 'approach to public issues and helped her to do serious, sustained work'.[61]

Following the armistice, Vanderlip began her work in international, humanitarian aid, with particular interest in women's higher education – the issue prioritized by international women's organizations in the interwar period.[62] In 1919, Vanderlip drafted the constitution of the International Federation of University Women (IFUW), whose purpose was to 'promote understanding and friendship between the university women of different nations and thereby further their interests and develop sympathy and material helpfulness between the peoples of the world'.[63] Historian Marie Sandell observes that the IFUW attracted more public support than other international women's organizations of the period, speculating that the international friendship developed in educational exchange was less controversial than issues such as feminism and anti-colonialism.[64] In 1920, the Vanderlips toured seven war-blighted European countries, interviewing recipients of US aid, compiling data and reporting to the American Relief Association. After returning to New York, Narcissa publicized the plight of missionary-established schools in the Near East and announced that she would personally fund six scholarships for young women in Turkey.[65]

In 1920, Shibusawa Eiichi invited the Vanderlips to lead a delegation of prominent businessmen and their wives on a Japan tour. Frank Vanderlip was the president of the New York City Japan Society and, in 1913, had led a syndicate purchasing the 16,000-acre Palos Verdes estate in California, leased by forty Japanese tenant-households.[66] In Japan, delegates attended daily briefings by government officials and business leaders on Japanese society and US-Japanese relations. Narcissa, however, claimed she owed her 'real insight into the Japanese life, and an honest affection for the Japanese people', to her interpreter, a JEJ faculty member. Gratified that they were 'sympathetic on almost every subject', Vanderlip mused, 'from the intimate contact, how sympathetically the whole world might get on if we only had a common means of communication and the opportunity to understand the fundamental principles of each other's civilizations'. Vanderlip was favourably impressed by JEJ, describing it a 'curious mixture of America and Japan. There was a vitality about the whole school that was striking', which she attributed to the teachers having been educated in the United States. Describing JEJ buildings as 'ramshackle', Vanderlip, nevertheless, enthused, 'the spirit of the whole place was of progress and aspiration'.[67]

Returning to the United States, Vanderlip hosted large-scale events through which she developed a Japan-advocacy network. She became a cultural-diplomacy impresario, booking Japanese performing artists and athletes. On behalf of the Japan Society of New York, the Vanderlips entertained 600 guests at an Orientalist extravaganza at their Beechwood estate. The Vanderlips, dressed in bespoke kimono, and their guests watched judo exhibitions, heard a recital by a soprano from the Imperial Opera Company of Tokyo, and viewed a play starring Japanese students from Columbia University.[68] Beechwood became a civil-society diplomacy headquarters where Vanderlip entertained Shibusawa, who was observing the 1921 Washington Armaments Conference; delegates to the conference of the International Council of Women, an advocacy organization established with the assistance of US suffragists to promote human rights for women; and members of the Council for the Limitation of Armaments, composed of thirty women's organizations, on whose executive board Vanderlip served. She compiled lists of Asian-American and Asian women in New York, whom she invited to her large-scale hospitality events with women political activists and Euro-American women's educators, promoting personal relationships and collaboration.

Immediately after the 1923 earthquake, Shibusawa telegrammed, requesting urgent assistance from the Vanderlips. Narcissa responded, 'naturally, our first thought was how we could supply these people with roofs, with clothes, with food; how we could quickly carry to them the bare necessities that would keep them alive'.[69] She was delighted with the irony of US war ships delivering humanitarian, relief supplies to the Japanese.[70] American and Japanese cultural diplomats were astounded that so soon after the outpouring of US disaster-relief aid, Congress passed the Immigration Act of 1924, which included the Asian Exclusion Act prohibiting Japanese immigration to the United States.[71] Publicly expressed support for Japan became unthinkable; the Japan Society of New York, for example, was discredited with allegations of direct ties with the Japanese government.[72] Newspapers advocated exclusion, including *The New York Times*, which merely expressed hope for a kinder way to address the issue.[73] Facing this hostility, Vanderlip sought a strategy with which to engage women in improving US-Japanese relations – the rebuilding of JEJ.

Vanderlip began her appointment as chair of the Tsuda Emergency Committee – New York branch, by hosting a luncheon introducing Yonako Abiko to potential donors. Vanderlip-planned fundraising events were held at fashionable venues, especially decorated with faux Japanese lanterns and screens, and featured Japanese women performing light entertainments, followed by an informative presentation about Japanese culture. *The New York Times* regularly reported on Vanderlip-hosted events, listing prominent attendees, who provided celebrity endorsement of JEJ. In 1924, Vanderlip hosted a blockbuster JEJ benefit, a Beechwood garden fête, replicating Japanese cultural performances she had observed in Japan. Ostensibly a JEJ benefit, Vanderlip publicized it as a means of expressing opposition to Japanese exclusion, 'many of us who understand the exquisite culture of the Japanese civilization have felt extremely sorry to offend in any way the proud sensitivities of the Japanese'.[74] Publicizing ticket sales, handbills were dropped from a plane and Vanderlip led a parade of kimono-clad Japanese women down New York City's Fifth Avenue. Fujita Taki, the first Japanese woman to earn a doctorate in literature, and later, fourth Tsuda College president, was conveyed in an ornate rickshaw, borrowed from the Metropolitan Opera House. She was 'embarrassed', but acknowledged that 'the name of Tsuda became famous overnight'.[75] Vanderlip released carrier pigeons to deliver invitations to the US secretary of state and the Japanese ambassador. More than 2,000 attended Vanderlip's garden fête, ticket sales yielding $3,500. Representing Japan as a non-threatening form of light entertainment, this blockbuster became the model for socialites whom Vanderlip recruited to host similar events, depicting 'the culture, beauty and charm of the land of the cherry blossom'.[76] Being recruited by Vanderlip to host a Japanese-themed garden party became a mark of elite status.[77] Vanderlip and the socialites whom she recruited, were the fundraising descendants of the 'Gilded Suffragettes' whom Johanna Neumann described, 'comfortable with power that wealth conferred, these women treated politics [and civil-society fundraising] as an extension of their realm as social figures. As hostesses of extravagant parties and managers of massive estates . . . they knew how to manage media'. Just as the

'Gilded Suffragists', according to Neumann, had given woman's suffrage legitimacy, making it appear less threatening, Vanderlip's garden fêtes and those hosted by her recruits, made Japanese fashionable and less menacing.[78] The following year, Vanderlip chaired a committee for 'a colossal Pageant of Peace, intended to symbolize man's [*sic*] progress toward cooperation and goodwill', supporting JEJ and seven other charities. Vanderlip's committee anticipated 10,000 participants, announced negotiations with a motion-picture studio and proposed that the Tsuda National Emergency Committee underwrite the project. The pageant was, however, never staged.[79]

Although her fundraising style was unconventional in comparison to those of the Philadelphia Committee, Anna Hartshorne, and Tsuda herself, Vanderlip was named President of the Tsuda College Association, which replaced the Emergency Committee for Miss Tsuda's School after Hartshorne returned to Japan in 1926. While having a weak personal connection with JEJ, Vanderlip had standing in US-Japan cultural diplomacy and international women's higher education. Tasked with creating a permanent, national, JEJ-fundraising organization and jumpstart what appeared to have been a stalled campaign for rebuilding the campus, Vanderlip began with a luncheon attended by one hundred women, during which she announced that educational philanthropist Edward Harkness had pledged $50,000.[80] Vanderlip selected a roster of speakers to engage in civil-society diplomacy: Harriet Burton Laidlaw, Vanderlip's suffrage and League-of-Women-Voters colleague, urged women to become informed about international relations; New York Japan Society President Henry W. Taft presented conciliatory positions on immigration and Sino-Japanese relations while commending Japanese peoples' character; Kawai Michi, a leader of Japanese Christians and the YWCA, an AWSJW recipient and a JEJ faculty member, who reported on the condition of women in Japan; and missionary Galen Fisher of the Rockefeller-funded Institute for Social and Religious Research, who described Christian-influenced reforms in Japan and cautioned that Japanese exclusion threatened peace in the Pacific. Vanderlip then addressed the question, 'what has a small college for the higher education of women in Tokyo to do with us?' She praised Japanese women's demeanour and character, describing them as 'priceless porcelains of the East', having 'a grace of person, a perfection of courtesy and breeding', 'beautiful behavior, [and] gentle charm', 'together with heroic courage and unselfishness', [going] 'forward to meet a wholly different future'. Noting JEJ's long-standing relationship with the United States, Vanderlip assured donors that the school was educating young women from Japan's finest families, using American methods, to nurture 'a true Christian life'. Illustrating cultural-diplomacy historian Jon Thares Davidann's observation that American liberals have seen 'too much of themselves in Japan', Vanderlip claimed that JEJ was educating Japan's future leaders, 'who love our Lincoln, Washington and Roosevelt – who feel akin to us in the life of the spirit [and] will make wars cease'.[81] Vanderlip's representation of JEJ women explicitly challenged exclusionists' assumptions that Japanese could not assimilate American values and supported the position of Americanization made by Japanese and American cultural diplomats.[82]

The establishment of the national Tsuda College Association reflected a trend in fundraising for 'American colleges abroad', in the 1920s. Established by Christian missionaries in the nineteenth century, these schools were primarily dependent on American missionary-board funding until the 1920s when they established modern fundraising organizations in the United States to wage ambitious, capital campaigns.[83] Fundraising consortia were established, particularly for women's higher education, to professionally solicit contributions from the increasing numbers of women college graduates in the United States. Following the Kantō earthquake, the international committee of the Association of American University Women raised two million dollars for Women's Christian Colleges in the Orient – JEJ however, was not a member.[84] Vanderlip made a modest contribution to the Kobe College Corporation, which was established in Chicago, in 1920, to raise funds for the women's school in western Japan and thereafter, was invited to join a seven-institution consortium, The Cooperating Committee for Women's Union Christian Colleges in Foreign Fields, headquartered in New York City. While Vanderlip made opposition to Japanese exclusion central to her fundraising for JEJ, the Kobe College Corporation merely published two protest resolutions, describing the 1924 legislation as 'an anti-Japanese measure antithetical to the spirit of Christianity and humanity'.[85] Vanderlip was more actively engaged in fundraising for the Near East College Association (NECA), which funded and administered six colleges. She had been named a trustee of Constantinople Women's College after establishing a scholarship programme, citing the need 'to secure sound and constructive education for women as well as fair and favorable economic and social conditions for them'.[86] To raise funds for the $15 million Permanent Endowment Fund for NECA in 1925, Vanderlip challenged a male trustee of the American University of Beirut to a contest to raise the final $200,000 in four days. Vanderlip won, demonstrating her capacity to quickly identify and successfully solicit wealthy donors. These fundraising organizations of 'American colleges abroad', developed in partnership with the new source of educational philanthropy – the non-profit foundation.

Large grants from the Laura Spelman Rockefeller Memorial Foundation, the Carnegie Endowment, the New York Japan Society, and the Commonwealth Fund, enabled the Tsuda College Association to achieve its $500,000 goal on 4 February 1928. Historian Katharina Rietzler has observed that, during the interwar years, American foundations aspired to the same goals as cultural diplomats – spreading the achievements of American civilization for the benefit of the world.[87] Foundation grants became a powerful endorsement for JEJ, particularly with respect to its role in promoting world peace. Vanderlip noted that JEJ had been celebrated 'by some of our greatest statesmen and educators, one of the most concrete contributions to a better understanding between our country and Japan now before us'.[88] Foundations' large contributions, however, rendered superfluous a national campaign appealing to large numbers of donors' smaller gifts, ending the role JEJ fundraising played in civil-society diplomacy. The fundraising goal achieved, Vanderlip consulted America's most prestigious collegiate architect, Ralph Adams Cram, who designed an Orientalist fantasy of a campus plan, with an upper courtyard symbolizing 'the delicate female geisha' and the lower, 'the bulky male samurai'.[89] Vanderlip promised, 'from the ashes of the fires following the earthquake, a wonderful new thing will develop – a harmonious mix of a charming traditional Japanese architectural style with a practical American architectural style. The Juku [JEJ] is a Phoenix.'[90] Because of its expense, JEJ rejected Cram's plan, fearing government condemnation; instead, a design by Satō Koichi completed the campus rebuilding in 1932. In the United States, however, Vanderlip was feted as an exemplary 'educational worker', at a luncheon in Pasadena, California, and her contributions to international educational philanthropy were listed in the *Pasadena Post*.[91] Mobilizing a vast network of organizations, Vanderlip not only expanded and diversified the JEJ donor pool but also the audience for whom the representation of JEJ women confounded the premises of Japanese exclusion.

# Notes

1   J. Charles Schencking, 'Giving Most and Giving Differently: Humanitarianism as Diplomacy Following Japan's 1923 Earthquake', *Diplomatic History* 43, no. 4 (2019): 729–31.

2   Andrea Walton, 'Introduction: Women and Philanthropy in Education – A Problem of Conceptions', in *Women and Philanthropy in Education*, ed. Walton (Bloomington: Indiana University Press, 2005), 9.

3   Ian Tyrrell, *Reforming the World: The Creation of America's Moral Empire* (Princeton: Princeton University Press, 2010), 3.

4   Quotations are ironic designations.
     Emily S. Rosenberg, 'Missions to the World: Philanthropy Abroad', in *Charity, Philanthropy, and Civility in American History*, ed. Lawrence J. Friedman and Mark D. McGarvie (Cambridge: Cambridge University Press, 2003), 246. Gail Bederman, *Manliness and Civilization: A Cultural History of Gender and Race in the United States, 1870–1917* (Chicago: University of Chicago Press, 1995), 23, 25.

5   Rotem Kowner, *From White to Yellow* (Montreal: McGill-Queen's University Press, 2014), xxiv.

6   Valeska Huber, Tamson Pietsch, and Katharina Rietzler, ' Women's International Thought and the New Professions, 1900–1940', *Modern Intellectual History* 18, no. 1 (2021): 121.

7   For example, *The Weekly Commonwealth* [Topeka, Kansas], 16 October 1872, 4.

8   Joyce Goodman, 'A Refined Womanhood as a Marker of Civilization', in *Women, Power Relations and Education in a Transnational World*, ed. Christine Mayer and Adelina Arrendondo (New York: Palgrave Macmillan, 2020), 28.

9   Affective labor' defined, Johanna Oksala, 'Affective Labor and Feminist Politics', *Signs: Journal of Women in Culture and Society* 41, no. 2 (2016): 284–5.

10  Emily S. Rosenberg, 'Rescuing Women and Children', *The Journal of American History* 89, no. 2 (2002): 458. Dana L. Robert, *American Women in Mission* (Macon: Baylor University Press, 1997), 133–7. Marie Sandell, *The Rise of Women's Transnational Activism* (London: I.B. Tauris, 2020), electronic-reader, chapter 2 'Education and Missionary Activities'. Patricia R. Hill, *The World Their Household: The American Women's Foreign Mission Movement and Cultural Transformation, 1870–1920* (Ann Arbor: University of Michigan Press, 1985), 134.

11 Cited by Toda Tetsuko, 'Starting as a Women's Organization: The Formation of the WFMA of Philadelphia', https://ci.nii.ac.jp/naid/110008151145 accessed 24 August 2021.

12 *Tsuda Umeko monjo* (The Writings of Tsuda Umeko) (Tokyo: Tsudajuku Daigaku, 1980), 21, 27, 92.

13 Between 1893 and 1917, Hampton was the wealthiest school for African Americans, having a comprehensive external relations programme. Troy A. Smith, 'Not Just Raising Money: Hampton Institute and Relationship Fundraising, 1893–1917', *History of Education Quarterly* 61, no. 1 (2021): 64–6, 71–2.

14 Alice Mabel Bacon, *A Japanese Interior* (Boston: Houghton Mifflin, 1893), 228.

15 Collaboration acknowledgement, Alice Mabel Bacon, *Japanese Girls and Women* (New York: Houghton Mifflin, 1891), viii. Editions in 1891, 1892, 1901, 1902, in United States and United Kingdom.

16 *Tsuda monjo*, 73–5. While scholarship on Tsuda's teaching is abundant, this study differs by analysing her role as a fundraiser and diplomat. For an analysis of a related issue of ways in which the JEJ curriculum and student policies were shaped by 'civilization' ideology, see Linda L. Johnson, 'The Civilizing Mission of Tsuda Umeko and Alice M. Bacon', *Ajia bungaku kenkyū* 38 (2012): 1–16.

17 Bacon, *Japanese Girls and Women*, 226.

18 Beverly Skegs, 'Uneasy Alignments, Resourcing Respectable Subjectivity', *GLQ: A Journal of Lesbian and Gay Studies* 10, no. 2 (2004): 292.

19 Kevin K. Gaines, *Southern Workman, Uplifting the Race* (Chapel Hill: University of North Carolina Press, 1996), xiii. Bacon, *Japanese Girls and Women*, 224.

20 M. Carey Thomas (dean, later, president, of Bryn Mawr) was AWSJW academic consultant, although her biographer, Helen Lefkowitz Horowitz, observed she had 'nothing but scorn for Japanese as a people', 'showed little personal interest' in AWSJW, and no 'curiosity about the recipients'. *The Power and Passion of M. Carey Thomas* (Urbana: University of Illinois Press, 1999), 382–3.

21 *The New York Evangelist*, 20 April 1899, 27.

22 'Japanese Women and the War', *The Independent*, 9 May 1895, 47.

23 *Tsuda monjo*, 484.

24 Quoted by Kameda Kuniko, *Tsuda Umeko* (Tokyo: Sōbunsha Shuppan, 2005), 159–60.

25 Leela Gandhi, *Postcolonial Theory*, 2nd edn. (New York: Columbia University Press, 2019), e-book. Tsuda quoted in Kameda, *Tsuda Umeko*, 154.

26 Tsudajuku Daigaku, 'Miss Tsuda's School for Girls, Tokyo, Japan' (Philadelphia? 1908?).

27 Febe Pamonag, 'A Bryn Mawr School in the East', *Pacific Historical Review* 81, no. 4 (2012): 559–60. *Tsuda monjo*, 92.

28 Margaret E. Burton, *The Education of Women in Japan* (New York: Fleming H. Revell, 1914), e-book.

29 Quoted by Febe Pamonag, 'Turn-of-the-Century Cross-Cultural Collaborations for Japanese Women's Higher Education', *US-Japan Women's Journal* 37 (2009): 47–8.

30 *American Journal of Sociology* 8 (1903): 693.

31 *Tsuda monjo*, 417.

32 Tsuda quoted by Barbara Rose, *Tsuda Umeko and Women's Education in Japan* (New Haven: Yale University Press, 1992), 129. 'Politics of respectability' defined, Evelyn Brooks Higginbotham, *Righteous Discontent: The Women's Movement in the Black Baptist Church, 1880–1920* (Cambridge, MA: Harvard University Press, 1994).

33  Tsuda Ume, 'The Ideal of Womanhood as a Factor in Missionary Work', *International Review of Missions* 2 (1913): 301–2.

34  *Tsuda monjo*, 504. Attributing Tsuda's conservatism to dependence on fundraising differs from historian Shibahara Taeko, who states, 'Tsuda was confused by her own inner-conflict between support for liberal and conservative ideologies'. Shibahara Taeko, 'Through Americanized Japanese Woman's Eyes', *Supplement to Doshisha American Studies* 18 (2012): 285.

35  *Tsuda monjo*, 114.

36  'Tsuda's School for Girls', 7, 14, 16.

37  *Tsuda monjo*, 92–3, 95.

38  *Outlook*, 104 (1913): 977.

39  *Tsuda monjo*, 143.

40  For example, *The Shreveport*, [Louisiana] *Journal*, 18 October 1915, 6.

41  For example, *Asheville* [North Carolina] *Citizen-Times*, 7 July 1917.

42  Syndicated, for example, 'A Famous Jap School ma'am', *Morning Tulsa* [Oklahoma] *Daily World*, 17 August 1917, 2.

43  Schencking, 'Giving Most and Giving Differently', 733.

44  James H. Collins, 'Drive Industry', *The Saturday Evening Post*, 14 August 1920.

45  Anon., *Outlook*, 8 June 1921, 253.

46  Tsudajuku Daigaku, *Tsudajuku Daigaku hyakunenshi* [Tsudajuku College 100-year history] (Tokyo: Tsudajuku Daigaku, 2003), 143–4.

47  Tsudajuku Daigaku, *Tsuda Umeko to juku no kujūnen* [Tsuda Umeko and the school's ninety years] (Tokyo: Tsudajuku Daigaku, 1990), 48.

48  Ibid., 160.

49  Eiichiro Azuma, 'Dancing with the Rising Sun', in *The Transnational Politics of Asian Americans*, ed. Christian Collet (Philadelphia: Temple University Press, 2009), 26.

50  Iino Masako, Kameda Kinuko, and Takahashi Yuko, *Tsuda Umeko o sasaeta hitoboto* [Tsuda Umeko's Supporters] (Tokyo: Tsudajuku Daigaku Hatsubaijo Yūhikaku, 2000), 251–2.

51  Tsudajuku Daigaku, *hyakunenshi*, 144–5.

52  Quoted in Johanna Neumann, *Gilded Suffragists: The New York Socialites Who Fought for Women's Right to Vote* (New York: New York University Press, 2017), 152.

53  Whitehouse quoted in Neumann, *Gilded Suffragists*, 135–7. Joan Marie Johnson, *Funding Feminism: Monied Women, Philanthropy, and the Women's Movement, 1870–1967* (Chapel Hill: University of North Carolina Press, 2017), 20–1.

54  Vanderlip, 'Woman's Influence in Public Life: Women in Politics', in *Narcissa Cox Vanderlip: Chairman, New York State League of Women Voters 1919–1923*, ed. Hilda Watrous (New York: Foundation for Citizen Education, 1982), 53. Vanderlip quoted in Jacqueline Van Voris, *Carrie Chapman Catt: A Public Life* (New York: Feminist Press, 1987), 143.

55  Neumann, *Gilded Suffragists*, 137.

56  Catt quoted in Ronald Schaffer, 'The New York State Woman Suffrage Party: 1909–1919', *New York History* 43, no.3 (July 1962): 283.

57  'National Women's Liberty Loan Committee', Treasury Department, 19 October 1918.

58  'Drive Industry', *Saturday Evening Post*, 14 August 1920.

59  Blanche Wiesen Cook, *Eleanor Roosevelt*, vol. 1 (New York: Penguin, 1992), 289.

60  Vanderlip quoted in Watrous, *Narcissa Cox Vanderlip*, 44.

61  Vanderlip quoted in Joseph P. Lash, *Eleanor and Franklin* (New York: W.W. Norton, 1971), 259–260.

62 Marie Sandell, *The Rise of Women's Transnational Activism: Identity and Sisterhood Between the World Wars* (London: I.B. Tauris, 2015). e-book chapter 5.

63 Narcissa Cox Vanderlip Papers, Columbia University Libraries, Rare Books and Manuscripts Collection.

64 *Women's Transnational Activism*, chapter 5.

65 'Mrs. Vanderlip Pleads for Students Abroad', *New York Times*, 30 November 1921, 7.

66 Vicki A. Mack, *Frank A. Vanderlip: The Banker Who Changed America* (Palos Verdes: Pinoles Press, 2013), 263–4.

67 Vanderlip Papers, 'Speech'.

68 Beginning in the mid-1880s, playing on popular culture motifs, 'Mikado ball' masquerades and 'Mahjong luncheons' were popular occasions for charitable fundraising. Josephine Lee, *Japan and Pure Invention: Gilbert and Sullivan's The Mikado* (Minneapolis: University of Minnesota Press, 2010). Annelise Heinz, *Mahjong: A Chinese Game and the Making of Modern American Culture* (New York: Oxford University Press, 2021).

69 Vanderlip Papers, 'Speech'.

70 Ibid.

71 Shibusawa Eiichi, *Shibusawa Eiichi denki shiryō* [Shibusawa Eiichi Biographical Materials] (Tokyo: Shibusawa Eiichi Denki Shiryō Kankōkai, 1960), vol. 35, 255; vol. 37, 62.

72 Michael R. Auslin and Edwin O. Reischauer, *Japan Society: Celebrating a Century, 1907–2007* (New York: Japan Society, 2007), 22–4.

73 Media scholar Bradley J. Hamm studied seven daily newspapers, in New York, Chicago and Louisville. Six advocated exclusion legislation, on the grounds of race, economy, national security and political decency. Hamm, 'Redefining Racism: Newspaper Justifications for the 1924 Exclusion of Japanese Immigrants', *American Journalism* (1999): 58. 'The Real Japanese Question', *New York Times*, 3 May 1924, 14.

74 'Fête Opens Drive for Tokio College: Party on Vanderlip Lawn Seen as a Protest Against Exclusion Methods', *New York Times*, 8 June 1924, 19.

75 Cited in Yoshiko Furuki, *The White Plum: A Biography of Ume Tsuda* (New York: Weatherhill, 1991), 132.

76 'Garden Party at Greenwich: Japanese Festival will be Given to Benefit the Tsuda College', *New York Times*, 6 September 1925, 9. JEJ garden benefits were held in Jackson Heights, New York City; Greenwich, Connecticut and the Japanese Botanical Garden in Brooklyn.

77 For an analysis of philanthropy as a mark of class status, see Francie Ostrower, *Why the Wealthy Give: The Culture of Elite Philanthropy* (Princeton: Princeton University Press, 1995), 6; Diana Kendall, *The Power of Good Deeds: Privileged Women and the Social Reproduction of the Upper Class* (New York: Rowman & Littlefield, 2002), 64–5.

78 Neumann, *Gilded Suffragists*, 155.

79 '10,000 to Appear in Peace Pageant', *New York Times*, 14 September 1925, 3.

80 Harkness's family financed the Commonwealth Fund and contributed to Columbia, Yale and Harvard.

81 John Thares Davidann, *The Limits of Westernization: American and East Asian Intellectuals Create Modernity, 1860–1960* (New York: Routledge, 2018), e-book; Vanderlip quoted in 'Tsuda College's Needs', *The New York Times*, 6 April 1927, 26.

82 For an explanation of positions taken by both sides of the exclusion debate, see Lon Kurashige, *Two Faces of Exclusion: The Untold History of Anti-Asian Racism in the*

*United States* (Chapel Hill: University of North Carolina Press, 2016), especially 135, 144–5.

83 Women's colleges in the United States also began capital campaigns in the 1920s. Laura Carpenter Bingham, 'Women, Higher Education, and Philanthropy', in *Philanthropy in America: A Comprehensive Historical Encyclopedia*, vol. 2, ed. Dwight F. Burlingame (Santa Barbara: ABC Clio 2004), 514.

84 Marie Sandell, 'Learning from the West: International Students and International Women's Organizations in the Interwar Period', *History of Education* 44 (2015): 17.

85 Noriko Kawamura Ishii, *American Women Missionaries at Kobe College, 1873–1909: New Dimensions in Gender* (New York: Routledge, 2004), 175.

86 Vanderlip quoted in Watrous, *Narcissa Cox Vanderlip*, 52.

87 Katharina Rietzler, 'Before the Cultural Cold Wars: American Philanthropy and Cultural Diplomacy in the Inter-War Years', *Historical Research* 84, no. 223 (2011): 164.

88 Vanderlip, *Los Angeles Times*, 8 September 1927.

89 Ethan Anthony, *Ralph Adams Cram and His Office* (New York: Norton, 2007), 178.

90 Vanderlip Papers.

91 'Educational Worker to be Honored', 29 March 1929, 6. Following the 1929 stock market crash, her husband's death and the Pacific War, Vanderlip focused her philanthropic and organizational leadership more locally, serving as president of the New York Women's and Children's Infirmary for forty years.

# 8

# Cultivating 'goodwill' through rural welfare

## The Near East Foundation in Iran, 1943–51

Ben Offiler

Following his unexpected victory in the 1948 presidential election, Harry S. Truman used his inaugural address to call for 'a bold new program for making the benefits of our scientific advances and industrial progress available for the improvement and growth of underdeveloped areas'. Put simply, the president stated, 'Our aim should be to help the free peoples of the world, through their own efforts, to produce more food, more clothing, more materials for housing, and more mechanical power to lighten their burdens.'[1] Point Four, as this aspiration became known, held the door wide open for private organizations, including philanthropic foundations, to contribute to US foreign policy goals. Truman's Point Four programme sought to embed two key principles into US foreign policy during the early Cold War. First, it emphasized the role of development as a means to inoculate countries against the appeal of communism. Second, it suggested that non-governmental organizations could be instrumental in this effort due to both their technical expertise and their local, on-the-ground knowledge. Private agencies were, then, integral to Harry Truman's strategy for containing communism and maintaining US economic, political and strategic interests in the developing world.

One such agency was the philanthropic Near East Foundation (NEF), formerly known as Near East Relief (NER). Founded in 1915 as a direct response to the emergency caused by the Armenian Genocide, NER had gained an international reputation for its humanitarian and relief programmes. But by 1930 it had transformed itself into the Near East Foundation from, in the words of Keith David Watenpaugh, 'an ad hoc food relief organization to . . . a bureaucratized, multidisciplinary, non-governmental "development" organization'.[2] By the time of Truman's Point Four declaration the Near East Foundation was operating in a number of countries, including Greece, Lebanon and Syria, but it was its Iran programme that caught the Truman administration's attention.

In the months that followed the pronouncement of Point Four, Truman administration officials approached the NEF to discuss the possibility of providing funds for the NEF's work 'to help the underprivileged countries of the Near East'.[3] Reporting his encounters with Department of State policymakers, one NEF officer noted that 'the Foundation's programmes had been quoted frequently as typical of the activities around which "Point Four" should be developed'.[4] Just a year later, when extolling the virtues and promise of Point Four, President Truman himself pointed directly to the NEF's Iran programme of leadership training, agricultural reform, rural education and sanitation projects as an 'example of what point 4 [*sic*] can mean'.[5]

The Near East Foundation was not the only American non-governmental organization or non-state actor that engaged with and contributed to Iranian development during the twentieth century. While many scholars have focused on formal diplomatic relations between the United States and Iran, especially during the Cold War era, John Lorentz, Thomas M. Ricks, Jasamin Rostam-Kolayi and Michael Zirinsky have illustrated the influence of American Presbyterian and evangelical missionaries in shaping Iran's education system through a series of mission schools and colleges.[6] Others have explored the role of non-state actors, including academics and students, in the evolution of US-Iranian relations beyond government policy, yet despite their intimate involvement in Iran's post-war development, few historians have focused on the contribution of philanthropic foundations and private NGOs.[7] Victor V. Nemchenok, Christopher T. Fisher and Gregory Brew have examined the activities of the Ford Foundation and David Lilienthal's Development and Resources Corporation, revealing the intricate relationship these and other NGOs had with Iran's official development programmes.[8] The Near East Foundation's Iran programmes, however, have not yet been explored in depth, despite the fact that not only did the NEF arrive in Iran at the invitation of Tehran before both Ford and Rockefeller, but they also received funding from these larger foundations throughout the 1950s to support their rural reform projects.[9] Moreover, that the NEF's work in Iran was considered emblematic of President Truman's Point Four goals and methods is an indication of how significant the Near East Foundation, and private agencies more broadly, were in US foreign relations during the 1940s and 1950s.

This chapter explores the origins of the NEF's Iran programme by first outlining how the Foundation's guiding principle of 'helping people to help themselves' was central to its understanding of philanthropy. It demonstrates how the concept of cultivating 'goodwill' underpinned both NEF methodology and philosophy. The chapter then discusses the conclusions of a 1943 Foundation survey of Iran's rural education that resulted in the negotiation and eventual signing of the initial contract that allowed the NEF to establish its first programme in Iran. The appointment of its first director, Lyle J. Hayden, in 1946 and the encroaching impact of the Cold War were important factors that shaped the early nature and direction of the programme. The chapter then focuses on 1947–8 when, under the stewardship of Hayden and his successor Theodore Noe, the programme was consolidated and expanded from its modest beginnings to incorporate a wider area of the country. These years were pivotal as the Foundation gained a special reputation within US policymaking circles, particularly inside the State Department, while they also marked the emergence of financial difficulties that would become increasingly apparent in 1949. Despite these challenges, the programme continued to expand and NEF staff were employed on various projects across Iran, highlighting the high regard with which the Foundation was viewed by the Iranian government. Finally, the chapter concludes by examining how the arrival of Point Four funding both provided opportunities for expansion and created new challenges for the Iran programme.

In his 1947 annual report to the Near East Foundation's Board of Directors, HB Allen, educational director, encapsulated both the NEF's methodological and philosophical approach to philanthropy when he wrote 'its primary interest is in long-range programs of education aimed at helping people to help themselves'.[10] According to Allen, Foundation programmes could be divided into three separate stages: 'the exploratory, the demonstration stage, and finally the period of integration'.[11] The exploratory stage usually involved a survey by NEF personnel of the basic needs of the country in question, assessing which areas required urgent attention, what relevant infrastructure already existed, and the level of local enthusiasm and government support for the proposed programme.

If a programme was deemed to be viable, then a demonstration could be established, which would quite literally demonstrate to local people, for example, different farming techniques or sanitation practices. As Allen noted, the Near East Foundation 'differed somewhat from that of most other American agencies operating in foreign countries' because it only required limited financial assistance from local governments to begin operating.[12] Once the demonstration programme was running effectively, however, its benefits would soon become apparent to both local communities and governments who, it was argued, would enthusiastically contribute financially and materially to the project.

The final stage, the period of integration, was when the programme, having demonstrated its effectiveness, could be integrated into the national development or reform project of the local government. 'A demonstration in rural extension is successful', wrote Allen in 1955, 'when its effectiveness with the people and its economy of operation lead the host government to adopt and support such a service for the national well-being and to extend this over the whole country'.[13]

By following these three stages, the NEF aimed to improve people's lives but it was also recognized that the role of private agencies and philanthropic organizations did more than simply help people. They acted as representatives of the United States, even in countries where US government policy, influence or intervention was unwelcome. Where government projects could be unwieldy, private agencies could be flexible and, Allen observed, 'The assistance given is usually accepted on its merits regardless of the current local attitude toward the policies of the American government'.[14] Moreover, US government missions rarely had the luxury of time, which was essential to allow for their 'acceptance and adoption into the way of life of a people'.[15] Private agencies were able to integrate completely into society to gain the trust and respect of local communities.

According to Allen then, 'Through simple, down-to-earth projects administered by [the NEF's] highly trained, hard-working leaders the helping hand of America is extended to our sometimes sceptical neighbors'.[16] By doing so, the Near East Foundation was contributing to what former presidential candidate Wendell Willkie referred to as 'that great reservoir of goodwill' that the United States enjoyed across the world. The concept of 'goodwill' was a guiding principle for the Near East Foundation as it sought to foster positive relations with the local people and governments that engaged with its rural welfare programmes. More than this, however, Allen believed that the activities of the Foundation contributed to the maintenance and defence of peace in a world only slowly recovering from the ravages of the Second World War and already embroiled in a new Cold War which appeared to be on the brink of turning hot at any moment. Noting the UNESCO constitution, which states 'since wars begin in the minds of men, it is in the minds of men that the defences of peace must be constructed', Allen declared in October 1948 that the 'Near East Foundation with its practical personalized, humanitarian approach must be constructing the strongest defences of all'.[17]

For the NEF, Iran became a test case of both its capacity to cultivate goodwill and strengthen its defences against totalitarianism. During the First World War, NER had provided aid to rural populations in the northwest of the country and, mostly, Christian refugees fleeing the Ottoman invasion. It was not until 1943, thirteen years after the Near East Foundation had pivoted towards providing long-term development instead of disaster relief, that the Iranian government invited the NEF to conduct a survey of the country with a view to establishing a rural education programme.

In his first report for the survey, written in August, Allen noted that there were a number of issues that needed direct attention, notably a provision of elementary education and a programme to improve local health and sanitation. As Dr Ora Morgan, a member of the Foundation's Program Committee, described it when commenting on Allen's report, there was a 'crying need for [an] extension service' whereby an organization like the NEF operated demonstration projects to educate and train local people in new techniques and skills. Allen also noted some positives. Not only were there the remnants of a state-sponsored 'rural uplift' programme whose infrastructure could be adapted, Allen was impressed by the intelligence and industriousness of the peasants he encountered, revealing an Orientalist perspective underlying his perspective on Iran.[18]

His final report summarizing his six-month survey, written in November, was less optimistic. Estimating that 85–90 per cent of Iran's population was 'living in poverty; many in abject misery', Allen noted several areas that required urgent attention.[19] On the question of home economics, at the time a largely female endeavour in both the United States and Iran, Allen observed that 'aid to women [is] deplorably lacking'. School facilities were 'quite inadequate', more needed to be done to recruit male and female teachers from villages, and a rural adult literacy programme was vital. Most poignantly, Allen observed that a 'Rural health program crys [*sic*] aloud for organization and implementation. . . . Diseases of Near East scourging the village population. Infant mortality 40%, 50%, even 60% in some unfortunate villages.' Summarizing Allen's reports, Morgan quoted the Iranian minister of foreign affairs, M. Saed, who had remarked to Allen that 'Iran is in dire need of the particular kind of help that is usually provided by Near East Foundation'. For Morgan, this was 'clear evidence that Near East Foundation is really wanted in Iran' and therefore validation for the possibility of an extension of NEF activity into the country.[20]

Upon receiving Allen's reports, members of the Foundation's Program Committee were 'willing to suggest a full-fledged program' in the country.[21] A few weeks later, E.C. Miller, NEF executive secretary, noted that the Foundation's proposed venture in

Iran had been 'received with unusual enthusiasm' within the US State Department.[22] Considering the international context of 1944 such recognition among US officials was an indication that once the war was over private agencies would play an important role in advancing both Washington's foreign policy goals and international development.

On 21 April 1944, the Iranian government extended an official invitation to the Near East Foundation to 'send a representative to Iran' to negotiate the creation of a programme along the lines set out by Allen.[23] At the June Board of Directors meeting, it was agreed 'That the matter of instituting Near East Foundation's programs in Iran be approved in principle, the details to be developed upon Dr. Allen's return to America.'[24] American and Iranian government support notwithstanding, the challenge before the NEF was nevertheless a significant one, as Allen's report to the board attested.

Despite having been invited by the Iranian government itself, Allen noted that when he arrived the previous year 'Iranian officials did not know who I was or what I was there for'.[25] The high turnover of ministers and officials meant that those with some familiarity with Allen's endeavour were no longer in the government. Between the beginning of 1944 and the end of 1946, Iran went through no less than seven different prime ministers. As Allen put it, 'The Iranian government was and is seriously disorganized. . . . Cabinets change frequently. . . . Other missions told me I might as well fold up and come home.'[26] He did, however, receive assistance and genuine interest from the Ministries of Education and Agriculture, as well as the minister of court and even the shah himself.

Nevertheless, Allen described the rural situation in Iran as 'tragic', with most of the population living as 'tenants under a medieval feudal system. . . . They work soil that does not belong to them under a feudal system that makes them virtually slaves.' According to Allen, it was apposite that the Iranian government had invited the NEF to survey the country as 'Unless the country puts its own house in order it is very apt to have someone from the outside come in and do this for them'.[27] Allen also noted that although the US State Department was in favour of an NEF programme, instability and corruption within Iran 'would make the job extremely difficult'. Trying to put a positive spin on such a gloomy description, Allen suggested that if the NEF could find the right man for the job, who necessarily required relevant agriculture educational and administrative experience, they would 'stand out in such a sharp contrast that he would get I believe wonderful cooperation from the job'.[28] While Allen's description once more revealed his Orientalist perspective of Iranians as generally corrupt and incompetent, it also illustrated the scale of the task facing the Near East Foundation.

Writing to the Iranian minister, M. Shayesteh, Allen explained the principles of how NEF demonstration programmes worked. He made it clear that 'we make no attempt to solve the rural problem for the whole country, or even in several places of a country'. Instead, the Foundation would 'develop methods that may be applicable to the whole country', with a focus on 'itinerant agricultural instruction, health activities which are largely in the nature of practical sanitation, carefully adapted programs for women and children, and finally, recreation'. By emphasizing practical experimentation that would develop replicable methods of instruction, Allen told Shayesteh, the Foundation sought to maximize the impact of smaller projects by ensuring that their principles and techniques could be easily adapted and rolled out elsewhere.[29]

Despite Allen's efforts to cultivate awareness within Tehran, however, two US officials wrote to him in September 1944 to warn that 'there is little real comprehension of your scheme or the basic principles of the Near East Foundation in government circles'. Their warning was not just in reference to the practical elements of a Foundation rural welfare programme but, equally significantly, the financial implications for the Iranian government. Allen was informed that Iranian officials were 'under the impression that … there was no suggestion that the expenses were to be shared' between the NEF and Tehran. Indeed, it was assumed that the NEF would bear the costs of the initial demonstration programme, thereby showing 'the government exactly what the program means'.[30] As early as February 1944, the Iranian Council of Ministers had determined that the invitation to the Near East Foundation to establish a programme of rural activity 'should evidently not create financial obligations for the Iranian Government'.[31] Dr Isa Sedigh, Minister of Education, reiterated that 'in a conversation some years ago with the then head of the Near East Foundation' he had been told that all that was required was an invitation from the government, 'No cash contribution was asked for'.[32] For Iranian officials, a demonstration was required before funding would be provided, while for the NEF government funding was essential to not only finance the operation but also, perhaps more importantly, illustrate the cooperative nature of the programme.

Allen's initial proposal for the new programme, which he shared with JM Upton from the State Department for feedback, emphasized the importance of local government investment and cooperation. However, he conceded that 'the government's material share be kept to a minimum during the early stages' and 'the financing and directing of the programs would be chiefly the responsibility of the Near East Foundation'. It was Allen's expectation that 'in the course of time these responsibilities would be gradually transferred to the Iranian government until the point is reached where the project is almost entirely maintained by the government'.[33] For the NEF, a financial commitment by the local government from the very beginning, no matter how small, was vital to illustrate the cooperation required for a programme to be successful.

Towards the end of 1944, a significant milestone was reached when Allen confirmed to the Program Committee that the search for a suitable director for the nascent Iran programme was over. Lyle J. Hayden, an agriculturist and administrator in his early forties, had been selected for the job.[34] In the months that followed, while Hayden waited to be released from his present instructional position in the US Naval Reserve, negotiations with the Iranian government over the contract for the NEF programme began.[35] During this process, Upton made a number of suggested revisions to Allen's original proposal.

Upton advised tweaking language, rather than substantive content, in order to ease its acceptance and circumvent the need for parliamentary legislation, which would likely be a longwinded exercise. For example, the original request for a 'Maintenance allowance for the director' was changed to 'Maintenance Aid' – essentially the provision of accommodation and servants, so as to avoid the necessity of parliamentary approval for putting a foreigner on the government payroll. Similarly, Upton suggested referring to Hayden as a 'voluntary technical assistant', rather than a 'counselor or advisor', as these latter terms were negatively associated with undue foreign influence in Iran.[36]

Allen replied to Upton to confirm that he had adopted all of his suggestions with two minor exceptions.[37] The following day, Allen wrote to Shayesteh to convey the NEF's proposed programme, explaining that the delay had been due to the important search for a director which had now been completed.[38] Three months later, having not received a response, Allen once again sought out his contacts in the US State Department and Embassy in Tehran, enquiring whether they had any knowledge that his proposal had even reached the relevant Iranian authorities.[39] Allen also wrote to Shayesteh again asking for confirmation that 'our proposals have been received, carefully studied, and favorably accepted' so that Hayden could depart for Iran to begin work.[40] Despite friendly relations with both American and Iranian officials, the Foundation was at times dependent on factors outside of its control before any projects could be set up.

At the same time, Hayden formally joined the Near East Foundation having served his notice with the navy and completed the final stages of his PhD at Cornell University. During the summer of 1945, Hayden 'spent July and August with Dr Allen in New York absorbing the Foundation's philosophy and studying the plans for the project in Iran'. In September he left the United States to visit NEF rural programmes in Lebanon, Syria and Cyprus before finally arriving at his post in Iran.[41] In November, Allen would briefly join Hayden to introduce him to relevant Iranian officials but then leave him to work things out by himself; Allen was, in his own words, letting him 'work out his own salvation, which seems to be the only sound procedure in a situation of this kind'.[42] However, despite Hayden's appointment and arrival in Iran, the contract between the Near East Foundation and the Iranian government was yet to be signed due to the burgeoning tensions of the Cold War.

Iran, occupied during the war by American, British and Soviet troops, had played a key strategic role in the Allied supply lines that helped secure victory. After Nazi Germany's defeat, it had been agreed that all three allies would withdraw their troops. However, Iran soon became a test of the Truman administration's resolve to contain communism when Soviet forces instead helped establish Azerbaijan, in the north of the country, as an autonomous and separatist province. With the Iranian government focused on the Soviet incursion, the official signing of the contract for the NEF programme, which should have taken place in January 1946, was delayed.[43]

In the meantime, the Foundation received help from the State Department in acquiring surplus army materials and in its ongoing negotiations with the Iranian government. The US ambassador to Iran, Wallace Murray, in particular, was very positive about the NEF, stating that it 'has the type of program I have dreamed of for Iran'.[44] Unsurprisingly, both Iranian and American officials were then too preoccupied with the crisis to spare much time for the Foundation but in April 1946 the contract establishing the rural welfare programme was at last completed.[45] Yet these positive steps were undermined by the difficulty the Foundation faced in actually implementing the contract with the Iranian government.

In June 1946, nearly two months after the contract had been formally signed, Hayden wrote to Allen to complain that further progress was delayed because the minister of agriculture was yet to add his signature as directed by the Iranian council of ministers. Hayden explained that internal divisions within the ministry were causing problems, suggesting that the minister was 'deliberately delaying the formal signing because he is unfavorable to the idea of the program, especially when it will be conducted by Americans. Like many others, he probably fears this is a clever piece of American propaganda to reduce the effect of Russian influence in Iran.'[46] Once more, the Cold War was encroaching on the NEF's efforts.

By October though, Allen felt confident to report that the recently inaugurated Iran programme 'has progressed far beyond the Foundation's most optimistic time schedule.'[47] While managing the ongoing negotiations with the Iranian government, Hayden had set up a demonstration project approximately 25–30 miles outside Tehran in the district of Veramin. The project at this stage consisted of five villages, 'the so-called Palisth group', owned by the 'Veramin Endowed Properties' and administered by 'a progressive committee' which used revenue from the land to finance a local orphanage for boys.[48] The project itself would consist of a ten-acre 'garden plot' rented by the Foundation from the Palisth group. Hayden would use this area, approximately the size of eight American football fields, 'for growing vegetable seeds, seedlings and nursery stock for distribution to farmers and for certain tests'. A further thirty acres of farmland would 'be used for demonstration and experimental purposes'.[49]

Hayden also agreed

> to provide agricultural instruction for all boys in the fifth and sixth grades; establish schools (with the assistance of the Minister of Education) in the three villages not now having educational facilities; establish for breeding and experimental purposes small flocks of sheep, poultry, possibly a few head of cattle; conduct variety, fertilized and tillage tests on the experimental plots, importing certain necessary machinery and equipment for this purpose.[50]

Acknowledging the importance and challenge of maintaining an adequate water supply in much of rural Iran, Hayden also prioritized experiments in irrigation using 'inexpensive, mechanical pumps', and hired an Iranian agriculturist, A. A. Yassi. It was also intended that the programme would 'be rounded out to include the home, public health through elementary sanitation, and certain types of social-cultural activities' with the appointment of an American rural sanitation technician being a vital first step.[51]

However, just three months after Allen's report financial constraints meant that Hayden's requested budget of $33,761.50 for the first half of 1947 had to be reduced by one-third to $22,750. In order to achieve this saving, Hayden delayed his request for a sanitation technician, half of the equipment he had planned on purchasing, and downscaled some of his projects.[52] In spite of these setbacks, in March 1947 Allen told the Program Committee that Hayden was doing a 'wonderful job'.[53] As the year progressed, Hayden reported that he was beginning to make inroads in his demonstration work. In addition to a forage and poultry project, he had also overseen the digging of one well to improve the water supply for one of the villages and was planning 'to sell it back to the village, and with this money he hopes to dig the second well'.[54] Through these sorts of activities, Hayden sought to not only help the local community gain access to a safe water supply but also cultivate goodwill by demonstrating the value and efficacy the programme.

The progress made on the ground was, however, not always matched by the cooperation of the Iranian government. According to Hayden, 'there seems to be no feeling on the part of any one with whom we have talked that the program has not been worthwhile or that there is any particular criticizm [sic].' Even so, due to debates about whether the original agreement remained valid, the agriculture minister refused to sign an extension to the contract until a special request had been submitted to the prime minister 'asking permission to continue the present agreement'. Hayden's frustrations were expressed in his observation that 'It is just one of those matters that move infintely [sic] slow in this part of the world', but the reality was that further funding from the Iranian government would not be forthcoming for at least another two months.[55] For an organization like NEF, which relied on local government cooperation and whose finances were less generous than those of the larger foundations, such as Ford and Rockefeller, every cent and every rial counted.

As such, although the NEF was largely funded by money received from small donors, alternative sources were always being considered, including the foundations just mentioned and the US government. By September, the passing of the Fulbright Bill, which used the sale of surplus war materials to support welfare activities, presented the Foundation with a new source of funding. In Iran's case, $2 million had been designated across a ten-year period, of which the NEF was to receive $68,000 per year to cover the cost of American and local personnel.[56]

In October, Allen reported that Hayden's project in Iran was 'an impressive example of how one should go about building a new program in a difficult area, constructing the foundations piece by piece and in such a manner as to insure ultimate success'.[57] Although primarily an agricultural, educational and sanitation programme, Hayden had built three 'modest dwellings' for his staff that also 'serve as demonstrations of slightly improved, economically constructed village homes', as well as a storage shed and poultry house. A small garden orchard was used for 'demonstrating pruning, spraying, and orchard management'.[58] In just fifteen months, Hayden had conducted over one hundred farm and home surveys, determining that 'ill health, the low level of home life and general illiteracy' were all major factors impeding progress in rural areas. He cleaned and repaired one village's 'umbar', an underground water storage system, and installed 'a simple but effective sand filter'.[59] Identifying malaria as a widespread scourge in the region, Hayden, assisted by three Iranian employees, sprayed every house, outbuilding, stable and standing pool in the demonstration area with DDT, the insecticide used in many developing countries during the 1940s and 1950s to try to eradicate malaria. School rooms were established in three of the five villages and evening literacy classes were set up for adults.[60]

According to Allen, 'Hayden was more and more in demand by the government, especially the Ministry of Agriculture, to advise on technical questions', and was requested to conduct eight reports on various issues for Tehran. Hayden had also appointed a new sanitation technician, Theodore Noe, and was mentoring an Iranian as his 'understudy'.[61] It is perhaps not surprising that Allen's report, written for the benefit of the Foundation's executive board, would be glowing in its appraisal of one of its area directors, especially one based in a country where the US government was showing considerable interest. Even so, Allen's fulsome praise of Hayden is indicative of the NEF philosophy that an effective programme needs to be embedded into the local community and demonstrate its worth through the introduction of practical and incremental improvements.

While Hayden and Allen's reports largely focused on the work at hand, describing in detail the progress of specific projects – how many egg-laying hens had been distributed to local villagers and so on – the activities of the Near East Foundation aligned closely with the thinking of US foreign policy officials at the time. Indeed, American policymakers regularly remarked upon the parallels between US national interests and the NEF's development efforts. Loy Henderson, director of the Office of Near Eastern and African Affairs at the Department of State, speaking at a Foundation luncheon in December 1947, outlined the Truman administration's perspective on how private agencies and philanthropic organizations contribute to US foreign policy goals.

Henderson stated that 'poverty, disease, and ignorance are disturbers of tranquillity and constant threats to peace and security', before implicitly referencing the threat of communism by arguing that 'Deprivation, economic chaos, and misery are the breeding grounds for the counsels of despair which lead to totalitarianism'. Although Henderson acknowledged that governments necessarily have a much greater capacity to provide certain kinds of relief than philanthropic organizations, he noted that the Truman administration and the NEF 'share one important aim – to help the peoples of the area to help themselves'.[62] The Truman administration was not being altruistic, of course, but sought to give people in the Middle East the tools, figuratively and literally, to improve their lives and thereby make them less vulnerable to the appeal of communism. Moreover, according to Henderson, 'the philanthropic and far-sighted projects of the Foundation have served as convincing evidence of American friendliness and good will.'[63]

Within Near East Foundation circles, the concept of 'goodwill' as being integral to the success of any given development programme was well understood. In January when reporting on the success of the well that Hayden had dug the previous year, HB Allen wrote: 'It is hard to measure either in dollars or in good will, the value of such contributions. This, however, is typical of the work in Iran.'[64] The cultivation of 'goodwill' was, then, vital for both US foreign policy goals and the NEF. For the Truman administration, it would help to create a positive image of the United States to counter the propaganda of its adversaries. For the Near East Foundation, it would help facilitate the development of its programmes on the ground and generate enthusiasm and support among local people, as well as government officials.

There were times, however, when its relationship with official US foreign policy could inhibit the work of the Foundation. If the NEF could cultivate goodwill that could help advance both NEF and US foreign policy goals, it stands to reason that ill will generated by US policies could impact the Foundation. For example, in June 1948 Hayden argued that President Truman's support for the creation of the state of Israel was making it impossible for him to secure additional funding from the Iranian government, which just a few months earlier had seemed close to being finalized. Hayden argued the delay was because of

Truman's stand on the Palestine question. So the reason we cannot expect expansion in Iran this year can all be traced directly back to Mr Truman. One month ago I said that the Palestine trouble had not reached Iran. Today that picture has radically changed. Newspapers are starting campaigns to help the Arabs, Mullahs are appealing to all good Moslems and mass meetings in the large Mosques are increasing.[65]

His assertion may or may not explain the problems he was encountering with the Iranian government at the time but it indicates the awareness within the Foundation that it was often impossible to keep private philanthropy and US government policy entirely separate. For NEF personnel, however, there was little they could do other than to concentrate on the job at hand.

Throughout 1948, the programme expanded from the original five villages to thirty-five to become 'a comprehensive integrated program of rural improvement which emphasizes the reduction of illiteracy among adults and the development of elementary education for the youth'.[66] Without wishing to list every aspect of Hayden's wide-ranging efforts, a few suffice to illustrate the nature of the programme: poultry demonstrations; the digging of wells and installation of water pumps and filters; demonstration of modern farm machinery and implements; development of techniques for managing ticks found in sheep and cattle; distribution of eggs and seeds; DDT spraying to control malaria; treatment of lice in 193 school children; establishment of ten additional elementary schools, which also saw 348 adults enrol in night classes to improve literacy; preparation of lessons on health, sanitation and agriculture; weekly teacher-training sessions; and publication of 5,000 copies of an education bulletin entitled 'Guide for Rural School Teachers of Iran' at the request of the Ministry of Education.

Allen concluded his report by stating simply, 'It should be quite unnecessary to point out the limitless value of fundamental work of this kind. That this type of education is appreciated in Iran is indicated by the eager cooperation of the villagers and the reaction of government officials'.[67] As a result, Allen wrote, 'The latter have seen to it that the contributors' dollar from America has been multiplied by Iranian rials in order that the benefits of this program may be extended as far as possible. This is the kind of investment that pays'.[68] As Allen and Loy Henderson had argued elsewhere, effective demonstration programmes cultivate goodwill which results in concrete support.

Yet, despite the considerable progress that Hayden had made in the two short years he had been serving in Iran, the future of the programme was, due to financial considerations, still uncertain. At one point in October 1948, the Foundation's Treasurer, Harold Hatch, noted 'that we have about used up our available funds', due to an apparent downturn in the number of donations. It was Hatch's recommendation that the NEF needed to take 'immediate and substantial retrenchment'.[69] All options were considered and the Iran programme was not immune from the threat of cuts or worse. The following week it was suggested that if Hayden, who was currently on his way home to the United States, decided not to return to his work in Iran, then 'the Iranian program should be closed but if he did return, the work in Syria or Lebanon should be eliminated'.[70]

Although Hayden was to take a leave of absence so that he could join the Economic Cooperation Administration (ECA) for a year, he strongly recommended that all three country programmes should be maintained; it was agreed that 'it would be a mistake to pick out one of the three areas and close it completely' but each would need to survive on a reduced budget until further funding became available, perhaps through the Fulbright Bill.[71] It was hoped that the Foundation's reputation among US policymakers might offer some salvation. Hayden's activities in Iran continued to be well-thought of within the State Department, while Allen and Miller were approached by US officials shortly after Truman announced his Point Four programme who suggested that the NEF may be a suitable recipient for funding to 'help the underprivileged countries of the Near East'.[72]

The NEF also remained popular within Iran. Theodore Noe, newly appointed as assistant area director while Hayden was with the ECA, cooperated with the Iranian government to expand its malaria control activities. Noe's efforts were warmly appreciated by Iranian officials, including the ambassador to the United States, Hossein Ala.[73] Overseas Consultants Inc., an American organization helping the Iranian government create what would become its seven-year development plans, also 'enthusiastically endorsed' the NEF programme and advocated for increased funding from Tehran.[74] The looming Cold War threat also created a potential opportunity for the Foundation, highlighting the role that private agencies such as the NEF might play in both advancing US interests and containing communism. As Miller observed, in Iranian government circles there was 'the constant fear of the next menacing move on the part of its neighbor, Soviet Russia', but the Truman administration's new emphasis on development as a key foreign policy goal placed private agencies and philanthropic organizations at the heart of its Point Four activities.[75]

As the Foundation's foreign director Laird Archer would put it in reference to NEF activities in Greece, 'We are, in a way, the advance technicians and light-bearers of the American Point IV.' The anti-communist ideology behind Point Four also aligned with thinking within the Foundation. Writing about Iran, Archer added that 'with alert, undeceived eyes constantly on its northern frontier and inner vision turned toward the west', the government in Tehran was 'planning its New Day in rural reconstruction with our advice and specific demonstrations, knowing the struggle it has before it to beat the communist race to capture with trick phrases the hopes of the underprivileged'.[76] Archer also noted that the Soviet Union's anti-religious, especially anti-Islam, purges had made by necessity allies out of the Christian and Muslim worlds.[77]

In his annual report for the same year, Theodore Noe confirmed that progress was being made in the Iran programme's three key areas of focus – education, sanitation and agriculture – although the latter was perhaps not as advanced as one would have hoped since the departure of Hayden who specialized in that field. By contrast, the Foundation's sanitation activities, Noe's area of expertise, were expanding across the country as the Iranian government requested further assistance, particularly regarding the spraying of DDT in the border provinces of Azerbaijan and Baluchistan in collaboration with the Ministry of Health and the Ministry of War, who provided the necessary equipment and personnel, respectively.[78] Not all of the programme's successes, however, were on such a national scale; indeed, they were more likely to be illustrated by case studies involving just a few individual people.

In his annual report, Allen cited the example of a landlord who had initially refused to pay the requisite fee after his field had been ploughed by the NEF using a tractor. When the landlord asked the following year if the NEF would repeat the service, Noe refused, explaining that he did not want an awkward situation to arise if he were to not pay again. In response, the landlord paid for the service in advance, as well as reimbursing Noe for last year's work. According to Allen, the landlord was determined to have his field ploughed by the NEF tractor again because 'his crop was so much better' and had since become 'one of the Foundation's best friends and recently started voluntarily, at his own expense, to make a fine addition to the school'.[79] It was this kind of goodwill that the Foundation sought to generate through its painstaking and meticulous approach to its demonstration programmes. The proof was in the pudding; peasants, farmers and landlords alike were able to see the improvements that were being made as a result of the Foundation's efforts and, it was hoped, would, in turn, become enthusiastic supporters of the programme.

Similarly, when Noe and his colleagues sprayed sixteen villages with DDT they did so with the cooperation of the villagers themselves, as well as the landlords. Otherwise, Allen noted, to do so without cooperation 'would represent simply a contributed service without adhering to the policy of helping the people to help themselves'.[80] This guiding principle of the Near East Foundation was, according to Allen, also borne out in the case of several NEF-trained Iranian staff who were engaged in sanitizing the city of Dezful, 'which has the unfortunate reputation of being one of the dirtiest places in Iran'.[81] The operation was funded partially by the shah himself who, according to Allen, 'requested that his appreciation be expressed to those American people who have supported this constructive effort which has already become a model for the country'.[82]

These positive developments coincided in the following months with a 'slight increase' in Foundation income, which Allen hoped might be the start of 'a more favourable trend'.[83] Even so, later in his report, he noted that while there was some enthusiasm inside Iran for expanding the Foundation's demonstration projects to other parts of the country, such an endeavour would require far more American technicians than were currently involved in the programme, which in turn would require considerably more funding.[84] At this time, the programme was still run by a single American, Theodore Noe who had replaced Lyle Hayden as director. Aside from the brief secondment of a home making supervisor to conduct a month-long survey and being ably supported by Iranian staff, including those involved in agricultural training, sanitation, teaching and teacher training, whom both Noe and Allen were always quick to commend in their reports, it remained a small-scale operation due to the financial implications of increasing the number of American staff.

As the end of 1950 approached, the Near East Foundation had reason to view the coming year with optimism. In June, President Truman had singled out the NEF's activities in Iran as a prime example of how private agencies could improve the lives of people in the developing world. By December, Edward C. Miller and Halsey B. Knapp were thrilled to declare that 'The Foundation possesses the highest standing over the widest field of any voluntary agency in the Near East'. After two decades of service, the NEF had 'accumulated a tremendous heritage of goodwill and appreciation', receiving praise from 'ambassadors and ministers of the United States, members of US official missions, prime ministers, ministry heads and undersecretaries of the various countries, and many others'.[85]

However, Foundation officers were all agreed that while recognition by government sources was valuable, not least for the funding that may accrue as a result, private agencies had a vital role to play that, despite their superior coffers, governments could not replicate. As Allen wrote in October, private philanthropy allowed for a 'slow, patient, personalized approach' that did not need to meet arbitrary deadlines in response to congressional appropriations; although Allen conceded that the latter method 'may have its advantages when building railroads, bridges, highways or destroyed harbors: it is a distinct handicap dealing with the human equation'.[86] Factoring in the 'human equation' was vital in order to cultivate the goodwill that was integral to both the methodology and success of the NEF's activities. Perhaps foreseeing the potential issues that may arise if the Foundation were to receive increased funds from the US government, Theodore Noe emphasized the importance of maintaining the slow, methodical approach favoured by the NEF and resisting pressure from external sources to expand or replicate the programme elsewhere.[87]

As hoped though, the new year brought positive news as Allen revealed that he had been informed by State Department officials that the Foundation would be among the recipients of Point Four funding, $50,000 of which would be allocated to expand the NEF programme in Iran.[88] The Near East Foundation's finances, however, remained precarious, leading to the closure of the Lebanon programme, a 'slight reduction of $1,500' to the Syria programme, and 'the reduction of the programs in Greece to a skeleton basis'. Only Iran escaped unscathed.[89] While further interest from Point Four officials about the possibility of additional funding for the NEF programme in Iran was welcomed, Foundation personnel also expressed some caution.

In March, after noting that discussions about expanding the programme beyond the Veramin district were being held with the Truman administration, the Board of Directors voted to authorize negotiation of another contract but only on the grounds that 'special funds . . . [and] proper safeguards' were outlined to ensure that the Foundation's work could continue to the same standard.[90] By May, two further Point Four contracts had been signed, one of $88,140 for Syria and a second for Iran of $247,000. Another for $25,000 'for an improved rural housing demonstration in Iran' was also being discussed with the State Department.[91]

In its press release announcing these contracts, the Technical Cooperation Administration (TCA) declared: 'The purpose of the Foundation's work is the same as that of the Point Four mission: to raise standards of living at the village level by a concerted effort to improve agriculture, health and education, and to train a body of Iranian experts to carry this work to other parts of the country'.[92] The new funds would allow for a significant expansion of the programme: 'In Iran it will mean increasing the number of village demonstration centres from 35 to 75. It will add ten American technicians to the staff and a large number of Iranians trained under United States supervision.'[93] There was, however, a clear sense among NEF personnel that although greater funding would mean a larger and better-staffed programme, it also brought with it potential problems.

Not least of these new challenges was the recognition that the Near East Foundation's slow and steady approach to rural development and extension education did not necessarily align with the State Department's need for quick results. As Cleveland E. Dodge noted at the June 1951 Finance Committee Meeting, 'the Foundation might have to adjust its policy from the slow careful development to a plan that would provide quicker results if we are to continue to have funds from the government.'[94] Allen also observed that while the Near East Foundation was held in high esteem in many quarters, the Point Four funding both made 'possible many refinements and additions long overdue' but also presented 'a serious challenge'. Point Four money could only be spent on *new* activities, it could not be used to supplement funding required to maintain existing programmes. In Allen's words, 'If the trend of the past few years of declining income, with the resultant cutting of basic work, were to continue, the foundations on which the new super-structure is to be erected would be seriously weakened.'[95]

Even so, thanks to funding from Point Four the programme was expanding far beyond its modest origins under Lyle J. Hayden's direction when he was the sole American technician working for the NEF in Iran. The agreement with the TCA now provided for 'the addition of three agricultural extension agents, a poultry specialist, a fruit specialist, two sanitarians, two rural educators for the supervision of village schools and the direction of the teacher-training course', in addition to a home welfare specialist.[96] The following year a third contract was signed by the Near East Foundation and Point Four authorities relating to the Iran programme. This latest agreement granted the Foundation $482,034, dwarfing the funding previously used to support the NEF programme in Iran. As had been predicted by Dodge and Allen, however, such a significant figure inevitably led to adjustments in the programme. Where Hayden's programme had originally overseen just five villages in the Veramin district it had since expanded to 135 as a result of the first two Point Four contracts and was now extended to over 300 villages by the new agreement. Allen observed that such an expansion 'departs somewhat from the basic policy of Near East Foundation' but because Point Four authorities aimed to 'cover the ten ostends or states of the country it is necessary for the organization to cooperate by providing complete coverage for one district'.[97]

The preceding six years of painstaking, small-scale project work had paid off. The Near East Foundation, which had become highly regarded among US policymakers, was now a key component of the Truman administration's Iran policy and the recipient of Point Four funding. Iranian officials were equally impressed with the efforts of Hayden, Noe and their Iranian colleagues. By emphasizing a focused and patient approach to development, the Foundation was able to cultivate goodwill among the local population through its practical demonstration projects. The NEF's philosophy of embedding its programmes within a society in order to gain people's trust and respect was effective in Iran. Hayden and Noe were able to establish a series of projects that would remain for the next thirty years.

From the beginning, the NEF's Iran programme was closely aligned with the goals of the US government. It developed a fruitful relationship with the State Department even while it managed to maintain its autonomy, benefiting from the expertise of US diplomats without needing to submit to their influence. Yet throughout this period the programme was beset by financial constraints and faced the possibility of closure at least once when Foundation funds nearly dried up. The Point Four funding that the programme received in 1951 and 1952 was therefore hugely significant in allowing it to continue to operate and even expand considerably. These opportunities also brought new challenges for the Foundation that would become increasingly apparent in the 1950s as it faced pressure from the US government to accelerate its development programmes. Throughout its time in Iran, the Near East Foundation tried to maintain a balance between retaining its high standard of projects and not overstretching the overall programme, while at the same time cultivating goodwill – among the local population and government officials, both American and Iranian – and continuing to make progress in broad development terms.

# Notes

1　Harry S. Truman, 'Inaugural Address', 20 January 1949. Online by Gerhard Peters and John T. Woolley, *The American Presidency Project*. https://www.presidency.ucsb.edu/ node/229929 (accessed 9 September 2019).

2　Keith David Watenpaugh, *Bread from Stones: The Middle East and the Making of Modern Humanitarianism* (Oakland: University of California Press, 2015), 93.

3　Minutes of the Program Committee Meeting of Near East Foundation, 21 February 1949, Box 46, Dockets - October 1948 to June 1949, Near East Foundation Records, Accessions 2010:002, RG 2, Rockefeller Archive Centre, Sleepy Hollow, NY, 1 (31). Hereafter referred to as NEF Records.

4　Minutes of the Program Committee Meeting of Near East Foundation, 1 June 1949, Box 46, Dockets - October 1948 to June 1949, NEF Records, 2 (37).

5　Harry S. Truman, 'Address Before the Annual Convention of the American Newspaper Guild', 28 June 1950. Online by Gerhard Peters and John T. Woolley, The American Presidency Project, https://www.presidency.ucsb.edu/documents/address -before-the-annual-convention-the-american-newspaper-guild (accessed 1 August 2021).

6　John H. Lorentz, 'Educational Development in Iran: The Pivotal Role of the Mission Schools and Alborz College', *Iranian Studies* 44, no. 5 (2011): 647–55; Thomas M. Ricks, 'Alborz College of Tehran, Dr. Samuel Martin Jordan and the American Faculty: Twentieth-Century Presbyterian Mission Education and Modernism in Iran (Persia)', *Iranian Studies* 44, no. 5 (2011): 627–46; Jasamin Rostam-Kolayi, 'From Evangelizing to Modernizing Iranians: The American Presbyterian Mission and its Iranian Students', *Iranian Studies* 41, no. 2 (2008): 213–40; Michael P. Zirinsky, 'A Panacea for the Ills of the Country: American Presbyterian Education in Inter-War Iran', *Iranian Studies* 26, no. 1/2 (1993): 119–37. On official diplomatic relations between the United States and Iran during the 1940s and 1950s, see James F. Goode, *The United States and Iran: In the Shadow of Musaddiq* (Houndmills: Palgrave Macmillan, 1997); Mark Hamilton Lytle, *The Origins of the Iranian-American Alliance, 1941–1953* (Boulder: Lynne Rienner Publishers, 1987); David R. Collier, *Democracy and the Nature of American Influence in Iran, 1941–1979* (Syracuse: Syracuse University

Press, 2017); Mark Gasiorowski, *US Foreign Policy and the Shah: Building a Client State in Iran* (Ithaca: Cornell University Press, 1991); James Bill, *The Eagle and the Lion: The Tragedy of American-Iranian Relations* (New Haven: Yale University Press, 1988); Barry Rubin, *Paved with Good Intentions: The American Experience in Iran* (Harmondsworth: Penguin, 1981).

7   Richard Garlitz, *A Mission for Development: Utah Universities and the Point Four Program in Iran* (Louisville: Utah State University Press, 2018); Matthew K. Shannon, *Losing Hearts and Minds: American-Iranian Relations and International Education during the Cold War* (Ithaca: Cornell University Press, 2017); *American-Iranian Dialogues: From Constitution to White Revolution, c. 1890s–1960s*, edited by Matthew K. Shannon (London: Bloomsbury, 2021).

8   Victor V. Nemchenok, "'That So Fair a Thing Should Be So Frail": The Ford Foundation and the Failure of Rural Development in Iran, 1953–1964', *Middle East Journal* 63, no. 2 (2009): 261–84; Christopher T. Fisher, "'Moral Purpose is the Important Thing": David Lilienthal, Iran, and the Meaning of Development in the US, 1956–1963', *The International History Review* 33, no. 3 (2011): 431–51; Gregory Brew, "'What They Need Is Management": American NGOs, the Second Seven Year Plan and Economic Development in Iran, 1954–1963', *The International History Review* 41, no. 1 (2019): 1–22.

9   Nemchenok does discuss some of the NEF's projects in relation to the funding they received from the Ford Foundation.

10  Annual Report of the Educational Director, October 1947, Box 6, Annual Reports, 1946–1956, NEF Records, 1–2.

11  Annual Report of the Educational Director, 21 October 1948, Ibid., 3.

12  Annual Report of the Educational Director, December 1954, Ibid., 8.

13  Annual Report of the Educational Director, December 1955, Ibid., 1.

14  Ibid., 20.

15  Edward C. Miller and Halsey B. Knapp, A Report to the Directors of Near East Foundation covering a trip to the field and an examination of Foundation Activities in Lebanon, Syria, Iran, Greece, during the period 20 October–3 December 1950. Box 46, Dockets, January 1951 to May 1951, NEF Records, 10.

16  Annual Report of the Educational Director, 21 October 1948, Box 6, Annual Reports, 1946–1956, NEF Records, 38–9.

17  Ibid., 39.

18  Report to Near East Foundation Program Committee on Dr H. B. Allen's Reports on Iran (Exhibit A), 19 January 1944, Minutes of the Program Committee Meeting of Near East Foundation, 19 January 1944, Box 5, 1944 Dockets of Board of Directors Meetings, NEF Records, 1.

19  Ibid., 2.

20  Ibid., 3.

21  Minutes of the Program Committee Meeting of Near East Foundation, 19 January 1944, Ibid., 7.

22  Minutes of the Program Committee Meeting of Near East Foundation, 17 February 1944, Ibid., 2.

23  M. Shayesteh, minister of Iran, to Near East Foundation, 21 April 1944, Box 63, Iran, Government 1944–1947, NEF Records.

24  Minutes of the Sixty-Second Regular Meeting of the Board of Directors of Near East Foundation, 15 June 1944, Box 45, Board of Directors Minutes, March 1944 – October 1947, NEF Records, 2.

25  Dr H. B. Allen's Report at Directors' Meeting, 15 June 1944, Ibid., 3.
26  Ibid., 4.
27  Ibid., 6.
28  Ibid., 7.
29  H. B. Allen to The Hon. M. Shayesteh, 19 July 1944, Box 63, Iran, Government 1944–1947, NEF Records, 2.
30  J. M. Upton to Dr H. B. Allen, 15 September 1944, Box 63, Iran, Rural Committee 1944, NEF Records, 1; Donald Wilber to Dr Allen, 6 September 1944, Ibid.
31  Decree of the Council of Ministers, 16 February 1944, included as an attachment to Ibid.
32  J. M. Upton to Dr Allen, 10 November 1944, Ibid., 1.
33  Considerations Relative to a Program of Rural Development for Iran, included as an attachment from H. B. Allen to Mr J. M. Upton, 26 December 1944, Ibid.
34  Minutes of the Program Committee Meeting of Near East Foundation, 22 November 1944, Box 5, 1945 Dockets of Board of Directors Meetings, NEF Records, 2.
35  Minutes of the Program Committee Meeting of Near East Foundation, 15 March 1945, Ibid., 7.
36  J. M. Upton to Dr Allen, 11 February 1945, Box 63, Iran, Rural Committee 1944, NEF Records, 1–3.
37  H. B. Allen to Mr J. M. Upton, 10 April 1945, Ibid.
38  H. B. Allen to The Hon. M. Shayesteh, 11 April 1945, Box 63, Iran, Government 1944–1947, NEF Records.
39  H. B. Allen to Mr J. M. Upton, 9 July 1945, Box 63, Iran, Rural Committee 1944, NEF Records.
40  H. B. Allen to The Hon. M. Shayesteh, 18 July 1945, Box 63, Iran, Government 1944–1947, NEF Records.
41  C. I. Crowther to Harold A. Hatch, 27 September 1945, Ibid., 7.
42  Annual Report of the Educational Director (Dr H. B. Allen), 4 October 1945, Ibid., 28.
43  Dr Allen's Report Delivered to Board of Directors of Near East Foundation, 4 April 1946, 1946–7 Dockets of Board of Directors Meetings, NEF Records, 2–4.
44  Ibid., 3.
45  Ibid., 4.
46  Lyle J. Hayden, Director, Iranian Area, to Dr H. B. Allen, Educational Director, No. T-27, 16 June 1946, Box 63, Iran, Government 1944–1947, NEF Records, 1.
47  Annual Report of the Educational Director, October 1946, Box 6, Annual Reports, 1946–1956, NEF Records, 2.
48  Ibid., 4.
49  Ibid., 5.
50  Ibid., 5–6.
51  Ibid., 6.
52  C. I. Crowther, Comptroller, to Harold A. Hatch, Chairman, Finance Committee, 22 January 1947, Box 45, Dockets, October 1946 to June 1947, NEF Records, 5.
53  Minutes of the Program Committee of the Near East Foundation, 18 March 1947, Ibid., 1.
54  Minutes of the Program Committee of the Near East Foundation, 15 May 1947, Ibid., 3.
55  L. J. Hayden to Executive Secretary, Ref. No. T-50, 30 July 1946, Box 63, Iran, Government 1944–1947, NEF Records, 1–2.

56 Minutes of the Program Committee of the Near East Foundation, 11 September 1947, Box 46, Dockets - October 1947 to July 1948, NEF Records, 3 (46).

57 Annual Report of the Educational Director, October 1947, Box 6, Annual Reports, 1946–1956, NEF Records, 41.

58 Ibid., 42.

59 Ibid., 44.

60 Ibid., 45.

61 Ibid., 46.

62 Speech by Mr Loy Henderson of the State Department, Washington, DC, at a Near East Foundation Luncheon of about 400 guests held at the Mayflower Hotel, Washington, DC, on 9 December 1947, Box 46, Dockets - October 1947 to July 1948, NEF Records, 1.

63 Ibid., 2.

64 Report of Educational Director on Middle East Tour, 19 January 1948, Ibid., 9.

65 Report of Educational Director to the Board of Directors of Near East Foundation, 28 June 1948, Ibid., 5.

66 Annual Report of the Educational Director, October 1948, Box 6, Annual Reports 1946–1956, NEF Records, 34.

67 Ibid., 34–7.

68 Ibid., 37.

69 Minutes of the Eighteenth Annual (Seventy-Seventh Regular) Meeting of the Board of Directors of Near East Foundation, 21 October 1948, Box 46, Dockets, October 1948 to June 1949, NEF Records, 7.

70 Minutes of the Finance Committee Meeting of Near East Foundation, 27 October 1948, Ibid., 3.

71 C. I. Crowther, Comptroller, to Mr Harold A. Hatch, Chairman Finance Committee, 23 December 1948, Ibid., 4.

72 Report of the Executive Secretary of the Board of Directors of Near East Foundation, 17 January 1949, Ibid., 3. Minutes of the Program Committee Meeting of Near East Foundation, 21 February 1949, Ibid., 1.

73 Hossein Ala, Ambassador of Iran, to Dr H. B. Allen, No. 4677, 16 March 1949, Ibid.

74 Part III – Comments by E. C. Miller, Executive Secretary, Meeting of Board of Directors Near East Foundation, 8 June 1949, Ibid., 4.

75 Ibid., 1.

76 Annual Report of the Foreign Director, 1948–1949, 15 August 1949, Box 5, Annual Reports, 1947–1950, 7.

77 Ibid., 8.

78 Near East Foundation Iranian Area Annual Report, 1 July 1948 to 30 June 1949, 10 July 1949, Box 46, Dockets, June 1950 to December 1950, NEF Records, 1–7.

79 Annual Report of the Educational Director, December 1949, Box 6, Annual Reports, 1946–1956, NEF Records, 5–6.

80 Ibid., 6.

81 Ibid., 7.

82 Ibid., 8.

83 Report of Educational Director to the Board of Directors of Near East Foundation, 10 April 1950, Box 46, Dockets, October 1949 to April 1950, NEF Records, 1.

84 Ibid., 7.

85 Edward C. Miller and Halsey B. Knapp, A Report to the Directors of Near East Foundation covering a trip to the field and an examination of Foundation Activities

in Lebanon, Syria, Iran, Greece, during the period 20 October–3 December 1950. Box 46, Dockets, January 1951 to May 1951, NEF Records, 2.

86  Annual Report of Educational Director, October 1950, Box 5, Annual Reports, 1947–1950, NEF Records, 2.

87  Ibid., 28.

88  Minutes of the Program Committee Meeting of Near East Foundation, 9 January 1951, Box 46, Dockets, January 1951 to May 1951, NEF Records, 1.

89  Ibid., 3.

90  Minutes of the Eighty-Fifth Regular Meeting of the Board of Directors of Near East Foundation, 22 March 1951, Ibid., 4.

91  Minutes of the Eighty-Sixth Regular Meeting of the Board of Directors of Near East Foundation, 24 May 1951, Ibid., 2.

92  Press Release: Point Four Agreements with Near East Foundation for Rural Programs in Iran and Syria, Technical Cooperation Administration, Department of State, 3 May 1951, Ibid., 2.

93  Ibid., 1.

94  Minutes of the Finance Committee Meeting of Near East Foundation, 12 June 1951, Box 46, October 1951 to December 1951, NEF Records, 1.

95  Annual Report of Educational Director, 8 October 1951, Box 6, Annual Reports, 1946–1956, NEF Records, 3.

96  Ibid., 19.

97  Annual Report of Educational Director, December 1952, Ibid., 2.

# 9

# From books to land rovers

## The informal, small philanthropy of the AFL-CIO and the ICFTU in Africa during the early Cold War

### Kevin E. Grimm

In December 1960, Maida Springer, an international affairs representative with the AFL-CIO, wrote to Jacob Namfua, the general secretary of the Tanganyika (Tanzania) Federation of Labor, offering Western aid in revealing ways. A key segment of her letter read,

> In order to help the work of the branches of the TFL., [*sic*] we are in the process of selecting a number of books for trade union kits on union bargaining procedures, education, etc. They will be available to centers for distribution to the local branches away from the central office. More immediately, we are now able to send a number of typewriters and mimeograph machines to unions in need of such equipment.[1]

The post-war West experienced dramatic economic gains and witnessed unions at the height of their size and influence in many ways, but as African nations gained their freedom, their unions, both local and national, were either virtually non-existent or so new that they had usually only come into being during decolonization in the 1950s and 1960s. Therefore items ubiquitous in the West were luxuries to fledgling unions, and even the very processes by which to build and grow a union might be relatively unknown depending on the country. Springer's letter reveals both the material and informational elements of the small, informal philanthropy of Western labour in Africa during the 1950s and 1960s when she mentions providing office equipment to aid the union as well as books for 'distribution' that will spread knowledge of Western unionism. In addition, her notation that 'local branches' will receive some material indicated, as will be seen later as well, that at times Western unions were able to help areas beyond union headquarters in urban centres. In addition, the International Confederation of Free Trade Unions, to which the AFL-CIO belonged, also provided this type of labour philanthropy to African unions, although the ICFTU was more often on the ground in Africa and their help tended to take the form of libraries, as will be shown. The ICFTU had formed in 1949 when American, Western European, Latin American, and some Asian national trade union centres broke from the World Federation of Trade Unions (WFTU) due to its increasingly communist lean. The WFTU continued to function, although it was then made up of unions from Eastern bloc nations. This story, however, is largely about the ways the AFL-CIO and the ICFTU provided vehicles, office equipment, film projectors and informational filmstrips, funding for a Kenyan headquarters building, and information through a variety of avenues, including individual book dispatches, libraries and AFL-CIO publications. While the end goal was certainly to orient African unions towards the West and to help them develop on Western lines, thus hopefully negating the influence of more radical African unionists or the WFTU, even those Africans who worked with Western labour at times used such philanthropy for their own purposes. In addition, there existed a high level of active African agency in requesting aid from Western unions, both material and informational, since they knew who would likely help them in their own union-strengthening goals. The interplay between donor and recipient could be delicate at times and, quite often, the donors in this case had little control over what the recipient did with the aid after it arrived.

The literature on American philanthropy rarely touches on the role of trade unions overseas. Olivier Zunz has noted how some elements of American labour participated in 'mass philanthropy' at home starting in the second half of the 1940s and Gary Hess has addressed 'the expanded efforts of the Ford, Rockefeller, and Carnegie foundations in Africa' during the decolonization era, but this chapter seeks to unite Western labour with its small and informal, yet consistent, philanthropy in Africa during the 1950s and 1960s.[2] In addition, while this chapter agrees with Hess's assertion about those foundations that 'their programs contributed to Western orientation of the preponderance of developing societies', he tends to focus on how 'members of Third World elites owed much of their education to American sources'.[3] Similarly when talking about the dominance of 'mass philanthropy' in the 1950s due to 'the rise in disposable income among the middle and working classes', most of the related campaigns Zunz highlights were domestic and the few international ones focused on Europe.[4] While union officials in the AFL-CIO and ICFTU were certainly better off financially than the average rank-and-file Western worker, both groups were made up of working-class Westerners in contact with working-class Africans in a mode of labour philanthropy outside of what is normally seen as the usual philanthropic structures of larger organizations or even mass-based initiatives led by members of the Western middle class. The AFL-CIO performed its domestic American functions *and* provided philanthropy to African unions. The ICFTU's main goals involved enhancing the primacy of the role of labour in Western societies, insisting on free and democratic trade unionism contrary to the communist model, *and* helping develop trade unions in decolonizing areas. So, while not, at their core, philanthropic organizations, they often functioned as such as they interacted with, and received numerous requests from, Africans who sought the material and informational philanthropy that Western labour could provide in small, often informal ways.

# Physical manifestations of labour philanthropy

Due to the policies of colonial powers, the nascent state of union organizing in Africa, and the difficulty in collecting dues, even basic items such as office machinery could be hard to come by for new African unions. Sometimes unions printed a newsletter, of which few copies usually remain, or distributed voting forms for officers at their annual constitutional conventions. Even producing typewritten letters was at first a challenge and the archives of both the ICFTU and the AFL-CIO contain letters from multiple African union officials across West, Central and East Africa that are a mix of typed and handwritten updates and requests. Therefore, although such equipment was so commonplace as to be unmentionable in the post-war West, in Africa they were luxuries for struggling African unions and Western union gifts of typewriters were especially valuable.

About a year after its transition in spring 1953 from a temporary to a permanent office in Accra, Ghana, the ICFTU provided a typewriter to the officials in its West Africa Trade Union Information and Advisory Center. In July 1954 the ICFTU indicated that the office should buy 'a very light, inexpensive portable machine in Accra and . . . show this purchase under "Office Equipment" in your July accounts'.[5] The office consistently produced a newsletter titled the *West African Worker* for several years and although printing had to be done elsewhere, presumably having a typewriter helped. While an English union official initially led the office, in 1957 a Ghanaian named Seth Dawson effectively took over until the Ghana Trades Union Congress (GTUC) disaffiliated from the ICFTU in late 1959.[6] The office and its material were transferred to the more friendly environs of Lagos, Nigeria where pro-ICFTU unions were stronger, although curiously 'in view of his seven years' service with the ICFTU', Dawson was allowed to keep the typewriter 'for his personal use', as he remained with the GTUC and thus was no longer working for the ICFTU.[7] Starting in 1960, however, the ICFTU finally formed an official African Regional Organization (AFRO), which, while never very strong and always facing contestation from more radical African unions in nations such as Ghana and Guinea, gave the ICFTU an ongoing institutional presence in Africa.[8] Operating out of Lagos, AFRO was so weak by the mid-1960s that ICFTU headquarters took it back over, but, for the purposes of this chapter, the ICFTU had in the meantime continued supplying office machinery because in January 1965 the Nigerian head of AFRO, Knight Maripe, reported a typewriter was stolen from AFRO's headquarters.[9] While less dramatic, the AFL-CIO likewise gave typewriters during the first half of the 1960s to the Gambia Workers Union, the Uganda Trades Union Congress, the Sierra Leone Council of Labor (SLCL) for 'a training program', and the Kenya Federation of Labor.[10] In addition, the United Labor Congress (ULC) of Nigeria and the Tanganyika Federation of Labor (TFL) received both typewriters and early forms of copying machines.[11] These were, of course, places where the ICFTU and the AFL-CIO had a stronger influence than in other African nations, but the unions there benefited as a result.

Western unions also sought to provide film projectors to aid trade union training courses. As early as October 1954, for instance, the ICFTU gave the Union Generale Libya de Travail (UGLT) of Libya and the Union Generale Tunisienne de Travail

(UGTT) of Tunisia projectors and a report on the distribution of such material noted that 'those receiving the equipment are now asking that we should place at their disposal audio-visual means, including films, film strips and records. Some requests have also been received that the equipment already provided should be complete (in particular, those who have received projection apparatus for film strips would like to have a pick-up amplifier added).'[12] The report also then listed out a number of film strips to distribute, as well as 'two record albums of European workers' songs'.[13] In March 1963 the AFL-CIO sent the Sierra Leone Council of Labor a projector, and had also sent in October 1963 'various types of radio equipment and a tape recorder', with the requests for these items, and a Land Rover station wagon to be mentioned later, coming from the SLCL general secretary H.N. Georgestone after conversations with AFL-CIO president George Meany in August 1962.[14] By 1964, a projector had also been sent to the Nigerian ULC, although it was held up in customs issues for at least a year.[15] In addition to the actual machines, filmstrips were available for use by African union officials or ICFTU officials working in Africa. As early as August 1953, the British official in charge of the ICFTU's West Africa Center in Accra, Albert Hammerton, noted that while he had to rent a projector, he had shown 'A Union Goes to School', presumably about union training, and he requested other film strips that were available.[16] In February 1959 Arthur Ochwada, the deputy general secretary of the Kenya Federation of Labor, requested a 'projector and any films' available, 'namely for Organising and education'.[17] In early 1964, P. Sithole of the Textile and Allied Workers' Union of Southern Rhodesia asked Maida Springer for 'some educational material' since '16 millimeter projectors are available even from [the] Government Educational services'; Springer replied that a film was among the material she would send.[18] The next year, Oulare Ansoumane of the Guinean CNTG-USPA requested films from the AFL-CIO and they complied.[19]

While it is hard to tell which filmstrips were shown in each country, the ICFTU periodically circulated lists of available films and filmstrips that it could send out. For instance, most relevant for our purposes here would be a December 1962 list broken down by categories, ranging from industry sectors, such as mines and railways, to general union activities, such as 'industrial safety' or strikes, to larger political and social concerns, such as filmstrips on 'political questions', refugees and 'social problems'.[20] The ICFTU thus sought to provide not only information on how a union should function but also what place it might take within new nations. In addition, the requests for films or more equipment by Africans in at least Libya, Tunisia, Southern Rhodesia, and Guinea showed widespread African agency across the continent in gaining this knowledge and in training their unionists via such ICFTU and AFL-CIO equipment and film strip philanthropy.

A larger physical manifestation of Western labour philanthropy involved aid in purchasing automobiles for African union centres. In a context in which funds were hard to come by and dues collections could be haphazard, the use of a car or jeep to travel to different union branches throughout a country was a major asset. As is apparent by now, the earliest and most well-funded project in Africa was the West Africa Center in Ghana, and in late 1952 or early 1953, the temporary ICFTU representative in Accra, British unionist David Newman, purchased a Fiat Belvedere Station Wagon, although he soon requested a 'larger Fiat model' because he found that 'the roads in the Gold Coast, however, are not up to European standard and driving two-hundred miles or more in one day in this car is a rather fatiguing process'.[21] Instead, by August 1954, Hammerton, Newman's replacement, was able to buy a Land Rover using CIO money and by the next month claimed to have 'covered over 2,500 miles visiting centres in Nigeria and on the Coast', noting as well that it would now be easier to connect with and do work in 'the more remote areas'.[22] Interestingly, he noted that 'a gift of this kind helps more to foster goodwill and international solidarity than all the pious resolutions so often passed at conferences and quickly forgotten'.[23] The car facilitated the West Africa Center's ability to aid Ghanaian, Nigerian, and, at times, other West African unions in their training and development. Indeed, by April 1959, when Dawson was in charge, the office had added a Volkswagen and in September the office sold the older Land Rover to the National Union of General Agricultural Workers in Ghana for a small price.[24] It is unclear when the Fiat was sold, although it was owned by the office until at least 1955 or 1956 and the Volkswagen continued its ICFTU service when it was transferred to Lagos in January 1960 after the Ghana TUC's disaffiliation from the ICFTU.[25] As late as 1962, the new ICFTU representative in West Africa, a Trinidadian named McDonald Moses, was still using the Volkswagen in Nigeria.[26] In addition, the ICFTU's ongoing operations in Nigeria included at least the insurance for two Jeeps for the ULC of Nigeria during the same year.[27]

The ICFTU and the AFL-CIO also provided funding for vehicles for numerous other African unions during the late 1950s and early 1960s and such philanthropy again demonstrated both African agency and the uses to which such physical goods were put. As early as 1956, the United Auto Workers funded the purchase of a Jeep station wagon for ICFTU 'organizational work in Kenya', but most activity occurred during the early 1960s.[28] In April 1961, the AFL-CIO bought a Land Rover for the Southern Rhodesia Trades Union Congress and its president general, Reuben Jamela, believed the vehicle, along with a 'duplicator and the type-writer', would 'go a long way towards meeting some of our needs in our organizational campaign'.[29] Just to the north, John Chisata, president of the Northern Rhodesia African Mineworkers Trade Union, requested funding in late 1961 for a Land Rover and received AFL-CIO money for one in early 1962.[30] In late 1963 a close ICFTU ally, Mamadou Jallow, who was president of the Gambia Workers Union, requested and received a Citroen D.S. 19 car.[31] Around the same time, the AFL-CO helped the Uganda Public Employees Union obtain a Peugeot Estate car and E. Kibuka, the general secretary, replied it was 'a relief as far as the problem of transport is concerned and we have every reason to believe that our Organization will be successful'.[32] In mid-1964 the head of the Francistown African Employees Union in Bechuanaland (Botswana), Gabriel Mmusi, requested a Chevrolet van from the ICFTU and presumably received it, since an emergency funding request was circulated by the ICFTU general secretary at the time, Omer Becu, and these were rarely turned down by ICFTU board members.[33] These vehicles tended to cost in the range of two to five thousand dollars each, depending on the year of the request and the type of vehicle, so the monetary outlays by the ICFTU and the AFL-CIO were not unsubstantial as they helped African union heads travel their nations and organize and educate their unions. In addition, Africans were actively asking for help and, even when it was unclear if they received a vehicle or not, they knew who to approach in order to obtain aid for their unions. In 1962, for instance, D.A. Wan Obi, the secretary-general of the West Cameroons Union of Teachers, asked the AFL-CIO for a Land Rover 'that would help us to tour the country regularly for effective organization'.[34] Finally, an official in the Tanganyika Federation of Labour in March 1960 wrote the AFL-CIO that although he had a 'sound Film Projector', he needed at least 'a second hand car' in order 'to have an extensive tour on the educational programme [*sic*]'.[35] It seems like the TFL had also asked the ICFTU for help purchasing a Land Rover in late 1959 as well.[36] While it is unclear if vehicles for the latter two unions were provided, the point again is that Africans were actively engaging American labour philanthropy in the service of building their unions and, in most cases, were receiving significant help.

The AFL-CIO also helped in ways that were even more integral to the operations of African unions. The most spectacular example was the funding of a new headquarters building for the Kenya Federation of Labor. Yvette Richards has noted how after the ICFTU turned down repeated Kenyan requests for funds, 'Histadrut [the Israeli national labor center], the German labor federation (DGB), and the British TUC did make come contributions'.[37] Yet it was the AFL-CIO that provided the bulk of the outside funding, at least $56,000.[38] Work began in mid-1959 and was completed by early 1960.[39] Although the AFL-CIO funded the project, the ICFTU was initially involved and a proposal submitted in June 1958 to the ICFTU's International Solidarity Fund revealed the extent of what Western labour provided the Kenya Federation of Labor (KFL). The building housed an 'Assembly Hall for 1,000 people', twenty-five offices, a library, a conference room, and even 'a canteen for light snacks' as well as 'a small flat for the Caretaker of the Building'.[40] After completion, Irving Brown, a constant AFL-CIO presence in Africa throughout the late 1950s and early 1960s, urged the head of the KFL, Tom Mboya, to advertise the building to every union, press outlet and political organization in Africa, considering it 'an excellent ICFTU regional activity', although of course the ICFTU did not directly fund the building.[41] The KFL did issue a statement, but it was quite neutral in tone and largely talked about African non-alignment, African independence, African unity and the needs of African nations themselves, most likely dashing Brown's hopes for the images involved in a kind of diplomatic union coup.[42] Overall, the episode showed that Africans pressed repeatedly for funding and then refused to cooperate completely in how to make use of the building for Western union propaganda purposes.

## Informational manifestations of labour philanthropy

Another way to aid African unions was through practical experience or educational scholarships. While the ICFTU, through both funding and its labour college in Uganda, and the AFL-CIO, through both funding and its organization known as the African American Labor Center, helped train African unionists in many countries, at times Africans were either brought to the United States or, showing their agency in obtaining aid from the West, sought out scholarships from Western labour groups. Yvette Richards has covered well the African pressure on AFL-CIO officials that led to the development of an American Trade Union Scholarship Program for Africa in 1957, yet it was short-lived and effectively ended when the ICFTU insisted the AFL-CIO cease independent activity regarding scholarships in Africa and a compromise, sometimes called the Atlantic City Compromise, was reached in which Western unionists would only work through the ICFTU in Africa.[43] In exchange, the ICFTU promised to build what would become its labour college in Kampala, Uganda.[44] In the end, however, even this agreement really only lasted until about 1961 when the AFL-CIO began undertaking, with Maida Springer's central involvement, a number of new programmes in Africa during the early 1960s. As Richards notes, 'Springer's persistent lobbying, however, was decisive in U.S. labor's decision to support a summer employment program for African students, a garment workers' scholarship program, and two training centers, the Kenyan Institute of Tailoring and Cutting, and the Nigerian Motor Drivers' School.'[45] The AFL-CIO thus provided many avenues for training and a significant amount of monetary aid to set up the latter two organizations, but at first it appears as if they largely, apart from the garment workers programme, abided by the Atlantic City Compromise on scholarships.

In fact, however, an ongoing pattern emerged in which African requests for scholarships were directed towards several other non-governmental organizations, and not the ICFTU, showing a kind of low-level dissent by AFL-CIO officials and an enduring willingness to help Africans get to the United States. Richards even notes that 'holding that ICFTU policies and programs in Africa were compromised by its European leaders' sympathies for the colonial powers, the Africans ignored the compromise by continuing to request bilateral programs with the AFL-CIO', but she does not go into detail on this point.[46] Key among the NGOs who certain AFL-CIO figures worked with were the African American Institute (AAI), which had both employment and scholarship programmes for Africans, the African Service Institute (ASI), and the Phelps-Stokes Fund. Maida Springer received numerous requests from Africans for assistance due both to her trips around the continent in the late 1950s and early 1960s as well as her position as an AFL-CIO international affairs representative between 1960 and 1966, although other American unionists were involved as well.[47] For instance, the head of the AAI's Summer Employment Project for African Students thanked Springer in May 1961 for 'a copy of Mr. Meany's letter to trade union leaders as well as his willingness that we should use the letter in finding summer employment in business and industry for African students. In its early stages the project yields encouraging results.'[48] In addition, in July 1961 Springer sent the AAI 'a few letters which I think come under the general terms of your scholarship interest'.[49] In March 1962 Harry Goldberg in the AFL-CIO's international affairs department told none other than Seth Dawson of Ghana, the former head of the ICFTU's West Africa Center, to approach the AAI for help with an academic scholarship.[50] In 1961 and 1962 Springer likewise told Africans from Tanzania and Uganda to write to the AAI for aid.[51] Between 1961 and 1966 she also directed several people from Ghana and others from Tanzania, Uganda and Southern Rhodesia to approach the ASI, the Institute of International Education, or the Phelps-Stokes Fund for aid in gaining scholarships for academic or technical studies in the United States.[52] Springer even wrote the ASI directly on behalf of a Ugandan named Francis Chitayi regarding engineering programmes in the United

States.[53] When Henry Kirsch took over after Springer's exit, he continued similar practices in the second half of the 1960s, directing people from Nigeria, Uganda and Ghana to one or more of these NGOs.[54] While it is unclear if these specific individuals ended up studying in the United States, there was certainly a consistent, yet subtle, effort to help out Africans writing to the AFL-CIO for scholarship aid. In fact, African unionists were often asking for help with higher education, not just technical training, and the AFL-CIO thus informally facilitated connections between Africans and those who could help them obtain a university education.

AFL-CIO figures also facilitated the flow of information to African unionists, although usually in more direct ways. For instance, while the ICFTU and the AFL-CIO mostly provided books on trade unionism, between 1961 and 1964 the AFL-CIO repeatedly sent out a specific set of books from an organization called Freedom House Bookshelf Committee. These books were on American history and mostly covered the American presidency as well as key historical figures such as Woodrow Wilson, Supreme Court Justice Oliver Wendell Holmes, Thomas Jefferson and Alexander Hamilton. Overall, the books indicated the embrace of some of the champions of mid-twentieth-century American liberalism, and between 1961 and 1964 unionists in Kenya, Nyasaland (Malawi), Southern Rhodesia, Sierra Leone, Ghana, Gambia, Basutoland (Botswana), Tanganyika (Tanzania), and Mauritius received these sets.[55] Similarly, apart from Freedom House, the AFL-CIO sent 'ten books on social and philosophical thought' to a union official in Southern Rhodesia in March 1961 and sent 'a set of books on social thought, economics, and politics' to one in Mauritius in November of the same year.[56] The AFL-CIO usually indicated that these were for a union's education department, the union's library, or a personal library, demonstrating a desire, no doubt, to portray America in a good light to African workers.

The provision of books also revealed yet more African agency in obtaining American labour philanthropy. Some representative examples include an April 1961 request from the acting secretary of the Nyasaland Commercial and General Workers Union, K.B. Zidana, for 'books and literatures' to help in building a union library, a personal request from a Nigerian at the ICFTU's Kampala College in March 1963 for books from the AFL-CIO on trade union topics, a November 1964 request from the head of the Swaziland Commercial, Technical, and Allied Workers Union for 'Books for the Union's Library', and, even though the Ghana TUC had disaffiliated from the ICFTU the year before, a 1960 request from the secretary-treasurer of the Oda/Akwatia District Council of Labor in Ghana for AFL-CIO publications.[57] African unionists knew the AFL-CIO was a ready supplier of books, and indeed it was, but a list of the individuals who received books on union topics would be too lengthy to include here. They usually involved the Anglophone countries mentioned throughout this chapter and another illustrative example of the types of union topics the books covered will hopefully suffice. In May 1962, upon request, Springer sent Joseph Wandera, the head of the Railway African Union in Uganda, books with the following titles, '*This is the AFL-CIO, Freedom Forever, ABC's of Trade Unionism, Why Unions?, AFL-CIO Manual for Shop Stewards, How to Run a Union Meeting, Questions and Answers of American Labor and World Affairs, and How to Reach the Union Member*'.[58] Finally, as an example of how the books were used, in November 1964 P. Sithole of Southern

Rhodesia, seen above requesting filmstrips, told Maida Springer that the books they had received 'are of great value to us [*sic*] we are already having branch classes on trade union education using these books as textbooks'.[59] Books, especially on trade union matters, were a small form of philanthropy that reached even beyond the capital cities of African nations, as seen especially in the Ghanaian and Southern Rhodesian examples, to local union leaders.

While the ICFTU fielded fewer individual book requests, they provided an enormous amount of information to African unionists through accessible libraries, first at the West Africa Center and then through a larger collection at the ICFTU's Kampala College in Uganda. When Dawson resigned from leading the former in November 1959 and upon its move from Ghana to Nigeria, he put together a detailed list of the 'Stationery and Books/Pamphlets' available at the office, totalling some 264 titles.[60] They ranged from American, European, and African history topics to trade union topics such as collective bargaining and workplace safety to various ICFTU reports on its activities and conferences. Hammerton, in charge before Dawson, provided a portrait earlier in the 1950s as to how the books were used. The West Africa Center's library opened in March 1953 with 'nearly 100 books covering various aspects of trade unionism'.[61] By November 1954, Hammerton reported,

> Visitors to the Reading Room have increased during the past three months, [*sic*] the average being between 50 and 60 per day. . . . At present, the library consists of some 150 volumes and 200 pamphlets. On average about 40 to 50 books and pamphlets are issued on loan per week to local readers. The library also supplies books to subscribers by post for a period of one month.[62]

He also described how 'the number of inquiries received seeking information and advice has risen to over 250 per month. This figure does not include people who visit the Centre personally seeking information'.[63] Finally, by the first half of 1956 Hammerton could claim, 'The library consists of over 300 books covering a wide range of trade union topics and a good number of trade union journals from all parts of the world are on display'.[64] He had ceased giving numbers on visits and remarked only that 'the number of trade unionists taking advantage of the facilities has steadily increased' and that 'since January, on the average, each book has been taken out five times'.[65] The ICFTU was providing, and Africans were taking advantage of, a significant amount of reading material during the 1950s.

Two other key locations for organized libraries were the ICFTU's AFRO headquarters in Nigeria and its labour training college in Kampala, Uganda. The college, designed specifically to train union officials from all over Africa, opened in a 'temporary headquarters in November 1958' and only received its own official building in 1961.[66] While the library there would only benefit the students studying at the institution, it contained a wide range of material, especially after November 1961 when the director of labour affairs for the State Department's Agency for International Development, John Meskimen, donated 'approximately 150 books' of his own and the delivery, facilitated through Maida Springer, was accepted by the school's principal J. Odero-Jowi.[67] The accompanying list Meskimen provided ran to eight pages and just listing the categories into which he broke down his holdings can illustrate the wide breadth of material then available at the college – Economics, Political Science, Psychology/Sociology, Labour and Labour Movements, Personnel Management, Biography, Miscellaneous Books, Pamphlets and even National Planning Association Publications.[68] In addition, AFRO developed a library in the early 1960s. While AFRO had been an idea since at least 1957, it did not come into being until 1960 and even though it took until October 1963 to open a library, at that point books were so few that borrowing was not allowed.[69] Still, in a circular advertising the library's opening, the college noted that the reading room hours would be Monday to Friday between 8.00 am and 6.30 pm and that the library would 'give yourself the correct [*sic*] trade union and general workers' education by reading the books which provide you with the fundamental studies of democratic free trade unionism'.[70] Thus it was advertised in the language that the AFL-CIO, and especially the ICFTU, used to distinguish their union models from communist or radical African nationalist unions. The initial list of books provided with the circular included works on the history of unions in Europe, Asia, and North and South America as well as on multiple practical union issues such as 'How to Organise a Trade Union Educational Programme', 'How to Conduct a Union Meeting', 'Trade Union Finance', 'Collective Bargaining' and about a dozen others.[71] Through both its formal training institution in Uganda and its more publicly accessible library at AFRO headquarters in Nigeria, the ICFTU during the early 1960s continued to provide information to Africans on a broad array of topics, although, as to be expected, its works concentrated most heavily on how to form, operate and grow unions.

African union figures also consistently read and requested AFL-CIO publications such as *The American Federationist* and the *AFL-CIO Free Trade Union News*. These were less about labour organizing principles and more about current events in various labour fields, but the information still helped Africans learn about labour in other parts of the world as well as feel a connection to other labour movements. While these were often widely distributed, some representative examples that also demonstrate African agency through requests will be noted here. For example, in 1959 General Secretary H. N. Moyo of the Zanzibar & Pemba Federation of Labor and in 1965 P. Sithole of Southern Rhodesia were added to *The American Federationist*'s mailing list.[72] In correspondence in 1958 with Michael Ross, the head of the AFL-CIO's International Affairs Department before Maida Springer, Dawson of the West Africa Center noted they received the *Federationist*, 'Economic Trend and Outlook', and 'Economic Review' and then stated, 'We shall be grateful to receive any other publications you have'.[73] Likewise in 1962, the assistant secretary-general of the Nyasaland Trades Union Congress told Springer, 'In your recent issue of the Federationist, I have noted of some [*sic*] recent publications which one no doubt of interest [*sic*] to a trade union movement. we [*sic*] would be very much pleased if you could afford to send us those you think can be of some help to us'.[74] Examples related to the *AFL-CIO Free Trade Union News* include how the United Labour Congress Youth Wing in Nigeria requested copies in 1967, K. Zidana of the Plantation and Agricultural Workers Union in Malawi received copies in 1965, and both a 'Field Organiser of the Railway Union of [*sic*] T.U.C. (Ghana)' in 1962 and the general secretary of the Nigerian Workers Council in 1967 noted that they consistently read the publication.[75] Spreading information about contemporary union activity around the world helped enhance the connection between American and African trade unionists and revealed yet another type of information philanthropy that Western unions pursued.

# Conclusion

In early 1967, a former student of the ICFTU's Kampala College and general secretary of the Kenya Shoe and Leather Workers Union, James Awich, wrote an international organization for help with his union.[76] The request ended up with the AFL-CIO, and they provided him with publications titled 'Foreign Aid for Peace and Freedom, Questions and Answers on American Labor and World Affairs, Labor Fights the Enemies of Democracy, American and Soviet Economy Contrast and Comparison, and Labor's Role in a Free Society'.[77] Now Awich knew who to approach and when in early 1968 he asked for works on various aspects of union organizing, the AFL-CIO sent him works titled 'Collective Bargaining/Democracy on the Job, Labor and Politics, Bargaining Gains: Review and Preview, Collective Bargaining Report, and AFL-CIO Collective Bargaining Report'.[78] He thus received material on both the practical functioning of unions as well as the relationship of unions to the larger Cold War struggle, showing how such topics were often intertwined for Western unionists and the African figures working with them. The AFL-CIO and the ICFTU did a lot of other things in Africa during the 1950s and 1960s, including providing funds for training courses, for aid during strikes and for a variety of other activities, but the practices discussed in this chapter were some of the more small and informal ways that they operated philanthropically. While certainly not starved for funds, the AFL-CIO and the ICFTU could never send out as much money as one of the large, well-known philanthropic organizations and they were not primarily philanthropic groups. Yet as they sought to connect to trade unionists in Africa, usually in Anglophone colonies and then nations, Western labour actors did seek to provide goods and information that would orient these unions towards the West in the global Cold War. Funding both the purchases of vehicles and office equipment as well as the building of a union headquarters in Kenya, facilitating connections between Africans and groups providing scholarships for education or training abroad, and providing books, library access and publications on a variety of topics, both about unions and about other topics, were consistent actions designed to build up African trade unions. AFL-CIO and ICFTU actions in this arena show us not only more about how Western philanthropy operated on the ground in Africa during the early Cold War period. They also show us how some organizations blurred the line between their non-philanthropic and philanthropic activities. These episodes also reveal a very consistent level of African agency in asking for funding or material, indicating African actors knew precisely who to go to for the help they needed. Providing that help at times demonstrated the give and take between Western and African labour actors, with the latter not always following the desires of the former, although no enormous rifts occurred over philanthropic actions. A labour philanthropy of both material and information that connected leaders of working-class Western organizations to working-class Africans constituted one of the many ways Americans and Europeans interacted with Africans in the early Cold War.

# Notes

1  Maida Springer to Jacob Namfua, 13 December 1960, Box 13, Folder 6: 'Tanzania, 1957–1961', RG18-001. International Affairs Department. Country Files, 1945–1971, The George Meany Memorial AFL-CIO Archives, University of Maryland, College Park, MD (hereafter cited as Country Files).

2  Olivier Zunz, *Philanthropy in America: A History* (Princeton: Princeton University Press, 2012), 177–8; Gary R. Hess, 'Waging the Cold War in the Third World: The Foundations and the Challenges of Development', in *Charity, Philanthropy, and Civility in American History*, ed. Lawrence J. Friedman and Mark D. McGarvie (New York: Cambridge University Press, 2003), 327–9.

3  Hess, 'Waging the Cold War in the Third World', 336.

4  Zunz, *Philanthropy in America*, 2, 367.

5  Fred Strauss to Albert Hammerton, 9 July 1954, Folder 4166: 'Accra Office (West African Trade Union Information and Advisory Centre). General Correspondence. With Reports. 1952–1960: 1954–1955', (hereafter cited as 4166), ICFTU/ITUC Archives, International Institute of Social History, Amsterdam, Netherlands (hereafter cited as ICFTU Files).

6  Yvette Richards, *Maida Springer: Pan-Africanist and International Labor Leader* (Pittsburgh: University of Pittsburgh Press, 2000), 197.

7  Charles Millard to McDonald Moses, 28 July 1960, Folder 4172: 'Lagos Office: General Correspondence. with Reports. 1958–1962: 1958–1960', (hereafter cited as 4172), ICFTU Files.

8  Wogu Ananaba, *The Trade Union Movement in Africa: Promise and Performance* (London: C. Hurst & Company), 120.

9  Ibid., 123; To Sabena, attention L. Walravens, 11 March 1965, Folder 3953: 'African Regional Organization (AFRO). Correspondence Concerning AFRO Staff Members and Staff Matters. 1960–1976', ICFTU Files.

10  J. D. Cole to Maida Springer, 11 March 1961, 3, Box 9, Folder 22: 'Gambia, 1960–1966', (hereafter cited as 9/22), Country Files; E. W. W. Nakibinge to Lee Minton, 20 February 1961, Box 13, Folder 18: 'Uganda, 1955–1970', (hereafter cited as 13/18), Country Files; Maida Springer to George E. E. Palmer, 11 June 1963, Box 12, Folder 19: 'Sierra Leone, 1960–1966', (hereafter cited as 12/19), Country Files; Maida Springer to William Ross, 2 March 1963, Box 11, Folder 3: 'British Trade Union Congress, 1959', RG18-003. International Affairs Department. Jay Lovestone Files, 1939–1974, The George Meany Memorial AFL-CIO Archives, University of Maryland, College Park, MD (hereafter cited as Lovestone Files).

11  Maida Springer to L. L. Borha, 15 April 1963, Box 11, Folder 22: 'Nigeria, 1956–1966', (hereafter cited as 11/22), Country Files; CARE receipt, 18 April 1961, Box 13, Folder 9: 'Tanzania, 1964–1970', (hereafter cited as 13/9), Country Files.

12  15 October 1954, 'Supply of Audio-Visual and Film Equipment to Certain Regional Offices and Affiliated Organisations in Economically Under-Developed Countries', 10RFC/20a, 1, Box 6, Folder 2: 'Regional Fund Activities Committee, 20–22 October 1954 (Mike Ross File)', RG18-007. International Affairs Department. International

Labor Organizations Activities, 1946–1985, The George Meany Memorial AFL-CIO Archives, University of Maryland, College Park, MD (hereafter cited as ILOA Files).

13  Ibid., 2.

14  H. Georgestone to George Meany, 25 August 1962, 1, George Meany to A. S. J. Carnahan, October 1, 1962, and A. S. J. Carnahan to Michael Ross, 29 March 1963, all in 12/19, Country Files.

15  B. M. Udokporo to Maida Springer, 3 December 1965 and Maida Springer to ben Udokporo, 23 April 1965, both in 11/22, Country Files.

16  Albert Hammerton to J. A. Riddell, 26 August 1953, Folder 4165: 'Accra Office (West African Trade Union Information and Advisory Centre). General Correspondence. With Reports. 1952–1960: 1952–1953', (hereafter cited as 4165), ICFTU Files.

17  Arthur Aggrey Ochwada to William Schnitzler, 18 February 1959, 2, Box 11, Folder 6: 'Kenya: Arthur A. Ochwada, 1957–1960', Country Files.

18  P. Sithole to Maida Springer, 24 March 1964 and Maida Springer to P. Sithole, 24 April 1964, Box 12, Folder 11: 'Rhodesia, 1963–1964', (hereafter cited as 12/11), Country Files.

19  Oulare Ansoumane to George Meany, 23 January 1965 and Henry Kirsch to Oulare Ansoumane, 4 February 1965, both in Box 10, Folder 5: 'Guinea, 1959–1965', Country Files.

20  13 December 1962, Circular ILFI/7 (1962) by Omer Becu, 'Distribution of Films in the Possession of the ILFI Film Library', Alphabetical Section, 2–3, Box 26, Folder 13: 'Circulars, 1961–1963', ILOA Files.

21  David Newman to J. H. Oldenbroek, 4 March 1953, 4165, ICFTU Files.

22  Albert Hammerton to Walter Reuther, 17 September 1954, 4166, ICFTU Files.

23  Ibid.

24  Fred Strauss to Seth Dawson, 'Office Car', 16 April 1959 and Fred Strauss to Seth Dawson, 'Sale of Landrover', 21 September 1959, both in Folder 4169: 'Accra Office (West African Trade Union Information and Advisory Centre). General Correspondence. With Reports. 1952–1960: 1959–1960', ICFTU Files.

25  Fred Strauss to Albert Hammerton, 'Re: Car expenses during 1955', 10 April 1956, Folder 4167: 'Accra Office (West African Trade Union Information and Advisory Centre). General Correspondence. With Reports. 1952–1960: 1956–1957', ICFTU Files; Fred Strauss to McDonald Moses, 19 August 1960, 4172, ICFTU Files.

26  McDonald Moses to Manager, Mssrs. Mandilas & Karaberis, 'Volkswagen Car LF 5352', 6 July 1962, Folder 3933: 'African Regional Organization (AFRO). General Correspondence. With Reports. 1960–1973: 1961', ICFTU Files.

27  E. M. O. Akala to McDonald Moses, 'Insurance of Two Jeeps', 7 September 1962, Folder 3861: 'Africa and Arabia. General. OGB. 1959–1970', ICFTU Files.

28  Walter Reuther to J. H. Oldenbroek, 26 January 1956, Box 10, Folder 22: 'Correspondence, 1956', ILOA Files.

29  Reuben Jamela to George Meany, 19 May 1961, Box 12, Folder 8: 'Rhodesia, 1956–1962', (hereafter cited as 12/8), Country Files.

30  J. Chisata to George Meany, 4 January 1962 and Michael Ross to J. Chisata, 11 January 1962, both in Box 13, Folder 24: 'Zambia (See also Northern Rhodesia), 1959–1970', Country Files.

31  George Meany to Mamadou Jallow, 16 December 1963, 9/22, Country Files.

32  E. R. Kibuka to Maida Springer, 20 November 1963 (or 1964), Box 13, Folder 19: 'Uganda, 1955–1970', hereafter cited as 13/19), Country Files.

33  Omer Becu to George Meany, 'ISF Emergency Procedure: Bechuanaland', 16 July 1964, 1–2, Box 11, Folder 16: 'Correspondence, 1964', ILOA Files.

34  D. A. Wan Obit to Chairman, AFL-CIO International Affairs Committee (Mike Ross), 3 September 1962, 1–2, 9/22, Country Files.

35  Letter (perhaps Mpangala or Kawawa) to Michael Ross, 10 March 1960, Box 13, Folder 7: 'Tanzania, 1957–1961', (hereafter cited as 13/7), Country Files.

36  Charles Millard to R. W. Kawawa, 4 February 1960, 1, 13/7, Country Files.

37  Richards, *Maida Springer*, 203–4.

38  William Schnitzler to J. H. Oldenbroek, 20 February 1960, Box 11, Folder 6: 'Correspondence, 1960', ILOA Files.

39  Arthur Ochwada to Michael Ross, 29 May 1959, Box 11, Folder 5: 'Kenya: Tom Mboya, 1958–1962', (hereafter cited as 11/5), Country Files; George Meany to Tom Mboya, 22 March 1960, Box 30, Folder 11: 'Mboya, Tom: Kenya, 1958–1962', (hereafter cited as 30/11), RG18-004. International Affairs Department. Irving Brown Files, 1943–1989, The George Meany Memorial AFL-CIO Archives, University of Maryland, College Park, MD (hereafter cite as Brown Files).

40  H. Richard Hughes, 'Proposed Solidarity Building for the Kenya Federation of Labour', 12 June 1958, part of ISFC16-12 new projects for aid app. 11, Box 12, Folder 22: 'International Solidarity Fund CTTE, July 1958', ILOA Files.

41  Irving Brown to Tom Mboya, 5 August 1960, 30/11. Brown Files.

42  'Kenya Federation of Labor – Solidarity Building: Press Statement', 1960, Box 45, Folder 23: 'Kenya, 1960–1961', Lovestone Files.

43  Richards, *Maida Springer*, 130–4, 143–52.

44  Ibid., 147.

45  Ibid., 222.

46  Ibid., 150–151.

47  Ibid., 198, 262.

48  William C. Bryant, II to Maida Springer, 12 May 1961, Box 14, Folder 12: African American Institute, 1961–1966', (hereafter cited as 14/12), Country Files.

49  Maida Springer to Robert Sherman, 26 July 1961, 14/12, Country Files.

50  Harry Goldberg to Seth Dawson, 7 March 1962, Box 10, Folder 1: 'Ghana, 1961–1970', (hereafter cited as 10/1), Country Files.

51  Maida Springer to Michael Mwasantembe, 20 November 1961, 13–16, Country Files; Maida Springer to Damian Wabwoba, 15 February 1962, 1, 13/18, Country Files.

52  Maida Springer to Peter Adu (Ghana), 12 November 1963, Maida Springer to Charles Taylor Adu (Ghana), 19 November 1962, Maida Springer to Gilbert K. MacNtow (Ghana), 25 July 1963, Maida Springer to Charles Ofori Okine (Ghana), 26 August 1963, and Maida Springer to Frederick O. Boakye (Ghana), 6 January 1966, all in 10/1, Country Files; Maida Springer to A. G. Chahali (Tanzania), 21 August 1962, Box 13, Folder 8: 'Tanzania, 1962–1963', Country Files; Maida Springer to Paul G. M. Matovu (Uganda), 14 September 1964, 13/19, Country Files; Maida Springer to Z. S. Powai, 20 August 1964, 12/11, Country Files.

53  Maida Springer to Paul Baddoo, 12 March 1963, Box 11, Folder 3: 'Kenya: Institute of Tailoring and Cutting, 1962–1964', Country Files.

54  Henry Kirsch to Dominic C. Olikeze (Nigeria), 30 September 1965, 11/22, Country Files; Henry Kirsch to Olumuyiwa Oladimeji (Nigeria), 6 February 1967, Box 11, Folder 23: 'Nigeria, 1967–1970', (hereafter cited as 11/23), Country Files; Henry

Kirsch to Isaac Kayondo (Uganda), 16 March 1967, 13/19, Country Files; Henry Kirsch to Francis Harry Nettey (Ghana) 23 January 1970, 10/1, Country Files.

55   Maida Springer to Tom Mboya (Kenya), 22 March 1961, 11/5, Country Files; Maida Springer to K. B. Zidana (Nyasaland), 5 May 1961, Box 11, Folder 14: 'Malawi (See also Rhodesia and Nyasaland), 1960–1969', (hereafter cited as 11/14), Country Files; Maida Springer to Reuben Jamela (Southern Rhodesia), 4 April 1961, 12/8, Country Files; Maida Springer to H. M. Georgestone (Sierra Leone), 22 March 1961, 12/19, Country Files; Maida Springer to J. Q. Quartey (Ghana), 21 March 1961, 10/1, Country Files; Maida Springer to John Davidson Cole (Gambia), 20 March 1961, 9/22, Country Files; Maida Springer to G. P. Ramoreboli (Basutoland), 16 September 1964, Box 11, Folder 8: 'Lesotho, 1961–1966', Country Files; Maida Springer to Joel Mgogo (Tanganyika), 21 August 1964, 13/9, Country Files; Maida Springer to A. Moignac (Mauritius), 31 August 1964, Box 11, Folder 18: 'Mauritius, 1954–1968', (hereafter cited as 11/18), Country Files.

56   Maida Springer to J. T. Maluleke, 13 March 1961, 12/8, Country Files; Maida Springer to Joseph Marcel Mason, 2 November 1961, 11/18, Country Files.

57   K. B. Zidana to AFL-CIO, 10 April 1961, 11/14, Country Files; S. B. Gidado to AFL-CIO, 14 March 1963, 13/18, Country Files; K. A. Shange to AFL-CIO, 14 November 1964, 11/22, Country Files; J. Q. Quartey to AFL-CIO, 15 November 1960, Box 9, Folder 23: Ghana, 1953–1960', Country Files.

58   Receipt, Springer shipment to Wandera, 14 May 1962, 13/18, Country Files.

59   P. Sithole to Maida Springer, 18 November 1964, 12/11, Country Files.

60   Seth Dawson to Charles Millard, 20 November 1959, attachment 'Names of Books on the Shelf', 17 November 1959, 1–8, Folder 4259: 'Ghana. General Correspondence. With reports, clippings and other documents. 1950–1974: 1968–1969)', ICFTU Files.

61   'ICFTU West African Trade Union Information and Advisory Centre, Accra: Report, April–October 1953', 29–31 March 1954, 2, Box 5, Folder 26, ILOA Files.

62   'Report of the ICFTU West African Trade Union Information and Advisory Centre (April – October 1954)', 17 November 1954, 5, Box 2, Folder 5: 'Executive Board, 24–28 Nov 1954 (Mike Ross File)', ILOA Files.

63   Ibid.

64   'Information and Advisory Centre, West Africa – Report on Activities for the period January–May 1946', 26 June 1956, 3 Box 2, Folder 13: 'Executive Board, 2–7 July 1956', ILOA Files.

65   Ibid.

66   Richards, *Maida Springer*, 153, 155.

67   John K. Meskimen to Howard V. Funk, Jr., 27 November 1961 and J. Odero-Jowi to Maida Springer, 27 November 1961, both in 13/18, Country Files.

68   Ibid., List of Books, 1–8.

69   S. B. Ujomu to Stefan Nedzynski, 'ICFTU/AFRO Library Opened', 10 October 1963, Folder 3980: 'African Regional Organization (AFRO). Correspondence Concerning the ICFTU/ARO Library. 1963–1964', ICFTU Files.

70   Ibid.

71   Ibid., List of Books.

72   Michael Ross to Publications, Research, Education, Federationist, 29 October 1959, Box 14, Folder 1: 'Zanzibar, 1955–1964', Country Files; Violet Lewis to Mary Petock, 30 March 1965, 12/11, Country Files.

73   Seth Dawson to Michael Ross, 7 May 1958, Box 11, Folder 2: 'Correspondence, 1958', ILOA Files.

74  Richard Sembereka (or Sembeseka) to Maida Springer, 20 July 1962, 11/14, Country Files.
75  Secretary-General, United Labour Congress Youth Wing to AFL-CIO Department of International Affairs, 8 February 1967, 11/23, Country Files; Henry Kirsch to K. Zidana, 1 October 1965, 11/14, Country Files; Peter Osborne Ferguson to George Meany, 11 April 1962, 10/1, Country Files; N. Chukwura to Jay Lovestone, 1 June 1967, 11/23, Country Files.
76  Rosemary Conley (American Society of International Law) to AFL-CIO, 10 (or 18) January 1967, Box 12, Folder 21: 'Somali Republic: Printed Material, 1967–1968', Country Files.
77  Henry Kirsch to James Awich, 1 February 1967, Box 10, Folder 21: 'Kenya, 1966–1970', (hereafter cited as 10/21), Country Files.
78  James Awich to William Schnitzler, 23 January 1968 and Henry Kirsch to James Awich, 6 March 1968, both in 10/21, Country Files.

# Challenging philanthropy

# Identifying a menace to the national welfare

## The final report of the United States Commission on Industrial Relations and the Progressive Era critique of philanthropic foundations

Margaret Nettesheim Hoffmann

On 9 September 1914, General Harrison Gray Otis, the ageing publisher of the *Los Angeles Times* newspaper, submitted personal testimony to the federal investigators leading the United States Commission on Industrial Relations (USIR). Otis argued, 'Business managers are generally and naturally reluctant to disclose inside information concerning the details of their business operations', and that on a personal level, Otis 'shared in their reluctance'.[1] General Otis's testimony before the commission was just one of over 700 public statements offered during the nearly three-year investigation into the causes of national 'industrial unrest'.[2] First proposed during the waning months of William Howard Taft's administration, the USIR convened in August 1912 to investigate the status of labour conditions throughout the United States. Otis's statement before the commission was notable, not for the content of his remarks, but rather because of his business connections to a bombing conspiracy led by three union activists at the *Los Angeles Times* building in 1910. Labelled the 'crime of the century', twenty-one people perished in the fire and subsequent collapse of Otis's newspaper building. The violence and horror detailed in national coverage of the newspaper bombing prompted a campaign that sought answers for deteriorating labour conditions throughout the United States. How had the tensions between industrial leaders and labour organizers devolved into acts of terrorism and urban warfare? What caused the conditions leading to industrial unrest? What could the nation do to alleviate these tensions? These were just some of the questions Otis sought to address in his personal remarks and testimony in September 1914.

The history of the USIR, and its subsequent final report published in 1915, is well known to labour historians and historians of the Progressive Era.[3] With a broad investigatory mandate, the commission's investigation and report caused a deep rift within the ranks of the commissioners themselves, in particular among the progressive reformer assigned to head the research division, Charles M. McCarthy, and the commission's chair, Frank P. Walsh.[4] As historian Leon Fink suggests, the fracture between the commissioners met its breaking point when Walsh, fearful of a financial conspiracy to block the investigation between McCarthy and the Rockefeller Foundation, fired McCarthy as the director of research. The commissioners' public tensions 'squandered much of its goodwill' with the nation, and its recommendations were 'the most radical social wisdom ever to emanate from an official federal authority in American history', completely, 'fell on deaf ears'.[5] Walter Lippmann represented the hopes of the nation and the public advocates of the commission: 'If they do their work with imagination and courage, they will do more than any other group of people in this country to shape our history'.[6]

The investigatory fissure within the ranks of the USIR resulted in the publication of three separate reports released in August 1915. Social reformers and progressive activists hoped the commission would finally provide definitive answers surrounding the civil, economic and social upheaval brought upon by American industrial development in the late nineteenth and early twentieth centuries. Unfortunately, the belief that the commission failed in their quest, became the prevailing contemporary opinion regarding the USIR's conclusions.[7] However, their final report, in particular the volume written by Basil Manly, the commission's director of research hired in the aftermath of Charles McCarthy's termination, outlined the emergence of a capitalist economic system within the United States that concentrated wealth within the hands of a few leading industrial families. While the final report offered Congress a number of legislative actions, the most radical elements in the report detailed an evolving threat that Manly and Walsh described as 'a menace to the national welfare' in the form of philanthropic foundations, most notably the Rockefeller Foundation.[8] Although the commission's work did not result in any legislative acts, the full report and its critique of philanthropic foundations provided profound insights into the role of philanthropy within the development of modern capitalism and outlined how the concentration of wealth within foundations impacted the American working-class.

The USIR, for the first time in American history, directly linked the history of labour unrest to the activities of philanthropic foundations. In this sense, the commission's final report condemned the centralization of wealth within foundations and painted an intricately woven philanthropic connection to the exploitation of American labourers. These intricacies depict a complex story that is often concealed within American capitalism. As the report detailed, foundations offered a mechanism for capitalists to further consolidate their wealth beyond the oversight of government and the public within their philanthropic trusts, while simultaneously controlling research into the system their industrial profits constructed. For reformers including Basil Manly and Frank Walsh, charitable activity would not justify the accumulation of wealth earned through workplace hazards, low wages, high costs on consumer goods, or the denial of labourers' rights to organize. Walsh and Manly feared that foundations served as an unchecked form of power while they enjoyed the public reputation as a model of charity. In the report's section on 'The Concentration of Wealth and Influence' the commissioners detailed how foundations posed a direct threat to American democracy:

> The entrance of the foundations into the field of industrial relations, through the creation of a special division by the Rockefeller Foundation, constitutes a menace

to the national welfare to which the attention of not only Congress but of the entire country should be directed. Backed by the $100,000,000 of the Rockefeller Foundation, this movement has the power to influence the entire country in the determination of its most vital policy.[9]

Walsh and Manly made a compelling argument that capitalists used their philanthropic foundations to construct a new type of relationship between industrialists and labourers, between social reformers and foundations, and between capitalists with American democracy. They feared these new relationships, established on what they argued was an old-world system of patronage and feudalism, would threaten democratic participation and lead to an industrial oligarchy. In particular, grants from foundations often directly funded the construction of public policy via gifts to scholars researching social and economic unrest. Philanthropists remained monopolists who used their charitable endeavours to justify the outcome of the new American economic system.

The commission's analysis offers insights into the power, development and ultimate influence of philanthropic foundations in the nation's history. Their recommendations advocated for public funding of social reform and scholarship, in opposition to the Progressive Era's growing historical trend towards private funding of public needs. Most importantly, the report identified the connections between the wealth of the foundations to the exploitation of labourers, while detailing that philanthropy sought solutions in a system directly responsible for its development, an irony not lost upon Frank P. Walsh and Basil Manly.

## The 'crime of the century'

The spark igniting the work of the USIR occurred during the early morning hours of Saturday, 1 October 1910, when two dynamite bombs exploded in the *Los Angeles Times* newspaper building located in the city's downtown. At the time of the explosion, as many as one hundred workers occupied the building, working on the upcoming Sunday morning edition of the paper.[10] Senior editors and reporters had recently left for the evening, but a few members of management remained, including Assistant City Editor, Harvey C. Elder.[11] The bombs had been strategically planted just outside the building in an alleyway filled with newspaper ink barrels, an area workers commonly referred to as 'Ink Alley'.[12] The alley stood directly above natural gas lines that fed into the newspaper's headquarters, and as intended, the initial blast ignited the barrels of ink.[13] The force of the firebomb engulfed the block, while producing a fire so massive, the three-storey building collapsed. The explosion and fire also destroyed an adjoining six-storey structure occupied by printing and engraving companies affiliated with the newspaper.[14] Eyewitness accounts described the horror of the explosion: 'all at once a terrific force from below seemed to raise a section of the floor clear to the roof', and the thrust of the bomb cracked wooden frames, while 'broken timbers flew in all directions'.[15]

Los Angeles fire and police officials estimated that as many as nineteen workers failed to escape the burning *Times* edifice before its collapse. Flames roared up several stairwells, blocking exit paths for trapped workers, including Harvey Elder. Elder's only path to safety was out a third-story window, towards firemen holding jump nets on the ground below. Elder leapt from the window, but his jump just missed the fire nets; his body landed on the sidewalk pavement. Elder survived his plunge, but passed away hours later at the hospital from burns and internal injuries.[16] Other workers also found their paths blocked by burning stairwells and feverishly yelled for help out windows to the waiting rescuers. The firemen 'failed to get their ladders up quickly enough' and the flames engulfed the men. Other workers were more fortunate; printer Mark Bentley had been 'making ready to run off a section of the Sunday paper when the roar of the explosion sounded and the floors overhead fell'.[17] Bentley and a group of fellow workers believed they 'were doomed to die in the basement when one of the men remembered that a hole had been cut near the sidewalk'.[18] The men crawled to safety via this temporary construction hole.

Workers spent more than thirty hours in the aftermath, sifting through the remnants of the building, diligently searching for their missing colleagues. Discovered bodies 'burned beyond recognition' were identified by their placement in connection with their workstations. Horrified searchers described locating the remains of their lost colleagues 'as best as they could be determined throughout the debris field'.[19] Twenty-one workers, ranging from editors to printers, and the secretary to the general manager of the paper, perished in the bombing; many others were wounded.[20] The magnitude of the event impacted the survivors. Paul Braud, a police reporter for the newspaper, 'who tried to aid the entrapped men in the burning building, gave way to the nervous strain'. Braud was hospitalized later that day.[21] Harvey Elder's wife travelled from their home in San Francisco the morning following the bombing. She collapsed when she learned of her husband's final moments, and subsequent newspaper accounts described Mrs Elder's condition at the hospital as 'serious'.[22]

While rescuers searched for unaccounted *Times* workers, the Los Angeles police discovered additional dynamite devices located throughout the city. They found the first bomb at the home of Felix J. Zeehandelaar, secretary for the Merchants and Manufacturers Association, a Los Angeles corporate lobbying organization affiliated with the *Times's* publisher, General Harrison Grey Otis.[23] Reports suggested there was sufficient dynamite in this explosive device to destroy the Zeehandelaar home as well as multiple homes along the residential block.[24] An intricate clock attachment 'set for 1 am', the same time as the explosion at the *Times*, was attached to fifteen sticks of dynamite.[25] Police investigators learned the bomb failed to detonate because 'the clockwork was wound too tight'.[26] Concerned by the increasing probability of a coordinated attack on business interests aligned with the *Times*, Los Angeles police sent detectives to search the home of General Otis. Otis was not in Los Angeles on the night of the attack; he was returning from Mexico where he had represented the Taft Administration during the Mexican centennial events in Mexico City. The publisher was nearly home when he learned of the attack on the newspaper.[27] During their scan of the Otis property, police uncovered another undetonated dynamite device concealed within a suitcase 'hidden in a bunch of vines underneath a bay window'. Following a lengthy debate about how to dispose of the bomb safely, the detective in charge of the scene proceeded to cut into the suitcase and heard the 'buzz of a mechanism', upon which 'smoke oozed out'.[28] Detectives hurriedly sprinted to a nearby park, carrying the smouldering suitcase 'where its explosion could do but comparatively little damage'.[29] The bomb safely exploded in the park.

National accounts of the bombing described the coordinated attack against the *Los Angeles Times* as the 'Crime of the Century'.[30] Almost immediately, General Otis accused labour organizers in Los Angeles of plotting to blow up his newspaper. Workplace tensions and union strikes had long dominated the headlines of the *Times* throughout 1910. As a well-known anti-labour union advocate, Otis's newspaper coverage, during a series of general strikes in Los Angeles throughout 1910, castigated striking workers as instruments opposed to what he and fellow business leaders within the Merchants and Manufacturers Association labelled as their 'industrial freedom'. Historian Joseph A. McCartin, in an analysis of the labour movement during the second decade of the twentieth century in *Labor's Great War*, characterized tensions between labour and capitalists as a series of crises that 'allowed and encouraged Americans to recast the labor question around the demand for industrial democracy during the era of the Great War'.[31] Where labourers sought the expansion of American democratic principles into the industrial workplace, capitalists including Otis, Zeehandelaar, and members of the Merchants and Manufacturers Association countered union efforts with an appeal to another deeply held American value: freedom. Visions of industrial democratic participation came into conflict with the values of individual freedom; the Los Angeles strikes of 1910 were but one scene in labour's national unrest during the decade. The catastrophic bombing of the *Los Angeles Times* threatened to turn the tragedy into a rationale for resisting unionization efforts.

That fall, the mayor of Los Angeles hired celebrated criminal detective William J. Burns to lead the investigation into the bombing. Hailed by national newspapers as the greatest detective ever produced in the United States, Burns had for many months prior to the explosion at the *Times* been searching for the conspirators of an industrial bombing in Peoria, Illinois.[32] He saw a familiar pattern with several other incidents of dynamite explosions across the nation beginning in 1905. Cities targeted in these incidents included New York City, Newark, Cleveland and Buffalo.[33] Historian Graham Adams, Jr. notes that during the period of 1905–9 'someone had unleashed seventy dynamite attacks, all against companies which employed non-union labor'.[34] Notably, Burns had also been hired to investigate a railroad bombing in September 1910 on the Peoria & Pekin Union Railway in East Peoria, Illinois. In particular, Burns determined rather quickly upon examining evidence in the Los Angeles explosion that 'the men responsible for the Peoria explosions were the ones who had operated in Los Angeles'.[35] Investigators noticed strong parallels in the two cases, including the use of clockwork bombs in the East Peoria explosion, a bomb mechanism that matched the unexploded dynamite device located at Felix Zeehandelaar's home in Los Angeles.

On 12 April 1911, following a six-month investigation, a team of Burns' investigators located in Detroit arrested two men they believed conspired to bomb both the Peoria & Pekin Union Railway and the *Los Angeles Times*. Burns theorized that 'the Los Angeles explosion had been planned in Indiana' by members of the International Association of Bridge and Structural Iron Workers, who had in recent years diligently fought anti-unionization efforts led in part by the United States Steel Corporation.[36] Based upon the evidence gathered from the gunpowder used in both the Peoria and Los Angeles attacks, Burns linked the conspiracy to the secretary-treasurer of the International Association of Bridge and Structural Iron Workers, John J. McNamara.[37] Burns' team arrested John's brother, James, along with union member Ortie McManigal in mid-April 1912. At the time of their arrest, Burns' men lied to McNamara and McManigal telling them 'they were wanted for robbery in Chicago'. While on the train transporting them, unknowingly, to Los Angeles, 'James deduced that the lawmen had really arrested them as suspects in the Los Angeles case.'[38] Within a couple of weeks, Ortie McManigal confessed to his role in the conspiracy, and investigators 'persuaded the Governor of Indiana to sign the papers necessary to extradite' John J. McNamara to California.[39] By the end of April 1911, the McNamara brothers and Ortie McManigal were imprisoned, accused of conspiring to blow up *the Los Angeles Times* building and murdering twenty-one people.

Details surrounding the imprisonment and extradition of the McNamara brothers outraged national union activists. Samuel Gompers declared the investigation a grand conspiracy against labour, and suggested that General Otis and other industrial leaders hired Burns in a great 'frame-up and plot' to subvert labour.[40] Eugene Debs declared the arrest of the McNamara brothers, by a detective with ties to leading industrialists, as a capitalist plot 'to discredit and destroy organized labor in the United States'.[41] Union leaders advocated with the courts in Los Angeles to bring criminal charges against Detective Burns for what they believed to be the illegal kidnapping of John J. McNamara from Indiana.[42] Organizers from the American Federation of Labor, the Building Trades Council and the National Socialist Party formed fundraising campaigns to offset the legal defence costs for the McNamara brothers.[43] Convinced of their innocence by constant reassurances from John and James, Samuel Gompers personally asked attorney Clarence Darrow to represent the brothers, even though 'he feared that the prosecution had an airtight case'.[44]

As Darrow prepared McNamara's legal case, accusations of juror tampering and bribery hampered the defence of the brothers and of labour in the United States.[45] Coverage of the case in Los Angeles pit the forces of pro-industrialists against the advocates of labour and led to an atmosphere of 'vituperative charges and bitter counteraccusations' across the city and the nation.[46] On 1 December 1911, organized labour's worst fears manifested themselves, as John and James McNamara pled guilty to murder and conspiracy. As historian Graham Adams Jr. notes, the news 'broke like a thunderclap over all Los Angeles'.[47] Samuel Gompers and Eugene Debs felt personally betrayed by the McNamara brothers, while labour advocates across the nation, previously firm in their commitment to standing behind the brothers and the virtues of organized labour, sighed grievously at what many viewed as a betrayal of the movement.[48]

## *The Survey*

While Los Angeles and California grappled with the aftermath of the bombing on the *Times* building, the subsequent trial and confession by the McNamara brothers for the 'crime of the century' aroused a series of troubling questions for the nation: what caused such tensions between labourers and business? What led union activists to commit industrial violence? Was the nation raising a generation of mass murderers? And more importantly, could the nation construct public policy to alleviate the tensions that led to this social and economic unrest? Lincoln Steffens of *McClure's Magazine* summed up the national mood when he asked:

> What are we Americans going to do about conditions which are bringing up healthy, good-tempered boys like these McNamara boys to really believe, as they most sincerely do – they and a growing group of labor – that the only recourse they have for improving the conditions of the wage earner is to use dynamite against property and life?[49]

Social reformers across the nation viewed the McNamara brothers' confession through the lens of progressive action. Paul Kellogg, an editor of one of the leading social reform journals in the nation, *The Survey*, stepped up his campaign advocating on behalf of forming a federal commission tasked with investigating the nature of industrial relations across the country. In a piece published in December 1911, Kellogg wrote that a commission could undertake 'such fundamental research into the relations of employers and employees', and could 'gauge the breakdown of existing laws under the pressure of industrial development'.[50] Reformers such as Kellogg hoped that a federal commission would not only investigate the systemic causes of industrial unrest but could provide expert research and scholarship leading to legislative action. As *The Survey's* editor described, such a commission 'will form the basis for a constructive public program'.[51]

Advocates for an industrial relations commission petitioned President William Howard Taft, and articulated the value in the proposed commission's ability to inform political decision making and the construction of sound public policy grounded in research and inquiry. Led by some of the era's most notable progressive reformers, including Louis Brandeis and Jane Addams, supporters of an investigatory committee believed researchers could unpack the complex and various reasons which led labourers, such as John and James McNamara, to commit mass violence. Instead of placing blame either on industry or labour, Brandeis and his co-signers suggested to Taft:

> with our stupendous manufacturing development, the industrial workers assembled in many cities exceed by thousands the entire populations of whole states generations ago. Our statutes in the main were originally enacted for the different conditions existing before these industrial changes, and naturally such evolution as there has been has been dominated by the readily mobilized forces and influences by capital. Here, in part, lies the explanation of that serious distrust which has come to be felt by great masses of workers toward the fabric of our law and the structure and control of the machinery through which we apply it.[52]

The signatories of the petition recognized that a much larger, systemic issue led workers to the types of violence perpetrated at the *Los Angeles Times* and to the industrial bombings around the nation *c.* 1905–10. Instead of castigating labour, these reformers sought answers in the economic system of the era.

Founded in 1897, the New York Charity Organization originally published *The Survey* as a voice for 'reform-minded social research', which 'emerged to help charity organization workers with advice and information'.[53] Kellogg in particular viewed his work thusly:

> The philosophy of the *Survey* is to set forth before the community all the facts that bare on a problem, and to rely upon the common understanding, the common forethought, the common purpose of the people as the first great resource in working that problem out.[54]

By 1911, Kellogg's progressive form of social research aimed at transmitting the conception of 'truth' to the public, received funding from a variety of prominent philanthropic foundations, including the Russell Sage Foundation and the Carnegie Foundation.[55] The journal's connection to philanthropic grants testified to the mechanisms by which social reformers funded their research and inquiries.

## Labor's tribune

In mid-April 1913, Kansas City attorney and labour activist, Frank P. Walsh, wrote a thank you letter to Local Union 100, the Beer and Soda Drivers union, acknowledging an award presented to Walsh that same year. Walsh wrote, 'There is no earthly accomplishment which I could more dearly prize than the affectionate esteem in which I must be held by your organization.'[56] Walsh argued to the labourers, whom he had represented in a variety of negotiations throughout his nearly thirty-year legal career, that his efforts had 'always been a labor of love with me, and I consider their friendship and confidence, expressed in many ways, as the most satisfactory accomplishment of my professional life'.[57] Incidents of industrial and workplace violence grew ever more common throughout the early twentieth century as tensions increased between workers and corporations, and labour activists such as Frank Walsh argued that the growth of the industry in the United States threatened the stability of the nation's political democracy.[58] As he would argue as the chair of the USIR in 1915, 'the question of industrial relations assigned by Congress to the commission is more fundamental and of greater importance to the welfare of the Nation than any other question except the form of our government'.[59] His personal commitment to the nation and to the needs of working-class Americans earned Walsh the nickname 'Labor's Tribune'.[60]

Frank Walsh's dedication to the American labour movement came from first-hand experiences forged at a tender age. Francis Patrick Walsh was born in St. Louis, Missouri on 20 July 1864, where his father James owned and operated a hay and grain business.[61] For a brief period, his father's business allowed Frank the opportunity to attend school at the Christian Brothers St. Patrick's Academy located in St. Louis.[62] When Frank was ten, his father unexpectedly passed away, forcing the young Frank to quit school and work in order to support his mother and siblings.[63] He worked in a variety of manual labour positions including finding jobs in a barbed-wire factory and as a water boy employed for the Colorado and Midland Railroad.[64] As one biographer detailed, these youthful experiences 'helped to sharpen that intense hatred of poverty which became so characteristic of him'.[65] Historian Graham Adams Jr. notes that these years of hard labour took a toll on the pubescent Walsh and his friends: 'of thirty boys he remembered in his neighborhood, only three had survived to manhood'.[66] Within time, Frank moved from manual labour to office work, first with a St. Louis trade journal called the *Age of Steel*, followed by employment as a clerk with a number of banks and railroad companies in the city.[67]

At the age of twenty-one, Walsh moved to Kansas City, Missouri, and found employment as a clerk for a law firm in the city, Gardiner Lathrop.[68] While employed at Gardiner Lathrop, Walsh formally studied law and was admitted to the state bar of Missouri in 1889.[69] Walsh developed a highly successful general practice law firm over the course of thirty years, representing a variety of clients including Jesse James, Jr., and Dr Bennet Clark Hyde in a high-profile murder case in the city. He also represented a number of corporate business clients, a practice model which, in time, Walsh came to detest. He once wrote: 'I represented every corporation worth representing in Kansas City: street railways, steam railways, stock yard companies, telephone companies and the like, for ten years growing more ashamed of the results as time went on'.[70] Eventually, Walsh rejected all corporate clients, eliminating them entirely from his practice.

While expanding his law practice, Walsh also became highly involved in local Kansas City and Missouri Democratic Party politics. Walsh's rejection of corporate legal work coincided with his expanding participation within Missouri party politics. He became affiliated with the 'rabbit' wing of the Democratic state party and found himself asked to work on city housing and sanitary commissions. On one commission project, Walsh 'helped expose the rat-ridden, unsanitary squalor which contaminated large areas of the city'.[71] The early years of harsh physical labour, combined with deep poverty and the loss of so many childhood friends, deeply influenced Walsh's social reform projects. He also worked on behalf of labourers as president of Kansas City's Civil Service Board and the Board of Public Welfare 'which established and enforced better conditions for industrial workers'.[72]

Frank Walsh's participation in social reform commissions, deep commitment to advancing the needs of American labourers, and involvement with the Wilson campaign during the election of 1912, gained the newly elected president's consideration as Wilson selected members for the USIR. Journalist George Creel wrote of Walsh: 'a great lawyer, a persuasive speaker, and the most authentic liberal I have ever known', he was convinced that social reform could only be achieved as an 'agitator outside' versus 'a plodding administrator inside'.[73] Advised by his secretary of labour, President Wilson submitted Frank Walsh's name to head the commission in early 1913. Formally nominated by President Wilson in June 1913, Walsh's nomination faced considerable pushback from national political figures and leading reformers. Louis Brandeis, whom Wilson had considered for the commission's chairmanship, worried Walsh's 'lack of a national reputation' and political clout could hinder the investigation, all necessary requirements for the commission to be successful.[74] Senators in Congress allowed 'Walsh's nomination to languish in committee for three months' before Walsh 'enlisted the help of Democratic boss Joe Shannon of Kansas City and Senator William J. Stone'.[75] Walsh's determination to see his nomination advanced set a tone for the type of investigation he would lead and demonstrated that he had a degree of political clout among the Missouri contingent. He was formally confirmed by the Senate in September 1913.

With the chair selected, Wilson took up the task of rounding out the nine-member panel. Representatives from the fields of labour, industry and the public were selected. President Wilson also asked University of Wisconsin economist, John R. Commons, to serve beside Walsh on the commission as a member representing the public contingent on the commission's board. Initially, Commons rejected the opportunity to serve when Wilson invited him via a telegram sent by Wisconsin senator, Robert M. La Follette.[76] However, according to Commons, a strange coincidence occurred that happened to place him in Kansas City at the very moment Walsh received his invitation from President Wilson.[77] The serendipitous meeting between Commons and Walsh transformed the economist's earlier rejection of Wilson's offer, and he agreed to serve. Commons rejected Louis Brandeis's concerns about Walsh's lack of a national reputation, arguing to Wisconsin senator Robert M. La Follette in a follow-up letter that he would wholeheartedly 'accept membership if Walsh is chairman'.[78] During their meeting, Walsh promised Commons that as chair, he would take on 'all responsibilities' for the commission itself, leaving the economist the ability to act as a formal adviser to the chair, an arrangement Commons readily accepted.[79] In fact, Commons remarked to Senator La Follette that 'he should not have considered' the opportunity to serve on the commission 'if it were not for Walsh'.[80] Commons was optimistic about Walsh leading the investigation, a prospect that he believed would allow the 'commission to amount to something' based solely on Common's observations of Walsh's personal integrity, strength and deep commitment to public service.[81] As the commission headed into its formal research and investigation phase, the agitator Walsh and the researcher Commons appeared united for the common good. While John R. Commons eagerly awaited the prospect of working with Frank Walsh, his prior research and connections to philanthropic funding would cause tensions between the two progressives as they started their investigation. As with the work of Paul Kellogg at *The Survey*, John Commons fostered a complex relationship with capitalists, as philanthropic grants funded much of his scholarship during this period.

## A rift among progressives

Frank Walsh, John R. Commons, and their fellow commissioners canvassed the nation during their two-year investigation, held public hearings from California to New York and cities in between, interviewed over 700 witnesses and documented 6.5 million words of testimony. Formal public testimony began in 1914, with Walsh taking the lead in examining notable witnesses including Andrew Carnegie and John D. Rockefeller Jr. While Walsh and John Commons sought answers for the industrial unrest rooted within the industrial capitalism of the era, a deep rift emerged between the two progressives during the course of the investigation rooted largely in questions surrounding the commission's operating budget. The two reformers also quarrelled over the research branches of the investigation. Should the commission prioritize public hearings or closed meeting inquiries led by a unit of academic investigators? The mechanism through which the commission operated, the appropriations budget offered by Congress, broke down politically as conservative members of the Senate sought to withhold funds from the investigation. How would the commission's small budget be used? Walsh desired public hearings publicizing to the nation the sins of the system. For John R. Commons, and the newly hired director of research, Charles M. McCarthy, the answer would be to fund intense research modelled on the type of inquiry advanced at the University of Wisconsin. The divide between balancing public hearings or intensive research with a small budget from Congress fractured the commission's progressive alliance.

In December 1913, Charles M. McCarthy, then the chief librarian of the Wisconsin Legislative Reference Library, a research library dedicated to providing educational resources to state legislators, wrote a think-piece essay regarding a proposed research path for the USIR.[82] In the essay, the author of the 'Wisconsin Idea' suggested that the vast majority of the investigatory work for the federal commission should be conducted within the specific legal contexts of the individual states and their laws, as opposed to federal regulations which created the commission itself. McCarthy suggested the complexities of each state in the American system of federalism could slow down the speed of the investigation. McCarthy also recognized the potential problems associated with managing an investigation at this scale, across the nation, and understood the time and resources required to manage the commission accordingly. The commission, in McCarthy's interpretation, would therefore require a series of clarifying questions directing its research. He argued: 'It does little good to this country for a commission to get out a report of twenty to thirty volumes to be put upon library shelves and examined by future generations of political economists.'[83]

McCarthy proposed a separate research branch of the commission, modelled upon the system he built in Wisconsin, one led by skilled experts dedicated to academic inquiries necessary to unpack the broad mandate of exploring industrial unrest. For the author of the 'Wisconsin Idea' the essay unpacked a national investigation, which would research the system and design appropriate legislation to rectify the worst injustices, but McCarthy did not operate under any illusion they could solve everything. His essay noted, 'These bills should be drafted on the principle that they are not going to settle the great questions now before the people, but that they are going to be 'germ' legislation, that is, something which causes other improvements to occur.'[84]

By June 1914, partially influenced by McCarthy's 1913 essay, John R. Commons recommended hiring the Wisconsin-based reformer to serve as the commission's director of research, replacing W. Jett Lauck who had not advanced the investigations adequately according to critical national coverage, including comments from Paul Kellogg in *The Survey*. Kellogg argued: 'It is an open secret that for ten months following the commission's appointment it floundered badly, without a clear-cut program of work, without clear-cut division of responsibility, and with great areas of the field before it practically untouched.'[85] While Commons influenced Walsh's decision to hire McCarthy, a series of correspondence between Walsh and McCarthy demonstrates the latter's strong personal desire to lead the investigation himself. He wrote to Walsh on the type of man who could lead the research investigation: 'It takes a man who has the broad viewpoint and who can also administer and command men.'[86] McCarthy then recommended he should be that natural leader: 'I have come to the conclusion that the only thing that can be done with it is for me to take hold of it in some way.'[87]

With the selection of Charles McCarthy arranged, John R. Commons also personally handpicked the rest of the investigation's staff.[88] McCarthy divided up the team of researchers into nine divisions under categories including: 'legal and legislative, labor organizations and collective bargaining, unemployment, agricultural problems, education and preparation for life, welfare and social insurance, safety and sanitation, underlying causes of industrial unrest, and women in industry'.[89] By all accounts, McCarthy's research division operated an investigation dedicated to unpacking the truth while meticulously documenting all available evidence. In one memo to the research staff, McCarthy reminded his team to remember that 'accuracy is essential in all this work and that all statements made by the investigators shall be fact checked and verified'.[90] Staff appreciated McCarthy's attention to detail and mentoring capabilities and believed him to be a 'very successful director'.[91]

McCarthy's brand of research and inquiry, however, came to exemplify the administrative bloat Frank Walsh detested, with his deep-rooted scepticism towards expert scientific testimonies traded for payment, and to Commons's and McCarthy's prioritization of a research-intensive inquiry over public hearings. But, for Walsh, a successful labour 'agitator' trained in a legal system based on judgement by one's peers, justice came from exposing systemic corruption via public examination. Justice would be found in these public hearings where his fellow Americans could witness for themselves, almost as a jury, the corruption of capitalists. Over the course of 1914–15, Walsh emphasized the importance of public hearings over the research being conducted by McCarthy's team of investigators. When the Senate finally appropriated budget funds to the commission, Walsh made the decision to use the majority of those funds for hearings, over Charles McCarthy's furious protestations.

Within a few weeks of his hiring, McCarthy sent a series of letters to Walsh lamenting the state of the commission's budget, in particular the appropriations for the research division. On 22 June 1914, less than a month into his new position, McCarthy fretted about the state of the budget to Walsh. He wrote: 'I am constantly working toward the report. The greatest difficulty which I have had is the impossibility of planning because of the limitations imposed by the budget.'[92] McCarthy then recommended to Walsh that the only method for rectifying the budget problems would be to restrict the number of public hearings, and argued, 'I am anxiously awaiting to hear what you can do about the hearings', and further suggested, 'I am certain enough we don't haven't money enough to carry this investigation along at the rate at which we are going, unless we cut the hearings down, or do away with them at the present.'[93] Three days later, when McCarthy had not yet heard a reply from Walsh regarding cancelling the public hearings, McCarthy sent another letter, describing in detail his plan to replace the hearings to Walsh. The nervous director wrote:

There is no reason why commissioners could not make examinations, that is, two of them could go together and look up certain things. For instance, I think two or three could go to the Ford Works at Detroit and stay a week there and look around and talk with employees, etc., and get evidence. A well-balanced committee could be put studying other places in the same way.[94]

McCarthy's near obsession over details regarding the commission's budget plan, and subsequent request to fully shut down the public hearings, would arouse deep suspicion within Frank Walsh at a particularly delicate moment during the investigation's hearings. Walsh replied to McCarthy: 'You have always worried too much about the finances of this Commission', and in the end if McCarthy could hang in with Walsh, 'we will come out all right'.[95]

While Charles McCarthy plotted to end the commission's public hearings amidst his budget concerns, Frank Walsh and the USIR arranged plans to visit Denver, Colorado in the wake of a six-month-long Colorado mine strike that ended in an attack on the coal miners by state troopers in April 1914. Frank Walsh's close friend, journalist George Creel, detailed the horror:

The reign of terror culminated on April 20, 1914, in what came to be known as the 'Ludlow massacre'. At a given signal, troops and mine guards opened fire on a tent colony and kept it up until dark. The strikers fought back from arroyos, while the women and children sought the refuge of safety pits dug under the tents – a ghastly blunder, as it turned out, for machine guns ignited the flimsy shelters. The flaming canvas then dropped down on the pits, scorching scores and burning two mothers and eleven children to a crisp.[96]

National reports of the atrocities committed at Ludlow described the attack on the coalminers as 'worse than the order that sent the Light Brigade into the jaws of death', and muckraker George Creel 'urged a mass meeting on the statehouse lawn'.[97] More than 10,000 people attended the protest, a surprise even to Creel himself as there was a 'driving rainstorm' that day.[98]

The commissioners on the USIR petitioned Frank Walsh to hold an immediate hearing to investigate Ludlow. Reformer Jane Addams urged her friend Florence Harriman, a member of the commission, to 'interrupt their normal schedule in order to hold an impromptu meeting'.[99] While the commission organized a two-day meeting interviewing some of the survivors of the fire, Walsh postponed a more intensive hearing in Denver due to 'federal mediators whom President Wilson had recently dispatched to Colorado to effect a settlement'.[100] The tensions in Colorado following the fire at Ludlow were so tense some members of the commission declared 'there was a positive danger of a national revolution growing out of this strike'.[101]

George Creel placed blame for Ludlow squarely on the shoulders of the Rockefeller family, controlling partners in the Colorado Fuel and Iron Company. During the mass protest in Denver that April, Creel's anger was palpable. He 'denounced the governor, the lieutenant governor, and particularly the Rockefellers'.[102] Creel remembered the 'violence of [his] attack' and in his autobiography described: 'I can still feel Senator

Charlie Thomas tugging at my legs and hear him pleading, "George! George! For God's sake, tone it down".[103] Influenced deeply by George Creel, Frank Walsh set about to arrange an in-depth hearing into the Ludlow massacre for that fall. John D. Rockefeller Jr. was witness number one on Walsh's list sought for the hearings.

With the events of Ludlow in April, the new director of research, Charles M. McCarthy continued his advocacy for the complete elimination of the hearings, an odd development at a moment when the nation clamoured for answers in the Colorado strike. That October, Frank Walsh learned of the Rockefeller Foundation's plan to create a separate task force to investigate the Ludlow massacre, directed by William Mackenzie King, a former Canadian minister of labour. Walsh also learned that his director of research, Charles McCarthy, was close friends with John D. Rockefeller Jr., a relationship forged during their years in college at Brown University. The two developed a deep bond, one of the closest in McCarthy's life.[104] According to his biographer, 'McCarthy never courted popularity. He had few intimates', while noting that Rockefeller was one of only three friends McCarthy made during his years at Brown.[105]

When Frank Walsh and Charles McCarthy learned of the Rockefeller Foundation's plan to start their own investigation into industry and capital, McCarthy single-mindedly renewed his concerns about the commission's budget. He wondered to Walsh: 'if John D. Rockefeller is willing to put several millions of dollars into an investigation of this kind after having stated his own position upon industrial matters surely the United States Government should not be afraid to put in a couple hundred thousand more.'[106] McCarthy used the Rockefeller Foundation's investigation as a rationale to ask for increased appropriations. Frank Walsh, on the other hand, wondered if the nation's largest foundation planned their investigation into industrial relations as a way in which to avoid a federal subpoena compelling them to testify. On the same day McCarthy wrote to the chairman asking for more funds, Walsh also wrote to Basil Manly, detailing a conversation that a commission representative held with the Foundation. The Rockefellers responded that they 'could not cooperate with us because we were a political party'.[107] Walsh hinted at his concerns to Manly about a competing private Rockefeller investigation to a federal investigation mandated by law. He argued to Manly that if the Rockefellers' failed to respond, 'to our summons, we may be able to make such a showing without them as to recommend to Congress the passage of a law which prevents their activities'.[108]

In the fall of 1914, three issues confronted Frank Walsh as he worked to subpoena John D. Rockefeller's testimony before the USIR. First, he learned the Rockefeller Foundation planned to arrange their own investigation into the issues of industrial unrest, a proposal which John Rockefeller Jr. shared with Charles McCarthy that October. The junior Rockefeller wrote: 'Our purpose is to promote an exhaustive, scientific investigation, based primarily upon facts, rather than opinion.'[109] Second, Walsh faced an increasingly sceptical Congress: 'There was a very general feeling in committee that no good was being derived corresponding to that appropriation,' according to Senator Thomas B. Martin.[110] Third, he began to grow sceptical of the relationship between Charles M. McCarthy and John D. Rockefeller Jr., particularly as the former continued to advocate for the elimination of public hearings. As Walsh wrote to a friend in April 1915, 'The adoption of the final McCarthy policy would have shut off our hearings', and 'the chloroforming of the sort of report you expect, and which I am exceedingly anxious to have made'.[111] More concerning for John R. Commons and McCarthy, the research division of the commission made Walsh critical of the Wisconsin Idea's methodological approach to collaborative work between employers and labor. Walsh described the process thusly:

> Another branch of the 'Idea' is the putting together of what they call 'large constructive programs' covering every branch of work. These consist of interminable 'bill drafting'; the proposed measures containing legal machinery which would provide for countless employees, experts, and the like, 'of thorough scientific training', the thought of which should throw the legal profession into spasms of delight, and the proletariat into hopeless despair. While this is going on, fundamentals remain practically untouched.[112]

For Walsh, the only method by which to change the 'fundamentals' would be to expose the system to the nation in a series of robust public hearings.

On 27 January 1915, Frank Walsh received the public hearing he desired when John D. Rockefeller Jr. testified before the USIR. Walsh was fully prepared as a prosecutor on behalf of the nation.[113] Rockefeller was also prepared and answered the majority of Walsh's questions, related to his role as the director of the Colorado Fuel and Iron Company (CFI). According to Rockefeller Jr., 'directors did not shape a firm's managerial policies, he insisted; they concentrated almost exclusively on its financial affairs. For this reason he denied that he had influenced CFI's attitudes toward labor.'[114] In other words, while the Rockefeller family personally profited from the policies, the cruel exploitation of workers was 'abhorrent to me personally' and 'contrary to the spirit of my whole purpose and training'.[115] Rockefeller also claimed, in relation to the events at Ludlow, that 'I have no desire to defend any conditions that are justly subject to criticism. I only ask that the responsibility for them be apportioned fairly'.[116] By all accounts, the composed, cool, and rational Rockefeller bested Walsh during the examination, and 'scored a smash hit'.[117] One union representative stated, 'Mr. Rockefeller is not the kind of man laboring men thought he was.'[118] Even Mother Jones remarked about Rockefeller: 'We have been misrepresenting him terribly.'[119]

Not to be undone by the public backlash against his treatment of Rockefeller Jr., Walsh redoubled his efforts to gather evidence that would implicate the business and philanthropic interests associated with the family for what the chairman viewed as their complicity within the events at Ludlow. 'Walsh had good reason for confidence', according to historian Graham Adams Jr.[120] Walsh had compiled a series of correspondence directly implicating Rockefeller, including a letter from the executive chairman of the CFI, L.M. Bowers. These documents 'outlined in detail the causes and major events of the altercation', in Colorado.[121] Within the series of correspondence 'Bowers told Rockefeller that the company refused to recognize', the coal miners, and more damningly for Rockefeller, Bowers indicated they would hold this stance 'until our bones were bleached as white as chalk in these Rocky Mountains'.[122]

Within the compilation of Rockefeller Jr. letters included a letter from Charles M. McCarthy listed as 'personal and confidential' to his good friend from Brown University. When Frank Walsh learned of the existence of these letters from McCarthy to Rockefeller Jr. is not clear. He directed McCarthy in October 1914 to reach out to Rockefeller in order to ask him to testify to the committee, but the letter marked 'personal and confidential' combined with McCarthy's policy recommendation to end the hearings seemed to convince Walsh that McCarthy had been 'acting with bad faith, duplicity, and reckless mishandling of the truth'.[123] In the letter to his old college friend, the researcher tried to diminish his role in the commission: 'In all these relations I wish you to understand, as I wrote in a previous letter, that I have charge of the investigational work and have nothing to do with the hearings of this kind'.[124] He continued, 'I want to again assure you of the same old personal relations, and the same regard exists, and behind all formalities which may come up, or red tape, you will find the same old Mac'.[125]

These portions of the letter from McCarthy convinced Walsh that the researcher had been engaging in 'a plan little short of espionage' as directed by McCarthy's adherence to the Wisconsin Idea.[126] For Frank Walsh, McCarthy's adherence to a research methodology requiring collaboration with organizations and individuals generating the economic unrest and corrupt business practices which led to the formation of the commission spoke to the systemic injustice he sought to root out. The Rockefeller Foundation proposed a separate investigation in order to counter the conclusions provided by the USIR; it was not designed to sort out the heart of industrial unrest, but to cover their complicity in causing the unrest directly. Frank Walsh fired Charles McCarthy in a meeting in February 1915, framed in the premise of budget cuts to the research division, but designed to remove a member deeply influenced by that same corruption, whether or not McCarthy fully understood his complicity. During the meeting, McCarthy once again 'moved that the Commission terminate its hearing and pour all its remaining funds into research'.[127] Walsh instead, 'decided to the contrary', and 'instructed the astounded Director to grant two weeks' notice to his staff and to close his office as soon as possible'.[128]

Frank Walsh hired Basil Manly in the immediate aftermath of Charles McCarthy's termination. Manly, a natural ally to Walsh, had been the head of the commission's hearing division since the beginning of their work.[129] All that remained for Walsh and Manly was to lay out their understanding of the causes of industrial unrest. To them, there was no real need for endless research, collaborative endeavours with corrupt business partners, nor the advancement of their careers based on their conclusions. Instead, to Walsh and Manly, the concentration of wealth led directly to industrial unrest.

## Final report

The Manly-Walsh report argued that the real threat to the nation was the concentration of wealth itself within the hands of a few Americans within industries such as mining, manufacturing, transportation, banking and finance.[130] According to their analysis, the control of these industries rested 'in the hands of a small number of wealthy and powerful financiers', and that these represented 'the basic industries upon which the welfare of the country must finally rest'.[131] Not only did the welfare of the nation reside within those industries, but because the power controlling those corporations lived within the hands of a few individuals, those men, including the Rockefellers, Carnegie and the Vanderbilts, could control the lives of individual American wage earners. They argued, 'the lives of millions of wage earners are, therefore, subject to the dictation of a relatively small number of men'.[132]

Walsh also concluded that the men who controlled wealth in the United States, 'are totally ignorant of every aspect of the industries they control', and that they are 'totally unconcerned with regard to the living and working conditions of the employees in those industries'.[133] Instead, the report argued that the creation of foundations, while premised in the idea of the public good to the nation, in essence sought to 'control the education and "social service" of the Nation'.[134] The commissioners pointed to the monies donated through 'the endowment of colleges and universities, by the creation of funds for the pensioning of teachers by contributions to private charities, as well as through controlling or influencing the public press'.[135] Finally, Walsh and Manly expressed concern that the hundreds of millions of dollars owned through the foundations lay beyond the realm of public taxation, while the directors and benefactors of the foundations, such as John D. Rockefeller, 'remained in absolute control of the funds and activities of the institutions now and in perpetuity'.[136] Therefore, foundations represented to Frank Walsh, the emergence of an economic oligarchy that constructed a legal framework legitimizing their existence forever, one legally constructed beyond the hands of American democracy.

Walsh and Manly offered Congress and the American people a number of recommendations to limit the control and power of American philanthropic foundations. First, they recommended that Congress pass legislation requiring foundations 'whose present charters empower them to perform more than a single specific function and whose funds exceed one million dollars, be required to secure a Federal charter'.[137] With this provision, Congress would gain crucial oversight concerning the function and operations of foundations. Second, Walsh and Manly recommended that Congress enact laws requiring any foundation or religious institution 'whose property holdings or income exceeds a moderate amount' be required to share their accounting records, bank holdings and all pertinent financial information with Congress.[138] Lastly, the chair advised Congress to establish new governmental agencies 'for education and social service' as counter organizations to the growing influence of foundations. In this last provision, Walsh and Manly clearly articulated the idea that the public, through their government, ought to control the work of social reform, and not leave it in the hands of private philanthropic foundations guided by the subjective whims of their wealthy benefactors.

## Conclusions

The USIR's conclusions condemning the rise of centralized wealth within philanthropic foundations, as an element within an evolving industrial economic system in the

United States, proved untenable for social reformers. Progressive scholars, including John Commons, Charles M. McCarthy, and Paul Kellogg, increasingly relied upon philanthropic grants to conduct their investigations into the United States' economic, social and civic unrest. The advance of their scholarship, as well as their careers, required money. McCarthy in particular spent considerable time thinking through these financial realities during his tenure as the commission's director of research. In fact, McCarthy's near obsession with the commission's budget, and the dedicated amounts appropriated to his research division, ruined his relationship with Frank Walsh and diminished the research he and his colleagues collected. As George Creel commented in 1947, Frank Walsh came to view reform methodologies, including the Wisconsin Idea, as 'plodding administrative' studies focused on the advancement of scholarly careers as much as the economic reform of American society.

The Walsh-Manly report asked the nation the following important question: who ought to fund the search for truth, as Paul Kellogg characterized social reform research? Ought the nation turn to private philanthropic foundations or was it the public's responsibility through their legislative bodies to fund academic research? The Rockefeller Foundation's attempt to arrange a competing investigation into industrial unrest only highlighted Frank Walsh's fears regarding the fine line between democratically appointed research versus private philanthropically funded investigations. The events in Colorado in April 1914 illustrated the problem of accepting money from a foundation which earned profit through the exploitation of labour, and, in the case of Ludlow, the coordinated and planned attack on innocent women and children. Could the potential 'good' conducted by philanthropic funding wipe away their deaths? These were the real-time considerations informing Frank Walsh's argument against philanthropy.

While contemporary Americans largely ignored the United States Commission on Industrial Relation's conclusions, the impact of the Walsh-Manly report criticizing philanthropic foundations did not disappear. Within ten years, a renewal of their warning emerged from an unlikely source. Wisconsin's most notable progressive politician, Robert M. La Follette, viewed by many as the father of the Wisconsin Idea, forged a deep friendship with Basil Manly during the post-war economic boom of the 1920s. Manly's influence on the ageing Wisconsin political giant informed La Follette's final run for president in 1924. In particular, Manly's experience writing the commission's final report shaped La Follette's expanding conceptualization of the ways philanthropic foundations buttressed the monopoly system. Newly inspired by Manly, Robert M. La Follette began an attack against foundations within the pages of his eponymous monthly magazine during the early months of 1925. Instead of a public shrug, in 1925, politicians in Wisconsin heeded La Follette's concerns and took action to limit the influence of foundations at the University of Wisconsin. For a brief period in Wisconsin, the answer to the question of who ought to fund social research seemed clear.

# Notes

1  General Harrison Gray Otis, 'General Otis Shares Candid Statements', *Los Angeles Times*, 9 September 1914.

2  Final Report of the United States Commission on Industrial Relations (Washington, DC: Government Printing House, 1916), 6.

3  For detailed labour and political analyses of the United States Commission on Industrial Relations, see Graham Adams Jr., *Age of Industrial Violence, 1910–1915* (New York: Columbia University Press, 1966); Leon Fink, 'Expert Advice: Progressive Intellectuals and the Unraveling of Labor Reform, 1912–1915', in *Intellectuals and Public Life: Between Radicalism and Reform*, ed. Leon Fink, Stephen T. Leonard, and Donald M. Reid (Ithaca: Cornell University Press, 1996); Joseph A. McCartin, *Labor's Great War: The Struggle for Industrial Democracy and the Origins of Modern American Labor Relations, 1912–1921* (Chapel Hill: The University of North Carolina Press, 1997); Shelton Stromquist, 'Class Wars: Frank Walsh, the Reformers, and the Crisis of Progressivism', in *Labor Histories: Class, Politics, and the Working-Class Experience*, ed. Eric Arnesen, Julie Greene, and Bruce Laurie (Urbana: University of Illinois Press, 1998).

4  Fink, 'Expert Advice', 182–3.

5  Ibid.

6  Adams, *The Age of Industrial Violence*, 50.

7  Leon Fink in 'Expert Advice' describes the commission's reform efforts as 'painstaking plans for labor reform' but also notes that they 'proved to be political nonstarters, championed neither by the workers they might have benefitted nor by public officials unwilling (outside wartime exigency) to challenge marketplace regulation', 212. Historian McCartin in *Labor's Great War* suggests, that while fractures in the commission impacted its contemporary audience, the radical the final report was 'one of the most remarkable ever released by a federal agency' and 'one of organized labor's greatest triumphs in the Progressive era', 12–18.

8  Final Report of the United States Commission on Industrial Relations, 121.

9  Ibid.

10  Adams, *The Age of Industrial Violence*, 1.

11  'Fire Kills 19; Unions Accused', *New York Times*, 2 October 1910.

12  Ibid.

13  'The Los Angeles Times Bombing', The McNamara Brothers, Archives and Rare Books Library, University of Cincinnati, accessed 11 January 2018. http://digital .libraries.uc.edu/exhibits/arb/mcnamara/bombing.php.

14  'Fire Kills 19; Unions Accused'.

15  Ibid.

16  Ibid.

17  Ibid.

18  'Los Angeles Ruins Yield Five Bodies', *New York Times*, 2 October 1910.

19  Ibid.

20  'The Los Angeles Times Bombing', and Howard Blum, *American Lightning: Terror, Mystery, Movie-Making, and the Crime of the Century* (New York: Crown Publishers, 2008), 50.

21  'Los Angeles Ruins Yield Five Bodies'.

22  Ibid.

23  'Fire Kills 19; Unions Accused'.

24  Ibid.

25  Ibid.

26  Ibid.

27  Ibid.

28  Ibid.

29  Ibid.

30  McCartin, *Labor's Great War*, 18.

31  Ibid., 4.

32  'How Burns Caught the Dynamiters: The Great Detective Reviews the McNamara Case from the First Clue to the Confession', *McClure's Magazine* XXXVIII, no. 3 (January 1912): 325.

33  Ibid., 326.

34  Adams, *The Age of Industrial Violence*, 10.

35  'How Burns Caught the Dynamiters', 326.

36  Adams, *The Age of Industrial Violence*, 10.

37  For a detailed analysis describing Burns's investigation and the arrest of the McNamara Brothers, please see Graham Adams Jr.'s *The Age of Industrial Violence*, 9–12.

38  Adams, *The Age of Industrial Violence*, 11.

39  Ibid.

40  Ibid.

41  Ibid., 12.

42  'Burns Surrenders; Released on Bail', *New York Times*, 25 April 1911.

43  Adams, *The Age of Industrial Violence*, 13.

44  Ibid., 13.

45  Ibid., 14.

46  Ibid.

47  Ibid.

48  Adams quotes Samuel Gompers who declared, 'The McNamara's have betrayed labor. We have been deceived, we have been put upon', Ibid., 19.

49  Ibid., 25.

50  'The Common Welfare: Federal Industrial Commission Urged', *The Survey* XXVII, no. 11 (30 December 1911), 1407.

51  Ibid.

52  'Petition to the President for a Federal Commission on Industrial Relations', published in *The Survey* XXVII, no. 11 (30 December 1911), 1430.

53  Fink, 'Expert Advice', 201 and 'The Survey Journal', Social Welfare History Project, VCU Libraries, https://socialwelfare.library.vcu.edu/organizations/the-survey/, accessed 25 May 2018.

54  Kellogg quoted in: Caroline Lanza, 'Truth Plus Publicity: Paul U. Kellogg and Hybrid Practice, 1902–1937', (PhD diss., University of Washington, 2016): 1.

55  Adams, *The Age of Industrial Violence*, 26

56  Frank P. Walsh to Beer Drivers, Soda Drivers and Helpers Local Union No. 100, 11 April 1913, Box 1, Folder 'General Correspondence, 1913, April 1–12', Frank P. Walsh Papers, 1896–1939, New York Public Library. Hereafter identified as FPW.

57  Ibid.

58  McCartin, *Labor's Great War*, characterizes Frank Walsh as one of the leading radicals of the era by advocating for the extension of democratic principles into the industrial workplace.

59  Final Report of the United States Commission on Industrial Relations, 17.

60  Judy Ancel, 'Frank P. Walsh: Labor's Tribune', *The Kansas City Labor History Tour*, 17 October 1992.

61  Letter to Landry Harwood from Frank P. Walsh, 14 January 1915, Box 1, Folder 'General Correspondence, Jan.–Feb. 1913', FPW Papers.

62  Sister Maria Eucharia Meehan, C.S.J., 'Frank P. Walsh and the American Labor Movement' (PhD diss., New York University, 1962), 9.

63  Ibid., 9.

64  Letter to Landry Harwood from Frank P. Walsh, 14 January 1915, Box 1, Folder 'General Correspondence, Jan.–Feb. 1913', FPW Papers.

65  Meehan, 'Frank P. Walsh', 9.

66  Adams, *The Age of Industrial Violence*, 69.

67  Meehan, 'Frank P. Walsh', 9; Letter to Landry Harwood from Frank P. Walsh, 14 January 1915, Box 1, Folder 'General Correspondence, Jan.–Feb. 1913', FPW Papers.

68  Ibid., 10.

69  Ancel, 'Frank P. Walsh: Labor's Tribune', 2.

70  'Letter from Frank P. Walsh to Lilienthal, 10 January 1921, FPW Papers', as quoted in Meehan, 'Frank P. Walsh', 12. Historian Graham Adams Jr. also notes that Walsh's law practice did not suffer as a result of removing corporate law from his professional portfolio. Adams writes: 'he still earned up to $50,000 a year in legal fees' following his decision in 1900.

71  Adams, *The Age of Industrial Violence*, 71.

72  Ibid.

73  George Creel, *Rebel at Large: Recollections of Fifty Crowded Years* (New York: G.P. Putnam's Sons, 1947), 48.

74  McCartin, *Labor's Great War*, 20.

75  Ibid., 21.

76  John R. Commons, *Myself: The Autobiography of John R. Commons* (Madison: The University of Wisconsin Press, 1963), 166.

77  Ibid., 167.

78  Telegram from John R. Commons to Robert M. La Follette, 20 June 1913, Box B73, Folder 'Special Correspondence, 1913', Robert M. La Follette Sr. Papers, 1844–1925, Library of Congress. Hereinafter RML.

79  Letter from John R. Commons to Robert M. La Follette, 21 June 1913, Box B73, Folder 'Special Correspondence, 1913', RML Papers.

80  Ibid.

81  Ibid.

82  'McCarthy, Charles 1873–1921', Historical Essay, *Wisconsin Historical Society*, https://www.wisconsinhistory.org/Records/Article/CS10376 accessed 26 January 2018.

83  Charles McCarthy, 'Suggestions for the Federal Industrial Relations Commission', December 1913, Box 24, Folder 13 'McCarthy Subject Files – US Commission on Industrial Relations, General 1913–1916', Charles M. McCarthy Papers, 1889, 1906–1931, Wisconsin Historical Society, 1. Hereafter CMM.

84  Ibid., 2.

85  Paul Kellogg, *The Survey*, 10 October 1914.

86  Letter from Charles M. McCarthy to Frank P. Walsh, 29 May 1914, Box 6, Folder 3, CMM Papers.

87  Ibid.

88  Edward A. Fitzpatrick, *McCarthy of Wisconsin* (New York: Columbia University, 1944), 190–1. Please note, the author of this definitive biography of Charles McCarthy also served as a researcher working under McCarthy for the United States Commission on Industrial Relations, a fact Fitzpatrick reports on page 191.

89  Ibid., 190–1.

90 Charles McCarthy, 'To all Investigators in the Research and Investigation Department', July 1914, Box 24, Folder 13, CMM Papers.
91 Fitzpatrick, *McCarthy of Wisconsin*, 191.
92 Letter to Frank P. Walsh from Charles M. McCarthy, 22 June 1914, Box 6, Folder 4, CMM Papers.
93 Ibid.
94 Letter to Frank P. Walsh from Charles M. McCarthy, 25 June 1914, Box 6, Folder 4, CMM Papers.
95 Letter from Frank Walsh to Charles McCarthy, 23 December 1914, Box 7, Folder 4, CMM Papers.
96 Creel, *Rebel at Large*, 127.
97 Adams, *The Age of Industrial Violence*, 164; Creel, *Rebel at Large*, 128.
98 Creel, *Rebel at Large*, 128.
99 Adams, *The Age of Industrial Violence*, 146.
100 Ibid., 147.
101 Ibid.
102 Ibid., 146.
103 Creel, *Rebel at Large*, 128.
104 Fitzpatrick, *McCarthy of Wisconsin*, 13.
105 Ibid.
106 Letter to Frank Walsh from Charles McCarthy, 6 October 1914, Box 7, Folder 4, CMM Papers.
107 Letter from Frank Walsh to Basil Manly, 6 October 1914, FPW Papers.
108 Ibid.
109 Letter to Charles M. McCarthy from John D. Rockefeller, Jr., 20 October 1914, Box 7, Folder 4, CMM Papers.
110 Quoted in Adams, *The Age of Industrial Violence*, 207.
111 Letter from Frank Walsh to William Marion Reedy, 17 April 1915, FPW Papers.
112 Ibid.
113 Adams, *The Age of Industrial Violence*, 162.
114 Ibid.
115 Ibid.
116 Ibid.
117 Ibid.
118 Ibid.
119 Ibid.
120 Ibid.
121 Ibid., 165.
122 Ibid.
123 Ibid., 212.
124 Letter to John D. Rockefeller Jr. from Charles McCarthy, 17 October 1914, CMM Papers.
125 Ibid.
126 Letter from Frank Walsh to William Marion Reedy, 17 April 1915, FPW Papers, 1–2.
127 Adams, *The Age of Industrial Violence*, 209.
128 Ibid.
129 Letter from Frank Walsh to William Marion Reedy, 17 April 1915, FPW Papers, 2.
130 Final Report of the United States Commission on Industrial Relations, 116.
131 Ibid.

132 Ibid., 117.
133 Ibid., 118.
134 Ibid.
135 Ibid.
136 Ibid.
137 Ibid., 125.
138 Ibid., 126.

# 11

# Klanishness and American fraternalism

## Examining charity and philanthropy in the Second Ku Klux Klan

Miguel Hernandez

On 11 October 1921, the members of the House Committee on Rules gathered for a hearing to scrutinize a series of claims made against the recently revived Knights of the Ku Klux Klan. The hearings, led by Congressman Phillip P. Campbell, were tasked with examining allegations of Klan violence and fraud made by newspapers such as the *New York World*. In doing so, the committee questioned current members of the Klan, including the founder and Imperial Wizard William Joseph Simmons. They also heard from O.B. Williamson, a post office inspector who had visited this Second Ku Klux Klan's headquarters in Atlanta to review their finances. After discussing a series of suspicious private property purchases by this order's leadership, Campbell asked Williamson directly how much of the Klan's profits were spent 'for the benefit of needy people, or for helpful purposes in communities – charitable purposes?' Williamson replied, jokingly, 'Well, if you call Mr. Simmons a needy person, then some thousands of dollars have been spent for him. But general charity, I do not think, has received any of it.'[1]

Although the hearings dedicated most of their attention to the more serious allegations of Klan vigilantism, the order's charitable status was repeatedly questioned and defended by various witnesses. The Second Klan's continued growth rested on its carefully constructed public image, and its charitable work was an intrinsic part of this. Addressing Williamson's allegations, Imperial Wizard Simmons claimed that he could present thousands of witnesses who could speak to the Klan's charity work, and that the only reason the national body had yet to dispense 'vast sums of money' was because they were still relatively early in their development. One congressman, after hearing of the substantial profits gained through sales of membership and Klan paraphernalia, asked whether the order had paid any federal income tax. Simmons stated that they had not, but defended his organization by explaining that since the Klan was a charitable fraternity they were tax-exempt.[2] The Imperial Wizard repeatedly employed his Klan's status as a benevolent and charitable fraternity to justify many of their more peculiar habits, such as their masks and restricted membership. In the end, this defence prevented the House Rules Committee from recommending any further action against the Klan, although the political furore over the revived movement continued for several years as more Americans joined its ranks. As a private organization with a xenophobic and chauvinistic vision of 'social good', the Second Klan pushed the nation to reconsider what a benevolent and charitable organization it was. These hearings and the Second Klan itself provide an insight into the debates Americans were having about the boundaries and relationships between political action, voluntary associations and charity in the aftermath of the First World War.

The Second Klan had been granted a charter in Georgia in 1916 which established that the order would be 'purely benevolent and eleemosynary, and there shall be no capital stock or profit or gain to the members'. The charter also recognized that the Knights of the Ku Klux Klan was a fraternal organization, and awarded 'such rights, powers, and privileges as are now extended to' existing fraternities such as the Freemasons and the Knights of Pythias. The peculiar history and cultural development of fraternities in the landscape of American voluntary associations and charities afforded unique protections which the Klan exploited to expand their small brotherhood into a decidedly political mass movement of anywhere from two to four million members. Nonetheless, the Klan also pushed and redefined the boundaries of what fraternities were supposed to do.[3] Thus, as many white Protestant Americans were drawn to the promises of this so-called Invisible Empire, the broader public repeatedly questioned the role and influence of exclusive fraternities and their 'charitable' efforts in a nominally democratic society.

The scholarship on American charities and philanthropy has tended to centre on the larger campaigns and foundations or the lives of notable individuals who contributed to this sector. As Lila Corwin Berman has pointed out, this focus can be partially explained by the generous support of such scholarship by foundations themselves, which in turn 'have led to a preponderance of institutional and celebratory histories'.[4] One example of this trend is the work of Olivier Zunz. His study of the broader trends in American philanthropy in the twentieth century remains valuable for helping to understand such areas as the legal and fiscal framework of philanthropy or the interactions between the state and the major foundations. However, such a synthesis inevitably requires generalizations. In Zunz's case, his study often overlooks or underemphasizes the charity of those with more exclusionary visions of a perfect society and produces a somewhat triumphalist narrative of American philanthropy.[5] But the history of American charity and philanthropy is messier. In relation to this issue Lawrence Friedman noted that 'There were marked differences over how homogenous or diverse the "good society" was to be, how inclusive or exclusive, and what its values were to be'.[6] In order to reach a better understanding of how Americans worked to craft a better society through voluntary efforts, it is worth examining how such reactionary groups as the Second Ku Klux Klan employed charity to shape life in communities across the United States. Furthermore, the Second Klan re-emerged at a crucial point in the evolution of both fraternities and charitability – the First World War – that allows us to examine how Americans responded to such drastic changes within the broader culture of giving.

In order to understand how the Second Klan came to claim and exploit the title of a charitable brotherhood and what this signifies for wider trends in the history of American charity and philanthropy, this chapter will first trace the establishment of fraternities as a feature of US society and the evolution of their charity from an inward-facing and reciprocal form of benefits to a more universal form of 'service'. The analysis will then turn to the development of the Second Klan, examining its many competing notions and uses of charity within its broader and often violent programme of unabashed white supremacy, Protestant evangelicalism and '100% American' patriotism. In addition, this chapter will dissect public reactions to this militant fraternity's civic and charitable efforts to 'improve' American society in the early 1920s. Ultimately, this chapter will highlight how the Klan came to exploit America's long-standing passion for fraternalism and charity to advance their decidedly political goals for a white Protestant and nativist future.

Fraternities had of course been a staple feature of American life throughout the nineteenth century, with groups such as the Freemasons and the Odd Fellows playing a vital role in the social and political development of America's communities in the early Republic. The period after the Civil War though saw a veritable explosion in the number and membership of such groups. By the turn of the century, the phenomenon had become so widespread that one writer, W. S. Harwood, commented: 'So numerous, so powerful, have these orders become, that these closing years of the century might well be called the Golden Age of fraternity.' He estimated that anywhere from a fifth to an eighth of the adult male population in the United States belonged to a fraternity, and the major orders he surveyed had paid out $650 million in benefits to its members in the year 1896 alone.[7] The widespread popularity of fraternal orders among American men in this era and the public good they offered made them cornerstones of the social life and welfare networks in many American communities. Some still criticized the private power fraternities wielded, but most Americans had long forgotten the anti-Masonic panic of the 1830s, and such orders received public approval and even governmental support for their charitable work through their tax-exempt status. Despite this, scholars have continued to question the nature of their charity.

In his study of benevolent fraternities, David T. Beito has noted that the benefits provided to members in case of illness or death cannot be properly classified as charity, but more closely resemble a contractual relationship. Members could expect benefits in their time of need but were required to provide the same to others and uphold the morals and values of the order. 'In contrast to the hierarchical methods of public and private charity', Beito explains, 'fraternal aid rested on an ethical principle of reciprocity. Donors and recipients often came from the same, or nearly the same, walks of life.'[8] While Beito is correct that the main fraternal benefits were restricted to members and their dependents, fraternities still provided extensive charity to the wider community. One writer in 1907 noted that the B'nai B'rith had spent $98 million in charity since their foundation in 1843. Of this total, $15 million had been spent on the construction and improvement of charitable institutions in the community and $35 million was given to 'other charities'.[9] Yet, even though they gave to good causes, fraternities at the turn of the century still replicated the same concerns as other reformers of the time as to the dangers of pauperization and ineffective charity. The very foundation of fraternalism was based on the principle of exclusivity. To join and partake in the beneficiary system that many fraternities instituted, Americans had to demonstrate their worthiness and lead a thrifty and respectable life. So, while fraternities at the turn of the century gave to others, their notions of universal brotherhood and charity extended primarily to those they deemed laudable, prioritizing their own tried and tested members and their families first and then the general welfare of the worthy yet unfortunate in American society.

It is also important to note that fraternities were segregated according to gender, race, ethnicity and class, which in turn shaped who was entitled to their charity. Beito's notion that 'Donors and recipients often came from the same, or nearly the same, walks of life' is only true in a broad sense. While white men of different classes could belong to the same fraternity, the composition of individual lodges was generally rather homogenous, which in turn was one of its primary appeals.[10] Consequently, while America's communities had a multitude of fraternal orders helping the needy, their efforts were divided and not all those seeking help would receive equal attention. Irish immigrants, for instance, would probably find more assistance from ethnic fraternities like the Ancient Order of Hibernians than a nativist fraternity such as the Junior Order of United American Mechanics.

The segregated lodge system produced a patchwork of local charitable efforts where you were often required to be associated either directly through membership or indirectly through your community or ethnic identity. This may not be what we now consider as charity, but at the time it was recognized as such by the American public and was protected by legal frameworks and charters that offered unique rights and protections. Furthermore, at the turn of the century, fraternities were widely respected and membership in the more exclusive orders was highly sought after by men looking to enhance their social, political or economic standing. 'From the president of the nation down to the humblest citizen the fascination of the grip and password enthrals,' wrote one author in *The Atlantic Monthly* in 1906, 'So rapidly does [the lodge] increase in popularity that it shows little indication of ever wielding less power.'[11] Yet fraternities were not immune to the wider cultural and political trends occurring in America during the Progressive Era that advocated for a new approach to social welfare such as the Social Gospel and 'scientific' charity. Lynn Dumenil highlights this gradual shift in her work on Freemasonry, explaining that 'In the Progressive period, some spokesmen occasionally insisted that Masonry as an institution take an active part in meeting the social problems of the day, but they were relatively few'.[12] Fraternities were by their very nature quite detached and resistant to change, so at the dawn of the twentieth century, this was a position advocated only by a minority. However, the demands of the First World War accelerated this gradual shift within American fraternalism, forcing seasoned members to seriously consider the social ills ravaging the world beyond their lodges.

The First World War proved to be a profound moment of change for the American civilian population on the home front and for mass philanthropy. Fraternities were among the many voluntary associations who answered Woodrow Wilson's clarion call to action, but in so doing broke with their traditional aversion to external affairs. The Freemasons and other fraternal orders urged their members to participate in organized war efforts and to donate to general charity drives. James N. Saunders, the Masonic Grand Master of Kentucky, speaking to his brethren in 1917 said of their charity: 'This is not generosity; it is high privilege and sacred duty. Let us by patriotic act evidence the sincerity of our patriotic speech. Kentucky Masons are not slackers.'[13] Saunders' appeal also highlights how mass voluntary charity took on a new coercive dimension during the war. As Christopher Capozzola explains, 'Being a good citizen meant fulfilling your political obligations and doing so through voluntary associations. Lending a hand to the war effort thus became not just a good deed but a duty, and serious consequences ensued for those who failed to join in.'[14] Among fraternities, there was even a competitive tension between orders to see who could do the most to aid those suffering the ravages of the war. Freemasonry, arguably the most respected and powerful fraternity in America, grew especially irritated when Wilson's government disallowed their order from providing charitable relief directly as a Masonic venture. Their latent anti-Catholicism was further inflamed by the fact that the only fraternity to receive such official approval was their rivals, the Knights of Columbus.[15] The home front enlisted the help of all Americans in aiding their nation and those suffering overseas, further solidifying the shift to mass philanthropy among ordinary citizens. But it would also accelerate a shift within fraternities. Borne out of the excitement of the war and their inability to prove their patriotism distinctly, more militant segments of various fraternities began to push more forcefully against the reclusive nature of their orders, particularly in terms of where they directed their charitable efforts. Rather than face inwards as their customs dictated, fraternities in the post-war era increasingly turned their attention to the wider public and the general well-being of society. The catchword for this attitude and form of charity and philanthropy was 'service' – that is, service to the fraternity, service to their community and service to the nation as a whole.

It was during this critical juncture in the evolution of both American fraternalism and charity that William Joseph Simmons founded his organization, the Knights of the Ku Klux Klan. Initially, the group was modelled on the traditions and aims of the older fraternities Simmons had been previously been involved in, like the Freemasons or the Woodmen of the World. Simmons, a former preacher and professional lodge organizer, claimed that it was his father's participation in Alabama in the original Reconstruction Klan that inspired him to revive the order in Atlanta in 1915.[16] Nonetheless, it is likely that Simmons also hoped to cash-in on America's new-found appreciation for the Reconstruction Klan, which had reached its apex that year with the release of D.W. Griffith's blockbuster *Birth of a Nation*.

From the outset, this Second Klan encouraged its members to practice 'Klanishness', a term that encompassed the same mutual aid and reciprocal charity that older fraternities had practised. As one early pamphlet from 1917 instructed: 'While it has due respect for the acts of large favors and conspicuous benefits, [Klanishness] especially gives attention to the countless small acts of beneficial practices and kind words.' Though this Second Klan practised traditional forms of charity and fraternalism, the order also advocated a more militant and political approach to improving society. Merely providing for other members in their time of need, as was the custom for fraternities, was not enough. Simmons instructed his followers to cultivate 'patriotic Klanishness', a 'Real, true Americanism, unadulterated' and to specifically 'keep our government forever free from the alien touch of foreign alliances and influences'. Klansmen were also supposed to practice 'racial Klanishness' maintaining white supremacy 'first, last and all the time' by protecting society from 'the haughty ambitions and arrogant aggressiveness of colored races who seek to mix their breed with the blood of our government and civilization'.[17] In summary, the Second Invisible Empire practised older forms of reciprocal charity but infused their fraternity with newer forms of direct and political action that suited the recent turn among American voluntary associations to this broader conception of 'service'.

Despite scholarly assertions to the contrary, fraternities continued to grow in size and power during the 1920s, though it was the more adaptable and modern orders that gained the most recruits. Newer voluntary associations, particularly luncheon clubs such as the Lions, Rotary and Kiwanis, which embraced this post-war zeitgeist of 'service' became especially popular.[18] The Klan managed to ride this new surge in membership by effectively incorporating the familiar elements of traditional fraternities and infusing them with the public's new-found interest in the concept of 'service' and militant political action. The second Imperial Wizard, Hiram Wesley Evans, claimed this made their organization unique and that 'The Klan is so constructed that inactivity would mean its decease, in any community . . . it is operative, and it's not presumption to forecast increasing service all along the fraternal line within the near future'.[19] Furthermore, basing their organization on the Reconstruction Klan, a familiar order with a particular cultural and historical resonance for the white American audience of the early twentieth century helps to further explain why this organization attracted so much interest. Nowhere in the Second Klan's teachings was there an indication of the brutality or terrorism of their Reconstruction predecessors. Instead, the Klansmen of the twentieth century learnt that the original order had 'rescued the entire country from utter disgrace and ruin', by answering the 'penetrating sobs of distressed women and plaintive cry of [the] hungry, cladless child'.[20] The 1920s Klan invoked the mythologized heroes of the first Klan to attract new members and to instruct them in their proper duty to safeguard the good of the nation and white civilization.

Before they could become the mass movement that the House Committee on Rules interrogated in 1921, however, Simmons' Klan would undergo a series of structural and leadership changes. During the war, the coercive atmosphere of the home front prompted Klansmen to police their neighbours and guard against 'slackers', which in itself was a departure from the regular activities of a fraternal order. The more significant changes came in the post-war era when Simmons, desperate for outside help to assist him in selling his order to the masses, signed a contract with promoters Edward Young Clarke and Elizabeth Tyler of the Southern Publicity Association. The contract was signed in June 1920 and made the two promoters solely responsible for the promotion and propagation of the order, all in exchange for an $8 share of each new member's $10 initiation fee. The Southern Publicity Association was a well-established firm that had successfully marketed campaigns for other charitable organizations such as the Red Cross, the YMCA and the Salvation Army. Through their new Propagation Department, Clarke and Tyler instituted a series of changes in the Klan's promotion strategy that helped to spread the order. This department was staffed by commissioned salesmen, called 'kleagles', that would sell membership in the Klan for a portion of the $8.[21] The two promoters would revamp the Klan for a mass audience, paying close attention to their public image in order to market the organization effectively.

This Propagation Department kept in close contact with their network of kleagles, which by the summer of 1921 was composed of hundreds of salesmen distributed across the country and structured in a hierarchical fashion with state and regional leaders. This network allowed Clarke and Tyler to implement their public relations and sales strategy, while still allowing individual salesmen relative freedom to adjust their pitch according to local circumstances. It is evident by the sheer frequency of examples that public donations to charity were an intrinsic part of the Propagation Department's national strategy. Throughout the country, the formation of a new chapter of the order, known as a 'klaverns', was followed by a public donation to the local church. For greater effect, these conspicuous donations were made by groups of robed Klansmen in the middle of a service. Critics of the order quickly recognized the true nature of such charity. As one writer explained, 'It is hard to quarrel with charity in any guise, and the Klan never hit upon a better advertising device than this.'[22] Such performative gifts, alongside their visually striking public parades, allowed the Klan to establish itself within a community as a respectable and charitable organization that patriotic white Protestant citizens should join.

The Klan's charitable efforts in the 1920s were often specifically targeted, and historians have analysed such gifts to better understand the aims and development of the Invisible Empire. For instance, the Second Klan made some donations to African American causes, but only if and when these African Americans did not advocate for racial equality. Thomas Pegram has explained that such paternalistic charity 'reinforced white domination and communicated the Klan's insistence on monitoring the behaviour of the black community'.[23] Protestant churches in need were certainly a high priority for the religious Second Klan, but the group often made donations to causes that were standard for other voluntary associations, such as the construction of orphanages or hospitals. Klansmen in Anderson, Indiana for example, raised $10,000 for a hospital fund in 1923, but made sure to note in their publications that the Freemasons had only donated half as much, and that the Klan's donation 'was the largest single donation that has been made to the fund by any organization'. By advertising such donations in their newspapers and juxtaposing the two, the Klan was implying their own order was working in conjunction with the widely respected Freemasons, but also that the Klan was the more generous fraternity and of better service to the community.[24] The charitable causes Klansmen worked towards also varied according to local circumstances, but there were some general trends. As Kelly Baker has noted, 'The Klan's benevolence could occasionally breach racial lines, but its charitable donations did not cross religious boundaries.'[25] Klaverns also frequently donated to public education initiatives, particularly any efforts to promote the study of the Bible or to inculcate patriotism. As such, Klansmen at all levels employed charity to further their narrow vision of the common good, one that prioritized the needs of conservative white Protestant citizens and which sought to reshape American society.

The Klan's distinctive brand of militant fraternalism, coupled with its effective sales strategy and public image management, helped to attract thousands of white American men to the ranks of this Second Invisible Empire. Yet many public figures soon began to realize that the immense profits many were making from this rush of applicants suggested that they were not as charitable as they claimed. One critic of the organization complained that its leaders were not 'inspired by a zeal for welfare', and that 'the Ku Klux Klan is a huge money-making hoax – a gold mine'.[26] Scholars have long recognized how profit and financial embezzlement built the Second Klan and eventually played a part in its collapse around 1925. Simmons himself estimated that the infamous D. C. Stephenson managed to amass around \$3,000,000 during his tenure as a salesman and leader of the powerful Indiana Klan.[27] The order's fiscal strategy to protect such revenues from state and federal tax regulations, however, has been neglected in the historiography of the Invisible Empire.

As mentioned earlier, the Second Klan had been chartered as a fraternity in Georgia, awarding it all the fiscal benefits and protections that this form of voluntary association was entitled to. Before the House Rules Committee, Simmons claimed that when the federal income tax legislation was introduced he sought guidance from a federal agent to ascertain whether his fledgling Klan would be exempt considering its status as a 'fraternal, eleemosynary institution'. The agent replied that the legislation did not apply, and Simmons assured congressmen that he had taken every precaution to ensure they were following the law. The Klan also designated the \$10 membership fee as a charitable 'donation', which ensured that such revenues would not be considered profits that the government could collect tax on. When asked about this suspicious measure, Simmons replied dramatically that 'I will say to you in all honor and under God that that thought has never come into the mind of a single man'. It is difficult to verify such claims since Simmons was prone to exaggeration and outright dishonesty. Furthermore, he was not an adept record-keeper.[28] Yet there is no evidence that this 'donation' qualification ever existed while Simmons led the Klan between 1915 and 1920. The more likely conclusion is that it was Clarke and Tyler that introduced this legally grey protection since both were significantly more adept in these matters than Simmons and stood to lose the most financially if it meant that income would be taxed.

As Zunz has demonstrated, the regulatory state played a critical role in the development of mass philanthropy through its ability to shape tax exemption, interceding in different ways and adding provisions to legislation to ensure this non-profit sector would contribute to society in ways it considered appropriate. Different governments had their own vision for the role and scope of such efforts, but a pressing concern was how powerful philanthropic foundations and charitable organizations could interfere in matters considered to be strictly political. As the tax code expanded in the years after the passage of the Sixteenth Amendment, the Treasury Department introduced a new proviso to regulate such political advocacy in 1919 which stated that 'associations formed to disseminate controversial or partisan propaganda are not education within the meaning of the statute' and were thus, not tax-exempt.[29]

The application of this legislation, however, was much more circumspect and reflected the conservatism of the white establishment regarding what was to be considered political. In the Klan's case, the obvious profitability of their scheme and the decidedly political nature of their organization did not appear to warrant any further investigation by the federal government or the withdrawal of their charitable tax-exempt status in the 1920s. Congressman Peter F. Tague tried to encourage the House

Rules Committee to take action on this tax avoidance, accusing the Klan of providing no returns 'under the internal revenue laws for more than $30,000,000'. Yet the committee was reluctant to intercede and to clearly define what constituted political action and tax avoidance within this case. With regards to the committee's decision, George Lewis has argued that the Klan avoided further attention by emphasizing their 'Americanism', a vague yet powerful qualification that placed the order above reproach. Furthermore, Lewis establishes that support for the Klan 'came not from the margins but from the very centre of the mainstream political process'.[30] In addition though, it was also the Klan's status as a charitable fraternity that prevented Congress from pursuing the issue, as such voluntary associations had always been afforded special legal protections in American society. Fraternities would even be specifically excluded from later legislation like the 1934 Revenue Act that established stricter guidelines to remove tax-exemption status from organizations engaged in political education and propaganda. In the 1920s though, the government was more than willing to use its regulatory power to undermine charitable organizations they regarded to be subversive, such as Margaret Sanger's controversial American Birth Control League, whose tax-exempt status was the subject of intense scrutiny in this decade.[31] This selective enforcement belies the problematic nature of such exemptions, which permitted the government to intercede in ways it saw fit; in this case, its inaction encouraged the development of the Second Klan, a charity that worked towards a white supremacist and nativist vision of the 'common good'.

The federal government questioned the Klan's benevolence, but did not formally reprimand the organization for the lavish profits its officers managed to accrue in the name of charity or the political nature of their efforts. This inaction was partly due to a combination of the secrecy and public relations campaign of the group's leaders that prevented outsiders from understanding the true nature of this appropriately named Invisible Empire. The American public was also divided on the alleged threat this charitable voluntary association posed to the political and social well-being of their nation, but many individuals and organizations refused to be complicit in such performative acts of charity. With regards to the Klan's public donations to Protestant churches, the popular non-denominational magazine *The Christian Century* castigated those who accepted such gifts, alleging that such ministers must do so 'with some purpose not consonant with the aims and ends of the gospel of the Christ'.[32] Even the Black community was forced to occasionally chastise African Americans for benefiting from the Klan's charity. In 1925, the NAACP produced a press release criticizing a Reverend O. R. Gordon of North Carolina, calling him a 'modern Judas', for welcoming the Klan into his church and their $20 donation.[33] While the Klan's targets – Catholics, African Americans and various immigrant groups – were often vociferous in their condemnation of this fraternity and its charitability, the white Protestant majority was not sufficiently united to undermine the order and to condemn its charity work. In individual locales and states, coalitions did eventually form to halt the Klan's growth, but these often took place after the order had taken hold in their communities.

Assessing the altruistic intent of ordinary members of the Klan was difficult at the time because of the secrecy of the order, the contradictory actions of different klaverns, and the cacophony of voices criticizing or highlighting the Invisible Empire's charity in public discourse. Historical studies of the Klan at a local level have since been able to somewhat clarify this. For example, Donald Holley's study of the local Klan in Monticello, Arkansas, revealed that the order gave a donation to the Mid-East fund to help Armenians in Turkey during the genocide and that the klavern organized a Christmas Cheer Committee to distribute fruit and toys among the needy in this small community. It is precisely this sort of charitable work, alongside the Klan's local reform impulses, that led Shawn Lay to argue in one landmark study of this order that 'beneath the threatening white robes and hoods walked millions of otherwise respectable Americans, many of them earnestly striving to forge a better life for themselves and their families'. Nonetheless, it is necessary to consider how the violence and coercion that ordinary Klansmen employed worked alongside the more peaceful reform campaigns and charitable endeavours. In the case of the Monticello Klan, alongside the Christmas Cheer Committee the klavern formed the Shock Committee, which among other forms of coercion sent harassing letters to any known moonshiners and bootleggers in the area and offered a reward of $50 for information leading to the arrest of those that broke the dry law. Holley concludes that this suggests that 'the liquor problem was clearly a legal and political strategy, not one of violence'.[34] Yet, while a previous generation of scholars insists that the order was non-violent, this conclusion is based on an overreliance on archival materials which misrepresent how the Klan functioned as a secret vigilante group.[35] Violent Klansmen did not disclose or record their vigilante attacks, and Klan leaders were quite adept at dismissing or obfuscating acts of terrorism. Klansmen certainly used coercion and even violence to police their neighbours, but these aggressive and intimidatory tactics do not necessarily preclude them from being considered charitable or 'ordinary Americans'. The scholarship on white supremacy in American society has long recognized that lynch mobs or the architects of *de facto* and *de jure* segregation justified such acts as not only necessary but also even vital for the welfare of the country. If anything, militant Klansmen would have regarded both their charity and defence of white supremacy – whatever the means – as working in tandem, as it had for the Reconstruction Klansmen they revered.

Where ordinary Klansmen did recognize some faults in their organization was in the contradictions between the order's stated purposes and the actions of many of its leaders. Clarke and Simmons' leadership had been repeatedly challenged unsuccessfully by Klansmen who were angered by the mounting evidence of executive mismanagement and financial corruption. At the first national convention, the 'Imperial Klonvokation', in November 1922 though, one faction managed to trick Simmons into giving up the office of Imperial Wizard and allowing Hiram Wesley Evans to replace him. The dispute between the two lasted several months thereafter but was eventually settled. Once in control, Evans quickly made several reforms intended to rebuild public trust and to combat the notion that the Klan was violent or that they were a money-making scheme. The most important of these was the dismissal of Clarke and Tyler, but he also lowered the price of Klan robes and various other fees.

Evans's Klan embarked on a more coordinated campaign to win political victories in 1923 and 1924, even as it continued expanding in key states like Indiana and Colorado. However, Evans did not institute major changes to the order's approach to charity, and even the reforms to the Propagation Department were largely superficial. An audit of the order at the Second Imperial Klonvocation revealed, just as Williamson had once done in 1921, that none of the national funds had been allocated specifically for charitable endeavours.[36] Of course, Klan leadership continued to exhort members to act charitably. 'Let us not forget that this is essentially a great fraternal and benevolent Order' said one officer in *The Imperial Night-Hawk*, the Klan's national weekly, 'Charity is great virtue. We should seek to build hospitals and homes for the needy and relieve the suffering of the poor.'[37] By and large, the Klan's charity work under Evans continued in much the same way as it had under Simmons; namely that it was directed by local klaverns. Dallas Klan No.66 for instance spent $80,000 on the construction of an orphanage in the city called Hope Cottage. Yet, in line with the new political priorities of the order, the ceremonial opening of the orphanage took place just as Evans gathered Klansmen for the largest Klan rally in history, where he also took the opportunity to launch their political campaign to lobby Congress for further restrictions to immigration.[38]

The Klan employed acts of charity to build public trust, but underlying their efforts was a philanthropic vision about how to reform American society. In its campaigns to fund patriotic public education and warn of the dangers of immigrants of different races, Evans's Klan was attempting to address what it diagnosed to be the gravest social ills that could damage the welfare of the United States. They worked to inform the public of how best to save the nation from ruin by ensuring the continuance of white supremacy and a return to Protestant fundamentals and fervent patriotism. The order was also deeply suspicious of the philanthropic efforts of others, particularly those who were not white, Protestant or native-born. For Klansmen, the parochial schools run by Catholics were an effort to undermine the nation, as were the campaigns working against immigration restriction in the name of benevolence. Evans himself condemned such actions in 1924, stating that 'They seek to destroy Americanism in the name of philanthropy, by substituting patriotism for universalism under which freedom and representative democracy alike would die'. Though the Klan practised direct forms of charity, their philanthropic vision was one of a pure, Nordic and Protestant America whose racial makeup would lead to a revitalized nation. Anything else would be regressive and detrimental. Evans would go on to say, 'It is sheer idiocy for any man who pretends to look ahead to declare that we would be philanthropic, or achieve the greatest goal for the greatest number, if we destroyed the future of civilization for the sake of a few million immigrants.'[39]

The Second Klan would reach the apex of its power soon after, but a combination of various factors including further financial and political scandals would begin to eat away at its membership. Even with the creation of the Women's Ku Klux Klan in 1923 and ancillary orders for children, the strength of the Klan began to wane around 1924 and 1925 as state after state was unable to recruit new members faster than they left. The more militant members remained and would continue to practice their blend of violent vigilantism peppered with acts of charity throughout the late 1920s and up to the Second World War. It was in 1944 that the government chose to rectify the mistakes of the 1921 House Rules Committee and use its regulatory power to challenge the Klan. In April 1944 the IRS presented the order with a bill for $685,000 in back-taxes for profits earned in the 1920s, effectively denying their status as a charitable organization and forcing the already weakened Knights of the Ku Klux Klan to disband.[40]

The Second Klan managed to amass immense power and wealth during the 1920s, dispersing it as it saw fit through charitable endeavours and philanthropic campaigns to protect white supremacy, '100% American' patriotism and the nation's Protestant heritage. By employing charity and exploiting existing legal and fiscal frameworks to expand their movement, the Klan gnawed at the roots of America's democracy, allowing this mass movement to swing elections and terrorize segments of the population. Americans would eventually recognize the gravity of the situation, but for several years the Klan grew and festered without significant opposition from the white Protestant majority. The federal government, despite using its extensive powers to monitor radicals and subversives throughout the 1920s, allowed this fraternity to cross the usual boundaries between charitable organizations and the political sphere. Indeed, millions of white Protestant Americans, not all of them members of the Invisible Empire, appeared to approve of this flexibility when it meant this would reinforce their already privileged place in society.

America's fraternities have a long and storied record of charity and philanthropy. This impressive record has led some scholars to regret their decline in the twentieth century. David T. Beito concludes one such assessment stating that 'There has yet to arise a modern analogue to the fraternal society either as a provider of services, such as low-cost medical care, or as a device to encourage the spread of the survival values of thrift, neighbourhood cooperation and individual responsibility'. Along similar lines, Jeremy Beer described fraternalism as 'a decidedly nonprogressive phenomenon that adapted old-fashioned charity to help meet the physical, emotional, and spiritual needs of millions of American men and women in an egalitarian, noncoercive way'.[41] Such assessments praise the self-reliance of individuals to form their own associations to look after themselves and others, but romanticize the nature of fraternalism, which at its core was about exclusivity in this era. The Second Klan was an extreme expression of this impulse, but its widespread popularity in the 1920s suggests that millions of white Americans believed that only some could and should benefit from their welfare. Lawrence Friedman and Mark McGarvie have noted that 'philanthropic activity in America has its roots in the desires of individuals to impose their visions, ideals, or conceptions of truth upon their society'.[42] While we can celebrate achievements like the construction of libraries or the eradication of diseases, the history of American philanthropy is incomplete without addressing how groups like the Second Ku Klux Klan sought to build a better society at the exclusion of others.

# Notes

1  *The Ku Klux Klan: Hearings before the Committee on Rules, House of Representatives, 67th Congress, 1st Session* (Washington, DC: Government Printing Office, 1921), 38–9.
2  Ibid., 77, 134.
3  Miguel Hernandez, *The Ku Klux Klan and Freemasonry in 1920s America: Fighting Fraternities* (Abingdon: Routledge, 2019), 40–3.

4  Lila Corwin Berman, 'How Americans Give: The Financialization of American Jewish Philanthropy', *The American Historical Review* 122, no. 5 (2017): 1462.

5  Olivier Zunz, *Philanthropy in America: A History* (Princeton: Princeton University Press, 2012).

6  Lawrence J. Friedman, 'Philanthropy in America: Historicism and Discontents', *Charity, Philanthropy, and Civility in American History*, ed. Lawrence J. Friedman and Mark D. McGarvie (Cambridge: Cambridge University Press, 2003), 10.

7  W. S. Harwood, 'Secret Societies in America', *The North American Review* 164, no. 486 (1897): 618, 623.

8  David T. Beito, *From Mutual Aid to the Welfare State: Fraternal Societies and Social Services, 1890–1967* (Chapel Hill: University of North Carolina Press, 2000), 15.

9  Albert C. Stevens, *The Cyclopaedia of Fraternities* (New York: E.B. and Treat and Co., 1907), 208.

10  Jason Kaufman, *For the Common Good? American Civic Life and the Golden Age of Fraternity* (Oxford: Oxford University Press, 2003), 7–9.

11  Charles Moreau Harger, 'The Lodge', *The Atlantic Monthly*, April 1906, 494.

12  Lynn Dumenil, *Freemasonry and American Culture, 1880–1930* (Princeton: Princeton University Press, 1984), 116.

13  *1917 Proceedings of the Grand Lodge of Free and Accepted Masons of the State of Kentucky* (Louisville: N/A, 1917), 18.

14  Christopher Capozzola, *Uncle Sam Wants You: World War I and the Making of the Modern Citizen* (Oxford: Oxford University Press, 2008), 8.

15  Hernandez, *The Ku Klux Klan and Freemasonry in 1920s America*, 47–53.

16  William G. Shepherd, 'How I Put Over the Klan', *Collier's National Weekly*, 14 July 1928, 6.

17  W. J. Simmons, *The Practice of Klanishness* (1917; repr., Atlanta: K.K.K. Press, 1924), 6–7.

18  Miguel Hernandez, 'The Gilded Age of Fraternalism: Brotherhood and Modernism in 1920s America', *Journal for Research into Freemasonry and Fraternalism* 5, no.2 (2014): 209–11.

19  Ku Klux Klan, *Proceedings of the Second Imperial Klonvokation* (Atlanta: K.K.K. Press, 1924), 158.

20  W. J. Simmons, *Kloran of the Knights of the Ku Klux Klan* (Atlanta, 1916), 48–51.

21  John Mack Shotwell, 'Crystalizing Public Hatred: Ku Klux Klan Public Relations in the Early 1920s' (MA diss., University of Wisconsin, 1974), 12–20.

22  W. P. Beazell, 'The Rise of the Ku Klux Klan', in *KKK: The Kreed of the Klansmen*, ed. E.Haldeman-Julius (Girard: Haldeman-Julius Company, 1924), 11.

23  Thomas R. Pegram, *One Hundred Per Cent American: The Rebirth and Decline of the Ku Klux Klan in the 1920s* (Chicago: Ivan R. Dee, 2011), 24–5.

24  'Masons and Klan Aid Hospital Fund', *The Fellowship Forum*, 1 December 1923, 1.

25  Kelly J. Baker, *Gospel According to the Klan: The KKK's Appeal to Protestant America, 1915–1930* (Lawrence: University Press of Kansas, 2011), 51.

26  Ezra A. Cook, *Ku Klux Klan Secrets Exposed* (Chicago: E.A. Cook, 1922), 24.

27  Charles C. Alexander, 'Kleagles and Cash: The Ku Klux Klan as a Business Organization, 1915-1930', *The Business History Review* 39, no.3 (1965): 366.

28  *The Ku Klux Klan: Hearings before the Committee on Rules*, 41, 134–5.

29  Zunz, *Philanthropy in America*, 85–90.

30  George Lewis, '"An Amorphous Code": The Ku Klux Klan and Un-Americanism, 1915-1965', *Journal of American Studies* 47, no. 4 (2013): 975–9.

31  Zunz, *Philanthropy in America*, 92–102.

32  'The Ku Klux Klan and the Church', *The Literary Digest*, 8 April 1922, 33.

33  'Negro Preacher Welcomes Ku Klux Klan', unmarked NAACP press release, 6 July 1925, NAACP Papers, Box C313, folder 5.

34  Shawn Lay, 'Introduction', in *The Invisible Empire in the West*, ed. Shawn Lay (Chicago: University of Illinois Press, 2004), 12; Donald Holley, 'A Look Behind the Masks: The 1920s Ku Klux Klan in Monticello, Arkansas', *The Arkansas Historical Quarterly* 60, no. 2 (2001): 146–7.

35  See Hernandez, *The Ku Klux Klan and Freemasonry in 1920s America*, 141–2.

36  Ibid., 183.

37  W. C. Wright, 'The Twelfth Chapter of Romans as a Klansman's Law of Life', *The Imperial Night-Hawk*, 5 March 1924, 2.

38  Ku Klux Klan, *Official Souvenir of Klan Day at the State Fair of Texas* (Dallas: Standard American Publishing House, 1923).

39  Klan, *Proceedings of the Second Imperial Klonvokation*, 140–7.

40  Stetson Kennedy and David Pilgrim, *The Klan Unmasked* (Tuscaloosa: The University of Alabama Press, 2011), 87.

41  David T. Beito, '"This Enormous Army": The Mutual-Aid Tradition of American Fraternal Societies before the Twentieth Century', *The Voluntary City: Choice, Community and Civil Society*, ed. David Beito et al (Ann Arbor: The Independent Institute: 2002), 197; Jeremy Beer, *The Philanthropic Revolution: An Alternative History of American Charity* (Philadelphia: University of Pennsylvania Press, 2015), 77.

42  Friedman and McGarvie, *Charity, Philanthropy, and Civility in American History*, i.

# Select bibliography

Abzug, Robert H. *Cosmos Crumbling: American Reform and the Religious Imagination.* Oxford: Oxford University Press, 1994.

Ananaba, Wogu. *The Trade Union Movement in Africa: Promise and Performance.* London: C. Hurst & Company, 1979.

Arnove, Robert F. et al. *Philanthropy and Cultural Imperialism: The Foundations at Home and Abroad.* Bloomington: Indiana University Press, 1982.

Attie, Jeanie. *Patriotic Toil: Northern Women and the American Civil War.* Ithaca: Cornell University Press, 1998.

Baker, Kelly J. *Gospel According to the Klan: The KKK's Appeal to Protestant America, 1915–1930.* Lawrence: University Press of Kansas, 2011.

Barnhisel, Greg. *Cold War Modernists: Art, Literature, and American Cultural Diplomacy.* New York: Columbia University Press, 2015.

Beer, Jeremy. *The Philanthropic Revolution: An Alternative History of American Charity.* Philadelphia: University of Pennsylvania Press, 2015.

Beito, David T. *From Mutual Aid to the Welfare State: Fraternal Societies and Social Services, 1890–1967.* Chapel Hill: University of North Carolina Press, 2000.

Beito, David T. '"This Enormous Army": The Mutual-Aid Tradition of American Fraternal Societies before the Twentieth Century'. In *The Voluntary City: Choice, Community and Civil Society*, edited by David Beito et al., 182–3. Ann Arbor: The Independent Institute, 2002.

Berman, Edward H. *The Influence of the Carnegie, Ford, and Rockefeller Foundations on American Foreign Policy: The Ideology of Philanthropy.* Albany: State University of New York Press, 1983.

Berman, Lila Corwin. 'How Americans Give: The Financialization of American Jewish Philanthropy'. *The American Historical Review* 122, no. 5 (2017): 1459–89.

Bindas, Kenneth J. *All of This Music Belongs to the Nation: The WPA's Federal Music Project and American Society.* Knoxville: The University of Tennessee Press, 1995.

Bingham, Laura Carpenter. 'Women, Higher Education, and Philanthropy'. In *Philanthropy in America: A Comprehensive Historical Encyclopedia*, Vol. 2 edited by Dwight F. Burlingame, 514–19. Santa Barbara: ABC Clio, 2004.

Bremner, Robert H. *American Philanthropy.* Chicago and London: University of Chicago Press, 1960.

Bremner, Robert H. *Giving: Charity and Philanthropy in History.* New Brunswick and London: Transaction Publishers, 1996.

Bremner, Robert H. *The Public Good: Philanthropy and Welfare in the Civil War Era.* New York: Alfred A. Knopf, 1980.

Brew, Gregory. '"What They Need is Management": American NGOs, the Second Seven Year Plan and Economic Development in Iran, 1954–1963'. *The International History Review* 41, no. 1 (2019): 1–22.

Carpenter, Joel. and Wilbert Shenk, eds. *Earthen Vessels: American Evangelicals and Foreign Missions, 1880–1980*. Grand Rapids: William B. Eerdmans Publishing Co., 1990.

Clark, Elizabeth B. "'The Sacred Rights of the Weak": Pain, Sympathy, and the Culture of Individual Rights in Antebellum America'. *Journal of American History* 82, no. 2 (1995): 476–7.

Curtis, Heather D. 'Depicting Distant Suffering: Evangelicals and the Politics of Pictorial Humanitarianism in the Age of American Empire'. *Material Religion* 8, no. 2 (2012): 154–83.

Curtis, Heather D. *Holy Humanitarians: American Evangelicals and Global Aid*. Cambridge, MA: Harvard University Press, 2018.

Cutlip, Scott M. *Fund Raising in the United States: Its Role in America's Philanthropy*. New Brunswick: Rutgers University Press, 1965.

Daigaku, Tsudajuku. *Tsuda Umeko to juku no kujūnen* [Tsuda Umeko and the school's 90 years]. Tokyo: Tsudajuku Daigaku, 1990.

Daigaku, Tsudajuku. *Tsudajuku Daigaku hyakunenshi* [Tsudajuku College 100-year history]. Tokyo: Tsudajuku Daigaku, 2003.

Dromi, Shai M. *Above the Fray: The Red Cross and the Making of the Humanitarian Ngo Sector*. Chicago: University of Chicago Press, 2020.

Dumenil, Lynn. *Freemasonry and American Culture, 1880–1930*. Princeton: Princeton University Press, 1984.

English, James F. *The Economy of Prestige: Prizes, Awards, and the Circulation of Cultural Value*. Cambridge, MA: Harvard University Press, 2009.

Foulkes, Julia L. "'The Weakest Point in Our Record": Philanthropic Support of Dance and the Arts'. In *Patronizing the Public: American Philanthropy's Transformation of Culture, Communication, and the Humanities*, edited by William J. Buxton, 300–24. Lanham: Rowman & Littlefield Publishers, Inc., 2009.

Fraser, Steve and Gary Gerstle, eds. *Ruling America: A History of Wealth and Power in a Democracy*. Cambridge, MA: Harvard University Press, 2005.

Friedman, Lawrence J. 'Philanthropy in America: Historicism and Discontents'. In *Charity, Philanthropy, and Civility in American History*, edited by Lawrence J. Friedman and Mark D. McGarvie, 1–21. Cambridge: Cambridge University Press, 2003.

Gamber, Wendy. 'Antebellum Reform: Salvation, Self-Control, and Social Transformation'. In *Charity, Philanthropy, and Civility in American History*, edited by Lawrence J. Friedman and Mark D. McGarvie, 129–54. Cambridge: Cambridge University Press, 2003.

Giesberg, Judith Ann. *Civil War Sisterhood: The U.S. Sanitary Commission and Women's Politics in Transition*. Boston: Northeastern University Press, 2000.

Gubernick, Lisa Rebecca. *Squandered Fortune: The Life and Times of Huntington Hartford*. New York: G. P. Putnam's Sons, 1991.

Gura, Phillip F. *Man's Better Angels: Romantic Reformers and the Coming of the Civil War*. Cambridge, MA: Belknap Press of Harvard University Press, 2017.

Hernandez, Miguel. 'The Gilded Age of Fraternalism: Brotherhood and Modernism in 1920s America'. *Journal for Research into Freemasonry and Fraternalism* 5, no. 2 (2014): 200–24.

Hernandez, Miguel. *The Ku Klux Klan and Freemasonry in 1920s America: Fighting Fraternities*. Abingdon: Routledge, 2019.

Hess, Gary R. 'Waging the Cold War in the Third World: The Foundations and the Challenges of Development'. In *Charity, Philanthropy, and Civility in American*

*History*, edited by Lawrence J. Friedman and Mark D. McGarvie, 319–39. Cambridge: Cambridge University Press, 2003.

Hill, Patricia R. *The World Their Household: The American Women's Foreign Mission Movement and Cultural Transformation, 1870–1920*. Ann Arbor: University of Michigan Press, 1985.

Huber, Valeska, Tamson Pietsch, and Katharina Rietzler. 'Women's International Thought and the New Professions, 1900–1940'. *Modern Intellectual History* 18, no. 1 (2021): 121–45.

Hutchison, William. *Errand to the World: American Protestant Thought and Foreign Missions*. Chicago: University of Chicago Press, 1987.

Ishii, Noriko Kawamura. *American Women Missionaries at Kobe College, 1873–1909: New Dimensions in Gender*. New York: Routledge, 2004.

Jackson, Maurice. *Let This Voice be Heard: Anthony Benezet, Father of Atlantic Abolitionism*. Philadelphia: University of Pennsylvania Press, 2009.

Johnson, Joan Marie. *Funding Feminism: Monied Women, Philanthropy, and the Women's Movement, 1870–1967*. Chapel Hill: University of North Carolina Press, 2017.

Kaufman, Jason. *For the Common Good? American Civic Life and the Golden Age of Fraternity*. Oxford: Oxford University Press, 2003.

Kendall, Diana. *The Power of Good Deeds: Privileged Women and the Social Reproduction of the Upper Class*. New York: Rowman & Littlefield, 2002.

King, David. *God's Internationalists: World Vision and the Age of Evangelical Humanitarianism*. Philadelphia: University of Pennsylvania Press, 2019.

Laderman, Charlie. *Sharing the Burden: The Armenian Question, Humanitarian Intervention, and Anglo-American Visions of Global Order*. Oxford: Oxford University Press, 2019.

Laycock, Jo. *Imagining Armenia: Orientalism, Ambiguity and Intervention*. Manchester: Manchester University Press, 2009.

Levy, Jonathan. 'Altruism and the Origins of Nonprofit Philanthropy'. In *Philanthropy in Democratic Societies: History, Institutions, Values*, edited by Rob Reich, Lucy Bernholz, and Chiara Cordelli, 19–43. Chicago: University of Chicago Press, 2016.

Lorentz, John H. 'Educational Development in Iran: The Pivotal Role of the Mission Schools and Alborz College'. *Iranian Studies* 44, no. 5 (2011): 647–55.

McCarthy, Kathleen D. 'From Cold War to Cultural Development: The International Cultural Activities of the Ford Foundation, 1950–1980'. *Daedalus* 116, no. 1. Philanthropy, Patronage, Politics (Winter, 1987): 93–117.

McCleary, Rachel M. *Global Compassion: Private Voluntary Organizations and U.S. Foreign Policy since 1939*. Oxford: Oxford University Press, 2009.

Miller, John J. *A Gift of Freedom: How the John M. Olin Foundation Changed America*. San Francisco: Encounter Books, 2006.

Mintz, Stephen. *Moralists and Modernizers: America's Pre-Civil War Reformers*. Baltimore: Johns Hopkins University Press, 1995.

Moore, Sean D. *Slavery and the Making of Early American Libraries: British Literature, Political Thought, and the Transatlantic Book Trade, 1731–1814*. Oxford: Oxford University Press, 2019.

Nemchenok, Victor V. '"That So Fair a Thing Should Be So Frail": The Ford Foundation and the Failure of Rural Development in Iran, 1953–1964'. *Middle East Journal* 63, no. 2 (2009): 261–84.

Neumann, Johanna. *Gilded Suffragists: The New York Socialites Who Fought for Women's Right to Vote*. New York: New York University Press, 2017.

Ostrower, Francie. *Why the Wealthy Give: The Culture of Elite Philanthropy*. Princeton: Princeton University Press, 1995.

Parmar, Inderjeet. *Foundations of the American Century: The Ford, Carnegie, & Rockefeller Foundations in the Rise of American Power*. New York: Columbia University Press, 2014.

Payton, Robert. 'Philanthropic Values'. In *Philanthropic Giving: Studies in Varieties and Goals*, edited by Richard Magat, 29–45. New York: Oxford University Press, 1989.

Reeves-Ellington, Barbara, Kathryn Kish Sklar, and Connie Anne Shemo, eds. *Competing Kingdoms: Women, Mission, Nation, and the American Protestant Empire, 1812–1960*. Durham: Duke University Press, 2010.

Ricks, Thomas M. 'Alborz College of Tehran, Dr. Samuel Martin Jordan and the American Faculty: Twentieth-Century Presbyterian Mission Education and Modernism in Iran (Persia)'. *Iranian Studies* 44, no. 5 (2011): 627–46.

Rietzler, Katharina. 'Before the Cultural Cold Wars: American Philanthropy and Cultural Diplomacy in the Inter-War Years'. *Historical Research* 84 no. 223 (2011): 148–64.

Robert, Dana L. *American Women in Mission*. Macon: Baylor University Press, 1997.

Rose, Barbara. *Tsuda Umeko and Women's Education in Japan*. New Haven: Yale University Press, 1992.

Rosenberg, Emily S. 'Missions to the World: Philanthropy Abroad'. In *Charity, Philanthropy, and Civility in American History*, edited by Lawrence J. Friedman and Mark D. McGarvie, 241–57. Cambridge: Cambridge University Press, 2003.

Rostam-Kolayi, Jasamin. 'From Evangelizing to Modernizing Iranians: The American Presbyterian Mission and its Iranian Students'. *Iranian Studies* 41, no. 2 (2008): 213–40.

Ruble, Sarah. *The Gospel of Freedom and Power: Protestant Missionaries in American Culture After World War Two*. Chapel Hill: University of North Carolina Press, 2012.

Ryan, Susan M. *The Grammar of Good Intentions: Race and the Antebellum Culture of Benevolence*. Ithaca: Cornell University Press, 2003.

Saunders, Frances Stonor. *Who Paid the Piper?: The CIA and the Cultural Cold War*. London: Granta Books, 1999.

Schäfer, Axel. *Piety and Public Funding: Evangelicals and the State in Modern America*. Philadelphia: University of Pennsylvania Press, 2012.

Schencking, J. Charles. 'Giving Most and Giving Differently: Humanitarianism as Diplomacy Following Japan's 1923 Earthquake'. *Diplomatic History* 43, no. 4 (2019): 729–57.

Sinha, Manisha. *The Slave's Cause: A History of Abolition* New Haven and London: Yale University Press, 2016.

Smith, David A. *Money for Art: The Tangled Web of Art and Politics in American Democracy*. Chicago: Ivan R. Dee, 2008.

Smith, Troy A. 'Not Just the Raising of Money: Hampton Institute and Relationship Fundraising, 1893–1917'. *History of Education Quarterly* 61, no. 1 (2021): 63–93.

Tyrrell, Ian. *Reforming the World: The Creation of America's Moral Empire*. Princeton: Princeton University Press, 2010.

Van Slyck, Abigail Ayres. *Free to All: Carnegie Libraries and American Culture, 1890–1920*. Chicago and London: University of Chicago Press, 1995.

Walters, Ronald G. *American Reformers, 1815–1860*. New York: Hill and Wang, 1978.

Walther, Karine V. *Sacred Interests: The United States and the Islamic World, 1821–1921*. Chapel Hill: University of North Carolina Press, 2015.

Walton, Andrea. 'Introduction: Women and Philanthropy in Education – A Problem of Conceptions'. In *Women and Philanthropy in Education*, edited by Andrea Walton, 1–36. Bloomington: Indiana University Press, 2005.

Watenpaugh, Keith David. *Bread from Stones: The Middle East and the Making of Modern Humanitarianism*. Oakland: University of California Press, 2015.

Wiseman, Carter, ed. Place for the Arts: The MacDowell Colony, *1907–2007*. Peterborough: MacDowell Colony, 2006.

Zirinsky, Michael P. 'A Panacea for the Ills of the Country: American Presbyterian Education in Inter-War Iran'. *Iranian Studies* 26, no. 1/2 (1993): 119–37.

Zunz, Olivier. *Philanthropy in America: A History*. Princeton: Princeton University Press, 2012.

# Index

www.ingramcontent.com/pod-product-compliance
Lightning Source LLC
Chambersburg PA
CBHW050424280326
41932CB00013BA/1988